D1452183

Healthcare Architecture

IN AN ERA OF RADICAL TRANSFORMATION

Healthcare Architecture

IN AN ERA OF RADICAL TRANSFORMATION

STEPHEN VERDERBER

DAVID J. FINE

Yale University Press New Haven and London

Image digitalization and preliminary format by William Scott.
Designed by Bessas & Ackerman.
Set in Palatino and Syntax type by Bessas & Ackerman, Guilford, Connecticut.
Printed in China through World Print.

Library of Congress Cataloging-in-Publication Data
Verderber, Stephen.
Healthcare architecture in an era of radical transformation / Stephen Verderber and
David J. Fine.
   p.   cm.
Includes bibliographical references and index.
ISBN 0-300-07839-0 (hc: alk. paper)
1. Hospital architecture. 2. Health facilities—Design and construction.
I. Fine, David J. II. Title.
RA967.v473 2000
725'.51—dc21   99-23390
                                                                                                              CIP

A catalogue record for this book is available from the British Library.

10 9 8 7 6 5 4 3 2 1

FOR KINDY, ALEXANDER, AND ELYSSA LEIGH VERDERBER
FOR SUSAN, CHRISTOPHER, AND JEFFREY FINE
FOR OUR PARENTS
AND FOR THOSE IN NEED OF SHELTERED CARE

Contents

Preface

This book is the result of an unusual coincidence. Earliest discussions between the two authors occurred in the fall of 1991, when we realized we shared a deep interest in the history of health architecture. Some years before, however, the need for a book of this type had been expressed by the first author, who taught interdisciplinary courses to architecture, medical, public health, and healthcare administration students at Tulane University, beginning in spring 1986. The cornerstone of what would evolve into a sequence of courses titled "Architecture and Human Health" was a course on the history of health architecture from ancient times to the present, and on the transactions between users and healthcare settings, primarily from the standpoint of how buildings affect one's well-being in social, psychological, and physiological terms. It immediately became apparent that one could trace developments from antiquity to about 1970 with clarity and precision, but from that date to the present the literature was scattered and uneven in quality, with most information appearing in one-off articles or in professional journals. The occasional book appeared, but much of the material was either devoted to specific building types, such as nursing homes or hospitals, or appeared in the form of technical reports and manuals, such as those published by the American Hospital Association (later through its publication arm, American Hospital Publishing), or documents such as the *Minimum Requirements for Construction and Equipment for Hospital and Medical Facilities,* published by the U.S. Department of Health, Education, and Welfare, Public Health Service (now defunct).

The second author became fascinated with the architecture of health facilities while a student at Tufts University in 1970, when his father, Arnold Fine, left a thirty-year career in chemical and industrial engineering and management for a second career in hospital administration, with emphasis on design, construction, physical plant, and support services. From 1974 to 1996, the second author had extensive involvement with dozens of large- and small-scale capital improvement projects in hospitals and medical centers. One of the courses offered at Tufts was based in part on the prepublication manuscripts of the seminal book by John Thompson and Grace Golden, *The Hospital: A Social and Architectural History* (1975, Yale University Press). When the second author learned, coincidentally, that the first author had used this book in teaching his own course, we observed one afternoon, almost casually, "You know, we need to produce a book that picks up where they left off." Some months passed, and as this notion seeped into our minds, the project became perceived as ever more necessary—for *someone* to take on, if not us.

As we began the daunting task of scouring the vast yet fragmented international literature on the subject, we found some noteworthy recent research, but again, it continued to treat each building type, issue, or user constituency as exclusive of the others. The result was what we saw as a continued fragmentation of the field of healthcare architecture (the term *health architecture* had become a more accurate descriptor of the de-clinicalization of many health-only building types, and indicated the emergence of the home health movement) into a series of over-specialized domains in which dialogue was becoming perilously internalized and where miniaturized bureaucracies had arisen, further distancing the mini-fields from one another. In the 1980s and 1990s this separation was most obvious among the specialists in aging, particularly researchers, many of whom pulled away from the "mainstream" (loosely defined) by opting to present their work at the annual gerontology conferences and related professional gatherings, as an alternative to the nearly 3,000-member American Institute of Architects' Academy of Architecture for Health. Further, health architecture continues to be excluded from serious discussions of architectural theory and criticism, with few exceptions.

By this time it was apparent to us that there was no single text that bundled these disparate mini-fields into a unified conceptual framework that allowed for critical appraisal of the recent history of health architecture or forecasting of trends. It might be argued that the explosion of specialized knowledge in each of these mini-fields demanded a new series of specialized books. Perhaps this is indeed needed, but again, such an approach would only emphasize the differences, and not those attributes and values held in common. One of the most intriguing insights revealed by this fragmented literature was that these specialized domains are actually more similar than they are different.

A second set of concerns stemmed from our early commitment to bring an international perspective to the discussion. This decision to explore key international developments added a second layer of complexity to the undertaking. The reader may construe that a coherent logic characterized international developments. In reality, this rarely occurred. Much of the time, because of the accelerated, complex, competitive nature of the health sector, decision makers are constantly driven by market forces, technological advances, and new organizational models. Because of this, they usually lack the time to ponder what is going on in another time zone, let alone in another country. This is manifest in what might be described as a pattern of independent invention, with the most noticeable gaps occurring, since 1965, between North America and the other continents, particularly Europe and Asia. For example, developments were more coherent and cross-referenced between Germany and France or between England and Italy than between the United States and France or between the United States and England.

In fact, the British viewed the American healthcare system, and Americans' near-obsession with the all-private-room hospital, suspiciously. The British, by contrast, continued, into the 1990s, to place their trust in the open-ward system of inpatient care. For us, the most visible countertrend to this discontinuity between British and American practices was the impact of the British hospice movement on the hospice movement in the United States and in other Western countries since the mid-1970s.

One result of the attempt to trace trends across international boundaries has been, at times, the accumulation of evidence suggesting that designers in the United States were cognizant of trends in England and elsewhere. Although events in America might have occurred contemporaneously, no connections are to be implied beyond the most obvious ones drawn—that is, underlying organizational philosophies as manifest in matters of aesthetics and formal characteristics.

A second conundrum revolved around the issue of language. What words would best describe a technical aspect of a building to an interdisciplinary audience? This is always a challenge for authors seeking to reach an audience beyond the usual specialists in the field. When discussing modernism, particularly the influence of the International Style on hospital and clinic architecture, the challenge was considerable. The matter became even more difficult when tracing the emergence of postmodernism across the healthcare landscape of the past twenty years. We apologize if architects or others whose work is cited are offended by the use of a particular term or period as a vehicle to discuss a work, but the intent has been to provide an overview to clarify trends, not to pigeonhole the work of an individual or firm in a particular stylistic category. We have identified individual institutions according to their formal name at the time of construction. Although some institutions have since been renamed because of mergers, consolidations, closures, and the like, we have endeavored to be as faithful as possible to each institution's identity at the time of its emergence in the healthcare landscape.

In researching this book, we sifted through archival sources (professional journals, books, technical reports, and photographic archives of hospitals and medical centers), reviewed case studies indicative of larger trends in history, visited sites, conducted numerous interviews, responded to the comments of external reviewers, and made personal observations. On the healthcare administration side, we focused on how projects are conceived and guided to completion and subsequent renovation. Case studies point to the transformation in health architecture over the past three decades from a period where the patient was a passive participant to one in which he or she emerged as an informed, active participant in what was actually built. Architecturally, we paid particular attention to buildings considered to be exemplary within a given time period, as evidenced through publication and other forms of professional recognition, for the iconoclasts, in retrospect, tend to be of enduring intrigue.

We are indebted to many persons and organizations whose support and guidance have made this project possible; in particular, the various professional organizations, including the American Hospital Association, the American Institute of Architects, the Environmental Design Research Association, the American Academy of Healthcare Executives; the professional journals, including the *Modern Hospital* and its successor publication, *Modern Healthcare;* and the architectural journals in the United States and abroad. Many of the firms whose work has been included provided assistance and insight, as did the external reviewers who commented on earlier versions of various chapters, including Robert Douglass, FAIA, who reviewed the earliest draft, D. Kirk Hamilton, FAIA, who reviewed Chapters 5 and 6, and Victor Regnier, FAIA, who reviewed Chapter 7.

An internal team was assembled at Tulane University to gather materials during the research phase, and to sift through countless articles and historical accounts of individual projects, many in languages other than English. Tracy Nelson, working as lead research assistant while in her final year of studies in architecture at Tulane, unearthed a wealth of information from journals dating from the early 1960s. Miguel Viteri, also a research assistant, carried on with this task after Ms. Nelson's graduation. He was responsible, with the unflinching assistance of Dee Wild of the Department of Health Systems Management at Tulane, for securing permission to reproduce more than four hundred illustrations from around the world, edited from an initial database of nearly eight hundred images culled from the literature and from the archives of architectural firms and health organizations. Dee also patiently typed multiple drafts of the manuscript stage of the book. The digitization of the images and the "first cut" graphic design of the text and illustrations was executed by the team's graphic production specialist, William Scott, an information systems specialist in the Department of Health Systems Management at Tulane. He played a key role in the book's preparation from the standpoint of information technology and multimedia applications for the anticipated CD-ROM version of the book.

The first author is indebted to the Tulane University Medical Center and to the Department of Health Systems Management in the School of Public Health and Tropical Medicine, where he has been a member of the faculty since 1985, for providing that most precious commodity—time—and generous research support, and to the School of Architecture at Tulane University.

The Center for Health Design, based in Martinez, California, and its founder and CEO, Wayne Ruga, have helped to clarify and refocus this field's core mission, which, ideally, is the improvement of the quality of life through supportive, patient-centered, therapeutic design. The center's annual *Journal of Healthcare Design* has adroitly articulated many of the most critical trends and emerging priorities in progressive facility planning and design in the past decade.

In a project such as this, scope and content are limited by logistics and various time constraints. We apologize to all whose worthy projects and insights drawn from experience throughout the world would have undoubtedly improved the book but were not able to be included.

Perhaps most important to the genesis of the present book has been the invaluable contribution of Thompson and Golden, whose above-mentioned book was our most influential precursor and source of inspiration. We hope that this book will be viewed as a sequel of sorts to their landmark contribution.

We are above all indebted to our families, and in particular our wives, Kindy Husting Verderber and Susan Gory Fine, who exhibited infinite patience and in so doing provided essential support, particularly at those moments when it was most needed.

In sharing our appreciation for the many contributions of all those mentioned above, the authors reserve for themselves final responsibility for the inevitable errors and omissions associated with a work of this complexity.

PART I **The Inevitable Implosion**

CHAPTER 1

Introduction
The Six Waves of Health Architecture

The adjectives used to describe hospitals include dehumanizing, de-personalizing, neutering, frightening, uncaring. I have never heard anyone describe a hospital as beautiful, peaceful, healing, warm, joyous.
—Roslyn Lindheim, 1979

To those among us who as children experienced the intimidating aura of the modern hospital, the experience probably left a lifelong imprint. It was common for the patient to be rolled on a stretcher through what would seem to be miles of dimly lit corridors, beneath a maze of tangled wires and exposed light fixtures, hearing the din of air hammers. The halls bustled with people, some of whom jostled the stretcher as if it were a cart filled with boxes. To the administrators and staff the message was clear and promising, although to an unsuspecting child it was anything but: the sign on the wall probably read "Please excuse the temporary inconvenience while we continue to make progress." Yet another renovation was under way.

The image of the hospital as a construction site, coupled with the natural fears of a child in a strange environment, remains ingrained in memory for many of us. The community hospital was in a nearly continual state of flux: reconfiguration, expansion, and upheaval characterized the era. The need to expand and modernize was not merely a matter of institutional self-interest but a matter of sheer will. Hospitals had a mandate and, many believed, a social duty to expand, rebuild, and reequip. Lyndon Johnson, in his Health and Education Message of March 1965, declared that one-third of the nation's hospital beds were in "obsolete" condition.[1]

Nearly a decade and a half later the situation had not significantly improved. Critics of the modern hospital claimed that more than 40 percent of the U.S. health budget went toward sophisticated but not always useful diagnostic and treatment procedures, and to the construction of complex clinical spaces for an ever-expanding battery of machines. But in less than one hundred years the hospital had been transformed from a place of disease, death, and disposal to one where a patient had a quite reasonable chance of survival and recovery.

From the tumultuous 1960s to the present, change—expansion—had become so constant in the healthcare milieu that its absence, even for a short period, often became cause for alarm in and of itself. Increasingly, if an organization did not grow, questions would be raised about its health and about the competency of its administrators. By the early 1990s, though, physical expansionism had given way to an era of internal restructuring. There has been a correspondingly diminished emphasis on building health facilities from scratch, with the notable exception of the boom in freestanding outpatient care centers, which have proliferated in the waning years of the century, shrinking certain other sectors of the industry, notably the traditional, massive acute-care hospital. As for the major providers, whose health networks were concentrated around dense, referral-driven, sophisticated medical centers, the volume and variety of consolidations and mergers alone were indicative of an industry in significant flux: "By one count, 1,318 corporate acquisitions took place in the health sector between 1989 and 1993. The 651 transactions for which financial data were disclosed publicly had a combined value of over $87 billion. An additional 2,152 health care joint ventures occurred during this time period. For the 72 of these alliances for which financial data were disclosed, the combined value exceeded $5 billion. . . . Experimentation and groping [is occurring] to find optimal structure and scale."[2]

The definition of a *progressive* provider organization has been extensively revised over the past three decades to mirror our culture and its fundamental definitions of sickness, disease, health, and wellness. Providers, by the end of the century, placed far more emphasis on preventive care than they did in 1965. The use of the hospital as the option of first resort was once common: one was admitted as an inpatient for a battery of sophisticated, costly tests, usually without hesitation. By the 1990s the hospital seemingly had been recast as the place for the care of the sickest of the sick, preceded by a complex system of gatekeeper facilities whose function was to assess the need for care of a more intensive nature. Meanwhile, the debate over the cost and availability of health care, alleged as well as proven transgressions within the HMO industry, and such medical breakthroughs as electronic stimulation for spinal cord injury, interspecies transplantation, and the Human Genome Project, with its vast promise for gene therapy, became touchstone issues in the 1990s.

The healthcare administrator has remained under intense pressure to reassess programs and policies, adopt new techniques, and start new programs in response to changing market forces. The healthcare administration literature, however, is dominated by new procedures, with relatively little rigorous attention devoted to the review of what worked or did not work in the past. The same assertion can be thrust on publications on health architecture: most books and journal articles on hospital and healthcare facilities are oriented exclusively toward the recent past or the future, and as a consequence, the review of theories and methods over a longer period of time has been neglected.[3]

With the overarching emphasis on new technologies and the need to rein in upwardly spiraling costs, collective uncertainty has become the modus operandi. The provider and the architect are caught in a whipsaw: the need to act today to stay up to date while somehow remaining self-reflective. This problem is no less acute for the administrator, direct-care provider, overseeing agency, or other decision-making entity than it is for the architect or health facility planner. Without an evaluative datum to move beyond or react against, it is difficult to function with much certainty. When this happens, mistakes are inevitable. A small but growing literature in the healthcare planning and design field has emerged to advocate the need for reform. Its goal has been to use design to transform the modernist mindset of the client, architect, healthcare planner, direct-care provider, and even the patient by promoting the notion of patient-centered care over provider-centered care.

This book is a response to a threefold void. First, a gap exists in the literature with respect to the recent architectural history of the hospital and its spawning of allied building types. What worked, what failed, and, perhaps most important, why? Attempts to summarize recent trends in a particular issue or building type, such as outpatient health clinics, mental health facilities, or units within acute-care settings (such as intensive care or emergency departments) have been overly technical or overcompartmentalized. The result has been a series of freestanding mini-literatures.[4] These publications have made it easy to sidestep broader concerns. At the other end of the spectrum, and far fewer in number, are the coffee-table books, which tend to provide scant narrative on planning and design and tend to eschew critical analysis except on a formal level.[5]

Second, there actually has not been a universal drift away from the traditional modern, post–World War II hospital as a functional entity with a valued purpose and mission, as critics so frequently suggest. In reality, forces currently reshaping the modern medical center are not centered on rejection per se but on a reinterpretation of function and mission. This change manifests itself in complex movements and countermovements flowing through, within, and at times against the modernist hospital. These cross-currents, or *transformations*, have occurred in fits and starts, with chronic uncertainty and confusion. Of the nearly six thousand hospitals in operation in the United States in 1995 it was expected that relatively few would completely shut down in the near future. Many would be adapted to new uses, however, including housing, while others might be demolished because of the value of the land they occupy. Throughout these changes, the hospital-based medical center, in its function and as a civic icon, has been the eye of the hurricane.[6]

Third, critical assessment of these movements and countermovements in health architecture has not occurred from the patient's perspective. The profound shift from a provider-driven system to a more patient-driven one—which by many accounts was exacerbated by the start of Medicaid and Medicare in 1965—is evolving into a system restructured toward increased self-regulation. The intent of self-reform is to focus on patient-centered care and consumers' unprecedented sophistication about health-related matters.

The merits of a system designed around the end-user constituency versus one designed around the best interests of the system itself—or, rephrased, a bottom-up versus a top-down system of care—is a topic of much debate. It is at the core of virtually every discussion of patient choice, access, and quality of care. Not surprisingly, a parallel debate in health architecture addresses the use of design to promote the dignity of the patient, appropriate sensory stimuli, self-selection, and control.[7] This is most often characterized as the complex relation between patient-centered care (and patient-centered architecture) and system-centered care (system-centered architecture).

These system-person constructs can be viewed as interdependent paradigms. The "patient empowerment paradigm" is about empowerment versus disempowerment concerning the patient. In the "system empowerment paradigm" the provider experiences empowerment at one extreme and disempowerment at the other. The relationship between these is held in tension, like the cables of a bridge, with each structured element supporting all others. But at what point are the scales tipped in the direction of the provider to the detriment of the recipient? And at what point are they tipped in favor of the care recipient at the provider's expense? In reality, neither dichotomy typically exists in life. In the course of researching this book we learned that the strongest, most enduring examples achieved a balance—that those buildings most supportive from a daily use standpoint and as civic symbols arrived at a state of equilibrium. It is this fascinating space of covariance that guides our discussion of the complex transformations across the health landscape of the last third of the twentieth century.

The argument for the humanization of health care and its institutions dates from the late 1950s. This stream of thought was by the late 1960s influenced by Abraham Maslow's needs hierarchy, which states that when basic physical needs are met, attention becomes focused on higher-level system needs, those associated with a higher concept of self-actualization.[8] In our discussion, this hierarchy is generally commensurate with the patient empowerment paradigm. The work of Maslow and others has been applied to the critical assessment of the needs and aspirations of nursing-home residents, who are capable of having peak experiences and reaching a high level of self-actualization despite often considerable physical and sensory limitations. The problem, as shown in Chapter 7, rested in the undue bureaucratization of the nursing-home experience, with the provider empowerment paradigm dictating innumerable layers of regulations and strictures. The effect of these policies was devastating for the nursing home architecturally and in human terms, given that architecture cannot aspire to anything more than our collective human aspirations will allow.

In this sense, J. Howard's definition of humanization in health care, as summarized by Lee H. Bowker, captures the essence of the argument and has direct import on the study of its parallels in health architecture.[9]

1. **Inherent worth.** Human beings are objects of value, to themselves if not to others. . . . If persons are forced to prove their worth, . . . the burden of proof is dehumanizing.
2. **Irreplaceability.** We are unique and irreplaceable. When people are stereotyped and treated in terms of commonalities rather than differences, dehumanization can logically follow.
3. **Holistic selves.** At any given moment the sum total of a person's experience influences that person's feelings, attitudes, and actions. . . . The patient's whole may be so fragmented that his or her problems become exclusive concerns of multiple practitioners who do not even communicate with one another.
4. **Freedom of action.** Humanized relationships are predicated on freedom of choice. Where the interaction is forced on participants or one or the other is bound against his will, the experience cannot be humanizing.
5. **Status equality.** Humanized relations involve equals on some level. If either sees his or her total self as superior or inferior to the other, the interaction cannot be fully humanizing.

6. Shared decision making and responsibility. [This concept] reflects the emerging ideology that all patients, regardless of education, have a right and perhaps a duty to participate as much as possible in decisions about their care.

7. Empathy. Humans have the ability to sympathize and identify with others. The more they compare themselves to others, the more easily they put themselves in others' shoes. . . . If practitioners contain their sympathy and avoid seeing the world from the vantage point of their patients, they cannot as readily understand the needs of those patients and appropriately respond to them as unique human beings.

8. Positive effects. Human beings are reservoirs and conveyors of emotion. Person-to-person interactions are most likely to involve emotional commitments because reciprocity and empathy can occur.[10]

These tenets of humanistic care are analogous to the values associated with a humanizing architecture for health care. If depicted as a biaxial matrix, two columns represent the two paradigms, viewed by each of three areas of concern: functional concerns, symbolic concerns, and aesthetic or formal concerns. Buildings associated with the system empowerment paradigm have been seen as over-complex, difficult to make sense of, and difficult to function within on a daily basis because of their convoluted layout, immense scale, awkwardness, and, in the extreme, threatening appearance. During the years of dominance of the International Style and its modernist offshoots, particularly the period up to 1980 in health architecture, the "less is more" dictum prevailed among architects. Ideologically, modernists hoped to improve the world, but by 1980 the basic principles of modernism had come under heavy scrutiny. Meanwhile, the hospital had become a proving ground for the application of modernist principles in a full-tilt effort to express and further the dictates of the era of technological medicine.

The seeds of the patient empowerment paradigm, with its widespread rejection of modernism in the late 1970s, were beginning to take root—the hospice movement was one example—but, not coincidentally, the influence of the anti-technologists was rather late in reaching the hospital as a building type. This would prove to be a lengthy bottom-up process, as new architectural freedoms trickled up through small-scale buildings, particularly in architectural work that would soon be known as postmodernism. Its adherents boldly (and some still claim mistakenly) proclaimed that modernism had failed to improve the world. The bases for postmodern reactionism in the healthcare milieu were, besides "patient-centered care," a new emphasis on surface, texture, and ornament, on traditional building massing and internal configuration through more legible interior spaces and circulation patterns (even at times recalling Florence Nightingale's provisions), on the reincorporation of nature as a therapeutic design element, and on the degree to which the building was attractive, uplifting, and comprehensible in the eyes of the patient. If architectural institutionalization had been the result of building on an inhuman scale, now, representational imagery in interior graphics (such as the pictures of children used in many new pediatric facilities), new expressions of the civic dimensions of health architecture (such as the location of a new clinic at the center of a town plan), and experimentation with residential images (the incorporation of elements of home) were acceptable. Nonetheless, time would serve as the true test. Seventeenth- and eighteenth-century advocates of totalitarian staff control of the patient probably believed no less fervently in their epoch than did the patient-centered-care advocates by the end of the twentieth century.

By 1965, the hospital as an institution was firmly centered within the healthcare system, but in subsequent years the hospital's dominance of the health landscape would diminish. One sees, therefore, when viewing the hospital through this paradigmatic dualism, a shift away from the highly centralized medical center to a decentralized system of community-based care settings with the hospital and its successor, the critical care center, at its hub. The increasing emphasis on outpatient care in places other than a hospital gave rise to, if nothing else, the possibility for a less threatening architectural language in health care.[11]

Movements and Countermovements

The last major text to address the history of the hospital was John Thompson and Grace Golden's *The Hospital: A Social and Architectural History* (1975).[12] It remains a seminal work on the origins and evolution of the hospital in Western culture, dating from the Greek Asclepia to the modern machine hospitals of the 1960s. But from 1975 to the present the literature lacks any comparable work continuing this line of critical inquiry. Thompson and Golden distinguished between what they referred to as "designed" and "derived" plans, defining designed hospitals as "those in which an attempt was made to plan for the function of nursing care." In derived hospitals the configuration and exterior were copied from another building type—monastery, palace, estate, prison, barracks—or synthesized from any number of building types.[13] Thompson and Golden focused almost exclusively on ward design and its evolution over the centuries, from the Asclepia to the Roman Valetudinarium military hospital to the open, cold, infected monastic hospitals of the Middle Ages, the palace hospitals of the Renaissance with their unvariegated geometry, the urban ghetto hospitals and insane asylums of the Industrial Revolution, the reformist Nightingale hospitals of the nineteenth and early twentieth centuries, and the large-scale, austere, and complex postwar modern machine hospitals. Throughout, the authors stated their adherence to what they regarded as the four basic tenets of any nursing unit: "The healthful environment it provides for patients, the amount of privacy it allows patients, the extent to which it exercises supervision and control over patients, and the efficiency with which it can be operated. These we call the four elements of ward design."[14]

Thompson and Golden operationalized this four-point framework in the analysis of historical developments, and their contribution remains peerless in the literature, up to its point of publication. However, and understandably, it became somewhat diffuse and fragmented when dealing with the most recent events in the field and placing them in context (and this will undoubtedly be true for this book as well). Regardless, their detailed attention to the Yale Studies in Hospital Planning and Administration remains a landmark, with Yale–New Haven Hospital functioning as the case study institution. Their groundbreaking studies, featured in the concluding chapters of their book, are still of interest, although the considerable attention afforded the design and staffing of the nursing unit came at the expense of prognostications on a broader scale (in fact, no direct mention was made of *any* outpatient facilities constructed in the 1960s or early 1970s).

Partly as a result of the relative inattention of Thompson and Golden to the seeds of change that would lead to a dramatic restructuring of the health landscape, together with the aforementioned start of Medicaid and Medicare, 1965 was chosen as the point in the time line from which to commence this analysis. This date was significant for three reasons: first, this time line overlaps Thompson and Golden's book by a decade in an attempt to cover events they chose not to discuss; second, it was the dawn of the rapid growth and impact of Medicaid and Medicare, which would soon exert profound impact on health architecture, and coincided with the sunset era of the Hill-Burton program of federal construction funds for capital improvements; and third, one year later Robert Venturi's *Complexity and Contradiction in Architecture* was published.[15] This third development is seen as pivotal in the emergence of postmodernism in architecture.

Venturi argued for a "messy," vital, complex, and contradictory approach to design, in opposition to the austere minimalism of modern architecture. His book came to be widely viewed as a postmodern treatise to a generation of architects inculcated in the International Style. Although it has been generally assumed that postmodernism did not affect health architecture until the 1980s, we challenge this assumption. In reality, postmodernism began to infiltrate health architecture in the late 1960s in the work of a few architects and clients who had become disenchanted with the status quo, although the earliest experiments were limited to small-scale freestanding health centers, hospices, dental clinics, and alternative care hospitals—such as the iconoclastic terraced-roof American Oncologic Hospital (1966–68) in Philadelphia (Chapter 2). The hospital architecture mainstream, however, cloistered itself (and its clients) from postmodernism for many more years because it was considered too radical for conservative-minded hospital administrators and their staffs. Its gradual assimilation into mainstream health architecture is discussed at length in subsequent chapters.

In the second chapter we recount the dominance, by the 1960s, of the International Style in hospital and clinic architecture, and the dissatisfaction that began to take root because of its restrictiveness. In the third chapter we discuss the entrenchment of the centralized, high-tech urban medical center, along with the effect of rampant expansionism and modernization, the emergence of investor-owned hospitals and managed care in the United States, and the rise of contemporary antihospitalism. In the fourth chapter, the search for the "perfect" hospital as a machine for healing is viewed as a search for utopia, as architecture was unable to keep up with the pace of change; it was not uncommon for a hospital to be deemed obsolete the day it opened and for construction crews to be brought in soon thereafter to update some aspect. We discuss utopian hospital prototypes against the backdrop of a society experiencing significant upheaval and consider the tenuous relation between the hospital as visionary machine and the patient.

The focus of Chapter 5 is the decentralization of services and the reappraisal of the modern hospital. This organizational shift would manifest itself in the movement away from autonomous, highly centralized institutions toward providers functioning in affiliated but decentralized networks, evolving into the eventual dominance of vast managed care systems.

In Chapter 6 we focus on the patient room, particularly on the rise of the private room, the all-private-room hospital, and the ultimate death of the open-ward hospital in the United States, despite the continued use of the ward in most other parts of the world. In Chapter 7 we discuss movements and countermovements in health architecture for the aged, ranging from precursors of the modern nursing home to the emergence of the assisted-living movement. The rise of the freestanding community care center, from precursors in the 1930s to the storefront urban advocacy clinics of the 1960s to the rise of highly specialized outpatient surgery centers in the suburbs, is the subject of Chapter 8.

In the concluding chapter, the period 1965–2000 is distilled into a number of trends that collectively constitute the new "health culture." These determinants include the rise of home health care, the reinvention of the medical center, the changing relationship between provider and care recipient, the imperative of adopting sustainable design strategies and principles, the use of nature as a therapeutic modality, the call for interdisciplinary education and professional alliances, and the influence of information technology.

Six Waves of Health Architecture in History

We have identified six periods in the history of health architecture that capture key developments through the centuries. These stages consist of five historical "waves" and an emerging sixth wave, which anticipates a period of rapid transformation in the new millennium. There is a certain degree of overlap among these periods, which we label the Ancient, the Medieval, the Renaissance, the Nightingale, the Modern Megahospital, and the Virtual Healthscape, which is emerging completely distinct from the fifth wave.

The Ancient

The first wave was expressed in the healing practices of the ancient Egyptians, the Greeks, and Middle Eastern and Eastern cultures. Nature and the afterlife played a role in the healing process; death was considered inevitable, although the earliest infirmaries were operated in conjunction with wellness and spiritual treatment centers. Wellness care was developed by the Greeks between 1,000 B.C. and A.D. 100. From the beginning of organized care the rich were treated to higher standards than were the lower economic classes. The private room first appeared nearly three thousand years ago in the Greek Asclepion. The shift from the first to the second wave generally coincided with the fall of Greece and the rise of Rome, and the second wave lasted until Rome's fall, in about A.D. 340. The most notable treatment settings were the Valetudinaria. These archetypal Roman military hospitals were built near the front lines throughout Europe and the near Middle East. The emphasis was on returning soldiers to battle as soon as possible. The fall of Rome created a void in orga-nized care across the vast regions previously dominated by the Roman Empire.

The Medieval

During the Middle Ages, the Catholic Church arose as the most powerful provider of hospital care. Immense monastic hospitals were built on the edges of villages and cities throughout the fifth through thirteenth centuries. These hospitals were the origins of the modern medical center. The one at St. Gall, Switzerland, was a walled city, headed by an administrator known as the abbot. Typically, towns grew to surround their monastic hospital, although those in population centers grew to as much as five times their original size. Hence the origins of hospital expansionism. The rise of the state-run insane asylum and state-operated urban hospitals began to signal the gradual shift to the next period.

The Renaissance

The Renaissance was epitomized by the stately palace hospitals of Europe, so named for their absolute adherence to neoclassical architecture. The era of clas-sicist and neoclassicist revival, dominated by symmetrical, axial configurations and regimented facades, lasted from the 1650s to the late nineteenth century. The exterior and plan configuration of London's Bethlehem Hospital (1676), also known as Bedlam, provide an example (fig. 1.1). The Ecole des Beaux Arts in Paris became a major center for neoclassical hospital design. In 1785, one of its atelier directors, Poyet, became responsible for proposing visionary replacement prototype hospital plans (some were built, others were not) for the obsolescent Hotel Dieu hospital, and for hospitals on the fringes of the city. Hotel Dieu had grown to house 2,600 beds scattered among numerous dilapidated buildings, including a women's ward built atop a bridge across the Seine.[16] Neoclassicism, rejected by the avant-garde during much of the twentieth century, reemerged as a viable influence in the period of postmodernism in the late twentieth cen-tury (fig. 1.2).

The Nightingale

The neoclassicism of the mid-nineteenth century coincided with the rise of the first truly modernist hospital-planning principles, through the work of Florence Nightingale. She emphasized function above form some two decades before the phrase "form follows function" was coined by Chicago architect Louis Sullivan to epitomize the new epoch of modern architecture. The exteriors of most Nightingale-influenced hospitals, however, remained rigidly neoclassicist, and her ideas were injected only to the extent that they did not interfere with the main architectural "statement."

The fourth wave originated in Florence Nightingale's work on the British front lines in the Crimean War during the 1850s. In two books, *Notes on Nursing* (1858) and *Notes on Hospitals* (1859), Nightingale spelled out her theories on the

1.2. Sylvester Comprehensive Cancer Center, Miami, 1990

practice of nursing, among other topics.[17] This work would have far-ranging implications for the next hundred years of hospital planning and design, guiding even the construction of the earliest Veterans Administration hospitals in the United States up to the beginning of World War II. Her principles—actually guidelines—for hospital reform, concerning such aspects as the maximum allowable width and length of a ward, the size of windows and their placement in relation to the bed, the overall ambiance, the ventilation and heating systems, and the use of specific materials and colors—for example, bright white walls and polished hardwood floors—were unprecedented and in many respects remain applicable. St. Thomas Hospital, London, which opened in 1871, used her theories of interior planning—the linear configuration of the patient ward,

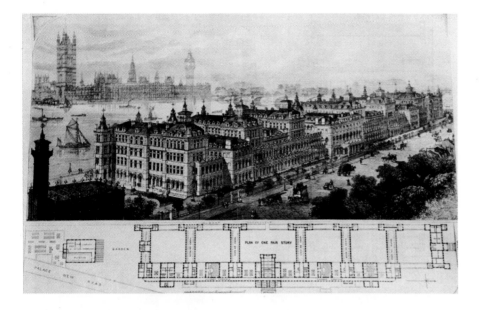

1.3. St. Thomas Hospital, London, 1871, elevation and plan

the supply-spine corridor for circulation of people and supplies, and the modern heating and natural ventilation—although the exterior was cloaked in full-blown Victorian regalia (fig. 1.3). Because Nightingale was neither an architect nor male, she was obliged to remain behind the scenes.

Nightingale's principles were based in large part on the need to bathe the interior spaces of the patient wards in abundant natural daylight. But once such major innovations as the electric light bulb and the Otis elevator were introduced in hospitals in the late 1880s, these concepts were increasingly compromised. Urban Nightingale wards were sometimes situated back to back on each patient floor and stacked up twelve to fifteen stories, thereby disregarding her requirement for light from at least two sides in each ward. However, the advent of the high-rise urban hospital was necessary because of the dramatic increase in land costs in urban centers.[18]

The Minimalist Megahospital

The decades following the end of World War II were the halcyon years of the megahospital. The muscular expressiveness of the International Style was hailed by hospital administrators as the perfect architectural expression in the age of high-tech medicine. It now was possible to reduce the hospital to its structural essence and allow it to become a sheer container of the volumetric machines for being healed, not unlike Le Corbusier's earlier proclamation of Villa Savoye as the archetypal machine for living in. In fact, Le Corbusier himself designed a hospital (unbuilt) for Venice (see Chapter 2), whose plans were grounded in his work dating from the Cité de Refuge project (1934–37), built in Paris for the Salvation Army.[19]

As the hospital grew more specialized, containing newly formed departmental groupings or "zones," each with unique functional planning requirements for diagnosis, treatment, surgery, administration, meals, and other support functions, it grew exponentially in size and spatial complexity. The advent of long-span structural systems and sophisticated heating, ventilation, and air conditioning (HVAC) systems encouraged the abandonment of the obsolete Nightingale wards in favor of large "block hospitals" with vast window-

1.4. The patient tower of the Massachusetts General Hospital, Boston, 1986, rising above the surrounding buildings

less regions at the center of each floor (fig. 1.4). The Weeks' system of hospital planning in England is a notable exception to the trend in the United States and other countries toward block hospitals in the 1960s and early 1970s.[20]

The megahospital reached its apotheosis in the large interstitial hospitals in the late 1980s, as epitomized by the 1,050-bed Veterans Administration Medical Center in Houston and its counterpart in Los Angeles. These and similar huge, self-contained "mothership" medical centers were to become anachronisms when they opened in an era of a restructured healthcare system soon to be refocused on community-based managed care. These hospitals therefore symbolized to critics everything wrong with the healthcare system in advanced industrialized nations.

The Virtual Healthscape

The emerging sixth wave of health architecture, the virtual healthscape, bloomed in about 1990. Part of the reaction against the minimalist megahospital has been a move toward residentialist imagery and design principles for hospitals and allied healthcare building types in the 1990s (fig. 1.5). If the machine hospital, in its enormity, functioned as a magnet, drawing to it all feasible services and subspecialties in the name of efficiency from the viewpoint of a provider-focused system, the postmodern hospital of the 1980s and 1990s has become a centrifuge, spinning off parts from its core to reinsert them in the surrounding community in an age of patient-centered care. At the same time, the information age is profoundly influencing how we define

health and how we care for ourselves. The virtual hospital and the virtual clinic are but two of the virtual health-related environments available in cyberspace.[21]

Together, these six periods in the history of health architecture provide the context for this book, and their articulation supplies the foundation for the following narrative.

1.5. Shenandoah Regional Campus, Manassas, Virginia, 1990, main building

CHAPTER 2

The Hospital as a Machine for Healing

The 1960s was a decade of unprecedented expansion of health organizations, in which new areas of specialization emerged and the institutions came to be used by an expanding cross-section of the population. The public was convinced that an up-to-date hospital was essential for the civic pride of a community. In architecture, by the early 1960s the International Style dominated mainstream hospital design. This style was characterized by flat roofs, minimal exterior ornamentation, monolithic volumes, the use of only one color (usually white or off-white), concrete and steel with large expanses of exterior glass, and a tripartite structure of a below-grade service base, an administrative base at grade level, and a patient tower on top. Austerity was in vogue, in stark contrast to the ornamentalism of opulent urban hospitals of the late nineteenth and early twentieth centuries. The traditional "pavilion" hospital had had a large identifiable main entrance leading to a generous lobby, which in turn led to the upper floors of the hospital, consisting of patient rooms whose smaller windows typically surrounded the exterior of the patient pavilion.

The architectural journals of the 1960s contained annual state-of-the-art reviews, typically in the format of an entire issue devoted to the hospital as a building type. The most common approach consisted of an introductory essay on current trends followed by numerous examples, with relatively little attention devoted to any individual project. The numerous photos were accompanied by usually no more than a few paragraphs on a project's background and development.

In these reviews, the modern—that is, International Style—hospital was lauded as the apotheosis of pure functionalism. At the same time, the hospital as a building type was, by and large, dismissed by the avant-garde because of its scale and sheer complexity, which left little, if any, room for personal artistic expression in terms of aesthetic or formal innovation. As a result, by the mid-1960s the modernist machine hospital drew its share of critics. Writing in the *Architectural Forum* in 1964, Richard A. Miller was one of the first critics to register alarm:

> If progress has complicated other building problems, it has hit hospital design
> with a vengeance. The hospital surgery, for example, was once a single room
> like the historic amphitheater at Massachusetts General Hospital. Today it is an

intricate complex laid out to facilitate . . . technique, equipped with elaborate mechanical, communication, and monitoring networks, linked to laboratories and other rooms for anesthesia, recovery, and intensive care. Yet radical as the innovations are, hospital architecture is being outpaced by still newer developments in medical care. . . . Program requirements, hard to pin down in the first place, change even as a new hospital is being designed. To complicate the matter further, any hospital building or modernization must also emerge from its own peculiar tangle of construction priorities, government and private financing, community planning controls, and mounting operating costs. Little wonder that architecture often gets short shrift, and that hospitals can be among the ungainliest, if not the ugliest, of large buildings today.[1]

In spite of these concerns, the community hospital solidified its role as a centerpiece of civic America after World War II. Numerous high-paying jobs were created through new construction, expansion of services, and new areas of technical specialization. The image of the shimmering glass-and-steel hospital tower was a source of pride for all who helped in its creation, including the many dedicated volunteers who served on fundraising committees and boards of directors. The mural in the staff dining room of Bishop Clarkson Memorial Hospital in Omaha, Nebraska, conveys the image of the International Style hospital as the apotheosis of postwar civic progressiveness (fig. 2.1).

The community hospital had been thoroughly interwoven into the fabric of postwar suburbia. In his book *The Levittowners*, Herbert Gans cited numerous building types that by the early 1960s had become the core educational, religious, commercial, and medical institutions of suburbia.[2] These icons of the rapidly evolving suburb of the late 1950s served as elements of comfort, as a reassuring presence in a brave new world. The blurring of the boundaries across these indices of suburban success was the subject of Stanley Tigerman's entry in the *Buildings for Best Products* exhibit shown at the Museum of Modern Art in New York in 1979. The entry, essentially a critique on civicness, was a large suburban tract house exploded in scale, whereby the local Best Products outlet became the benevolent community symbol of neighborliness, not unlike the community hospital (fig. 2.2).[3] The hospital, however, in reality sought, architecturally, its validation in sources far removed from the suburban residential milieu. Although this fact is ironic in retrospect, at the time almost any hospital administrator would have been hard-pressed to explain why a proposed new hospital might want to look like the houses that surrounded it rather than like a factory or office building.

As Gans pointed out, the local hospital, shopping mall, school, community center, parks, roads, and religious institutions were all symbols of the collective aspirations of the community. Yet the public, while supportive of the roles and services provided by these various civic building types, never wholeheartedly accepted modern architecture in general—including that of the austere International Style hospital. Tigerman's parody of the ubiquitous tract house crossing over into the ubiquitous chain department store could never have applied to the community hospital simply because the hospital took itself far too seriously for that, and its intentional separation from the everyday ver-

Opposite:
2.1. Bishop Clarkson Memorial Hospital, Omaha, Nebraska, 1964, staff dining room

2.2. Stanley Tigerman, entry in *Buildings for Best Products* **competition, Museum of Modern Art, New York City, 1979**

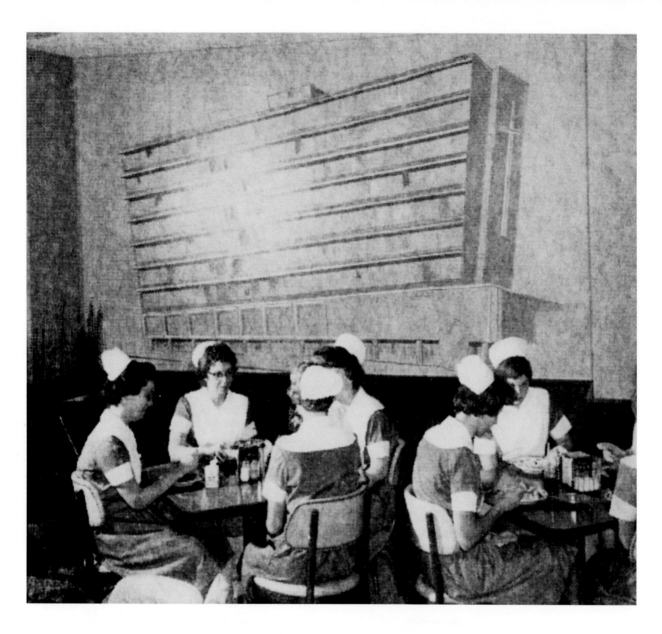

nacular of the suburban neighborhood is an enduring legacy of the International Style community hospital.

The Evolution of Modernism and the International Style

The International Style had its origins in Europe during the 1920s. The Bauhaus, the citadel of early twentieth-century modernism, was founded in 1919 in Dessau, Germany, and operated until Hitler shut it down in 1933.[4] The philosophical call to arms of the faculty of the Bauhaus—which included psychologists, color theorists, furniture designers, industrial designers, architects, and artists—was based on the near-total rejection of the academic and elementarist traditions of the arts-and-crafts movement of the late nineteenth century, and of all modes of neoclassicism as expressed in the arts and in architecture. In their place the Bauhaus proposed a new language of architecture based on forms derived from the rapid rise of industrialism. These forms were based on simple Euclidean geometry, on theories of Gestalt psychology, and on economy of expression in social, behavioral, and aesthetic terms.

The theories of the early modernists spread during the three decades immediately following World War II. Jon Lang and others have examined how a series of pithy phrases—including Louis Sullivan's now clichéd statement "form follows function," Ludwig Mies van der Rohe's definition of architecture as an endeavor where "less is more," and the French architect Le Corbusier's passionate view of the dwelling as a "machine for living in"—profoundly influenced three generations of architects, designers, and urban planners.[5] Le Corbusier was particularly fascinated with the functionalism of naval architecture, especially that of ocean liners.

Urban planning was similarly revolutionized by the call for expunging everything considered extraneous in the urban fabric. In this way a modern city, minimalist in configuration and aesthetic, would be created. This view was most clearly articulated by Le Corbusier in his proposal for Radiant City (1922) and the ideas of the Congrès Internationaux d'Architecture Moderne (CIAM) in the 1930s. Later, Frank Lloyd Wright's Broadacre City proposal (1958) would embody Wright's similar interpretation of modern town planning in an American context. Of the rationale behind the work of the avant-garde during this period, Lang writes:

> There is a tendency, in much recent criticism, to regard these architectural and urban design ideas and proposals as whimsical ego trips or autocratic exercises [rather than] . . . carefully worked out responses to what their proponents considered to be the major problems of their times. At the urban scale these included: the uncontrolled growth of the city; polluting industries; long trips to and from work for the poor; the lack of educational and recreational facilities; dismal housing and sanitary conditions; overcrowded dwellings; and the negative impact of automobiles on the existing infrastructure of cities. In architecture there was the question of how to house large populations in a short time; there were new activity patterns and social organizations to house and thus new building types . . . new technologies to harness . . . the machine age and the new polit-

ical realities. The overall goal was the laudable one of bringing to all people the standard of life that only the wealthy could afford in the nineteenth century.[6]

In the hands of less talented, less resolute followers, however, the results often fell short of the initial high ideals of the first generation of modernists. The modern hospital was by no means immune to this trend. Lang defined three phases of criticism of modern architecture. The first appeared in the late 1940s in the work and writings of a small but influential group known as Team 10. Second, in 1954 Peter and Alison Smithson noted that in "reeducating" their clients and public officials, modernists had created conditions even less humane than those they were rejecting. Five years later the critic Aldo Van Eyck denigrated modernism for its "'boredom of hygiene.' The material slum has gone—but what has replaced it? Just mile upon mile of unorganized nowhere, and nobody feeling he is somewhere."[7] This second wave of critical reaction resulted from the massive urban renewal programs of the 1950s and 1960s in the United States and overseas, and from the piecemeal yet methodical replacement of traditionally developed, socially cohesive neighborhoods with block upon block of austere high-rise housing projects surrounded by expanses of open spaces. As Lang notes, this criticism echoed the earlier rumblings of Team 10 and a few other critics but went much further: the theories of modernism for the first time came under direct attack by such first-wave "new urbanists" as Jane Jacobs, in her 1961 classic *The Death and Life of Great American Cities,* and by Herbert Gans, Martin Pawley, Peter Blake, and Brent Brolin, among others.[8] Concurrently, hospital administrators and their boards wrestled with the decision to stay or relocate, while looking over their shoulders at their peer institutions and competitors.

The third development cited by Lang, originating in the mid-1960s—at about the same time as the critical reaction to the modern hospital and the massive urban renewal efforts involving the urban hospital—is the emergence of the field known as environmental design research, or environment-behavior studies. Its early proponents, reacting against the shortcomings and outright failures of modern minimalism, called for the application of the behavioral sciences to the planning and design of the built environment. The work of the minimalists had done little to satisfy human day-to-day functional requirements. Thus, one of the objectives of the social scientists and designers who began to collaborate (and later of experts trained both in design and social science) was to create settings appropriate to human scale. At this point, hospital administrators struggled to accommodate pressure to expand without obliterating the core legibility, scale, and internal navigability of their institutions. As a means to ameliorate sheer gigantism, such stopgap interventions as multicolored directional bands on floors, bold supergraphics, and floor-coded colors and furnishings were developed in an ultimately futile effort to inject comprehensibility and hence humanism into the modern machine hospital.

The background for these developments was the social and cultural upheaval of the 1960s. In fact, many early adherents to the humanist perspective were grounded in the 1960s counterculture and later, to some extent, in postmodern sensibilities. The humanists' criticisms of modernist institutions were based on four major observations: (1) key decision makers, including both architects and administrators, remained curiously unaccountable to the daily needs of the people who were to use the building; (2) "function," as embedded within the dictum "form follows function," was interpreted in an overly restrictive way, and in the case of the hospital the needs of the patients seemed to be considered less important than those of the machines housed within; (3) architects had been trained to use a highly regimented, restrictive model of human behavior (dating from the reductivist behaviorism of the Bauhaus), as manifested by, for example, the patient room "machine" with virtually all-fixed furnishings; (4) designers lacked specific knowledge of (and interest in) the myriad implications of their healthcare buildings for patients and the general public. Further, no studies were made of the performance of these modernist hospitals across time. By the late 1960s, the dogma set down nearly fifty years earlier was still being unquestioningly applied. The cookie-cutter syndrome set in, and community hospitals began to look nearly identical inside and out.

Hill-Burton and the Modern Hospital

After World War II the medical establishment accepted International Style modernism with open arms. The vast funds allocated to postwar federal and state programs enabled the construction of new hospitals and clinics and had a profound impact on their size, outward appearance or "complexion," and configuration. At that time, it was implicitly assumed among architects and their clients that there was an acceptable (modern) aesthetic (fig. 2.3) and an unacceptable (historicist) one. Hence the International Style was able to assert dominance over the next forty years of health architecture.

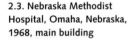

2.3. Nebraska Methodist Hospital, Omaha, Nebraska, 1968, main building

In the United States, the passage of the Hospital Construction Act of 1946, commonly known as the Hill-Burton Act, set the stage for four decades of health facility construction. Hill-Burton evolved from the New Deal programs of the 1930s. In the years 1941–46 teams of community representatives met with representatives of the U.S. Public Health Service to map all existing hospitals and allied health facilities on a regional basis. With the end of World War II came the immediate need to accommodate the return of veterans, the creation of new households, the exponential growth of the suburbs, the increasingly specialized facilities that hospitals required in order to keep pace with accelerating developments in medicine. These circumstances were viewed as a unique opportunity to coordinate a network of facilities across the nation. One of the first steps taken after passage of the legislation was the mapping of communities where services were noticeably lacking, particularly in light of shifts in population from rural to urban and from center cities to suburbs. During this period, the Veterans Administration, the U.S. Public Health Service, and the Indian Health Service received massive infusions of funds for construction.

The Hill-Burton legislation resulted in a series of overlapping rings laid across the nation, with a large, typically urban teaching institution at the center of each ring and a network of support or satellite clinics and specialty hospitals—for example, clinics for psychiatry, tuberculosis, chronic disease, and community health—arrayed in outlying zones. The intent of the Hill-Burton Standards, which consisted of preset floor plans, room arrangements, bed capacities, and minimum standards for diagnostic and treatment departments, was to assist communities, health planners, and architects to ensure minimum quality and content. At first the program was particularly aimed at underserved rural areas, but later it was expanded to include urban medical centers, and in its later years the program became associated with classic pork barrel politics.

From 1946 to 1965 the federal government's involvement in health care, then, was limited primarily to financing hospital construction. Thousands of facilities were built during this period, and many remain in use. In 1965, with the passage of the legislation that created Medicare and Medicaid, the Hill-Burton program diminished in importance because emphasis had been shifted from bricks-and-mortar initiatives to program-based initiatives, such as the creation of a new oncology program. The two new health entitlements, Medicare and Medicaid, had been initially designed to be small and containable programs but rapidly grew to immense, seemingly uncontrollable proportions. The implications of this growth are discussed further in the following chapter.

Le Corbusier's Machine for Healing

Hill-Burton facilities were modeled, almost automatically, on the principles of modernist functionalism. Still, it is surprising that few internationally known architects ever received a commission to design a hospital, and this fact probably accounted for the Zeitgeist's disinterest in the hospital. Le Corbusier, one of the most influential architects of the twentieth century and indisputably a leader of the modern movement, was an exception; he was offered a commis-

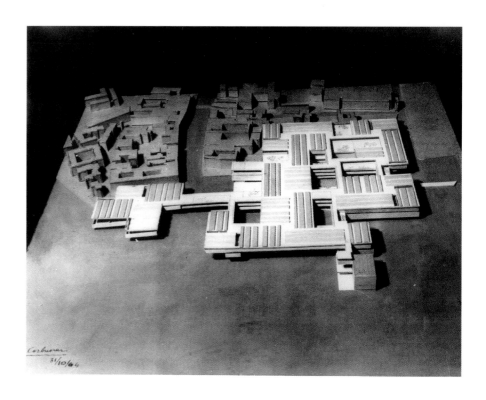

2.4. Le Corbusier, proposal for City Hospital of Venice, Italy, 1965 (model)

sion to design a new city hospital for Venice, Italy. He presented his design a few months before he died, in 1965 (figs. 2.4 and 2.5).

The building was to occupy a prominent site adjacent to a large lagoon. Le Corbusier designed a low, sprawling building of interconnected parts around courtyards, recalling Venice's intense network of buildings and open squares. Because of the frequent flooding in the city, he raised the hospital on piles, bringing to mind such vertical accents as gondola moorings, bridges, the underpinnings of buildings, and the city's horizontal silhouette. The hospital was to be constructed of cast-in-place concrete on columns, or *pilotís*.

According to an account in an American journal, "the hospital is planned in four levels, each housing a different aspect of medical services. The first floor contains arrival and registration facilities for all departments, in addition to commonly shared departments. . . . One alarming provision is for automobile parking for vehicles coming across a gangway from the Santa Lucia Station. . . . Venetians have been receiving adequate medical care for some time, however, and this proposal for introducing the camel's nose of the noxious automobile into the Venetian tent is inexcusable and should be abandoned."[9] The second level was designated for all diagnostic and treatment functions. The third floor was a services floor, containing staff preparation and staging areas. The fourth floor was the nursing floor for patient care, divided into the departments of general medicine, general surgery, neurology, neurosurgery, urology, dermatology, otolaryngology, stomatology, oncology, obstetrics, and pediatrics. A chapel was also to be housed on this floor. The patient rooms were designed to be "modulor," in accord with Le Corbusier's well-documented theories of the "modulor man."[10] These rooms were criticized for their lack of conventional windows (the only source of natural daylight was a clerestory extending along the inner, corridor wall of the room): "A significant departure—for hospitals, at least—is that patient rooms will be lit indirectly. . . . There will be no direct natural illumination or view, which constitutes an unkindness perhaps to patients who would otherwise be looking out at the lagoon."[11]

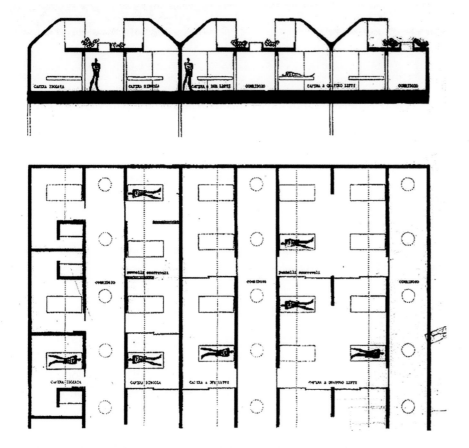

2.5. Le Corbusier, City Hospital of Venice, section and plan

Nevertheless, Le Corbusier was held in reverence by the cognoscenti in the architectural press, and the American reviewer ultimately rationalized the design by adding, "This system should give the hospital a cadenced roofline that will catch the rhythm of the pillars supporting the mass of the buildings. . . . If the automobile proposal can be shelved, Venice will achieve a building that could introduce an architectural vitality rivaling that of her great past." The planned site of the hospital was considered dominated by expendable buildings of minimal architectural merit. Thus the proposal was also viewed as a vehicle for urban renewal, even though the urban-planning ideology of Le Corbusier had by that time acquired numerous critics, perhaps the most vocal of whom was Jane Jacobs. In the end, funding for Le Corbusier's proposed design was never secured, and an alternate plan was developed and built by others on a different site.

Jacobs and others faulted Le Corbusier for taking an oversimplistic view of the city in terms of its day-to-day functions, and for his subdivision of the city into rigid, hierarchical, mutually exclusive precincts, with little attention paid to the complex, vast incongruities of urban life. Some of these critics have since accepted this limitation in his writings and buildings, and many of these same people now defend Le Corbusier for his ability to remain in the ideological vanguard up to his death. Architect and critic Charles Jencks, for example, has argued that the Venice hospital proposal contains many of the complex, urban attributes that critics of Le Corbusier had been clamoring for. According to Jencks, the building's semi-cloistered, monastic ambiance and the use of minimal, indirect light indicate "all the heroic qualities of calmness, isolation and pure form when patients would seem to need comforting qualities of human contact and variety. But obviously this depends on the patient, his condition and taste. No clear-cut answers will ever be achieved about the ultimate appropriateness of metaphors, and one epoch's disdain for an 'heroic' hospital conceived with the Parthenon spirit will turn into another's appreciation for these qualities."[12] Nevertheless, although Le Corbusier's Venice Hospital might have been successful from an urban design standpoint, it would likely have been less than a success in terms of the daily quality of life of its occupants. Regardless, the initial spirit of the International Style was diminishing, as evidenced by the work of architects of lesser stature than Le Corbusier. And this was also the case with hospital architecture.

Interpreting the International Style in the United States

In the United States, the dominant internal configuration for a hospital nursing unit throughout the 1950s, as virtually mandated by the Hill-Burton guidelines, was the double-loaded corridor. In this arrangement a central corridor is flanked by rooms that open onto it. Virtually all Veterans Administration hospitals, urban teaching hospitals, and community hospitals of the period followed this plan. By the early 1960s, however, the double-loaded corridor had given way to what would became known as the racetrack plan. This was created by pulling apart the room blocks along the two sides of the corridor and inserting in the center a core containing a panoply of support amenities. The plan of St. Joseph's Hospital in Burbank, California (1962–64), designed by Welton Becket and Associates, was an early example. The service core contained elevators, two nurses' stations, closets for clean and soiled linen, mechanical shafts, general storage, staff offices, treatment rooms, and conference rooms. It was a *reflective plan:* the two sides of the floor were mirror images. In this sole respect it was similar to the European palace hospitals of the sixteenth through eighteenth centuries. At St. Joseph's each of the four patient floors housed a mix of private and semi-private accommodations: numerous double-occupancy rooms plus six rooms each containing four beds separated by a partition along the center. The exterior of the building was of reinforced concrete and bands of ceramic tile spandrels. The patient floors were situated atop a support base of administrative, diagnostic, and treatment services, and a second level of surgical suites.

The modest scale of St. Joseph's main lobby was typical of 1960s community hospitals, as opposed to the grand lobbies of prewar hospitals. The chapel of St. Joseph's was somewhat atypical, however. In most hospitals the chapel was gradually being downsized to a waiting room off a bleak corridor, but St. Joseph's had a freestanding chapel across from the main entrance. The 256-bed main building and the chapel cost 5.5 million to build.[13]

To position the U.S. interpretation of the block style in context, it is useful to examine its counterpart overseas. In England the double-loaded, mid- to high-rise "ward block" hospital was the dominant configuration in the 1960s. A prime example of the influence of Le Corbusier, who in his Radiant City proposal of 1922 envisioned the high-rise housing block as set apart from its immediate context of undifferentiated open space, was the Princess Margaret Hospital, built at Swindon in 1960–65 for the Oxford Regional Hospital Board.

This medical center was designed by Powell and Moya, with Llewelyn-Davies, Weeks and Partners. In 1965, when the first phase of construction was completed, the hospital contained 388 beds in a linear block configuration; its structural expressiveness was accentuated through the use of reinforced concrete with floor-to-ceiling windows on the patient floors (figs. 2.6–2.9). The wards contained eighty beds per floor "in a long slab block that is naturally ventilated. . . . Each ward comprises two, twenty-bed nursing units sharing a cen-

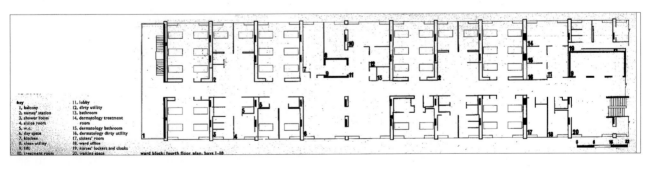

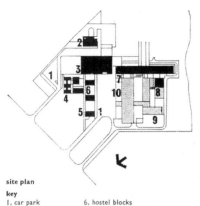

site plan
key
1, car park
2, boiler house
3, service zone
4, training school
5, flats .

6, hostel blocks
7, ward block
8, operating theatre
9, physical medicine
10, out-patients' department

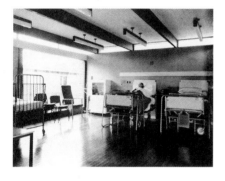

2.8. Princess Margaret Hospital, site plan

2.9. Princess Margaret Hospital, interior of ward

Opposite:
2.10. Archbishop Bergan Mercy Hospital, Omaha, Nebraska, 1965, plan of typical patient-care unit

tral day space, kitchen and treatment suite similar to the Nuffield experimental ward in Belfast."[14] Patient rooms housed up to six beds each. From the day this and similarly designed hospitals opened, the patients and staff frequently complained of the glare caused by the outer "window wall" and the harsh silhouettes caused by an unbalanced distribution of daylight.

By contrast, an interesting and popular feature, and a holdover from the solariums used for outdoor therapy in tuberculosis (TB) hospitals earlier in the century, was the open-air terrace at the end of each patient floor. This feature accentuated the main ward block's steamship-like appearance. In silhouette, it was reminiscent of Le Corbusier's Unité d'Habitation in Marseilles (1947–52), which also incorporated exterior space—vertical garden terraces (later, this feature was used in high-rise urban renewal housing blocks in the United States and elsewhere, with mixed results). Because of the complex political bureaucracy inherent in the British National Health Service and its counterpart in other developed nations, it often took a decade or more for a project to move from conception to completion, and in some cases architects were hired and fired along the way. In the case of the Princess Margaret, architects were appointed in 1951, and it took nearly ten years for construction to commence on the first phase of the medical center.

The mid-1960s United States equivalent to the European International Style ward block hospital was similarly driven by highly complex internal functional requirements, prescriptive federal guidelines, and the prevailing architectural ideology. But in the United States, pure, shiplike forms, while desirable, were not of obsessive importance. Problems had begun to arise in the United States and overseas when staff began to require so much equipment and allied services in the service support core that the linearity of the open-plan ward block nursing units—the last remaining vestiges of the Nightingale ward—was overwhelmed by a propensity to house more and more machines within the core. "Optimization" of staff and patient flow diagrams was emphasized; concurrently, new and expanded departments were added to the support base below. For the architect, the most difficult task was to provide an elegant building envelope for an ever-expanding, ungainly apparatus. As before, the central core contained staff functions, such vertical transportation systems as conveyors and elevators, and stairs. New additions to the core consisted of specialized treatment rooms, triage rooms, conference rooms, radiology suites, and numerous pre- and post-staging areas. The net effect of all these changes was that the plan of the core ballooned from a rectangle to more of a square box.

This trend away from the linear double-loaded corridor and toward the rectangular racetrack and later the racetrack square, or "block plan," evolved slowly over ten years. A midpoint between the two extremes of the double-loaded plan and the block racetrack plan was represented by the plan and appearance of the Archbishop Bergan Mercy Hospital (1963–65) in Omaha, Nebraska (fig. 2.10). This five-level community hospital, constructed of reinforced concrete with concrete floors and roof, contained only semi-private rooms on each patient floor, with patient rooms wrapped around the ends of a 52-bed nursing unit. The patient rooms had to be at the ends for two reasons: first, in order to position rooms as near to the nurses' station as possible, and

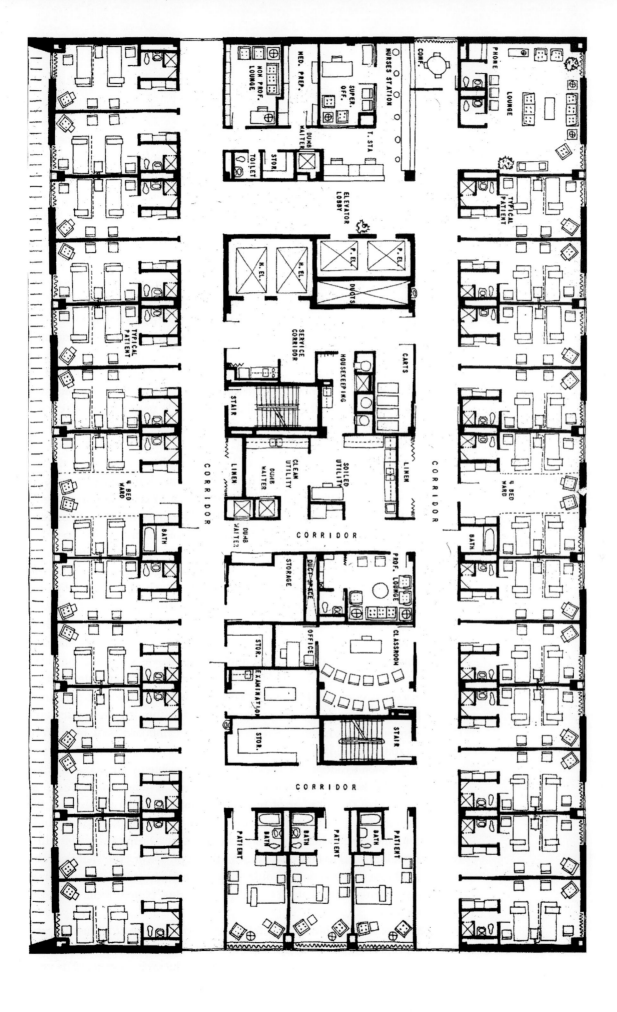

second, as a response to the expanded width of the staff service core. The diagnostic and treatment functions were located on the first floor, together with all outreach and administrative functions. An innovative architectural feature on the exterior was the addition of mechanized vertical aluminum louvers for use as sun screens, automated to move gradually during the course of a day in response to the position of the sun.[15]

The mid-1960s block—often referred to as "cube"—hospital perhaps reached its apotheosis in the Bellevue Hospital replacement facility in New York City (1964–66). Its high-rise block configuration was a response to the administration's concern that the horizontality of the existing complex had gradually led to highly inefficient traffic patterns between departments and between buildings, and this had translated into high costs in personnel and facility maintenance. The new twenty-five-floor hospital block was expected to result in significant savings because of the decentralization and verticalization of central support and distribution systems. This monolithic building contained 2,000 beds and replaced all eight pavilions previously used for patient care. It was the first of its type built in the United States at such a scale. In addition to its role as the main city hospital, it was to serve the staff and patients of multiple academic programs and was one of the first applications of the "progressive patient care" nursing model, defined as a system whereby variable numbers of staff were assigned to a care team as a patient's needs changed. Each floor measured an unprecedented 65,000 square feet and was to house its own battery of diagnostic, administrative, dietary, and laboratory services. The patient was to remain on the same floor for all diagnostic and treatment procedures except for major invasive treatment, such as surgery and radiation therapy. Thus elevator travel for patients was to be kept at a minimum, while the vertical transport systems reduced excessive travel distances for staff.

The exterior perimeter wall of the block contained windows; all other rooms were windowless. This decision was defended on the grounds that only the patient needed natural daylight and a view. It was expected that staff would perform their duties more efficiently in artificially illuminated spaces. As a consequence, all patient rooms were located along the four perimeter walls of the envelope, and all staff were housed within its interior regions. Patient-care support functions were located on the "inboard" side of the four perimeter zones (fig. 2.11).

The decision to adopt the block was made possible by advances in artificial lighting, the development of long-span structural systems that made it possible to minimize the number of interior columns and thereby expand the typical structural bay as a basic unit of planning, and by advances in heating, ventilation, and air-conditioning systems (HVAC). The hospital, as a building type, was well primed to take advantage of the trend toward the "hermetically sealed" building as a means to acquire unprecedented control over the three main care and treatment realms: technical apparatus, patient rooms, and the staff work area.

This replacement block hospital was the cornerstone of a massive construction program at Bellevue during the 1960s and 1970s. But the response to the Bellevue high-rise was less than enthusiastic. The staff questioned its vastness, impersonal scale, visual sterility, and the degree of isolation fostered by the design. The architectural media also criticized the replacement hospital's "stark concrete cube" exterior, although they noted that the lead architects, Pomerance and Breines, had made a minimal attempt to address its monolithism through "the textured rhythm of sill and floor heights."[16] In other words, these architects had accepted the box as the basic shape on the basis of its universal functionality, and therefore they had by default limited their role to that of exterior window-dressers. As the generic block hospital quickly filled to capacity with people, services, and high technology, comparatively little thought was given to traditional qualities of buildings—natural daylight, scale, or meaningful connections to the natural environment. This dilemma would force conditions of unprecedented compromise upon the hospital architect for years to come. It was not until 1979 that the generic block configuration would be openly attacked, and options proposed, in an article by Lord Taylor in the *British Medical Journal* (see Chapter 4).[17]

American Alternatives to the Block Hospital

The emergence of the urban high-tech block hospital all but signaled the end of the nineteenth and early twentieth century courtyard hospital, which had been planned and designed largely on Nightingale principles. These pavilion hospitals had dwindled in number since 1945 because of rapidly rising land costs in urban areas, obsolescence in the face of medical and technological progress, and the need to house more technical and staff support functions within and near the nursing unit. Aside from this, in the era of technological medicine, attitudes had shifted as to the virtue of nature as a therapeutic tool in the healthcare setting. While the urban teaching hospital was busy assembling high-tech equipment and experiencing unprecedented expansion on increasingly high-priced parcels of land, smaller hospitals in communities where land costs were lower were able to maintain smaller facilities in a more horizontal configuration. Therefore these hospitals were able to retain a more traditional linkage with nature, despite the pressure to expand.

A pivotal example of this dilemma of nature versus machine was illustrated in the plan of the Garland Memorial Hospital in Garland, Texas (1963–64). The building consisted of a front side that housed administrative, diagnostic, and treatment services and all central support functions, and a back side that housed the nursing units. The nursing units were fingers reaching out from a central access point. A combination of private and semi-private patient rooms was arrayed along a double-loaded corridor in each nursing unit, with the nurses' station at the end closest to the interior court and garden. An architectural review panel praised the innovative central interior open space as one of the first of its type. In fact, this large space—which would be later referred to as an atrium—was the precursor of a widely emulated element of hospital architecture.

As a whole, the hospital was semi-radial in plan, whereas each nursing unit was linear in plan. The partial pinwheel created by fanning out these linear elements yielded outdoor green spaces between each of the wings. This feature

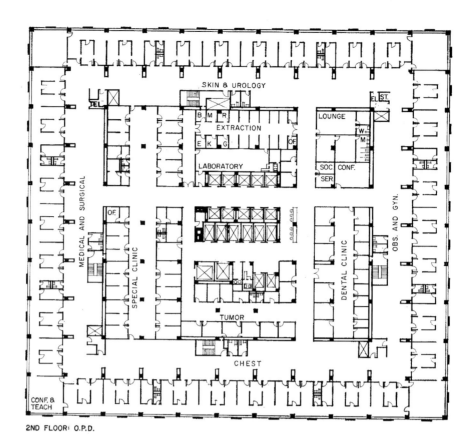

2.11. Bellevue Hospital,
New York City, 1964, plans of
second floor, ground floor,
fifteenth floor, and fourth floor

2ND FLOOR: O.P.D.

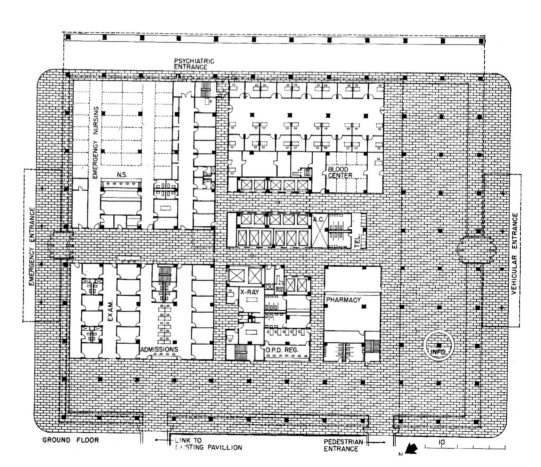

GROUND FLOOR

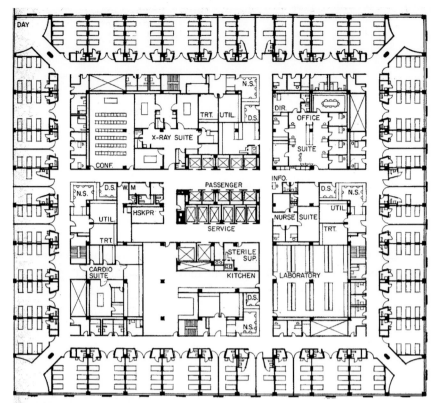

15TH FLOOR: MEDICAL & SURGICAL

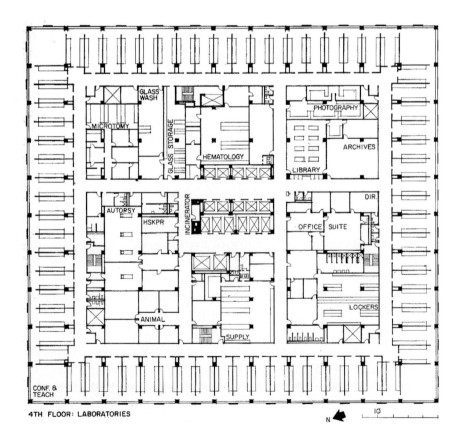

4TH FLOOR: LABORATORIES

N   10

was a direct holdover from the typical Nightingale open ward and the pavilion hospital. By planning the hospital around the functional grouping of major services "in the shape of a hand with two thumbs and six fingers," the architects provided options for horizontal expansion (by extending the length of these elements) as well as vertical expansion.[18]

The Radial

The struggle among staff efficiency—that is, the minimization of distances that staff must walk on the nursing unit and the maximization of direct visual contact with patients from the nurses' station—nature as a healing force (an increasingly discardable amenity in the eyes of decision makers), and the indispensable machine merged into the struggle against the status quo of orthogonality—obsessive use of right angles—in the planning of the typical modern hospital. The curves and wave forms made possible by advances in architectural technology gave rise to a new wave of experimentation with radial, semicircular, and cloverleaf floor plans for nursing units. The search for an ideal radial nursing unit in the 1960s hospital went through three early stages: the side-by-side concept, where the main hospital sat beside one or more radial patient towers; the piggyback concept, with the radial towers straddled above an orthogonal support base; and the radialization of nearly the entire hospital, including the base as well as its tower.

The Lorain Community Hospital, in Lorain, Ohio (1964–65), was one of the first radial side-by-side hospitals in the United States. Its conflict among the nursing units (that is, their relative freedom from the core functions), nature, and machine was manifested in a clear, though somewhat tentative, demarcation between two "worlds"—the main hospital and the nursing unit. Because of the mutual exclusivity of the two plan types and their proximity to one another, the two domains seemed almost suspicious of one another (fig. 2.12).

The front side of the hospital, built initially for 150 beds, contained administrative, central support, and dietary areas, and surgery, obstetrics and the emergency departments. A central spine connected to the main body of the hospital ran on an axis with the main public entrance; two radial nursing towers flanked this axis, housing the nursery, pediatrics, offices, and consultation rooms. The central nurses' station was situated between the two towers. The description of Lorain Community Hospital appears to be the first published account of a community hospital in the United States with radial nursing units.[19]

A second significant variant in the search to incorporate the radial concept in the United States was in the 315-bed Scott and White Memorial Hospital in Temple, Texas (1963–65). Three five-level patient towers sat atop a two-level support base (figs. 2.13 and 2.14). The base contained, as usual, all administrative, general support, diagnostic, and treatment functions. Each tower was designed to accommodate expansion by an additional three levels at a later date. One of the three towers was built slightly higher than the others; it housed thirty beds, whereas the smaller two housed sixteen beds each. At the time this replacement hospital opened, only 35 percent of the beds were in private rooms. The washrooms were on the "outboard" (outer wall) side of each patient

2.12. Lorain Community Hospital, Ohio, 1965, circular patient-care unit

room: "The octagonal nursing units . . . have the nursing station in the center so that a nurse is no farther than six steps from each patient's room and all beds are visible. . . . This appears to have a good psychological effect on the patients." The administrator, Vernon W. Forsman, added that radial units allowed for staffing reductions while simultaneously allowing for every patient to have "essentially intensive care." The standardization of the floor plan was also claimed to have a positive effect on employees because it required minimal staffing adjustments when assignments changed.[20]

This was eventually to become the standard line of argument for the radial: greater efficiency in terms of staffing ratios, reduced travel distances for staff, better observation of patients, and ease in expansion because future units could be stacked on top. An additional claim, which would later be viewed as the most questionable feature but was at first lauded as one of its key assets, was that patients actually preferred the radial unit over conventional orthogo-

2.13. Scott and White Memorial Hospital, Temple, Texas, 1964

2.14. Scott and White Memorial Hospital, plan of typical patient-care unit

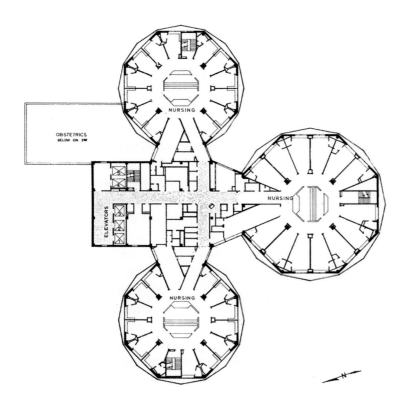

2.15. Central Kansas Medical
Center, Great Bend, Kansas,
1964

nal patient rooms and unit configurations. In fact, widely reported anecdotal evidence soon indicated that the patient often experienced a greater loss of privacy in the irregularly shaped rooms because the door was usually wide open to face the nurses' station. Furthermore, the bed itself often faced toward the station, thereby putting the patient's backside virtually against the window wall, rendering it virtually impossible to take in a meaningful view. Hence, this arrangement was a constant reminder of the patient's isolation and confinement to the inner realm of the hospital.

The third early variant on the radial concept was clearly expressed in the Central Kansas Medical Center, in Great Bend, Kansas, designed by Shaver and Company, with J. A. Hamilton and Associates (1963–64). The exterior appeared nearly absolute in its radiality. Three four-level towers were its dominant visual feature, anchoring a triangulated support base with circular exterior walls (fig. 2.15). The main floor, ninety feet in diameter, housed all central support, administrative, diagnostic, and treatment services. The triangulated corridor was anchored by three pods: emergency care, records and administrative, and laboratories and central support (fig. 2.16a). Each of the three patient towers housed a twenty-three-bed nursing unit on each floor, along with a glassed-in nurses' station and staff support amenities (such as linen closets) in the center of each unit. The triangulated central core on each floor housed the expected aggregation of stairs and elevators, consultation rooms, and supply and equipment rooms (fig. 2.16b).

Soon after the building opened, the chief administrator commented that because of the similarity of the circular units and their disorienting corridors, people seemed to be having problems finding their way, but "[these] comments come mainly from people who first visit the building. . . . I think it would be true of almost any building [of] its size."[21] To more accurately describe what

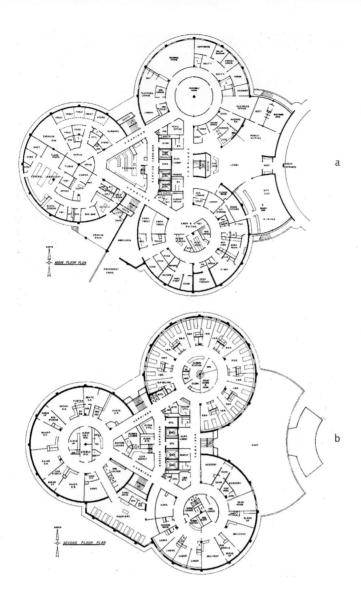

2.16. Central Kansas Medical
Center, plans: (*a*) main floor;
(*b*) second floor

was occurring, however, one might substitute *shape* for *size* in this administrator's account. An additional drawback to this first generation of radial hospitals was the glare caused by uneven levels of illumination on the two sides of the window between the patient's room and the nurses' station. Seen from outside the patient room, the window looked like a wall because of the bright fluorescent lighting at the nurses' station. This problem plagued many of the radial-plan nursing units during this period.

The Sawtooth

The radial concept, the most radical advance in nursing unit design in the 1960s, was by no means the only alternative to the traditional racetrack hospital. By 1965 a consensus had emerged among a small cadre of administrators, architects, and hospital planners that the rectangular box of the patient room could be altered and even enhanced without completely relinquishing the basic rectangularity of the overall floor plan. One way was to introduce partial triangulation by perforating the perimeter of the patient tower so that patients would have a better view from their beds (fig. 2.17). Architects on both sides of the Atlantic soon sought to alter the exterior skin of the hospital by incorporat-

ing sunscreens, aerodynamic-looking fins, angled windows, and setbacks from the structural frame, as if they were designing automobiles in Detroit or a space capsule for NASA.

West Coast hospitals in the United States led the way. An early, tentative example of a hospital with a perforated, or corrugated, exterior membrane was the Alexian Brothers Hospital in San Jose, California, by Robert R. Weber and Associates with John Carl Warnecke and Associates (1961–65). A four-level patient tower was placed on top of a one-level base containing the typical assortment of administrative, central support, diagnostic, and treatment departments. The patient beds and circulation arteries, however, retained the rectilinearity of the total floor plan. The sawtooth exterior wall was thus little more than an aesthetic device (and did not solve the problem of glare), but it did set the stage for more dramatic efforts that would include the repositioning of the patient bed on a diagonal to the main corridor, an innovation driven largely by new theories of nursing care and the continual drive to reduce the distances that staff had to travel to the farthest patient room on the unit.[22]

An early, more pronounced example was Mary's Help Hospital in Daly City, California, by Stone, Marraccini, and Patterson (1964–66). Many of the 250 beds in this ten-level hospital had an unobstructed view of the surrounding hills (fig. 2.18). Alternate bedrooms were positioned outboard by turning every second room at a forty-five-degree angle to the main racetrack corridor loop (fig. 2.19a–b). The turning of these cubes resulted in diagonal walls in the adjoining rooms; the views from these beds, however, were comparatively inaccessible to the patient. The tower was situated above the typical assortment of departmental services in the support base (fig. 2.19c–d). An interesting feature was the pair of four-bed open wards flanking the ends on some of the nursing units.[23]

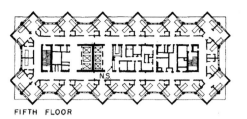

FIFTH FLOOR

a

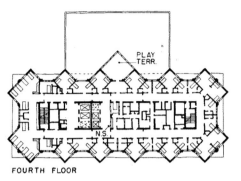

FOURTH FLOOR

b

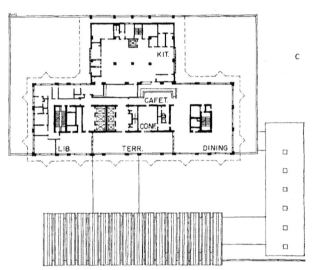

SECOND FLOOR

c

2.19. Mary's Help Hospital, plans: (*a*) fifth floor; (*b*) fourth floor; (*c*) second floor; (*d*) first floor

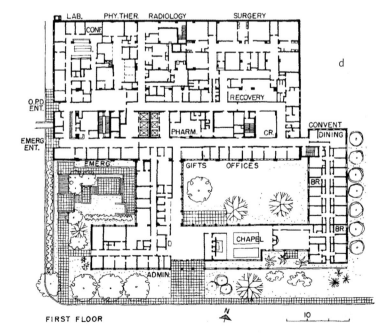

FIRST FLOOR

d

The Triangle

The triangulation of the nursing unit, which also first appeared in the mid-1960s, was justified largely on the basis of the Yale Index research (see Chapter 6), which found it a highly efficient, effective configuration from the standpoint of nursing staff. An early significant example was the Lane Pavilion of Point Pleasant Hospital, Point Pleasant, New Jersey, by Gordon Powers (1963–64). It was a two-level addition with sixty-four beds, of which three-fourths were private rooms (fig. 2.20). The shape was derived directly from the Yale Index method of measuring operating efficiency, especially staff walking distances. The triangle unit was defended as lending itself to "economical sizing of service core areas . . . unlike the circle [radial], which rapidly generates excessive core space as perimeter bedrooms are added. Straight lines of the triangle also serve to reduce construction costs . . . compared to circular units."[24]

Unfortunately, because the patient room washrooms were placed on the outboard side of the nursing units, more than 60 percent of the total exterior wall surface was unavailable for windows for patients; this resulted in an unusually narrow view from the patient's bed. Additional shortcomings were the placement of the patient's closet doors along the backside bed wall and the uncomfortably close spacing of the beds to one another, despite the provision of

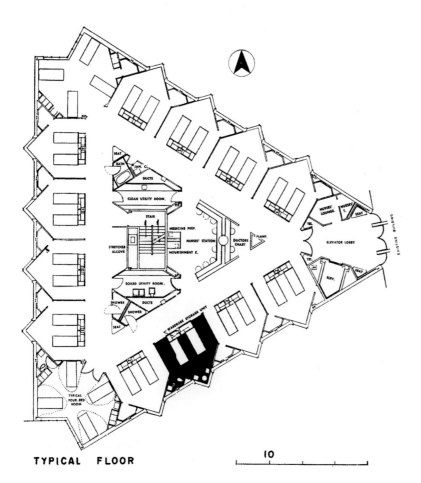

2.20. Lane Pavilion, Point Pleasant Hospital, New Jersey, 1964, typical patient-care unit

TYPICAL FLOOR

10

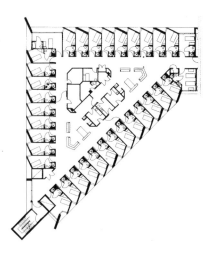

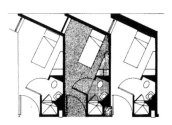

2.21. St. Mark's Hospital, Salt Lake City, Utah, 1971: (*top*) typical patient-care unit; (*bottom*) typical patient room

a rigid yet movable, folding partition mounted from overhead tracks between the beds in each room.

In 1969 a series of comparative studies of the triangulated plan versus the conventional racetrack plan were produced by the firm Kaplan/McLaughlin/Diaz. They proposed a triangular nursing unit for St. Mark's Hospital in Salt Lake City, Utah (1970–71), with an expandable number of beds. The original nursing unit was to contain thirty-two private beds and one semi-private room containing two beds. Each bed in the private rooms was shifted approximately 30 degrees to allow for a view from the bed through a narrow, full-height window to the outer edge, with the washroom on the inboard side (fig. 2.21).[25] Unfortunately but not atypically, the window was placed in the corner at an inconvenient viewing angle. In terms of site planning the units could be stacked on top of one another or flip-flopped in plan, yielding awkward exterior residual spaces that would barely pass for use of the term "exterior space" but would nonetheless be rationalized as "courtyards." Also, it was theoretically possible to "plug in" horizontal additional triangulated nursing units at the endpoints, although in practice this would often result in ungainly expansions. Regardless, the test of time would prove the triangular nursing unit to be a far more popular innovation than the radial nursing unit.

Other Variations

The block hospitals of the 1960s gave way to further experimentation with the massing and compositional attributes of acute-care hospitals. Designers were looking for new ways to give shape to the ever more complex requirements of their clients by introducing sometimes convoluted variations on the same theme. The Woodland Memorial Hospital in Woodland, California (1966–68), designed by Rex Whitaker Allen and Associates, was praised upon completion for its "inventive marshaling of mass and detail," its anticipation of growth, and its innovative patient room configuration (figs. 2.22 and 2.23). In its eighty-one-bed, six-level first phase of construction, the hospital boasted a design that would allow for nearly 100 percent occupancy at all times. This would be achieved through what was referred to as the "duo-room" concept: the patient rooms were separated by a movable partition. Each room could thus be a single room or a semi-private room. The basic structure and framing was of reinforced concrete, and the nursing pavilion walls were of precast concrete. The exposed-concrete aggregate panels on the patient tower served a dual purpose: they supported a system of gridded vertical and horizontal "fins" to shade excessive sunlight from the rooms within, and they provided ornamentation.[26]

Woodland Memorial Hospital's patient rooms might have been as efficient as their creators boasted, but the patient experienced only minimally better conditions. In fact, many patients voiced their concerns when their private room was suddenly changed to a double. Furthermore, because of the placement of the toilet, the window was to the back of the patient. This was a recurring problem in hospital planning. If the toilet was inboard, more freedom was possible in the building's fenestration. If it was outboard, the amount of windowed wall area would be severely restricted. Part of the trend to recompose

2.22. Woodland Memorial
Hospital, California, 1968

2.23. Woodland Memorial
Hospital, second-floor plan

SECOND FLOOR

the hospital during these years thus hinged on reconciling the relation between the hallway, the patient bed, the toilet, and the exterior perimeter wall. As architects began to experiment with these variables, the exteriors of the patient rooms began to have more irregular facades, with shadows and folds created by, for example, the aforementioned undulating pattern of a projecting room adjoining a recessed room.

Another published example of this trend was the new teaching hospital at Temple University in Philadelphia (1967–71). The dominant planning principle at Temple, as at Bellevue, was to create a system of layered hospital floors, each floor functioning as a semi-autonomous mini-hospital. Seven of these "hospitals" were stacked vertically as columns of patient rooms, surgery suites, labs, and so on. Clusters of eight patient rooms were configured into pods around a shared entry spur off the corridor. The toilets were outboard, and some walls of patient rooms were at 30-degree diagonals. The windows of patient rooms were small, and once again, the severe viewing angle was disconcerting for all but the most agile patient. One advantage of this configuration was that patients could remain in their beds for surgery and x-rays instead of being wheeled to another floor or forced to wait alone in a hallway. Doctors spent more time on the patient-care unit as a result of this arrangement. Also, it was usually claimed that the nursing staff provided more individual attention by monitoring patients in eight-bed clusters. This plan allowed for shorter corridors than traditional hospitals with a double-loaded corridor. And the walls between some of the patient rooms were removable, opening up a space to accommodate three or four beds. The hospital had a total capacity of 850 beds, and perhaps its most significant feature was that almost all were configurable as private rooms with an adjoining private bath.[27] The further evolution of the cluster-planning concept is discussed in greater detail in Chapter 6, in the context of the nursing unit.

In other instances a bold outward gesture, such as a sweeping curve, would become a hospital's trademark. The Stamford Hospital, in Stamford, Connecticut, was originally a pavilion hospital but had tacked on numerous additions over the years. A major expansion program in the mid-1960s resulted in a 192-bed addition (1966–69). This building was to function as the new image for the institution, with its curved facade and minimalist, sculpted appearance (figs. 2.24 and 2.25). The architects, E. Todd Wheeler and the Perkins and Will Partnership, justified its sweeping exterior essentially on the basis of interior planning determinants (a practice that remains common to this day). They cited the need to accommodate semi-private rooms on the outer back side and private rooms on the inner side of the "crescent" (fig. 2.26). Additionally, the arc of the corridors was said to make them seem shorter than those in the traditional linear, double-loaded-corridor hospital. Each floor was divided into two thirty-two-bed nursing units.[28]

In all the heroic efforts in the United States to create variations on the minimalism of the International Style, a criterion dating from the earliest cross-ward monastic hospitals of the Middle Ages continued to exert an influence on the modern hospital: the need to control the largest number of patients with the fewest number of staff. In America the open ward died in the 1960s private-

Opposite:
2.24. Stamford Hospital, Connecticut, 1968

2.25. Stamford Hospital, view
through colonnade

2.26. Stamford Hospital, plans
of typical nursing-unit floor and
main floor

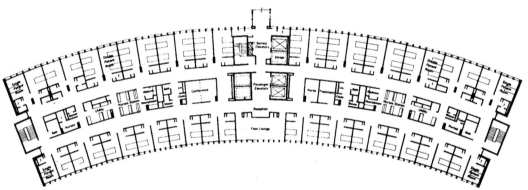

Typical Floor - Medical-Surgical Nursing Units

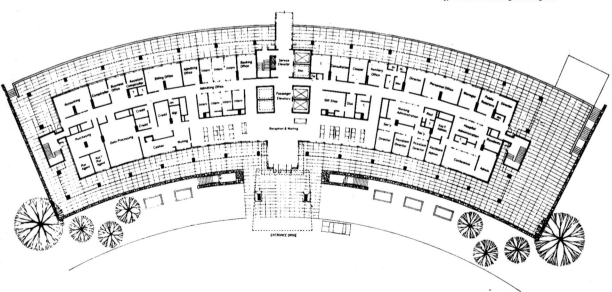

Main Floor - Entrance Level

sector community hospital, but other medieval planning concepts were alive and well. A new version of Jeremy Bentham's eighteenth-century panopticon was created in the plan of the Beloit (Wisconsin) Memorial Hospital, designed by John J. Flad and Associates (1967–69). Like Bentham's idealized plans for prototypical insane asylums, this plan was driven by the need for maximum staff control over the patient. In 1969 it was described as quite innovative, almost classical, in its formal properties—it was shaped like a snowflake (fig. 2.27). The new 260-bed addition featured an automated cart transportation system (which never worked properly), permitting a reduction in staff from an estimated 211 employees per 100 beds to only 166 per 100 beds. The system used a vertical dumbwaiter that fed into a series of conveyors on each floor for clean and soiled utilities, leading to and from the cart wash and storage area. Carts moved through the hospital to preselected destinations and were to be handled only at the unloading stations. An electronic selector system was to be activated by a sliding contact attached to the top of each cart.

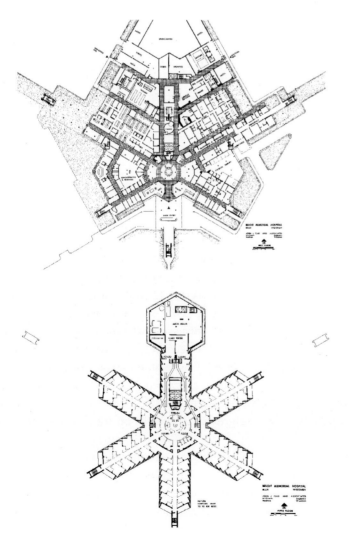

2.27. Beloit Memorial Hospital, Wisconsin, 1969, plans of first floor and typical patient-care floor

The hexagonal snowflake design was justified on the basis that it maximized the number of patients on each nursing unit. The patient rooms were staggered so every patient could take in a minimal view of Wisconsin's rolling dairy pastures through the bedside window. All patient rooms were double occupancy, with electronic curtains on ceiling tracks separating the pair of beds in each room. Later, many would be modified to private rooms. Maximum distance from the nursing station to a patient's room was 104 feet; the nursing stations were autonomous in terms of supplies and staff support amenities. Each served as many as 92 patients.[29] At Beloit, then, the hospital-as-machine metaphor coexisted with a full-blown reprise of neoclassical panopticism.

The European Urban Platform Hospital

In Europe, a number of urban replacement hospitals were built on a scale rivaling the grand asylums and city hospitals of the seventeenth and eighteenth centuries. The main difference was the role of high technology as a determinant of form. In the twentieth-century cases, technology drove the need to place autonomous nursing units above a high-tech platform, or base. This use of a monolithic base with patient towers above might best be termed "platform." One such example in Germany was the new teaching hospital for the Free University Hospital Center at the University of Berlin (1966–70), where the nursing units were perched atop a service and support podium that served its patient towers. Unfortunately, the hospital, because of its vast scale and alien appearance, overwhelmed the small-scale dwellings in the adjacent neighborhoods. Its designers, Arthur Q. Davis of the United States and Franz Mocken of Berlin, created a self-contained urban machine (fig. 2.28). This 1,416-bed facility was symmetrical in plan, similar to the male and female sides of the neoclassical palace hospitals of the sixteenth and seventeenth centuries in Europe. The dual patient towers extended out from the core block as two appendages (fig. 2.29). These contained private and semi-private rooms, and the core contained support functions and wards of up to four beds each. The sawtooth pattern along the perimeter wall, which had floor-to-ceiling windows, allowed the patient a view of the small-scaled dwellings of the surrounding town.[30]

The new 1,920-bed medical center for the University of Göttingen, Germany, designed by Neue Heimat (1967–71), also had a podium plan (or a "matchbox on a muffin" plan), with support functions on the lower levels. Research units were housed on the second and third levels, together with the open wards for patients. A series of eight outdoor courtyards were arrayed like soldiers along the main circulation axis, giving the hospital the appearance and feel of an eighteenth-century state asylum. The mechanical systems of the building were housed in eighteen structures on the roof, which looked like gigantic sugar cubes.[31]

A more flagrant variation on the International Style was the Gonesse Hospital Center, France (1967–70), designed by O. Rabaud and R. Marquet (fig. 2.30). But if nature was a valid expression of the machine aesthetic (as in the snowflake pattern at Beloit Memorial), then would not the human metaphor be equally valid? This building was perhaps the boldest, most iconographic exam-

Opposite:
2.28. Free University Hospital Center, Berlin, 1969, aerial view

2.29. Free University Hospital Center, plan of typical patient-care floor

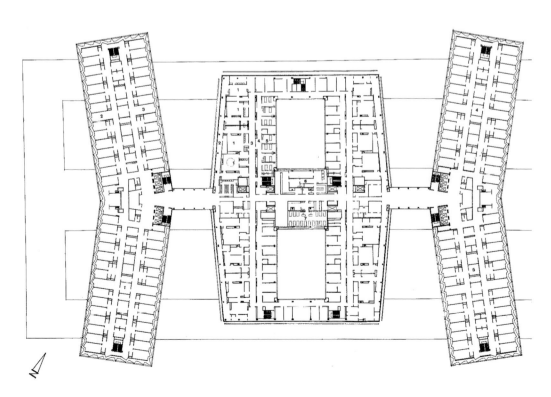

2.30. Gonesse Hospital Center, France, 1970

2.31. Gonesse Hospital Center, site plan

2.32. Gonesse Hospital Center, typical patient ward

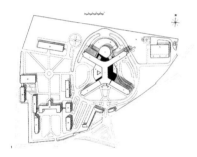

ple of reference to the human body in 1960s hospital architecture. Upon arrival, however, one would not have suspected the footprint of this 325-bed hospital to be configured as a human body. The exterior from the ground level provided little evidence of the architects' metaphorical intentions, beyond the obvious positioning of a round treatment unit atop the shoulders of the inpatient wards. The full subtlety of this metaphor cannot be fully appreciated until the plans are scrutinized (fig. 2.31). The arms and legs of the figure were occupied by patient rooms with one, two, or three beds each. Support functions were located across the corridor from patient rooms. The torso and portions of the head were occupied by the vertical circulation core, and the head also housed the intensive care units, stacked above one another on the upper four floors. The patient rooms had floor-to-ceiling windows, but furnishings were typically spartan and glare was again a considerable problem because of the harsh, reflective surfaces throughout the interior (fig. 2.32). The administration and the architects undoubtedly considered their floor plan totally functional—rational—yet highly ironic, almost whimsical (fig 2.33). Regardless, relatively few patients or staff could ever fully appreciate the metaphor and the underlying wit in intention, especially given that hospitals are among the most *serious* of all building types.[32] The theme of ironic intent would be extended with considerably greater narrative directness and panache in the mid-1980s by Cesar Pelli, with the hypodermic-needle summits of his St. Luke's Medical Tower in Houston (see Chapter 5).

Brutalist Hospitals

A distinct variant of the International Style was evolving at this time in England. This variant came to be known as brutalism for its extensive use of monolithic, gray, cast-in-place concrete forms, its minimalist vocabulary in materials of construction, and its grim overall appearance. Among the largest and boldest of the brutalist hospitals was the Norwick Park District General Hospital (1965–70), designed by Llewelyn-Davies Weeks Forestier with Walker Bor and Partners (fig. 2.34). The cost and size of the hospitals built in England by the National Health Service had been exploding throughout the 1960s. The stan-

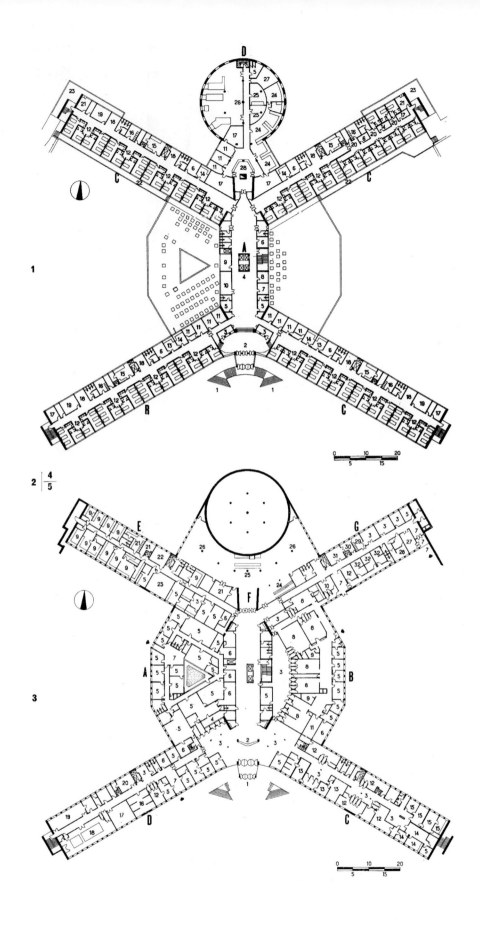

2.33. Gonesse Hospital Center, floor plans. *Top:* Ground floor: (1) arrival, (2) main vestibule, (3) gift shops, (4) main lobby, (5) personnel, (6) infirmary office, (7) observation, (8) interview, (9) central housekeeping, (10) mechanical support, (11) infirmary office, (12) private patient rooms, (13) clean and soiled utilities, (14) linen staging, (15) office, (16) supplies, (17) central storage and supplies, (18) parlor (dayroom), (19) staff office, (20) isolation suite, (21) transition (post-operative) room, (22) visitors' gallery, (23) isolation and egress, (24) laboratories, (25) central sterilization, (26) operating suite, (27) staff, (28) central distribution. *Bottom:* Typical patient-care floor: (1) main entrance, (2) orientation, (3) attendants, (4) admissions, (5) central administration, (6) medical records, (7) vestibule, (8) radiology (diagnostic), (9) laboratory, (10) radiology (treatment), (11) staff consultation, (12) examination (general), (13) examination (ear-nose-throat), (14) ophthalmology suite, (15) dentistry suite, (16) electrotherapy, (17) occupational therapy, (18) physical therapy, (19) gymnasium, (20) office, (21) restroom, (22) supplies, (23) nursing, (24) cafeteria, (25) information, (26) administration, (27) discharge, (28) admissions, (29) business office, (30) nursing, (31) pediatric examination, (32) treatment.

2.34. Norwick Park District
General Hospital, England, 1970

dard policy was to build as few freestanding hospitals as possible and to centralize as many functions as possible within a few large medical centers. Over the decade 1959–69 the operational costs of maintaining this system rose from 830 million pounds annually to 1,770 million pounds. The typical British hospital in the late 1950s had housed 200 beds; by the late 1960s the average new hospital had 600–800 beds. The aging prewar hospitals in England were in dire need of replacement: the mean age of hospitals by 1969 was 70 years. Three-fourths of the beds in hospitals-in-use had been designed before World War I, mainly for the sick poor, as most were successors of the old almshouse system.[33]

Numerous brutalist megahospitals were built during this period, such as the gigantic Hull Royal Infirmary, with its 542 neatly packaged beds in a uniform, high-rise block tower (1965–70), the Queen Elizabeth Medical Center at Birmingham, the Greenwich Hospital, and the growing network of "Best Buy" district hospitals. Norwick Park was the most expensive hospital in England when it opened. It was both a district hospital and a research center for the Medical Research Council, with 800 beds. Its fundamental composition was by then archetypal: T-shaped ward blocks situated on top of a support base. The hospital was built in a forty-eight-acre parcel of virgin parkland. Upon opening, it was harshly criticized in the British architectural and popular press. Its exterior facades were seen as immense, chaotic, and unrelenting, and the overall visual effect was viewed as oppressive and unduly repetitive.[34]

The trend toward brutalism in European hospital architecture had begun nearly ten years earlier, however, and had been "tested" at first in smaller district hospitals. A prime example was the Ulster Hospital in Belfast (1958–62) with its repetitive patient "cages"—balconies, actually—suspended from the sides of a standard ward block (fig. 2.35).[35]

2.35. Ulster Hospital, Belfast, Ireland, 1962

Brutalism also emerged in other parts of Europe. The private Pope Pius XI Clinic in Rome (1967–70), designed by Julio Lafuente and Gaetano Rebecchini and built on an open, rolling site, was significant for its use of suspended forms of poured concrete (fig. 2.36) and its undulations with the contours of the site. The main floor had a covered entrance area and a large, hotel-like atrium in the center of the core support building. The curves of the patient bed tower were attached at midsection to the support core (fig. 2.37), and the exterior concrete panels took on a corrugated texture, also serving as retaining walls for terraces on each patient floor. Patient rooms were arrayed along a single-loaded corridor, with central support and vertical circulation at the midpoint. The sculptural treatment of the mechanical systems on the roof were reminiscent of Le Corbusier's Unité d'Habitation in Marseilles.[36] In contrast to the brutalist hospitals built in England during this period, the Private Clinic exhibited somewhat more delicate compositional sensibilities, greater attention to human scale, and greater attention to the natural environment.

2.36. Pope Pius XI Clinic, Rome, 1969

2.37. Pope Pius XI Clinic, plan of maternity ward

The International Style was influential throughout the world by the late 1960s. In Chandigarh, India, Le Corbusier had received a commission to develop a master plan for the city and to design many of the key public buildings. Among the buildings he had planned to design himself but did not finish before his death was the major medical center and teaching hospital for the new university. This 1,000-bed Central Hospital, designed by Le Corbusier's successor firm in collaboration with Indian architects Jeanneret, Sharma, Malhotra, Chopra, and Mehta (1966–70), consisted of two long blocks of patient rooms, six levels in height, connected by a drum-shaped building with a dramatic, sweeping circular ramp leading to the upper floors. It contained administrative functions, the main entrance, a cafeteria, an auditorium, and the entrance to the maternity department (fig. 2.38). Patients were housed in wards on the second through sixth floors (fig. 2.39). Diagnostic and treatment support departments were housed in a pavilion attached to one of the patient towers.[37]

The International Style was also exported to Israel, in the large state-sponsored psychiatric hospital Tirat Hacarmal, in Haifa (1968–71). Its autonomy and indifference to its site is evident in its master site plan.[38] This aesthetic was also

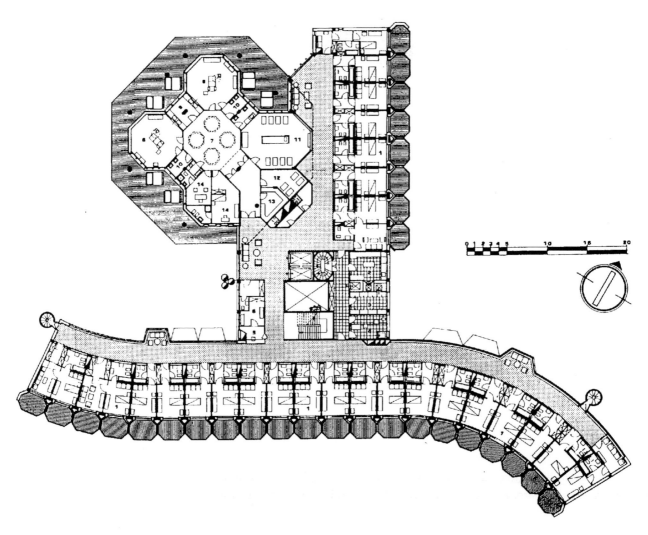

2.38. Central Hospital,
Chandigarh, India, 1970

2.39. Central Hospital, typical
patient ward

exported to dozens of other nations, such as Mauritania, whose Nouakchott National Hospital (1963–65) was designed by Renaudie, Riboulet, Thurnauer and Veret. The hurdles of adapting the International Style to extreme climates were easily surmounted by the modern architect; in this case the buildings were clustered as a series of modules in a grid system.[39] The hospital at Marsico Vetere, in southern Italy (1968–70), designed by Guido Gigli, was yet another example built in the brutalist vocabulary of reinforced concrete, with its low-slung profile nestled into its mountainside site. Its plan, however, was a curious mixture of the relentless grid system that was one of the main tenets of the International Style, and a response to the indigenous vernacular, that is, the architectural traditions, of this remote desert region. Hence, the patient wards and hospital support functions were clustered around a series of enclosed and semi-enclosed courtyards, with patient wards cantilevered over the base of the first floor, providing dramatic views out to the valley. The wards were configured in the increasingly common pattern of alternating inboard and outboard bathrooms.[40]

The minimalist influence of Mies van der Rohe, who was by then teaching and practicing in Chicago, was evident in the Women's Hospital in Kuwait City, Kuwait (1967–69), by the British architect John R. Harris. In this brutal climate, with temperatures typically reaching 120 degrees at midday, the orthogonality and stripped aesthetic and site plan of a 400-bed hospital on the shores of the Persian Gulf responded to the desire of the Kuwait Ministry of Public Works to Westernize. Such Western imports were common throughout the Middle East at the time, in countries as diverse as Egypt, Israel, Lebanon, Iraq, Iran, and Saudi Arabia. The Kuwaiti hospital contained eleven wards, each housing thirty beds. The building was four levels in height, with dramatic views to the Gulf. Significant features of this hospital included its operable windows, allowing sea breezes to cool the interior spaces at night. The window apertures were narrow (two feet and eight inches wide) to keep out excessive sun, and the walls were eighteen inches thick on the north and south faces of the hospital, allowing the windows to be recessed in the walls with the structural frame working as a screen. The plan was significant for its double-loaded-corridor circulation system combined with patient rooms on either side, with the same pattern of circulation and adjacent spaces carried into the administrative, diagnostic, and treatment buildings. Brick veneer panels were inset in a reinforced steel and concrete frame, roofs were flat, and the arrangement of the buildings on the campus was directly influenced by Mies's master plan for the campus of the Illinois Institute of Technology in Chicago (1948–65), with its rectangular block buildings set at right angles in a grid.[41]

These and similar buildings became the international mainstream standard, because national health ministers and other politicians, and leading healthcare professionals, believed that this approach was the more valid means to achieve parity with their Western counterparts. However, not all decision makers followed in lockstep when it came to the search for a meaningful synthesis of technology, culture, and humanism.

Countercurrents

Three countercurrents to the International Style became evident by the end of the 1960s: (1) small-scale inpatient-outpatient clinic-hospitals, (2) European spas typically built in seaside resort areas, and (3) a small number of iconoclastic hospitals that rejected the absolute minimalism of the conventional modern block hospital. The first of these building types was distinguished by its smallness. In France, the "machine clinic for the masses" reached its apotheosis in the residentially scaled Surgery Clinic at Bagneux (1963–65), designed by P. A. Chauveau. The exterior of this clinic-hospital shows the influence of the early twentieth-century modernists Gerrit Reitveld and J. P. P. Oud, and the later influence of the Bauhaus. The building was separated into two blocks connected by a narrow vertical circulation core, with administrative and clinical space housed in one block and the patient beds in the other, somewhat longer block. Aside from its scale, the Surgery Clinic was significant because it was not driven by high technology:

2.40. Thalassotherapy Institute, Quiberon, France, 1965, view from shoreline

2.41. Thalassotherapy Institute, indoor pool

its appearance, configuration, and size were drawn from the typology of the modernist house or apartment as much as from the imagery and functional determinism of the conventional modern hospital of the period.[42]

The second countercurrent, the seaside European spa, had its precursors in the ancient spas of Greece and Rome and spas built in the Mediterranean region as recently as the fifteenth century. In the 1960s, one spa stood out as a reaction against the International Style's dominance of hospital and health architecture: the first phase of the Thalassotherapy Institute, in Quibéron, France (1963–65), designed by R. Lopez, made dramatic use of its seaside location. In this wellness center, water was used in various therapeutic regimens, principally swimming and hydrotherapy. A second phase of the complex, designed by André Bruyère and completed in 1970, housed a large pool and a second hydrotherapy building. The building was organic, with many curves and an undulating roof in reference to its rocky site and a strong nautical motif in reference to the ocean. The exterior silhouette of the pool building formed a wave against the sky. The expressively ribbed roof was a bold contrast to the gray monolithism of brutalism and its variants (figs. 2.40 and 2.41).[43]

A third and, as time would prove, farsighted alternative to conventional modernist hospitals was the "anti-block" hospital of the late modern period, which appeared first in England. The Slough District General Hospital was designed by Powell and Moya, with Llewelyn-Davies, Weeks, and Partners. The architects for this 296-bed facility were appointed in 1955, but owing to the cumbersome bureaucracy of the National Health Service, the first stage was not built until 1962–65. The hospital, widely considered iconoclastic, was designed as a low-rise facility, with all major functions on one level with the exception of the administrative area and medical staff residential units, which were contained in a seven-level tower block (figs. 2.42 and 2.43). The tower rose directly above the entrance hall, which in turn formed the intersection of the two main hospital pedestrian streets, or spines—not unlike the connective arteries found in the late nineteenth-century Nightingale wards and pavilions—to which all departments and patient units were connected.

The wards were L-shaped and thus provided ample opportunity for a courtyard garden, which contributed to the intimate domestic scale of the entire hospital. Each ward contained 32 beds, with a central entrance, dayroom, and staff support areas contained in the "elbow" (figs. 2.44 and 2.45). The hospital was easily extendable horizontally. Moreover, the residential ambiance of the wards was unmarred by central administrative, diagnostic, or treatment areas, and a clear architectural vocabulary—that is, composition—was employed in terms of volume, scale, and the definition of each domain.[44] Above all, faithfulness to human scale, access to the outdoor environment, and attention to premodern precedents were at the heart of the philosophy expressed in Slough. In one architectural journal, Slough was favorably contrasted with Norwick Park:

> Norwick park may be a clinical success but its "duffel-coat" plan hides a malformed anatomy. . . . [It] disappoints. . . . By contrast, Slough District General

2.42. Slough District General Hospital, England, 1965

2.43. Slough District General Hospital, aerial view

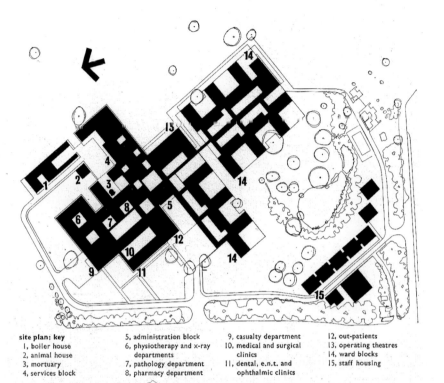

site plan: key

1, boiler house	5, administration block	9, casualty department	12, out-patients
2, animal house	6, physiotherapy and x-ray	10, medical and surgical	13, operating theatres
3, mortuary	departments	clinics	14, ward blocks
4, services block	7, pathology department	11, dental, e.n.t. and	15, staff housing
	8, pharmacy department	ophthalmic clinics	

2.44. Slough District General Hospital, site plan

2.45. Slough District General Hospital, plan of typical patient ward

ward plan (scale 1/32in : 1ft)

key

1, clean utility	7, cleaner
2, dirty utility	8, kitchen
3, sister's room	9, wheel chairs
4, treatment room	10, equipment
5, nurses' cloaks	11, bathroom
6, w.c.	12, nurse's station
	13, wash
	14, day space
	15, lobby

by Powell and Moya is well worth a revisit as a marvelous object lesson in minimizing maxi-scale. The sizes of the two are of course very different—Norwick 800 beds, Slough just under 300 but Slough is, beyond question, designed *for patients,* whereas Norwick seems to be designed neither for the staff nor for the patient. At Norwick walking distances are too great and too devious to form an easy working framework for staff. . . . Slough is (still) unbeatable . . . for the sheer humanity of its scale . . . firmly rooted in Philip Powell's personally held conviction that a hospital as a building itself has a duty to provide mental therapy for those who work or stay there. . . . In comparative studies of Slough and later Wythenshawe, P&M have shown conclusively that a multistory ward block would substantially add to every walking journey, even taking into account fast lifts and direct routes. . . . Slough is relevant to the thesis that hospitals should be pegged to architecturally, socially and economically manageable units.[45]

Slough was particularly significant because it represented a rediscovery of the Nightingale ward-pavilion of decades earlier. Moreover, it reapplied Nightingale's principle that every patient should have contact with nature from within the ward, and should be able to be outdoors without straying far from the bed within the nursing unit.

In the United States, few architects and administrators pursued true architectural innovation, but by the late 1960s the block hospital, with a base and a patient tower above, had become the prevailing trend. The American Oncologic Hospital in Philadelphia (1966–68), by Vincent G. Kling and Associates, was iconoclastic, as it broke away from this pattern. It was built on a forty-one-acre site as a replacement hospital for an institution founded in 1904. Mainstream block hospital and base-tower forms were rejected early on in the planning process in favor of a more daring, graduated massing and thus a more unusual internal spatial organization (figs. 2.46 and 2.47). Because of this decision, numerous possibilities opened up in terms of the building's relation with the world beyond its walls. For one, the patient rooms could be terraced through the use of stepped setbacks. No longer were the exterior walls of the hospital required to be vertical, unrelieved, multi-storied slabs, as at England's Hull Infirmary. Entire floors were now to be stepped back, creating a non-institutional effect not unlike that found in innovative multi-family housing prototypes of the period that were receiving worldwide attention, such as Moshe Safdie's Habitat at Expo '67 in Montreal (1965–67).

The hospital contained fifty-six beds in its first phase and a comprehensive outpatient care program for cancer diagnosis and treatment. Rooms were provided for family members to stay overnight, and the open, wooded site was considered a therapeutic adjunct to the care provided within. The shed roofs—with their homelike, or residentialist, shingles—and the terraces were intended to break down the division between home and hospital. Indeed, from a distance the structure looked like an apartment complex, library, or school. The terraces ran along the perimeter of each floor. On the interior, the patient rooms provided amenities that would not become common for twenty-five more years. These features included wooden doors and trim, area rugs on the floors, built-

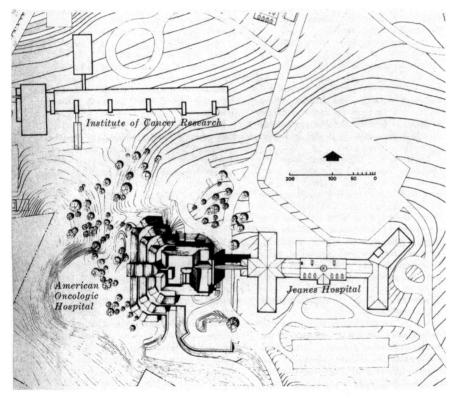

2.46. American Oncologic
Hospital, Philadelphia, 1968

2.47. American Oncologic
Hospital, site plan

in desk alcoves, artwork, plants, and residentialist furnishings (fig. 2.48).
Clerestories were created to provide daylight in the corridors and at the nursing
stations, and the atrium lobby looked like that of a hotel. The entrance was
unassuming, and the lobby was linked with the adjacent general hospital,
Jeanes Hospital. When the hospital opened, a reviewer for *Progressive Architecture* wrote:

> It is heartening to discover that neither hospitals in particular nor Government-
> financed structure in general are required, a priori, to be examples of mediocre
> architecture. Vincent Kling's . . . hospital (one-third financed by Hill-Burton

funds) is part of what is still a minority revolt against the hospital green and its aseptic adjuncts. Although the revolt has been brewing for some time, it has received more lip service than action. Today, however, there seems to be stronger willed architects, more receptive hospital clients, and enough money in the pot to build institutions where the patient's physical environment makes a significant contribution to his recuperative state of mind.[46]

2.48. American Oncologic Hospital, typical patient room

The Slough General Hospital in England and the American Oncologic Hospital in the United States were years ahead of their time. It is arguable that they were examples of late modern health architecture rather than the first signposts of postmodern health architecture. The two institutions, however, were astonishingly similar given their radically different origins and sponsorship: Slough was built by a massive government agency, whereas American Oncologic was one of the first upscale private institutions to break away from the mainstream in terms of its architecture. In sharp contrast to the status quo, both these environments considered the patient before the machine. This re-empowerment of the individual would become the core of what would, in the 1980s, become known as patient-centered care. In addition, the favorable reviews that these two buildings received in the architectural press demonstrated the appetite for hospitals to be considered as individual, expressive works of architecture. During the late 1960s, designs for hospitals, compared to other building types, were only infrequently published, indicating the rarity of breakthrough hospital designs that found their way to publication. The lack of new approaches justified to a certain extent the reputation of the hospital as among the most uninteresting and rigid of all building types, and partially accounted for the resultant dismissiveness on the part of leading architectural thinkers. Sadly, the efforts of the few architecturally pioneering hospitals and their administrators to search for new architectural expression in order to deinstitutionalize their physical settings would not be accepted by mainstream healthcare administrators and their architects for nearly twenty more years.

CHAPTER 3

An Imperfect Machine for an Imperfect System, 1970–80

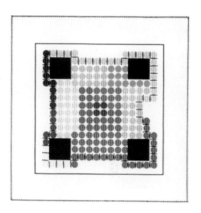

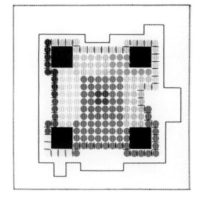

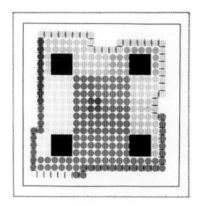

3.1. Consolidated clinical support prototype, 1970, showing system flow diagrams for people, equipment, and supplies. The three separate floors shown here are zoned according to differentiated functions and patterns of use.

By the early 1970s, hospital architecture was straining to keep abreast of the explosion in high technology and the need to update obsolescent facilities. The option to expand was taken for granted by most hospital administrators. In this chapter, events of the 1970s are discussed in light of five factors: the entrenchment of the high-tech medical center; the end of Hill-Burton funding; the emergence of investor-owned hospitals and managed care in the United States; the rise of contemporary antihospitalism and the search for alternatives to the modernist hospital as personified in the rise of the hospice movement and early examples of postmodernism; and efforts to ameliorate the inherent sterility of the hospital.

High Technology

During the 1970s the modern medical center expanded in size and complexity as new medical specializations appeared. The emphasis was on innovation, be it in the form of the electronic patient bed, exam tables with electronic extensions, the CAT scanner, or the relocation of an entire organization to replacement facilities. Manufacturers and product representatives were providing administrators with advice similar to that of hospital planners and architects: expand, renovate, replace, or be left behind. Possession of the Magnetic Resonance Imaging (MRI) unit was perhaps the most visible sign of status for an institution.

Facility planners experimented with new techniques in an attempt to make sense of the rapid changes taking place, and their diagrams and flow charts became nearly as complex as the reality they were attempting to transcribe. Systems diagrams produced by Sheila Clibbon and Marvin Sachs are a case in point (fig. 3.1).[1] The field of architectural research was slow to evolve, and the hospital was the subject of little systematic investigation. An additional development was the building system known as interstitial space—a plenum between two occupied floors that housed all the anatomical support systems of the building (HVAC, electrical, and materials transport systems). This system signaled the immense influence of technology on hospital architecture, as every other floor was now to be a technology-only floor (fig. 3.2).[2]

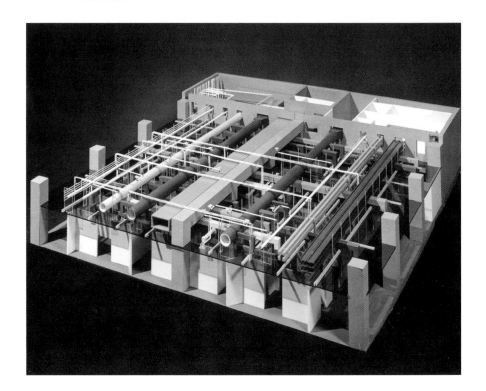

3.2. Interstitial space system
prototype (model), 1972

3.3. Herman Miller Co-Struc
system, 1972

In addition to the work of hospital designers, such product manufacturers as Hill-Rom of Batesville, Indiana, and Herman Miller of Grand Rapids, Michigan, also conducted their own research, sometimes in tandem with large architectural firms. Herman Miller's Co-Struc System, developed between 1970 and 1972, envisioned a fully coordinated palette of modular, clip-on/plug-in furnishings for the patient room (fig. 3.3).[3]

One hospital planner, Gordon Friesen, was known for introducing a new "service delivery system" every year. He would develop a prototype system or unit—a patient room, an intensive care unit, or a materials transport system— and proceed to market it with the intensity of an automobile manufacturer with a new model. The so-called Friesen System was extremely successful, and by the early 1970s it had become a source of status to have Friesen on board for your institution's capital improvement project. Friesen, based in Washington, D.C., was not a registered architect but worked closely with many leading architects and frequently wrote articles for architectural periodicals. His high level of visibility in the projects he was associated with can be viewed as signaling the decline of the architect as orchestrator, and accordingly, the growing role and influence of the specialized hospital facility consultant.[4] For the facility administrator, an alternative to hiring an architect and a health facility expert under two separate contracts was to retain a firm that possessed both these areas of expertise in-house. In this scenario the entire process could be managed by one team, from the project's inception to programming, equipment specification, interior design, schematic design, construction, and completion.[5]

Similar arrangements were evolving in Europe. In England and France, in particular, the government-built medical centers of the late 1960s were nearly always planned and designed with the help of an "interdisciplinary" government-based team of planners, which was responsible for generating such pertinent data as projections for use of the future unit or hospital. This information would be handed over to the programming and design arm of the team. In France, the Hôpital Ambroise-Paré in Boulogne (1967–71), a 650-bed medical

3.4. Hôpital Ambroise-Paré, Boulogne, France, 1971

3.5. Hôpital Ambroise-Paré, typical patient ward

center, was built in this manner. The main building was situated behind a gate, which functioned as a checkpoint but projected the image of a compound (fig. 3.4). The patient wards, each housing four patients, were sparse, with little space even for chairs (fig. 3.5). The floor plan was configured as a central trunk with four appendages, like a pair of arms and legs sans head (fig. 3.6).[6]

At the other end of the spectrum, many French community hospitals were built with as few as fifty beds, although they tended to be as minimalist as their larger counterparts. The Tarascon-sur-Rhône Hospital (1969–71) projected total

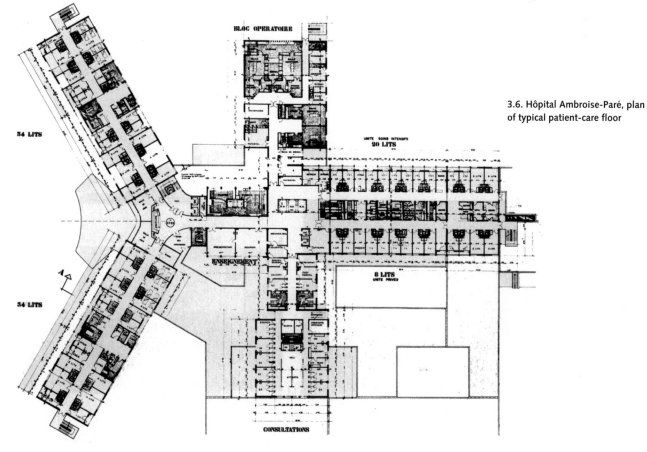

3.6. Hôpital Ambroise-Paré, plan of typical patient-care floor

Right: **3.7.** Meidling Rehabilitation
Center, Vienna, 1973

3.8. Meidling Rehabilitation
Center, roofscape mechanical
systems equipment treated in a
sculptural manner

3.9. Meidling Rehabilitation
Center: (*bottom*) first-floor plan;
(*middle*) second-floor plan; (*top*)
section

3.10. Meidling Rehabilitation
Center, typical corridor

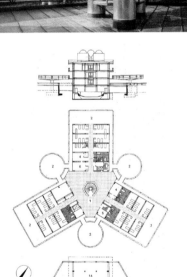

austerity. In fact, it was little more than a three-dimensional extrusion of its floor plan, although its honeycombed patient rooms signified some interest in giving patients a view of the outdoors.[7] In Austria, the Meidling Rehabilitation Center (1970–73), by Gustav Peichl and R. F. Weber, was a tour-de-force in high-tech modernism. This machine hospital was built initially to house fifty beds. Its appearance was ominous, with a long walkway bridge extending from the main entrance (fig. 3.7). The most striking feature was the treatment of the mechanical equipment on the roof. The machinery was housed in three large spherical forms clad in steel, creating an eerie impression of spacecraft having landed on the roof (fig. 3.8). The facility's plan was triangular, with an atrium at the center of its three wings (fig. 3.9). A variation of the interstitial space concept was incorporated, whereby each occupied floor was served by an exaggerated support layer housing all mechanical and electrical apparatus. This system enabled corridors to be relocated as adjacent departmental needs changed (fig. 3.10).[8]

In England, it was not uncommon for a firm to be contracted by the Ministry of Health to plan and design a hospital that might not open for ten or even fifteen years. In the case of the Royal Infirmary in Edinburgh, the team was contracted in 1955 and it took ten years for the "brief" (the program) to be approved, and it was four and half more years before the facility actually opened its doors (in 1969).[9] Yet the high-tech movement in architecture had also influenced small-scale health buildings, so architects in England were given opportunities to experiment in ways that were not possible with the massive machine hospitals because of the long duration of the projects. The high-tech movement was defined as a bold, visible expression of technology that had previously been hidden above ceilings and behind walls. Now ceilings were exposed to reveal their complex ductwork, lighting grids, and electrical and structural systems. These anatomical systems were often encoded in bright colors. Building technology and construction assemblies were treated as a form of formal expression and ornamentation, in a significant break from the dull, monochromatic buildings of the brutalist period of the 1960s. One clinic, the

Lakeside Health Centre (first stage 1970–72), was built in Thamesmead in the high-tech manner: it was a blend of the bold use of reinforced concrete and the suspended forms pioneered by Le Corbusier. This clinic filled a void in England because it linked the services of a community family health clinic with those of a larger hospital (Guy's Hospital) and was hailed as a breakthrough in social terms and as an architectural statement.[10] The building was considered high tech in part because the main clinic was suspended over an artificial pond (figs 3.11 and 3.12), with the exam rooms cantilevered over the water. Treatment and support spaces were also housed within this cantilevered podium. From the exterior, the building looked like a hovercraft suspended over the water (figs 3.13 and 3.14). This was in keeping with the high-tech movement's use of technology, and engineering systems in particular, to defy gravity and give emphasis to individual building components or, as in this case, to particular programmatic components.

The high-tech approach was also evident in other parts of Europe. In 1971 the Barraquer Dental Clinic opened in Barcelona in a structure built in 1936 in the center of the city. The architect, Joaquim Lloret, was commissioned to create a dynamic clinic within a large office building. His response was to create a dramatic stage set. The exam and treatment room had a viewing area where one could observe the patient receiving treatment (fig. 3.15). The "theatrical" relationship between the viewer (spectator) and the patient and dentist (actors) was highly orchestrated. The large glass bubble was reminiscent of an airplane or spacecraft. The lighting, imagery, and furnishings, however, were more than somewhat foreboding for the unsuspecting patient (fig. 3.16). A central spiral staircase contributed to the overall effect.[11]

A little later, the new community medical center at Wellingborough, England (1972–74), also applied the materials and attitude of high technology. This center, designed by Aldington and Craig, had an open plan within a large ground-level loft space. Mechanical systems were carried overhead in a space-frame ceiling-grid system (figs. 3.17 and 3.18). The Department of Health called for 25 percent circulation space, but the architects, through the use of this innovative system, were able to reduce the overall circulation to a remarkable 6 percent of total floor area. One architectural reviewer commented:

> It is the GP's answer to the Thamesmead Health Centre . . . which is the embodiment of the opposite, National Health Service, approach. . . . We are tempted to guess that the Wellingborough Medical Centre has a good chance of being accounted by history as one of the most truly functional buildings that the Modern Movement has given birth to. . . . It was a brilliant thought to run all the services in flexible trunking in the roof space, to make it accessible by putting it in full view, and to run each limb of trunking straight down into each consulting room: for this simplicity makes for effortless change. But, in terms of imagery, it was surely unwise. The services of a building bear a sort of analogy with the organs of the human body. To give the waiting patient, when he looks up, such a visceral panorama seems an error in perception. This is . . . the aftermath of the '60s, when Functionalism suddenly became deliberately ugly and harsh.[12]

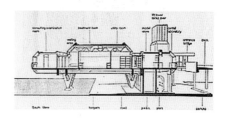

3.11. Lakeside Health Centre, Thamesmead, England, 1972. Courtesy of Derek Stow & Partners, London, England, Architects, Planners, Designers.

3.12. Lakeside Health Centre, section through pond. Courtesy of Derek Stow & Partners, London, England, Architects, Planners, Designers.

3.13. Lakeside Health Centre, view from pond. Courtesy of Derek Stow & Partners, London, England, Architects, Planners, Designers.

3.14. Lakeside Health Centre, clinic and waterway system. Courtesy of Derek Stow & Partners, London, England, Architects, Planners, Designers.

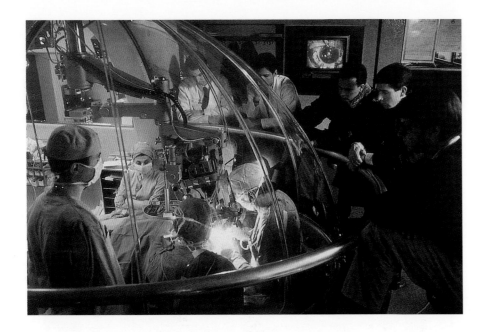

In the United States, significant examples of the high-tech movement within modernism included the Leonard Morse Hospital, in Natick, Massachusetts (1969–71), designed by Markus, Nocka, and Payette. The view from the exterior shows three nursing floors projecting outward. Each thirty-two-bed nursing unit was housed in a pod configuration, with units elevated above the lower service floors in the support base and cantilevered beyond the edge of the structural frame (fig. 3.19). The hospital was also significant for its use of carpet in most areas, desktop nursing stations, a coffered ceiling system, generous levels of daylight, and structural expressiveness (that is, the effort to clearly show the building's means for carrying its own weight).[13]

3.17. Medical Center, Wellingborough, England, 1974

3.18. Medical Center, waiting room

3.19. Leonard Morse Hospital, Natick, Massachusetts, 1971

3.20. Rehabilitation Institute of Chicago, 1974

Opposite:
3.21. Joseph O. Ruddy General Hospital, Whitby, Ontario, Canada, 1973

The direct influence of structural and systems expressionism in the buildings of Mies van der Rohe was conveyed by the Rehabilitation Institute of Chicago, widely known as RIC (1971–74), designed by C. F. Murphy and Associates (now Murphy-Jahn Architects) of Chicago (fig. 3.20). Its lead designer, Gene Summers, had been a student of Mies at the Illinois Institute of Technology and later worked for his firm (now Lohan and Associates). This seventeen-level tower was a straightforward International Style skyscraper hospital. Its site, on the lakeside campus of the Northwestern University Medical Center, afforded dramatic views to Lake Michigan directly to the east. This hospital remains a strong example of the Miesian aesthetic: bold, elegant use of glass and steel, attention to detail, and technical sophistication. Although these attributes continue to be viewed as the RIC's main architectural virtues in the eyes of adherents of high-style modernism, to critics this hospital conveyed a cold anonymity in that it could easily be mistaken for an office building.

In Canada, a similar bold structural expression influenced the exterior of the Joseph O. Ruddy General Hospital in Whitby, Ontario (1971–73), designed by Craig, Zeidler, and Strong. This hospital, however, had a somewhat softened exterior compared to that of the RIC. The exterior concrete frame was reminiscent of the art nouveau style of the late nineteenth century, as most evident in the work of Antonio Gaudí.[14] Its rounded corners and tucks (fig. 3.21) were a

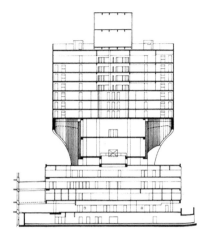

bare-bones reinterpretation of Gaudí's seminal Casa Mila apartment house in Barcelona (1905–7).

Concurrently, in the United States, the hospital and laboratory buildings designed by Chicago architect Bertrand Goldberg were attracting attention worldwide for their daring geometry and space-planning concepts. In the spirit of Le Corbusier and with the same passion for reinforced concrete, Goldberg designed a series of circular and radial hospitals in which the patient towers were compositionally distinct yet functionally connected to a support service below, vis-à-vis a vertical circulation core. Among the most striking of these hospitals was the Prentiss Hospital for Women and Psychiatric Institute at the Northwestern University Medical Center in Chicago (figs. 3.22 and 3.23), and Goldberg's most striking laboratory building was the Clinical Sciences Tower

3.22. Prentiss Hospital for Women and Psychiatric Institute, Chicago, 1975, section

3.23. Prentiss Hospital for Women and Psychiatric Institute

at the University Hospital of the State University of New York at Stony Brook.[15] At Prentiss (1973–75), Goldberg created a panopticon. The nursing station was at the center of a radial unit. The two nursing units per floor each housed twenty-five beds. The support core for vertical movement was split into halves, one on each side of the nursing station. The patient rooms were irregular in shape, with small bathrooms on the outboard side. Staff and patients immediately had difficulty with the circular windows on the exterior, and the unusually shaped patient rooms (figs. 3.24 and 3.25). The staff claimed that patients found the windows disorienting. Goldberg nonetheless pursued many of these same concepts in the new St. Mary's patient tower in Milwaukee, and at St. Joseph's Hospital in Tacoma, Washington (both 1974–76).

At Stony Brook (1974–76), Goldberg created an immense cube elevated on stilts above its support core. An open, concrete plaza functioned as the roof of the podium as well as an access point to the tower (figs. 3.26 and 3.27). Its central services core functioned as a tree trunk, from which four cubes seemed to be suspended. Goldberg's signature circular windows adorned only the four corners of the lab floors; otherwise, the floors were virtually windowless.

By the end of the 1970s some effort was made to put hospital architecture of the decade in perspective. Notably, in 1979 a French journal devoted an entire issue to the topic.[16] This series of essays by prominent French experts asked whether the hospital as a building type was careening out of control and

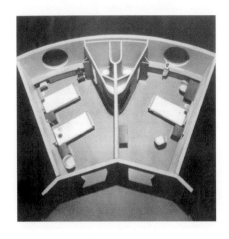

3.24. Prentiss Hospital for Women and Psychiatric Institute, model of patient rooms

3.25. Prentiss Hospital for Women and Psychiatric Institute, plan of typical patient-care floor

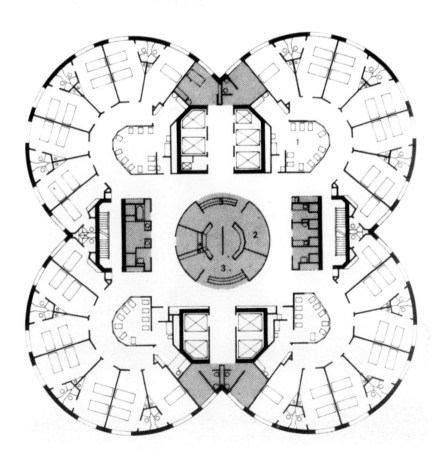

3.26. University Hospital, Stony Brook, New York, 1976

3.27. University Hospital, pilotis of patient tower atop support base

Opposite:
3.28. Patient-care unit of the 1970s, plan typologies

whether modern hospitals were any better than their premodern predecessors. In one essay, a physician-administrator presented a detailed visual compendium of plan types of recent hospitals, most of them in Europe. The pinwheel, or spoke, hospitals were featured (though not pictured) in another essay, followed by a series of plan types that might be best described as radial, panoptical, or modular in configuration (fig. 3.28). A third series, drawn from the two previous plan-based typological studies, focused on the patient room within the context of the medical-surgical nursing unit (fig. 3.29). This series emphasized the trend toward radial and cellular-modular room types in private and semi-private versions. If nothing else, these pieces illustrated the diversity of philosophies and approaches in hospital design during the 1970s.

Meanwhile, experimentation was occurring elsewhere on the relations among cost, the need for growth, climate, and hospital form. In South America, a hospital was built combining the modern machine aesthetic with the unique requirements of a tropical region. The Saint Vincent de Paul Regional Hospital, designed by J. M. Llauro, J. A. Urgell, and E. C. Facio (1977–79), was built as a regional hospital at Oran in the Province of Salta in Northwest Argentina. Because of the mountainous tropical climate, epidemics and diseases were common in the area. The hospital was composed of modular units stacked horizontally and vertically. From a distance, its large, suspended space-frame roof gave it the look of an airplane hangar (fig. 3.30). A plaza was provided to accommodate future expansion beneath the structural frame and roof. A modified interstitial floor system was incorporated as well (fig. 3.31). The plan was configured as a series of four wings joined by courtyards. This hospital was significant for its synthesis of traditional planning principles, its flexibility in anticipation of growth, and an affinity for nature evident in its low scale, its courtyards, and various opportunities for patients to be outdoors near their room, all integrated in a minimalist framework.[17]

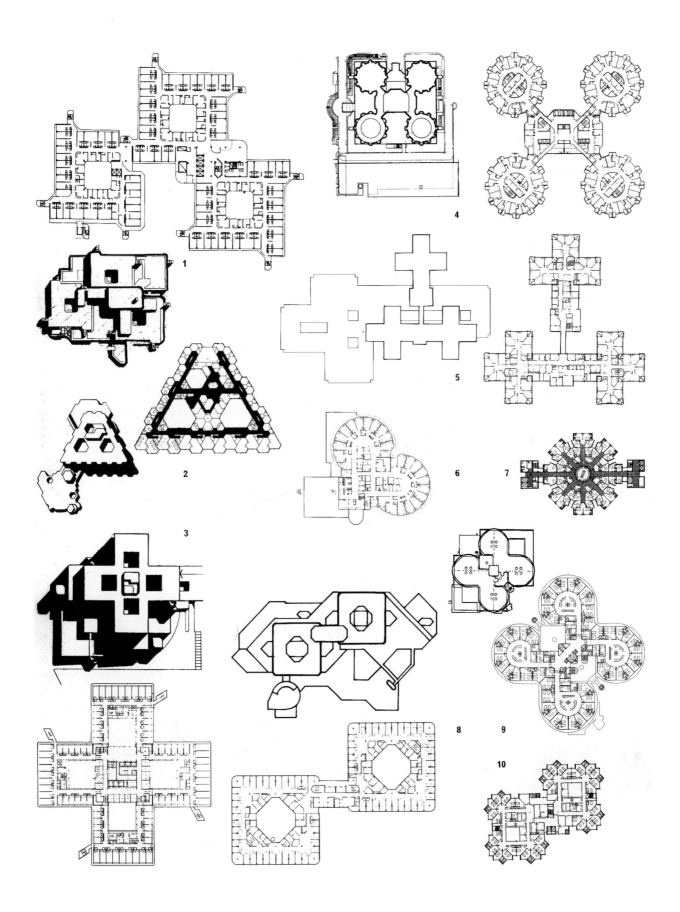

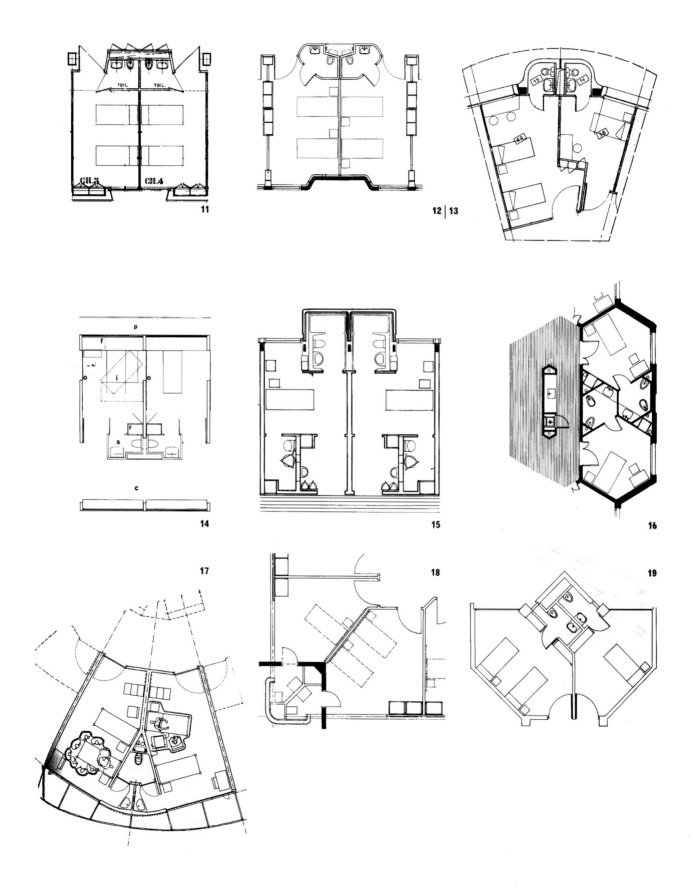

11

12 | 13

14

15

16

17

18

19

3.30. Saint Vincent de Paul Regional Hospital, Oran, Argentina, view of courtyard

3.31. Saint Vincent de Paul Regional Hospital, 1979, section

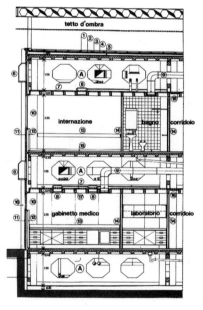

The End of the Line for Hill-Burton

Two factors fueling the period of exponential growth in the United States between 1970 and 1980 were federal urban renewal policies, dating from the 1950s, and the growth of Medicaid and Medicare, created in 1965. Medicare, in particular, sparked a national debate, which persists to this day, on the merits of a national healthcare program. It radically changed the healthcare delivery system and had a profound influence on what was built. Together, the Medicaid and Medicare entitlement programs soon became the main vehicle to fund capital improvements:

> Medicare made hospital managers and entrepreneurs acutely aware of the games that could be played to maximize hospital income by including the costs of borrowing money in third-party reimbursement rates. The availability of Medicare reimbursement accelerated the preexisting trends toward borrowing funds for hospital capital projects and de-emphasized the role of government grants and private gifts as the base funding for new buildings. Voluntary hospital administrators, as well as for-profit hospital managers, began to view their budgets in terms of the institution's entire financial requirements, including operating expenses and capital as one package. Demands for capital were increasing funding for the development and start-up costs of new projects, [as well as] money to replace buildings and equipment and to add new services and facilities.[18]

The Hill-Burton program had changed much since 1946. In 1954 the program had been broadened to provide grants for the construction of nursing homes and rehabilitation centers. Ten years later an amendment authorized a new grant program for modernization and total replacement projects. Finally, in 1970 the program was amended once again to provide assistance to neighborhood health centers and alcoholism treatment centers, and it assigned priority to poor communities, where the federal share of a project's cost typically rose as

Opposite:
3.29. Patient room of the 1970s, plan typologies

high as 90 percent. Changes aside, most observers felt that the program had been a success. By 1975 more than $4 billion of Hill-Burton funds had been applied to build, modernize, or expand nearly 11,000 facilities, costing a total of $13 billion. In 1948 more than 80 percent of projects had been for new construction, but by 1971 modernization and renovation accounted for 96.5 percent of all Hill-Burton projects.[19]

In its early years, the Hill-Burton program resulted in hospitals built to house as many beds as possible per floor, with the diagnostic and treatment functions housed on the lower floors. The bed towers were the dominant features. These facilities were nearly completely focused on costly inpatient care. As the hospital grew in size, it required larger areas for technology and for the growing armada of administrators and management support personnel. When, in 1965, adherence to the Hill-Burton standards became a requirement for Medicare and Medicaid reimbursement, the program became too costly to warrant continuance. In 1967 a conference on methods to control the skyrocketing cost of health care estimated that $10 billion was needed for hospital modernization, not taking into consideration new Medicare patients or increases in the sheer number of long-term care facilities. It was concluded that hospital services in the major cities were reaching a point of breakdown.[20]

In the 1970s the already large cost of constructing a health building came to represent an increasingly large portion of a facility's funds, compared with the 1950s and 1960s. In the United States most medical centers were urged by their architects and planning consultants to adopt a phased program for capital improvements. The term "master plan" soon became a buzzword, as one consultant and architect after another implored the administration and board to take a more holistic look at their inventory of facilities and to plan for rapid growth, arrange the most prudent investment of capital, and formulate an overall plan for the future. Rising land values often dictated that an institution, if reasonably satisfied with its present location, remain on its present site and expand upward or outward. This strategy might have made sense in the short term, but in many cases it resulted in a state of gross disfigurement, with the facility gradually acquiring a hodgepodge of appendages poking out from an original main building, often one dating from the early decades of the century. Examples of infrastructural disfigurement were to be found in nearly every city, and too often the neighborhoods surrounding the institution would never recover from the shock waves of rapid expansionism and its impact on neighborhood displacement (see Chapter 4).

Meanwhile, in upscale communities away from decaying city centers, a countermovement emerged, as hospitals not dependent on federal funds were free to provide any amenities their patients were willing to pay for. In such facilities as the Community Hospital in Carmel, California (1970–72), on the Monterey Peninsula, and the Eisenhower Memorial Hospital at Palm Desert, California (1971–72), first-time visitors would be certain that they had mistakenly walked into a hotel or resort. These hospitals foreshadowed by nearly twenty years the trend in hospital-hotels, with their saunas, full-size pools under glass domes, large atrium lobbies, porte cocheres at the main entry, lavish dining rooms, and many other amenities that would become widespread in a highly competitive environment in later decades.

The first phase of the Eisenhower Memorial Hospital, designed by Edward Durell Stone, consisted of a 140-bed acute-care facility overlooking artificial lakes on an eighty-acre resort in the California desert. From the exterior it bore a striking resemblance to the Kennedy Center for the Performing Arts in Washington, D.C. (fig. 3.32). A dramatic three-level atrium, one of the first in the United States, was the main feature of the interior (fig. 3.33). The patient floors were arranged like a racetrack in plan, with patient rooms on all four sides of the upper two floors. The rooms were thoroughly conventional in their

3.32. Eisenhower Memorial Hospital, Palm Desert, California, 1972

3.33. Eisenhower Memorial Hospital, atrium lobby

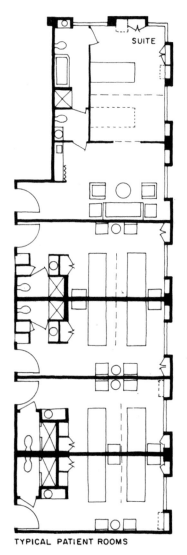

TYPICAL PATIENT ROOMS

3.34. Eisenhower Memorial Hospital, typical patient room

3.35. Eisenhower Memorial Hospital, plan of typical patient-care unit

design in most respects but were furnished in non-fixed furnishings—well-above-average sofas, chairs, tables, artwork, plants, carpet, floor lamps—and residential wall coverings, a far cry from the austerity of the typical hospital of the period (figs. 3.34 and 3.35). This was the most lavish new hospital in the United States when it opened in 1972. In retrospect, it was progressive for its hybridization of late modern architecture and features later to become inculcated in the postmodern hospital.[21]

Maintaining the nation's infrastructure of health facilities was an extremely expensive proposition. By the early 1970s existing physical plant assets in U.S. community hospitals averaged more than twenty thousand dollars per bed, and new construction would cost much more.[22] Had health facility planning been a major focus of Medicare, Congress might have initially made a clear separation between the funding of capital and the reimbursement of services for Medicare patients, as would later be the case. This would have made it possible to regulate the healthcare system by controlling the extent of its physical infrastructure. However, Medicare was initially designed merely to protect the incomes of the elderly against catastrophic hospital bills. Furthermore,

the federal government's major incursion into hospital construction, the Hill-Burton program, was now being roundly criticized. Despite shifts in the program over the years, including grants for hospital modernization and urban services from 1964, Hill-Burton had a minimal impact on hospitals in the inner cities, which were not a program priority; nor did Hill-Burton funds come anywhere near the total cost of the massive construction programs of the 1960s. Hill-Burton provided less than one-fifth of the overall construction costs in voluntary not-for-profit institutions in 1965 and less than one-fourth in state and local government institutions.[23]

In the early 1970s the federal government was faced with rapidly increasing hospital costs due largely to Medicaid and Medicare. It was determined that cost containment was essential if the programs were to survive. As a result, the Health Planning and Resources Development Act of 1974 was enacted. This legislation created the federal Certificate of Need (CON) program, which monitored and sought to regulate construction from 1974 through the mid-1980s, when this system also began to pull apart at the seams.

Increasingly, healthcare institutions began to turn to long-term debt as a vehicle to fuel renovation and new construction. In 1968 only 38 percent of hospital construction was funded through debt; by 1981 this figure had risen to 69 percent. The remaining funds were derived from a combination of philanthropy, government programs, and internal reserves.[24] A conflict in planning persisted, because Hill-Burton emphasized local institutions: two-thirds of all Hill-Burton funds for general hospital construction between the mid-1940s and the mid-1960s were given to small towns and rural areas. This greatly strengthened the rural and suburban hospitals but made coordinated regional planning difficult. Though typically under one hundred beds in size, these institutions were—in economic, administrative, and architectural terms—becoming small versions of megahospitals.[25] In the United States, the end of Hill-Burton subsidies was therefore hastened by the resulting capital-related costs passed through to the Medicaid and Medicare entitlement programs:

> Hill-Burton fell out as a casualty. In the Spring of 1969, heralding the new trends towards private enterprise, HEW Secretary Robert Finch proposed a "radical redirection" of the Hill-Burton program to one of guaranteed loans to stimulate private capital. As the Hill-Burton program came under fire from the Nixon administration in the late 1960s and was folded into the National Health Planning and Resources Development Act of 1974, federal hospital construction funds faded from the scene. Now as earlier (pre-1945), hospitals were responsible for their own capital formation. The difference was that now capital costs were regarded as a reasonable element of the cost to be reimbursed for patient care.[26]

In short, the federal government chose to refocus its immense resources away from brick-and-mortar initiatives to direct-care programs, and this policy shift would be quickly assimilated into the financial strategy of the more adroit providers.

The For-Profit Enterprise, Managed Care, and Architecture

The year 1972 marked the first serious mention in the architectural literature of the healthcare industry's change in emphasis from the treatment of sickness to the maintenance of health. Articles appeared projecting that in the ten-year period from 1972 to 1982 the United States was to spend between $30 and $40 billion on the construction of health facilities (the real figure turned out to be much higher). A nearly equal sum was projected for the developing nations over the same period. Architects were now echoing the prognostications of industry and government leaders of a coming era where patients would be treated in less costly outpatient settings, which would have a profound effect on the nation's inventory of health facilities.[27] The nation had become overbedded; although more hospitals existed than ever before, 20 percent of all hospital beds remained unoccupied every night (a modest figure compared to that by the end of the century).[28] Often, ineffective regional planning had led to widespread duplication, and early efforts to "mainstream" formerly hospitalized patients, particularly psychiatric patients, led to new federal programs to support the construction of community-based neighborhood health clinics. Community mental health programs were a frequently cited example of how to relocate patients previously housed in state asylums into the community, as a means to control inpatient-care costs and to "unwarehouse" this population. Industry leaders and observers called for a service-oriented system, or what would later be referred to as a patient-focused system of care (note that this term is not the same as *patient-centered* care, as used later in this book).[29] This was in direct opposition to the prevailing provider-focused system, where the patient was a subservient and passive entity. New types of health facilities were anticipated in the early 1970s: (1) outpatient multiphasic health-screening centers, (2) mobile health units, (3) community mental health centers, (4) health education programs and centers, (5) community-based multi-family housing for deinstitutionalized patients, (6) ambulatory care centers for diagnosis and treatment of minor injuries and surgery, (7) longer-term rehabilitation centers and home care programs to reduce the burden on more expensive, acute-care hospitals, and (8) subsidized long-term care facilities for the aged. Prognosticators maintained that in the future there would be larger but far fewer acute-care hospitals.[30] This prediction would be borne out by the 1980s.

Concurrently, a new type of provider organization began to appear. The large-scale investor-owned hospital chain came to the scene in the early 1970s. By 1972 about ninety such companies were in operation, and forty were publicly held. Combined, the chains controlled about 5 percent of the 1.6 million hospital beds in the United States.[31] Their early areas of concentration were the southern and western regions of the United States (at the time many northern states had laws prohibiting corporations based outside the state to own hospitals in their state). Critics who stated that investor-owned hospitals were interested in treating only "profitable" cases were surprised to learn that these corporations were building hospitals in areas that had been underserved for decades. Some investor-owned chains were criticized for duplicating services, but when efforts were made to work in cooperation with local hospitals and agencies to identify and provide truly needed services, the resulting hospital was attacked for not being a full-service facility.[32]

The architect was now engaged in a delicate balancing act of satisfying the wishes of the medical staff (that is, the "end-user" constituency) while meeting the needs of the corporation. The medical group, often composed of physicians who attended the same church or lived in the same neighborhood as the architect, sometimes had difficulty accepting that they had been supplanted as the "client"—that is, that the architect now worked for the corporation rather than for them. Under this new working arrangement the architect was subject to severe criticism by the local doctors.[33]

Moreover, the traditional method of designing health facilities vastly differed from the investor-owned approach, with its reliance on the provider's in-house facility planners and architects. It was now possible to standardize designs and replicate them across various regions in the United States, not unlike how a fast food franchise achieves efficiencies by standardizing nearly every aspect of its franchise outlets, especially the architecture. In the early 1970s, critics claimed that this practice was undermining local architects, was a negative trend in the long term, and was causing the indiscriminate use of generic hospital "templates."

In 1972 the Hospital Corporation of America (HCA) was working with eight architectural firms in five states. Since the corporation's founding in 1968, it had built facilities housing nearly 1,500 beds, and at the time it operated forty hospitals with a total of 5,000 beds. Later, more of its architectural work would be concentrated in fewer "lead" firms, who would often team up with local "bridesmaid" firms to handle local building-code issues, construction supervision, and so on. Capital was raised by selling shares of its stock to the public.[34]

Another provider, the fast-growing Extendicare (later Humana Corporation), based in Louisville, Kentucky, had worked with Earl S. Swensson Architects (now Earl S. Swensson Associates) on twelve hospitals by 1972. Swensson stated: "Extendicare's staff does not shove design plans down our throats. On the contrary, staffers work closely with us and with the local physicians . . . to establish particular needs of the staff. We work as a team. When it comes to being sure that we are helping to put the right facility in the right place, well, we don't know the answer to that one . . . however we have worked with experts on market studies for medical care facilities and with the state and federal agencies which control such decisions, and we find it hard to believe that our client would deliberately build a facility that is not needed."[35]

From these architects' point of view, working with an investor-owned firm meant that the project could move much faster because financing would be in place from the start, there was no need to go through the often tedious process of community fundraising or the sale of public bonds, and they could develop a long-term relationship with the client. The architectural firms claimed that this approach yielded many spin-off benefits, such as the opportunity to refine a new technique or concept by trying it out in many facilities.

The typical investor-owned corporation sought to succeed by finding a niche and applying business techniques. For example, in its early days HCA focused on small community hospitals of 50–100 beds and on psychiatric hospitals. The nonprofit health facilities, guided by a long-standing set of altruistic "ideals," mistrusted the for-profits. Yet the for-profit chains were introducing breakthroughs in management and staff efficiency, new construction techniques such as fast-tracking, innovations in equipment design in cooperation with equipment suppliers, construction management, and a lower-cost product to the patient as a result of their national scope as both purchasers and sellers of services. This translated into standardized construction and operating methods, and mass purchasing.

Another corporation, Medicenters of America, based in Memphis, was by 1971 one of the fastest-growing investor-owned providers in the field of recuperative extended care facilities (ECFs), which were short-lived alternatives to acute care and nursing-home care. The construction costs of the first ECFs ran from 30 to 60 percent below those of a typical community hospital, and many of the patients were eligible for Medicare or Medicaid. By 1971, forty-eight Medicenters were open, with dozens more in planning stages. The typical facility housed 120 beds, and many were in derived-plan buildings—some even in former roadside motels. The company touted its lower costs of operation and low level of technology compared with acute-care hospitals.[36]

The most interesting aspect of these ECFs was their rejection of the hospital, with its machines, bland interiors, monotony, and above all, its high cost of care. The ECF was typically no more than three levels in height and had the look, scale, configuration, and amenities of a motel or, at best, a multi-unit apartment building. These facilities were based almost entirely on a preexisting unrelated building type, such as the apartment complex. Visions aside, these providers were driven by a profitable market niche that did not exist before 1965. The ECF entrepreneurs were ineligible for Hill-Burton funds and often could not afford to finance the construction of new facilities themselves. As a result, the early investor-owned ECFs were anything but grand architecturally, and they usually had to make do with what was available within a very low capital acquisition and improvement budget.

The ECF turned out to be a fad, but the investor-owned hospital chain was a different story. The emergence and rapid growth of the for-profit healthcare chains were shocking to those in the voluntary hospital sector. In time, these newcomers would be wildly successful. Although the overall number of investor-owned hospitals remained relatively stable during shakeout years of the 1970s (there were 769 such hospitals in 1970 and 730 in 1980), substantial restructuring and consolidation were beginning to take place, with the goal of establishing niches and, where possible, market dominance.[37] The blueprint established in the 1970s by the chains, then considered a fringe element by the mainstream healthcare industry, would by the 1990s ascend to a position of prominence and considerable influence.

The Hospice Movement

Many hospitals in the United States had become muscle-bound by the mid-1970s. Hospital critics blamed the federal government—namely, the Health Care Financing Administration and the U.S. Public Health Service—for the bloated system. These overseers were accused of setting the tone for an unprecedented degree of institutionality inadvertently mandated through Hill-Burton. Worse, many states adopted the Hill-Burton minimum standards as maximum standards. Coupled with low-budget modernism, the result was many second-rate buildings. In addition, the hospital was being besieged by new technology with scant opportunity for decision makers to reflect on the situation. Through a curious convolution of forces—modernism, expansionism, technology, social indifference on the part of many communities, and an extremely strong medical profession as a lobbying force—an imperfect machine for healing was grafted onto an imperfect healthcare system.

An example of the widening gulf between the medical establishment and the patient—with the search for an appropriate architectural expression hanging in the balance—was the changing attitudes toward death and dying. Was architecture to continue to hold highest the virtues of the machine, or should this ideology be rejected in favor of an anti-machine aesthetic? A number of events transpiring at precisely the same time in the worlds of medicine and architecture would, together, give rise to the hospice movement. The seminal book *On Death and Dying,* by Elisabeth Kübler-Ross (1975), was a call for a thorough redefinition of societal attitudes toward dying and death in contemporary society.[38] Until that time, death had been tantamount to utter failure for a physician. When a patient died, he or she was whisked immediately to the morgue, in the most remote corner of the hospital. Death and dying were not taught in medical or nursing curricula, and many physicians and nurses felt it unethical to accept death even in the context of terminal illness because technology and the high-tech hospital must somehow find a way to triumph.[39]

The British hospice movement of the 1960s and 1970s was the first to emerge in an advanced industrialized society. It provided care for persons suffering from a terminal illness with a prognosis of six months or less of life. The philosophy of the hospice was centered on palliative, as opposed to restorative, care. That is, it aimed to provide a high degree of support to the patient while unequivocally accepting the conditions of the illness. Care was given as needed in outpatient as well as inpatient settings: a patient could be in residence for a few weeks and then return home, later repeating the pattern. An interdisciplinary team worked with the family, significant others, and the terminally ill individual on a twenty-four-hour basis. The typical British hospice was housed in a former single-family residence that had been donated to the program. The Tarner House, in Brighton, England (1973), exemplified the principle of caring for the terminally ill in a homelike setting (fig. 3.36). Residents were allowed to wear their own clothes and bring their own possessions, including furniture; without the formidable presence of such life-extending equipment as respirators, there was little to remind one of a medical institution. Relatively few architectural modifications were needed because the hospice did not house diagnostic and treatment machines per se. After the building-code standards for food preparation, safety, and handicap accessibility had been met, remaining rooms were generally not in need of significant renovation or retrofitting. These ancillary rooms consisted of a large living room or parlor and a number of bedrooms and other spaces devoted to social activities, dining, or counseling.

The contemporary British hospice movement had begun in 1967 with the opening of St. Christopher's Hospice in London, founded by Dr. Cicely Saunders.[40] The first U.S. freestanding hospice was the Connecticut Hospice, built in New Haven (1972–74). It was initially a forty-four-bed facility but was later expanded to fifty-two beds. The architect, Lo-Li Chan, introduced many innovations to the United States, including a grieving room (fig. 3.37). This hospice has since expanded to become a center of teaching and research.

Hospice care had been accepted in France since the 1840s, and in England since the late nineteenth century, but the hospice movement in the United States received much resistance at first.[41] By 1977 England had more than thirty inpatient hospices, while the United States had only two. Most U.S. hospice patients have some form of cancer, but since the mid-1980s a number of hospices for persons with HIV or AIDS have opened in the United States.[42] At the end of the 1970s the Joint Commission on the Accreditation of Hospitals began a survey of healthcare agencies across the United States, seeking information on the growth and size of the hospice movement. The survey identified more than 800 home-based care programs in various stages of development, with 440 of them functioning. No inpatient hospice had existed before 1974 in the United States, and most (51 percent) had begun to offer services to patients only in or after January 1980. Typically, the hospices were small: the average caseload for a program was sixteen.[43]

By 1980 there were five models of hospice care in the United States, all based on the Canadian and British models: (1) the freestanding, autonomous facility, as exemplified by the Hillhaven Hospice in Tucson, Arizona, and the Connecticut Hospice in New Haven; (2) the freestanding hospice with a hospital affiliation, such as the Riverside Hospice in Boonton, New Jersey; (3) the special-care unit within an acute-care or long-term-care facility, such as the first phase of the New Age Hospice in Houston (later renamed the Hospice of the

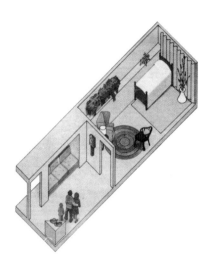

3.36. The Tarner House, Brighton, England, 1973

3.37. Connecticut Hospice, New Haven, 1975, axonometric view

Texas Medical Center); (4) the hospice team that cared for patients scattered throughout a hospital, as at St. Luke's Hospital in New York; and (5) the program with exclusively at-home care, such as the Hospice of Marin, California, and the Hospice Orlando in Florida.[44]

A case can be made for the assertion that the freestanding hospice, because of its antihospitalist underpinnings, was the first truly postmodern health building type. It had made a radical break from the hospital, rejecting its ideology, its architecture, and its revered place in society. Yet it wasn't a utopian reaction but a pragmatic, modest response to a lacuna in an increasingly imperfect healthcare landscape. The architecture most appropriate for this new building type was anything but heroic. It called for human-scaled buildings that could fit snugly into a community. Appropriately, new autonomous hospice facilities, such as the Connecticut Hospice, contained grieving rooms, gardens, a chapel, sleeping quarters for families, perhaps an indoor or outdoor pool or whirlpool, therapy rooms, offices, reading rooms, and opportunities for contact with nature.[45]

Postmodernism

The bulk of all health architecture built in the 1970s was unquestionably conservative. Nevertheless, new ideas trickled into the mainstream. The seeds of the postmodern hospital were planted through a combination of the foresight of a small group of iconoclastic administrators, the ideas of their architects, and sufficient fiscal resources for some degree of experimentation. The Slough District General Hospital, the American Oncologic Hospital, and the Eisenhower Memorial Hospital were three of these seeds. Medical centers, firmly entrenched, were the slowest to change. The restrictions inherent in the planning and design of an acute-care hospital made innovation and speedy construction particularly difficult. Worse, only hospital architects designed hospitals! If postmodernism was only a distant prospect on the fringe of a hospital architect's mind in the 1970s, then it was of no surprise that hospice clients and their financial benefactors rarely, if ever, turned to hospital architects to design a hospice.

The prospect of an alternative ideology and aesthetic language in architecture had already begun to make inroads in the 1970s; after fifty years of modernism, postmodernism was being applied to small-scale residences and public buildings. The seminal *Language of Post-Modern Architecture,* by Charles Jencks (1977), summarized key work up to that point, with full homage accorded to Robert Venturi's iconoclastic ideas of the 1960s.[46] If modern buildings were, according to their critics, severe, conservative, monotonous, minimalist, and restrictive, postmodern buildings could be the opposite: unorthodox in their composition and use of materials, colorful, ironic, ornamented, and historicist. The giant, highly centralized medical center was just about the last building type to experience this sea change. The Martha's Vineyard Hospital in Massachusetts (1973–75), by Payette Associates, was an early example of the incorporation of a residentialist aesthetic into the design of a hospital, largely in response to the residences in the surrounding community. The new addition

was two wings connected with walkways to a main building (figs. 3.38 and 3.39). The hospital was well received by staff, patients, and the public for its understatement, human scale, and image of repose.[47]

The impact of late modern mannerism was felt on an international level, although in those settings, too, it was equally slow to be included in mainstream health architecture. In Japan, many health clinics built in the late 1970s were late modernist in their planning and appearance. The best of these were sensitive to their site context, adaptable, clearly expressive of structure and materials, and human in scale. Some, however began to break out of the modernist mold altogether. The Togane Central Clinic (1977–79), designed by Shin Toki and Associates, was a prime example, with its simple composition, large windows, glass-block walls, interesting forms, and sense of human scale (figs. 3.40–3.43).[48] The Nakamura Plastic Surgery Hospital (1976–78), by Masahiro Ono and Associates, was somewhat less successful in these respects but managed to fit into its immediate community without being overbearing.[49]

In the United States, early expressions of change with an impact on the healthcare milieu occurred as part of the adaptive reuse movement, which began in earnest in the late 1970s. The adaptation of existing buildings for healthcare uses (derived plans, once again) was now in vogue. For example, the Hall Mercer Children's Center at McLean Hospital in Belmont, Massachusetts (1974–77), a building designed in the late modern style as a residential "village" for autistic children (but never actually used as such), was adapted in 1978 as a diagnostic center for children with emotional disorders. The building was designed by Perry, Dean, Stahl, and Rogers and inspired by the work of Louis Kahn. It housed forty inpatient beds for children up to age twelve, a preschool for up to 125 children, an outpatient counseling center, activity and recreation

3.38. Martha's Vineyard Hospital, Massachusetts, 1975

3.39. Martha's Vineyard Hospital, plan of ground floor and site

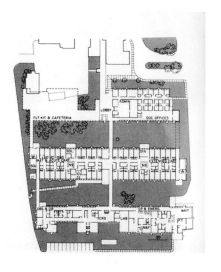

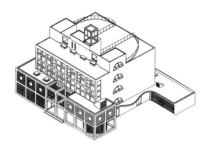

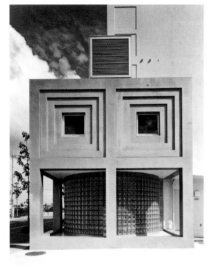

3.40. Togane Central Clinic, Japan, 1979, axonometric view

3.41. Togane Central Clinic, details of exterior

3.42. Togane Central Clinic, exterior view

3.43. Togane Central Clinic, waiting room

areas, and staff offices. It was somewhat in opposition to the stately nineteenth-century buildings on the campus of this upper-echelon psychiatric institution (fig. 3.44), and yet its informal cluster of smaller buildings enabled it to blend in. The site was planned to save as many trees as possible. Notably, the greeting "I Like You" was inscribed in the concrete tower flanking the main entrance (fig. 3.45). This was intended to reassure patients, but it is actually a striking denunciation of modern minimalist health architecture insofar as it indicates that the staff needed to soften the alienating qualities of the institution. It remains a point of debate whether this measure actually worked to humanize the brutalist monolithism. This facility, perhaps more than any other, symbolized the tug-of-war taking place between modern and postmodern architecture.[50]

The tug-of-war was taking place on the West Coast as well, in Morphosis' addition to the Baja Peninsula Hospital in Mexico (1976). The building attempted to provide a postmodernist contrast to the adjacent main hospital, an example of the modernist block hospital dating from the 1960s.[51]

One of the first conversions of a historic building into a health facility was the adaptation of a commercial arcade, built in 1870 in Providence, Rhode Island, into a 48,000-square-foot HMO outpatient clinic (1977–78). The conversion was designed by Steffian Bradley Architects. The obvious benefits included the renewal of a historic structure and the lower cost of renovation as opposed to new construction. The original, dilapidated building had been an eyesore in the community, and the new clinic fit successfully into its historic neighborhood.[52]

The Machine for Healing as Anachronism

The acute-care hospital, for the most part, remained immune to the shift taking place in architecture during the late 1970s. Modern architecture had been under siege from such critics as Ada Louise Huxtable, architecture critic for the *New York Times,* cultural critic-at-large and author Norman Mailer, and a young generation of architects disenchanted with what they considered a dead-end movement.[53] The hospital, meanwhile, was written off by elite architects because they felt that it had become unmanageably complex and prescriptive. The most well known architectural critics, when they addressed the hospital at all, harshly critiqued it—along with public housing—in line with their larger criticisms of modernism. Yet the management and boards of directors of medical centers often contained many of the most influential members of the community, prompting the popular press, among others, to ask "How could all these people be wrong?" Meanwhile, they continued going about business as usual, preoccupied with expansionism, technology, staffing, recruitment, and the growing importance of marketing. All this left little time to take stock of changes in architectural ideology.[54] Health facility planners, for their part, were not attuned to (or interested in) the particulars of aesthetics in general or postmodernism in particular. Also, most facility planners had very little to do with what the finished building would look like; such matters were left up to the architectural designer.

Because the largest medical centers were generally the most conservative of all clients, the most conservative architectural firm was usually the firm of

3.44. Hall Mercer Children's Center at McLean Hospital, Belmont, Massachusetts, 1977

3.45. Hall Mercer Children's Center, inscription in concrete tower

3.46. Carter Clinic, Roseburg, Oregon, 1979

first choice. In the largest public commissions of the era, such as the Bellevue and Veterans Administration replacement hospitals, postmodernism was not to be trusted. For the institutional client, postmodernism—which, when viewed optimistically, called for contextual responses to site, reinterpretation of nature, the return of ornament and color, and the general elements of "delight" within the Vitruvian equation of architecture as defined by a synthesis of commodity, firmness, and delight—remained oppositional to the status quo until at least 1980. The most freedom in health architecture was to be found in extremely small-scale projects designed by "non-health" architects. Such was the case with the Carter Clinic in Roseburg, Oregon (1978–79), by Martin/Soderstrom/Matteson. This dental clinic was designed completely in the mode of its region, with natural materials and a friendly scale and appearance (fig. 3.46).[55]

As for the larger institutions, well-intentioned facility planners did their best to respond to the wishes of clients who seemed to want everything immediately adjacent to everything else and wanted it open for operation yesterday. Even after "master planning" came into vogue in the early 1970s, few institutions were able to abide by their own plan's recommendations for growth. Under the excuse that things were changing too rapidly, few executives thought twice about veering away from their master plan, particularly when funding, status, market share, or staffing opportunities in a new area of specialization were at stake. Meanwhile, a small but growing amount of empirical evidence suggested that the modern machine hospital was itself unhealthful. Articles on wayfinding concluded that stress levels were elevated by an overly challenging internal circulation system in institutional settings.[56] The lack of effective directional signs was often cited as a source of confusion for staff, patients, and visitors.[57] And the systems of color-coded stripes on corridor floors were singled out as the most ineffective of all attempts to circulate persons through the maze of corridors and highly fragmented diagnostic and treatment "districts" within the typical megahospital.[58] Even the debate over the use of carpet in health facilities, begun in the 1960s, continued to rage throughout the 1970s.[59] All agreed, however, that noise had reached excessive levels in hospitals and other health facilities, owing to decades of the use of harsh "institutional materials"—that is, ceramic tiles along corridors, terrazzo floors, and nonabsorptive ceilings—combined with the omnipresent army of chattering machinery and monitoring equipment. In fact, eventually each region of the hospital had its own constellation of "specialized" critics because the building type had become so complex and overdifferentiated.[60]

The patient room was also subjected to unprecedented standardization during this period.[61] The move toward fixed equipment and furnishings in the patient room, along with the advent of the private room, started in the mid-1950s and had reached its apogee by 1980. Built-in, recessed closets and sinks; fixed light fixtures, seating, and televisions; and inoperable windows were justified in the name of efficiency, convenience, and ease of maintenance. Quietly, however, some administrators, architects, and facility planners began to voice their dissatisfaction, at first privately and later publicly.[62] Nevertheless, the trend continued unabated until healthcare costs exploded, inspiring an entirely new wave of cost containment measures in the early 1980s (see Chapter 5).

Some hospital administrators in the United States and elsewhere came to realize that the sheer size and complexity of their facility had become problematic. Consultants were brought in to make the facility more manageable, navigable, and coherent, if not more personalized. A direct outcome of this development was the aforementioned ineffective color coding of the 1970s. A giant floor-to-ceiling letter and a massive band of color would greet the person disembarking from the elevator. Sometimes even the furniture was color coded by floor. Other unsuccessful efforts were made to develop signage more comprehensible to the patient and visitor. These interventions, however, did nothing to solve the real problem, which centered on the dysfunctionality of the machine for healing.

One architect, Herbert McLaughlin, spoke out as early as 1976 on the issue of hospitals' relative inflexibility and monumentality:

> Architects, until quite recently, were trained to be essentially the sculptors of monuments. Secondarily, they have been taught, or they have learned, to think in terms of a simplistic notion of systems with the result that their monuments have come to be based on repetitive, modular units of measurement. The thing is, overtly monumental and systematic hospitals are usually functional disasters, yet this is the thinking that has dominated the field, particularly since the more sophisticated design firms entered what was considered, until about ten years ago anyway, a kind of conceptual backwater. The result has been . . . large scale sculpture [versus] the common, older hospital [but] also much less useful.
>
> The problem lies in the inability of monuments to deal with the two kinds of change which dominate the existence of a hospital—addition and demolition. A hospital is the most changing of building types, and its physical life is uniquely characterized by modification. Design should permit this change to occur in diverse patterns, but most hospital designs don't, can't—at least not in ways that are appropriate. Sure, you can move furniture around inside a hospital of this monumental variety, but you can't tack on a shanty, and hospitals *need* shanties added, regularly. The importance of this kind of change can not be too strongly stressed. The demand for regular and small scale expansion of virtually every department is necessary and incessant. It frequently doesn't occur,

however, because the design of most buildings makes such an incremental process almost impossible. . . . For the raw and regrettable fact is that hospitals, which averaged about 550 square feet per bed in 1950 and which now average about 1,000 square feet, are just getting bigger and bigger per bed and for no convincing reason. . . . The fact is that large-scale remodeling doesn't occur very often in a truly well-planned hospital. [Because] they seldom have to undergo the agony of large scale remodeling, as new spaces are added, old ones can be converted without major remodeling, within both the total fabric and individual departments.[63]

McLaughlin continued:

Another thing. While monuments are seldom designed for addition, they are never, never, never designed to be demolished. Yet this is an appropriate way to deal with change in the single most significant part of a larger hospital, the nursing tower. This fact, plus growth in the number of beds, invalidates the monumentalists' favorite scheme—what Isadore Rosenfield called the "matchbox on a muffin" which, despite all logic, has dominated hospital design for the last ten years. Worse, as many as four "matchboxes" on a giant "muffin" are built— clearly monumental, clearly systematic, clearly differentiated elements (shades of all those smart fellows at Harvard and their Gropiusian binuclear houses). The shaft of the nursing tower thrusts starkly above a sweeping horizontal base.[64]

McLaughlin particularly attacked the excessive cost of the newly introduced interstitial system (see Chapter 4 for a more detailed discussion of this concept), with its alternating layers of treatment and service floors. His firm, founded in the mid-1960s in San Francisco as Kaplan and McLaughlin, set out to question basic design assumptions such as these, and it soon attracted like-minded clients who sought to break out of the status quo. As the young firm's reputation spread, large institutional clients were attracted to its alternative views. One client in particular, St. Vincent Hospital in Santa Fe, provided the firm, by now renamed Kaplan/McLaughlin/Diaz, with considerable freedom in this respect.

St. Vincent was characterized by a horizontal arrangement whereby the diagnostic and treatment side was set apart from the patient-housing realm (fig. 3.47), in distinct opposition to the matchbox-on-a-muffin plan. In fact, the architects published a series of side-by-side comparisons refuting the patient-tower racetrack model in favor of a triangulated modified-radial concept, which borrowed some features from experiments in the design of medical-surgical units that McLaughlin had participated in during the late 1950s while in the army (these experiments tested the amenity of various floor-plan concepts and overall shapes: square, triangular, and variations on the rectangular racetrack plan). The triangulated nursing unit would in fact become an outgrowth of the radial concept, retaining its centrality while eschewing its formal inflexibility by "squaring off the edges," or outer perimeter wall, of the circular form. The firm's findings disputed those of the Yale Index in certain key respects (see Chapter 6). By this

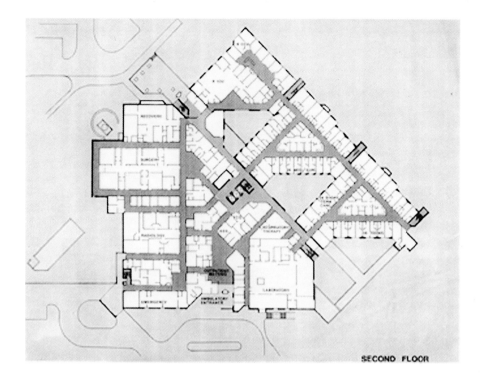

SECOND FLOOR

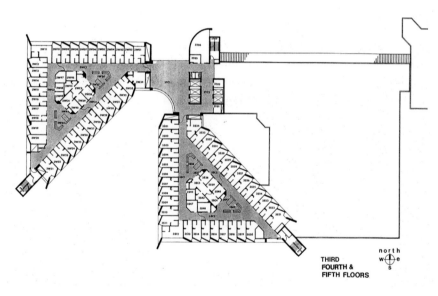

THIRD
FOURTH &
FIFTH FLOORS

north
w ⊕ e
s

3.47. St. Vincent Hospital, Santa Fe, New Mexico, 1975–77, second-floor plan

3.48. St. Vincent Hospital, typical plan, third–fifth floors

time, though, it had been generally concluded that the freestanding triangulated nursing unit allowed for change or even destruction without compromising the integrity of the various support regions of the hospital (fig. 3.48).[65]

St. Vincent was significant for three reasons. First, far more emphasis was placed on horizontal movement than vertical movement internally, thereby opening up courtyards situated between the two "sides" of the hospital. Second, the low-rise massing allowed for many irregularly shaped spaces to accommodate change and future growth of various departments. Of this McLaughlin wrote:

> In the matchbox-and-muffin scheme, the problems are extraordinary. Circulation and critical support elements are nestled tightly around a central elevator core serving the nursing tower, which is so placed that it is extremely difficult to expand. When standards change, the nursing units must either be maintained in place in an inefficient form or abandoned. . . . What then, should a hospital be?

The most apt analogy as far as I am concerned is that of a village, starting with a multi-layered industrial services building with labs, radiology, surgery, administration, and designed to make the addition of shanties very easy. The "service road" or horizontal transportation system is open-minded. . . . Visually and functionally [these features] should be conceived to anticipate additions and the architect might as well accept the fact that they may well be designed by others. . . . An urban design consciousness is useful because it must deal with tightly woven assemblages of varied but intermingling parts. The function of a hospital as a compact, changing village of such variety should be affirmed, not denied.[66]

The third significant attribute of St. Vincent, besides its horizontalism and expandability, was its regionalist appearance: the exterior massing and materials (stucco) and narrow windows on the south side acknowledged historical regional influences of the American Southwest (fig. 3.49).

These examples provide evidence that the hospital itself (now referred to as "medical center") was continually the subject of debate in terms of its layout and internal functional relationships; however, scant attention was given to connections between the hospital and outpatient care clinic. In other words, the hospital continued to be thought of as an autonomous entity, when in fact this autonomy would be seen by critics as its isolation: the hospital was an island disconnected from its context. By 1980, then, modernism in health architecture, and particularly the megahospital, had been criticized from several perspectives. And indeed, isolation from context, inflexibility, monumental scale, and the obsession with high technology would contribute to a thorough rethinking of this building type.

CHAPTER 4

Utopian Excursions

By the late 1960s the modern hospital was being pushed and pulled by a conflicting combination of internal and external utopian ideals. Society itself was experiencing a period of critical self-assessment and upheaval. The relevance and aims of nearly every institution were scrutinized. The mission of the urban hospital was particularly called into question. Yet even the 1967 urban riots, which erupted in city after city, did not stop these hospitals from expanding, resulting in massive aggregations of buildings, parking garages, automobiles, and congestion in urban neighborhoods. The urban renewal movement was in full stride.

In this chapter we demonstrate how techno-utopian thinking and a quest to perfect the internal workings of the hospital became obsessive. Mainstream health organizations failed to take into account the effects that other utopian visions—those of the counterculture, the civil rights movement, the efforts to ameliorate urban alienation, and the movement against the Vietnam War—would have on their own agendas. Moreover, when this unprecedented hospital expansionism slowed in the 1970s, many historic urban neighborhoods turned out to have been irrevocably altered, if not entirely obliterated.

Urban Renewal and the Medical Center

Many urban medical centers were faced with the choice of remaining in their present location or moving out to the booming suburbs, which needed schools, libraries, and roads in addition to new health facilities. The urban hospital had evolved into a highly centralized, imposing complex, but at a cost—it had to balance expansion of capacity and increased specialization without becoming totally set apart from its neighborhood. For decades, the relationship between the neighborhood and the urban voluntary hospital had been awkward, yet the community had usually accepted the "manifest destiny" of the institution. Now the hospital had to weigh, on the one hand, land constraints and pressures for expansion against, on the other hand, its avowed mission to serve its community.

A second factor in the decision to build up, out, or elsewhere was the institution's ambitions. Was it content to remain a high-quality neighborhood-based institution, or did it aspire to be a citywide or regional institution? Often a board of directors sought to increase status by focusing on a broader region, with the hospital becoming a powerful magnet to staff and patients far beyond the neighborhood. This attitude had several negative consequences.

First, as a rule a team of hospital consultants and architects was hired to develop a master plan for the institution. In an article defending the need for a master plan, Isadore and Zachary Rosenfield stated, "A hospital is organic, and when it is substantially enlarged it must also be reconstituted so that it may be brought into functional and organic balance."[1] Unfortunately, many hospitals had lacked functional or organic balance to begin with, and their disorganization—dysfunctionality—became further compounded when they were expanded. The Rosenfields' approach, typical for hospital consultants during this period, was to analyze community demographics, departmental loads, and projected patterns of growth. In the case of Griffin Hospital, in Derby, Connecticut, two years of study were devoted to creating the master plan. It was concluded that expansion of bed capacity was necessary, as were new programs in home care, health education, outpatient services, medical education, and physical medicine.

The recommendations of the team were brought to the board of directors, administration, department heads, medical board, and, in the Rosenfields' words, "all those who give the hospital its personality." The current facility was deemed inadequate, so a phased expansion program was proposed. The existing physical plant was judged to be chaotic, hampering the work of physicians and making the operation of the hospital more costly than it should be. Griffin Hospital, like most hospitals during this period, had previously simply added wings around a central core building (fig. 4.1). In this system, a new freestanding building was connected to the old with an elevated or underground walkway, or a combination of wings and walkways was built to connect separate buildings. Griffin had landlocked itself though prior expansions and had pushed itself right up to the sidewalk of a major traffic artery. And to complicate matters, the Hill-Burton Act stipulated that a fireproof building could not be attached to old, flammable ones.

The Rosenfields wrote, "In any case, the hospital and the community were not interested in half measures." The phased master plan was organized to avoid increases in the day-to-day costs of operations or interruptions in services. It was decided to increase bed capacity from 186 to 250, to relocate patient and central support services to more logical, convenient locations, to demolish all "flammable buildings," and to build on the cleared land a new patient tower with a two-level base containing support services and administration. The new configuration was a T-shaped double-loaded corridor versus, in their view, an "inefficient" racetrack-corridor configuration, with its "strung out" support services and its frequent intersections of corridors. Each of the paired nursing units had thirty-seven beds, yielding seventy-four beds per floor. Pairs of rooms had recessed doors off the corridor, thereby breaking up the "proverbially monotonous tunnel-like hospital corridor." The master plan of 1965 called for expansion up to 600 beds, and each floor was designed "to expand horizontally without disruption."

This and similar hospitals were becoming a system of subsystems, and hospital consultants were advocating the avoidance of physical obsolescence at all costs. The Hill-Harris amendments to the Hill-Burton Act (the Hospital and Medical Facilities Amendment of 1964) had focused attention on the need for modernization and replacement of public and private urban hospitals and other health facilities, and this legislation authorized the appropriation of $160 million between fiscal 1966 and 1969 for areas where the "greatest need" was considered to exist—in densely populated inner-city neighborhoods. In an article on the essential steps in hospital modernization, August Hoenack, a well-known architect allied with the Hill-Burton program, called for detailed feasibility studies of all internal systems and patient utilization levels within the hospital, detailed site analyses to determine likely future growth patterns, measures to protect the institution from possible "undesirable encroachment" from the neighborhood, and the need for more space to expand on-site parking.[2] Above all, according to A. C. Parette, an architect in the firm of Eggers and Higgins in New York, was the need for the administrator, the board, and all others involved to acknowledge the institution's manifest destiny:

> Unless enough time and thought are spent . . . the result will be a collection of services and not a hospital. To start the process, it is necessary to discover what existing functions in the hospital can be temporarily taken out of the hospital without creating a hazard. . . . [This] creates a store of possible empty spaces in which construction can begin. From there on, the method resembles a game of Chinese checkers. . . . The existing buildings should be considered purely as structure. Appearance, use, age and sentiment can have no value in the analysis of their worth. If they do not fit into the final solution in a way to make a direct contribution to that solution, they must be demolished. Since the total project will extend over a span of many years (15 at least) allowance for presently unknown treatment techniques must be provided in the form of vacant ground area. No conceivable . . . type of past construction could have provided flexibility for the installation of such hitherto unknowns as hyperbaric suites or linear accelerators.[3]

The quandary posed by the mindset of manifest destiny and its expression in unbridled expansionism was complicated by the automobile. In traditional, pedestrian-scaled neighborhoods, where patients and staff could walk or take public transportation to the hospital, the automobile clearly played a secondary role. But as the hospital expanded its ambitions and physical plant, it was logical to assume that people would now be driving much further distances from the suburbs, using the new interstate and urban freeways, to receive specialized treatment. On the dilemma this posed, one prominent health architect wrote: "There are, of course, offsetting issues [in modernization]. One is the availability of land. Parking has become crucial in our society, and the success of the shopping center demonstrates how far people will travel if they can park their cars. . . . Where land is available, it is our considered opinion that horizontal expansion costs less and provides the greatest flexibility for the future. . . . Streets can, of course, be leapfrogged. . . . [This can] ensure final decisions of at least relative wisdom."[4]

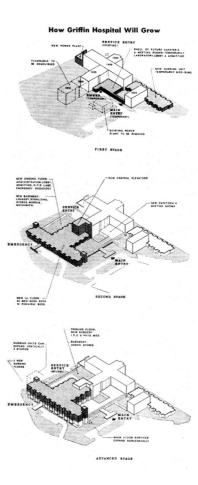

4.1. Griffin Hospital, Derby, Connecticut, 1965, three stages of expansion

4.2. Tufts–New England Medical Center, Boston, 1968: model (*top*) keyed to aerial view of site (*bottom*)

As a result of the encouragement of architects, administrators, and boards of directors, and of the oblique validation provided by the federal government, hospitals in the 1960s and early 1970s embraced the federal urban renewal movement with open arms. For its part, the federal government had already been in the business of razing inner-city neighborhoods for decades, replacing them with austere, low-budget versions of Le Corbusier's prototype high-rise housing block, first proposed for Paris in 1922. Now, with nearly all the experts advocating modernization and growth in the name of progress, on came the bulldozers. In city after city neighborhoods were demolished to make way for hospitals to expand. This was accomplished by land acquisition either through the purchase of individual parcels, piece by piece, or through the powers of eminent domain, which paved the way for multi-block areas to be razed in one fell swoop. A model of the proposed Tufts–New England Medical Center in Boston, keyed to the target neighborhood (fig. 4.2), illustrates the second approach, which continues to this day, although in a far more tempered manner.[5]

By 1970, as hospital expansionism hit full stride, critics began to advocate a more holistic approach. Herman H. Field, the chief planner of the Tufts–New England Medical Center, called for clear articulation of the institution's mission.[6] Besides the lack of an analysis of the delicate relation between the hospital and its immediate urban fabric, the chief problem was one of semantics. What geographic scale, for instance, was the term *community* to denote? Usually the terminology was tailored to serve the interest of the institution, which used such terms to defend its schemes for tearing down the neighborhood and forcing residential dislocation and upheaval. Hospital consultants were loathe to encourage the organized response of community groups—churches, universities or colleges, or neighborhood civic organizations—to their plans for expansion. Too often, the hospital would address its neighborhood only after plans were set in stone, and the result would be anger and sometimes legal resistance.

In a 1967 article in *The Modern Hospital*, Richard L. Johnson, a principal in the consulting firm of A. T. Kearney and Company, argued that the dilemma of the urban hospital had occurred because of demographic changes since the end of World War II: "The American inner city is decaying. The blight of the cities and the problems this creates for the hospitals in its path are all too apparent. Less clear to most of these hospitals is the path to survival. Hospitals located in deteriorating neighborhoods have three basic courses open to them: to flee to the suburbs, to stay in the city and adapt to changing conditions, or to stay in the city and change [status] from community to regional hospital. To the governing board concerned, the decisions can represent an agonizing, time consuming process . . . and in many instances there will be less than three choices."[7]

The factors that influenced a given hospital's decision included community-related, staff-related, facility-related, and educational issues. Community-related factors included the exodus of the socioeconomic group formerly served, an increase in the average age of those remaining in the neighborhood, the conversion of single-family dwellings into multi-family units, a decline in average family income, a static or declining assessed valuation in the area, and an increasing crime rate. Issues involving medical staff included an increase in the average age of staff physicians, a decline in applications for staff membership, and an increased caseload. Facility-related factors included obsolescence of the physical plant, largely depreciated but often unfunded capital accounts, crowded departments handicapping the work flow, inadequate parking space, rapidly increasing numbers of emergency room visits, and inadequate land for present needs, let alone future expansion requirements. Educational factors included the closure of most hospital-based nursing schools and, in many cases, unfilled postgraduate medical residency positions and the rising use of foreign medical school graduates.

Faced with the seriousness of these developments, some boards chose a course of inaction, casting the institution adrift while existing resources were further depleted. But, for the urban institution, the exodus of the hospital's traditional population base accelerated. The utopian ideal of urban renewal had been based partly on the assumption that cities would evolve into diverse multi-racial, multi-income-level societies in which the replacement or displacement of deteriorated buildings with planned housing would make life in the city more appealing for all. This did not occur: the further urban renewal went, the more the "white flight" syndrome took the hospital's former constituents away from their old neighborhoods, with concomitantly adverse financial consequences.

In his discussion of the three possibilities available for hospitals, Johnson felt that institutions should beware the superficial appeal of the first choice, that is, relocating to the suburbs: "The first ring of suburbs surrounding the city may already have enough hospitals and beds. Leapfrogging to the less populated outer ring presents a number of imponderables. Can funds be raised successfully in the new area? Will the occupancy be high enough to sustain long term indebtedness? Will the medical staff follow the hospital? Can key personnel be retained? What chance is there of maintaining patient and family loyalties?" With respect to the relatively few large voluntary teaching hospitals, he felt that the best course was "holding on and riding it out. . . . Governing boards are betting that reputation and resources will carry the institution until such time as the area is rebuilt and rehabilitated. But for the smaller, more typical . . . [institution] the task of survival can be a grim prospect."[8]

The second alternative posed by Johnson was for a hospital to reach for patients and staff beyond the immediate neighborhood, to acquire a regional character by developing research, teaching, and treatment programs. This scenario required a university affiliation and capital. Advanced medical technology would play a significant role in this metamorphosis, as would the readiness of staff to accept change.[9]

The third option outlined by Johnson was simply to remain put, accept the changed social conditions surrounding the hospital, adapt the mission, and simply serve the new community. He stated that this might be plausible on social or moral grounds but would be difficult to support fiscally because financing formulas based on the Hill-Harris method paradoxically tended to work against the inner-city hospital. With hospital use dropping in many urban areas and dramatically increasing in the suburbs, federal and third-party reimbursement favored the suburban hospital. Moreover, the urban hospital that waited too long to refocus often found that its fundraising sources had fled to suburbia, and the cost of acquiring land was significantly higher in the city than in suburbia.[10] For its part, the federal government in 1967 acknowledged the increasing obsolescence of the nation's urban hospitals but continued to advocate the centralization of services and the hospital's aggressive involvement in urban renewal programs.[11] Harold M. Graning, U.S. assistant surgeon general, remarked: "The advantages of centralization and regionalization . . . speak in unmistakable terms of better quality, lower cost, and faster service."[12] And a top-ranking official of the Department of Housing and Urban Development stated:

> Cutting wide swaths through the ghetto . . . and replacing crowded deterioration with widely spaced new structures, federal urban renewal is a program providing new hope to the city hospital. . . . Federal legislation offers specific encouragement to hospitals to become active partners, even initiators, of such community improvements. . . . Originating as the Slum Clearance and Renewal Act of 1949, urban renewal provides federal funds covering up to two-thirds the cost of buying, clearing and improving land and of relocating businesses and families. . . . Generous as this may seem . . . the hospital's [land] purchases [must] be consistent with a long range development plan of its own or of the city, that the land lie within a mile of the renewal project and a quarter mile of hospital boundaries.[13]

One institution to take this advice to heart swiftly was Michael Reese Hospital and Medical Center, in Chicago. This institution had grown in sixty-five years to 750 beds, and it had built a solid support base from local Jewish philanthropies. In 1966 there were twenty-one thousand admissions, twenty-three thousand outpatient visits, and thirty-three thousand emergency room visits. But from the late 1940s it had considered itself increasingly isolated amid the rapidly changing South Side of Chicago. The area, its streets once lined with stately mansions, had become, according to a former hospital director, disintegrated. The streets leading to and from the hospital were considered unsafe because of the rising crime rate in the area, and the hospital seriously considered relocating to the suburbs. Beginning with the work of a City Hall–based planning group in 1945, by 1952 the hospital became part of the South Side Development Association, joining forces with a number of other civic institutions. A seven-square-mile area was set as the target area.[14]

The subsequent urban removal effort attracted national attention for its completeness and scope. A set of before (1945) and after (1967) photographs describe the "success" of this final solution to the "nuisance" of urban decay (figs. 4.3–4.5). In a 1967 article praising the effort, and in particular the leadership of administrators, urban planners, and architects, it was proclaimed:

> What was 20 years ago a hospital island surrounded by slums is now . . . a large urban redevelopment center. South Chicago is still notorious for its ghetto areas, but the boundaries are now well removed from Michael Reese. . . . Close by Michael Reese are three impressive high rise apartment projects . . . with intervening parks. As for the hospital, the opportunity to purchase cleared land—on which some $11 million had been spent by 1954—has made possible a series

of major additions that have increased the scope of the hospital's position today as a major treatment, educational and research center. And continued gifts . . . are making possible new additions to the hospital campus projected well into the future.[15]

A similar elitism existed in Europe. The new thousand-bed acute-care facility for the Cologne University Hospital in Germany (1967–69) reflected the obsession of its architects with internal determinants; that is, the movement of supplies and people within this urban microcosm, or "city within a city." Featured prominently in published accounts of this new high-tech teaching medical center were its generous accommodations for the automobile (fig. 4.6).[16]

Perhaps acting out of conscience as much as fiscal concerns in the late 1960s, hospitals began to establish small satellite urban clinics in response to the civil unrest and riots of the period and claims that inner-city hospitals were not addressing the primary care needs of their increasingly minority constituencies. A number of hospitals in U.S. cities established outreach clinics, financed through Medicaid programs. The Mount Zion Hospital Outpatient Clinic in San Francisco (1964–66) was one of the first in the United States; it was followed by many, including the Mercy Hospital Neighborhood Health Center in Pittsburgh (1969–70).[17] Many were housed in former storefronts and were quite opposite, aesthetically, from the architectural heroics being pursued in the machine hospitals. They had low up-front investment costs and a comparatively low level of technology.

In sum, therefore, each hospital, whether a small-scale institution or a large teaching and research center, and whether in the United States or overseas, was forced to redefine the concept of *community* in the postwar era. Each institution had to refocus its mission, depending on whether it considered its community as the immediate neighborhood, a portion of the city, the entire city, the metropolitan area, or beyond.[18] Those that chose to stay in the city found themselves in a balancing act between an uncertain, complex, external urban environment and an equally uncertain, complex internal environment centered around the rapid proliferation of high technology.

The High-Tech Hospital as Utopia

The hospital had triumphed, in the Le Corbusian sense, as a machine whose primary mission was to accommodate other machines in the treatment of human sickness and disease. Internal determinants—or, rephrased, the quest for a techno-social utopia, a pure system of subsystems—were expressed in the diagram of the horizontal and vertical circulation systems of the Hospital Center in Montpellier, France (1963–66; fig. 4.7). This hospital had chosen to transform into a medical center, and like its peer institutions in other countries was in a state of constant change in the race to expand capacity and offer new diagnostic and treatment procedures. The need to avoid obsolescence drove the search for alternatives adaptable to constantly evolving functional requirements, and its flexible facilities were to be the utopian agents of change—grounded in the culture-at-large.

4.3. Michael Reese Hospital and Medical Center, Chicago, view of neighborhood, 1945

4.4. Michael Reese Hospital and Medical Center, "slum" clearance, 1960s

4.5. Michael Reese Hospital and Medical Center, effect of urban "renewal," 1967

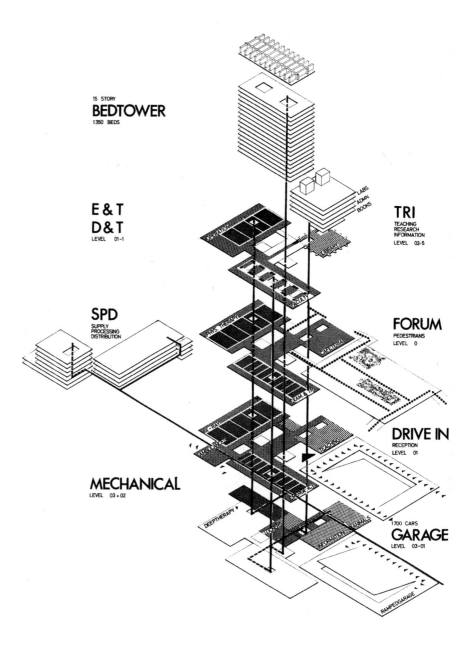

15 STORY
BEDTOWER
1350 BEDS

E & T
D & T
LEVEL 01-1

TRI
TEACHING
RESEARCH
INFORMATION
LEVEL 02-5

LABS
ADMN
BOOKS

SPD
SUPPLY
PROCESSING
DISTRIBUTION

FORUM
PEDESTRIANS
LEVEL 0

DRIVE IN
RECEPTION
LEVEL 01

MECHANICAL
LEVEL 03 + 02

1700 CARS
GARAGE
LEVEL 03-01

4.6. Cologne University
Hospital, Germany, 1967,
system flow diagram

Outside the hospital, and in sharp contrast to the ivory-towered autonomy of some high-tech urban medical centers, profound changes were occurring in the culture-at-large. At the same time, critics were starting to speak out
on the immensity of the hospital.[19] This happened for two reasons. First, the
typical hospital "mothership" had become a labyrinth. Even while critics
attacked the rigid sterility and overscaling of the hospital, its growth remained
obsessive. In 1972, Charles W. Brubaker, vice president of Perkins and Will,
asserted: "Today . . . hospitals often are massive piles of brick unrelieved by
gardens, with patients' windows overlooking parking lots, gravel roofs, and
walls, with all departments jammed together (making growth and change difficult for each), and with confused circulation systems." The "villain" in all this,
he stated, "is our overpowering reliance on vertical circulation systems—on elevators. As the hospital grows, adjunct and service facilities expand, and as additional nursing units are required, the simple vertical system begins to break
down. A mechanistic environment emerges, with too many building units hud-
dled together, surrounded by parking."[20] Brubaker's proposed solution was to
use horizontal mover systems to allow discrete units to be arranged without

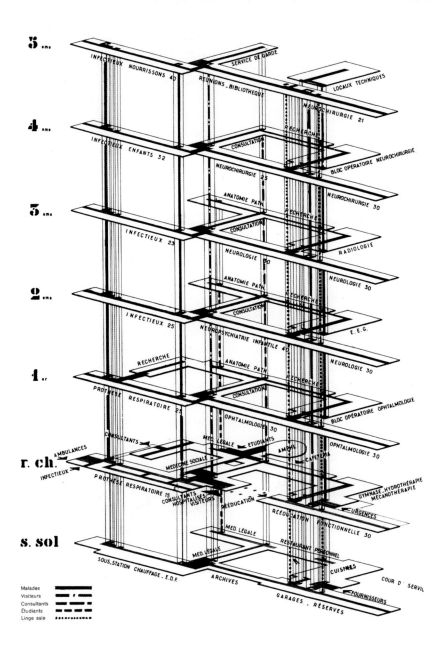

5 ᵉᵐ

4 ᵉᵐ

3 ᵉᵐ

2 ᵉᵐ

1 ᵉʳ

r. ch.

s. sol

INFECTIEUX NOURRISSONS 40
SERVICE DE GARDE
RÉUNIONS - BIBLIOTHÈQUE
LOCAUX TECHNIQUES
NEUROCHIRURGIE 21
RECHERCHE

INFECTIEUX ENFANTS 32
CONSULTATION
NEUROCHIRURGIE 25
BLOC OPÉRATOIRE NEUROCHIRURGIE
NEUROCHIRURGIE 30
ANATOMIE PATH
RECHERCHE

INFECTIEUX 23
CONSULTATION
RADIOLOGIE
NEUROLOGIE 30
ANATOMIE PATH
NEUROLOGIE 30
RECHERCHE

INFECTIEUX 25
CONSULTATION
NEUROPSYCHIATRIE INFANTILE 40
E.E.G.
ANATOMIE PATH
NEUROLOGIE 30
RECHERCHE

RECHERCHE
PROTHÈSE RESPIRATOIRE 25
CONSULTATION
OPHTALMOLOGIE 30
BLOC OPÉRATOIRE OPHTALMOLOGIE
CONSULTANTS
MED. LÉGALE ÉTUDIANTS
OPHTALMOLOGIE 30
AMBULANCES
INFECTIEUX
AMPHI CAFÉTÉRIA
MÉDECINE SOCIALE
PROTHÈSE RESPIRATOIRE 15
CONSULTANTS
HOSPITALISÉS
VISITEURS
RÉÉDUCATION
GYMNASE - HYDROTHÉRAPIE
MÉCANOTHÉRAPIE
RÉÉDUCATION FONCTIONNELLE 30
URGENCES
MED. LÉGALE
RESTAURANT PERSONNEL

SOUS-STATION CHAUFFAGE - E.D.F.
MED. LÉGALE
ARCHIVES
CUISINES
COUR D SERVIL
GARAGES - RÉSERVES
FOURNISSEURS

Malades
Visiteurs
Consultants
Étudiants
Linge sale

4.7. Hospital Center at
Montpellier, France, 1966,
system flow diagram

forcing all elements to huddle around too few circulation cores and to thereby allow for gardens, courtyards, and semi-independent building massings.

The debate between vertically oriented and horizontally oriented facilities continued. But few hospitals had the luxury of starting anew; most had to make the best of what they had. When administrators and architects gathered at professional meetings to compare notes on recent trends in renovation and modernization, they were preoccupied with accommodating more and more people, machines, and supplies.

A second reason for the growing disconnection between the hospital and society had to do with the bewildering array of new specializations in medicine, the myriad new medical tests and procedures, and the counterculture's disaffection with anything associated with the sociotechnical establishment. The healthcare industry's posture became defensive in the hope of allaying the fear of principal stakeholders. The 1960s were to be the decade of unlimited possibilities, an outgrowth of the 1950s boom years. The American quality of life soared; the children of those raised during the Depression of the 1930s experi-

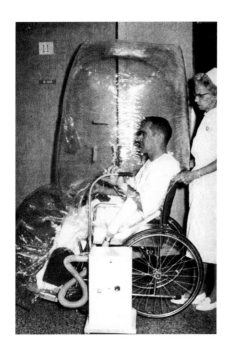

4.8. Neumatic Portable Satellite Unit (NPSU), Stanford University Hospital, California, 1965

4.9. NPSU

enced a far better standard of living than their parents had, and the Age of Consumerism was heralded. Yet, if Tom Wolfe's pithy "*we* decade" label aptly described the sociological mood of the 1960s, the term "*machine* decade" might have aptly described the same period in terms of the hospital.

Often, even the patient was treated as a machine. In most countries other than the United States, the open ward was still the accepted form of patient housing in the 1960s for those not at risk of highly contagious infection and not in need of intensive, continuous care. The medical profession, long insensitive to patient dissatisfaction, which had arisen in proportion to modern medicine's increased dependence on and faith in high technology, called for depersonalized approaches and deemphasized the emotional dimensions of providing care.[21] In 1962, a thin plastic bubble was developed at Stanford University to isolate patients with extreme susceptibility to infection. The prototype membrane was flexible, disposable, and portable (figs. 4.8 and 4.9). It was viewed as an alternative to the costly isolation suite: "Unlike the era of the pesthouse built on the outskirts of town the 'isolated' patient today may well need to be in the heart of a general hospital's activity, requiring intensive care, surgery, dialysis or x-ray diagnosis and therapy, and a whole team of physicians, nurses and technicians intimately involved in his care. His requirements for isolation may be most exacting, and a simple 'isolation' sign on the door will hardly control the transfer of infectious organisms in or out of the room where he happens to be."[22]

The major design issues, besides the considerable space required for isolation units, were the need to prevent cross-contamination, the need to accommodate basic bodily functions without disruption of the plastic membrane, the need for safety of the entire system, the need for patient acceptance, and (ironically) the need for self-empowerment through the minimization of social isolation. The system was found to be effective:

> Results have demonstrated that ordinary patient activities can be accomplished without difficulty. Isolation . . . was accomplished. Procedures such as physical examination, venipunctures and an electrocardiogram have been performed while maintaining physical separation for the patient, his bedding, and his wastes. Air passed through the service unit has been consistently sterile, as determined by blood agar plates against which the column of air was directed. . . . So far the most usual concern on the part of the observers—the question of patient claustrophobia . . . has not developed [nor has] social isolation. . . . The plastic isolator, in effect, telescopes a suite of isolation rooms into one. . . . [It] requires a large single bed room, but two isolators could function simultaneously in a two or three bed room of generous size. Storage space when not in use is little more than for an ordinary bed.[23]

The bubble was eventually tested at Stanford with more acutely ill patients, and although it was touted as highly cost-effective, this "visionary" replacement for the "impractical" patient room was never fully implemented.

In 1970, a prototype plastic capsule for patient care was developed in New York by William N. Breger, an architect and educator (fig. 4.10). The module,

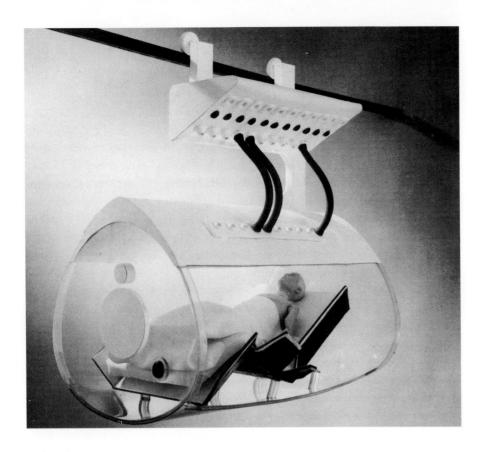

which looked like a space capsule and was influenced by the work being done at NASA, was designed for short-term intensive care. The self-propelled capsules were to move about the hospital on a monorail track. Breger was convinced that conventional hospital facilities were obsolete because the buildings were becoming monstrous in size. He stated that nurses spent up to 75 percent of their shift walking, and one in seven patients picked up new infections while in the hospital. His concept involved bringing the patient to the service rather than the service to the patient, as was the conventional practice. He believed that it was more logical to automate and mobilize the patient than to automate and mobilize supplies and equipment. The system was said to cut healthcare costs, reduce infection, and improve the rate of recovery.

Elements borrowed from emerging NASA space technology included techniques for air control and distribution, waste disposal techniques to enable one to exist in an enclosed moving space, propulsion, and communications (fig. 4.11). In 1970 the system was ready for testing in hospitals, merely awaiting the willingness of administrators and medical staff to apply this existing technology to new uses.

The patient would arrive at the hospital and immediately be encapsulated. For up to a week patients might not ever leave their capsules, which would be transported from station to station as needed. The hospital would become Big Brother:

> If the patient needs a new set of sheets, the nurse will take care of him at a nursing station, where she can treat each patient with assembly line efficiency. If a visitor comes, the patient will be notified and he will speed out to a visiting area for a chat, then return, still in his capsule, to the recovery area. . . . Movement and other adjustments will be centrally controlled by the professional staff, who communicate to the patient with intercoms, TV, etc. The patient will also . . . be

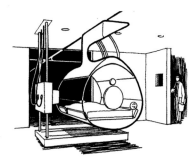

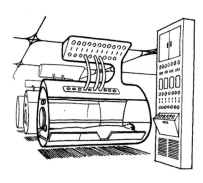

4.11. PPC in various modes of deployment

able to turn on a light or a TV set. Inside the capsule . . . [the] patient would have a synthetic or air mattress. . . . If bedsores were a threat, there could be a layer of air that would allow the patient to float above the mattress. . . . The waste system would be designed to prevent reinfection and aid patient comfort. . . . A self-contained incineration system installed underneath [would have] access through a trap door in the mattress. . . . Eventually, sewerage would be eliminated through hydrolysis, or, like spaceships, the capsule could have a recycling system. . . . The environmental control system would include a [self-contained] air system that could be adjusted to meet the patient's pathological requirements. A heart patient could have cool, high oxygen-content atmosphere; and an elderly person could have a warm environment. . . . Illumination could be adjusted centrally or by the patient. Color may also be used in or around the capsule. The patient would enjoy some entertainment and . . . amenities in the capsule as well as the security of having his bodily functions fully monitored at all times. . . . Programmed music may also be used therapeutically. The capsules will move like trolley cars . . . but eventually they may have air compression systems [and] small unit fuel cells or nuclear propulsion. The main question about movement is the effect of acceleration and deceleration on the patient.[24]

The designers of the capsule system anticipated that skeptics might attack it for being too expensive and perhaps having harmful psychological side effects. Their response was that the patient would ultimately accept the capsule "if it could get him out of the hospital faster, healthier and cheaper." They were dismissive of the relatively "few" patients who would break down: "There would be exceptions. . . . Some patients might retreat into the capsule like a womb; others might remain unalterably claustrophobic."[25] Yet Breger maintained that because of this system, the architect could concentrate on creating a total environment, including landscaping, private views, and new methods of facility planning. The capsules would eliminate building and space requirements by putting resources into these machines rather than into massive duplicative facilities. And he viewed the automation of the patient as inevitable.

Others saw the situation differently. E. Todd Wheeler predicted that the patient room would remain an entity but could afford much more therapeutic amenity. This could be achieved thorough modularization of components, flexible patient rooms for changing specialized needs, and movable rather than fixed equipment. Even portable patient rooms were a possibility.[26]

Visionary Hospitals

The techno-social euphoria of the 1960s eventually found its way into visionary architectural proposals for hospitals fantastic even by present-day standards. In a chapter in his 1971 book *Hospital Modernization and Expansion* entitled "Pitfalls, Dividends, and the Future," Wheeler put forth a series of proposals later referred to in the health literature as "tents," "trees," "inverted pyramids," and "bathyspheres."[27] He used the term *organic hospital* to describe his revolutionary architectural responses to the static, fixed conventional hospital on a land-starved urban site. In his designs, he focused on three areas of physical change in future hospitals. The first was the control of the physical environment, involving the use of what he referred to as psychotherapeutic techniques in order to regulate the patient's immediate atmosphere. For example, he proposed a tent design for hyperbaric medicine (fig. 4.12). Made of a durable, translucent plastic strung on steel cylinder "poles" encasing elevators and service facilities, the tent ensured total atmospheric control, as humidity and temperature were to be variable throughout the "building." Therapeutic surgical chambers would provide pressure conditions up to twelve atmospheres. Expansion would be simplified by the addition of more columns and plastic sheathing. Parking was to be provided on four levels along the perimeter, and the masts could be conformed to a sloping site "like trees on a hillside." Wheeler wrote: "In this design the interior is comfortable year round. A double plastic envelope provides heat and light insulation. For patients needing only atmospheric comfort the rooms are open above and free to expand, contract, connect, and even rotate as desired about the supporting trunks, within which are elevators, stairs, and services. All levels are connected by bridges. Within the tent is a great tropical garden. . . . Its amorphous shape permits . . . more floor space almost at will. Internal transportation is by powered carts, conveyors, and tubes."[28]

The second innovation he predicted was the introduction of machines in all forms. He almost offhandedly cautioned, however, that "man's attitude towards the machine" would be critical.[29] His third prognostication centered on communications systems, specifically the telemetric measurement and monitoring of the patient. Wheeler predicted the extensive use of computers and what would later be known as artificial intelligence, and remote sensing devices combined with staff assessment as a mediating modality. He anticipated that the patient would at first be fearful of these new machines but would gradually come to trust and appreciate them.

Wheeler's tree hospital was yet another visionary proposal, this one expandable to four hundred beds within its own structural framework (fig. 4.13). Of this he wrote:

> The desire for a flexible hospital is really a wish to have the hospital renewable in its working parts even as the body components renew themselves . . . like a tree with a permanent central trunk, with the surrounding rooms, like limbs, serving their functions but provided with room to grow. . . . Prefabricated room units are fitted together within a network of hangers from the roof trusses. . . . The central core contains utilities, elevators, and stairs. . . . Future expansion is accomplished by fitting new units into the open spaces or by projecting the prefabricated units outward. . . . At its top a grid of trusses provides support for telescoping steel hangars to which are attached the various prefabricated room elements.[30]

Wheeler's inverted pyramid hospital (fig. 4.14) illustrated a way to fit a large hospital into a crowded urban neighborhood. Five floors were to be built below grade in a conventional pyramid shape to provide structural support and

4.12. Tent hospital, E. Todd Wheeler/Perkins and Will, 1971

4.13. Tree hospital, E. Todd Wheeler/Perkins and Will, 1971

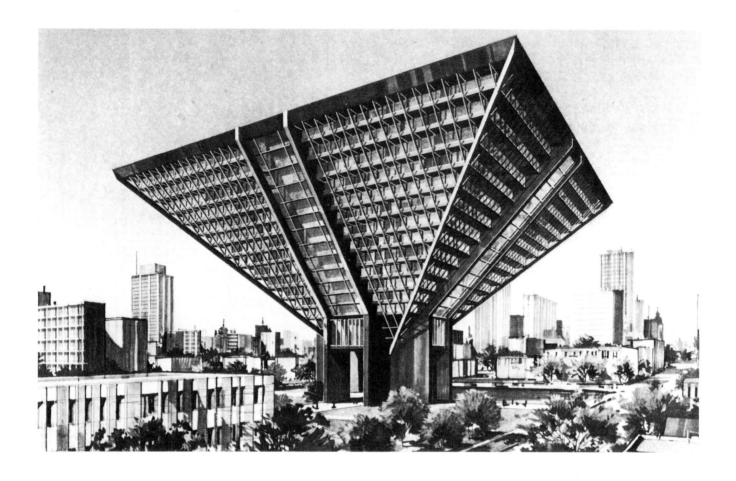

4.14. Inverted pyramid hospital, E. Todd Wheeler/Perkins and Will, 1971

parking. The inverted pyramid was built on top, on a cruciform base of four L-shaped sections. Elevator space would move vertically through the structure to a central lobby, fifty feet above the ground, then on an incline to the outer edges of the L-shaped sections. Wheeler admitted that expansion of this design would be difficult, if not impossible. Curiously, no mention was made of the psychological implications of suspending patients and staff in mid-air over the city, nor of the possible problems caused by wind velocity. Yet the scheme implied that the "old neighborhood" would be left intact beneath the super-structure.

The prototype for the underwater bathysphere hospital was, like the tent hospital, a vision of total control over the atmospheric environment (fig. 4.15). It provided a stable temperature and low noise level and allowed for the controlling effects of radiation equipment and hyperbaric operating chambers. The steel-clad hospital would have structural ribs on the outside to minimize interior obstructions, and adjustable anchor cables to raise or lower the hospital. The facility could be expanded by adding bulkheads to the structure and submerging it deeper or by building additional vessels parallel to the main unit, connected by passageways. The plan of the marine hospital shows how additions could be tethered to the mothership (fig. 4.16). An underwater tube connected hospital with shore. The hospital could be disconnected from this umbilical cord and relocated if necessary. Of this vision, Wheeler wrote: "In the design of an underwater hospital an ancient fact is recognized—below the surface the sea is relatively stable in temperature, pressure, and movement. The marine hospital, like a giant submarine with its environment fully controlled internally, exposes only a small deck to the natural elements, borrowing both

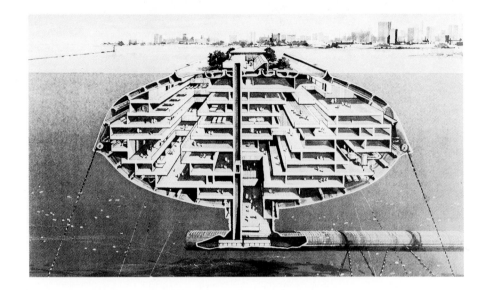

heating and cooling from the underwater environment. Cables to the bottom offset the slight design buoyancy to prevent movement."[31]

These futuristic hospitals, regrettably, responded primarily to internal technological challenges of the 1960s urban hospital. Therefore, in retrospect they remain virtual follies at best. Nevertheless, experiments were taking shape contemporaneously on other more realistic fronts, and substantial progress was being made in the area of prefabricated and industrialized buildings for health-care, albeit on a far more modest scale than the fantastic schemes proposed by E. Todd Wheeler and his firm, Perkins and Will.

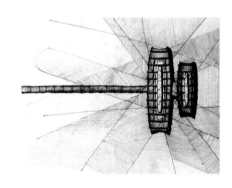

The Atomedic Hospital

To meet a need for low-cost health facilities for small and mid-size communi-ties, a utopian, prefabricated hospital dubbed the Atomedic Hospital was devel-oped by Dr. Hugh C. Maguire of Montgomery, Alabama. Conceived in 1956 but first publicly announced in 1960, it was both scorned and praised. The proto-type hospital, for forty patients, required less than one employee per bed, and it was touted as ideal for small communities or as a satellite hospital or special-care-unit addition. It came complete with fixed and movable equipment, including a laboratory, an X-ray suite, furnishings, and surgical instruments, and was ready for operation sixty days from the start of site preparation. The cost as of 1965 was $760,000. The second prototype Atomedic Hospital served as the official hospital at the New York World's Fair in 1964. The services provided to potential customers included consultation on layout and setting and other services perfected earlier by the mobile-health-unit industry, which had built hundreds of vehicles for clinical use by TB programs and various immuniza-tion and blood-donor programs during the 1950s.

The exterior of the Atomedic Hospital looked like a flying saucer, an image accentuated by its elevation on a circular support podium (fig. 4.17). A

4.17. Atomedic Hospital, 1964,
prefabricated unit

4.18. Atomedic Hospital, plan

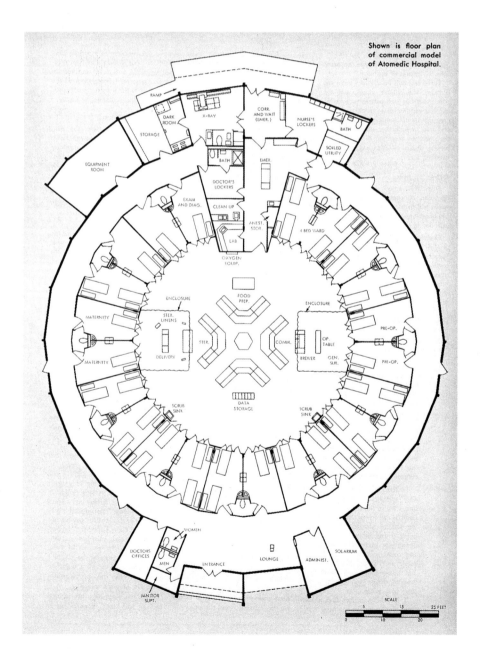

stairway with five steps led to the entrance, and a ramp led to the rear entrance. The original Atomedic Hospital was erected in Montgomery and by 1965 had been adapted as a wing for medical-surgical research in the Jackson Hospital and Clinic. This utopian, nomadic facility was radial in plan, with a ring of patient rooms surrounding a staff service and nursing core containing a surgical area, a labor and delivery area, a records area, and a central nursing station with direct access to each patient room (fig. 4.18). The plan was a series of concentric rings, with an outer corridor for visitors. Each patient room had two doors, one from the outer corridor and a second opening onto the inner core. One of these was a half-door through which the patient, bed and all, could be transported into the center core for intensive care (fig. 4.19). A bathroom not unlike that of a Boeing 707 airliner included a toilet stool that also functioned as a shower seat.

The labor and delivery suite adjoined a pair of maternity rooms, and the surgical suite adjoined a pair of pre-operative rooms. These rooms were sealed from the core by a movable, semi-rigid fabric partition. The core was open in plan, separated only by four L-shaped consoles for laboratory, sterile supply, communications, and dietary service based on pre-prepared (frozen) meals. The staff support side of the radial contained a small laboratory, an emergency room, a cleanup area, lockers, washrooms, an X-ray suite, and materials storage rooms for clean and soiled utility (clothing and laundry). The nurses' station included a control console with automated life-support-system monitoring equipment (fig. 4.20). The "front" side housed admitting and administration. The building was round, metal, and one level in height, built on a reinforced concrete slab, and the main structure contained no external windows. Advanced lightweight steel framing techniques were employed, and all interior and exterior walls were composed of aluminum and polystyrene-foam sandwich panels. A state-of-the-art HVAC system was developed specifically for this hospital. The success of the Atomedic Hospital would be dependent upon the use of disposable dishes, utensils, linens, lab supplies, and various other items made of paper or plastic. This was done to minimize storage space and eliminate the need for a kitchen or laundry.[32]

The Atomedic Hospital faced several serious hurdles from the start. First, it was expensive. In 1965, the cost was about $19,000 per bed, and the figure was higher in extreme climates or where local fire codes required automated smoke detectors, sprinkler systems, smoke barriers, or fire-rated doors. Finally, the hospital did not meet Hill-Burton eligibility standards for federal construction funding. In addition, many potential customers regarded it to be best used as a special-care unit for burn victims, pediatric care, or cardiac care—not as a general-care facility for the suburbs or rural communities, as its creators had envisioned.

The origins of the Atomedic Hospital could be traced back to the portable Dymaxion House developed by Buckminster Fuller in the 1930s, and in the stainless steel, sleek technology perfected by the creators of the Airstream trailer.[33] Although early proponents of the concept believed that this alternative to conventional hospital facilities could be built and operated for half the cost of traditional facilities of comparable size and function, their optimism was

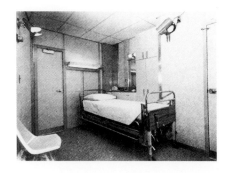

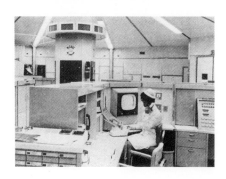

4.19. Atomedic Hospital, typical patient room

4.20. Atomedic Hospital, console with high-tech monitoring apparatus at nursing station never allowed to be tested on a wide-scale basis. A number of units were purchased by existing hospitals for use as temporary expansion quarters, or as an extension for chronically overcrowded nursing units. But, to the frustration of its creators, the potential for the Atomedic Hospital to be exported to developing countries or used by the U.S. military were never to be realized. The unit was conceived as a utopian, mass-produced, affordable medical-care machine—innovative, efficient, yet radically different—but its creator was to become the butt of jokes.

Prefabricated Medical Units

4.21. U.S. Army inflatable hospital, Vietnam, 1966

Meanwhile, the U.S. Army was busy developing a portable, prefabricated hospital of its own, based on a pneumatic air inflation system tethered to the ground with numerous cables to stabilize it during high winds and inclement weather (fig. 4.21). A prototype was unveiled at the annual meeting of the American Hospital Association in 1965. The army named the project Operation MUST (Medical Unit, Self-contained, Transportable). After numerous false starts, the first inflatable combat hospital reached the South Vietnam battlefield in November 1966. No sooner had the first $2 million unit been set up ninety miles northeast of Saigon, near the Cambodian border, when it came under heavy mortar attack. One inflatable patient-housing unit was pierced in more than a hundred places, but within a week the hospital was operational once again. Its outer walls had been patched with conventional rubber.[34]

Like the U.S. military, which sponsored research into new building systems to meet the urgent demands of combat, the health ministries of nations in Francophone Africa and in Central and South America were also eager to import prefabrication technology, in their case to decrease infant mortality and the various diseases that plagued their people (fig. 4.22). Over a five-year period beginning in 1966, two British firms, the Oxford Architects partnership and the International Professional Consortium for Health Services, worked closely with the Brazilian government to provide and install forty-two prefabricated buildings in the State of Amazonas. This complete network of health facilities included medical and surgical equipment. The project cost 10 million British pounds and had a major impact on health conditions in the region in subsequent years. The first installation was in 1968 in Manaus. In 1971 the State of Amazonas had a population of 1 million, with a ratio of 60,000 persons per doctor and 1 hospital bed per 5,000 persons—some of the lowest ratios in the world at the time. By 1975, however, there was about 1 doctor per 12,000 persons and 1 hospital bed for every 1,500 persons.

Under this ingenious plan, the units were manufactured in England, shipped to Brazil, and installed on a selected site. Five basic building types were created, from a thirty-bed hospital to a public health outpost. A "domino" concept of referrals from the community clinic to the hospital was employed. The most sophisticated units, called Type 4, were hospitals of twenty-five thousand square feet; however, the twenty-four public health units, called Type 1, were the backbone of the system. Ten river boats were purchased to transport medical staff to the various program sites.[35] The units could be repaired with a

4.22. Transportation of a prefabricated hospital, Mariani and Associates, 1978

screwdriver, and all building materials were carefully chosen and pretested to avoid insect infestation. Furthermore, each unit had its own electrical generator. The major obstacle was in recruiting enough qualified medical staff to operate the forty-two units. To this day, staffing remains one of the most problematic issues in Amazonas and similar settings.

In the United States, apart from the utopian Atomedic Hospital, the industrialized building movement had only a marginal influence on the development of prefabricated medical clinics. In 1968 a series of three prototypes called the Cashion-Horie clinics were constructed. These single-story clinics, developed by the architectural firm Cashion-Horie of Pomona, California, were assembled from prefinished, truckable units built by Designed Facilities Corporation of El Monte, California. The company was not a specialist in this building type; its prior modular units had been built for branch banks, small offices, and classrooms, and the clinic units bore a striking resemblance to branch banks designed by the firm Ziegelman and Ziegelman a year earlier.[36]

The three clinics were located in West Oakland, the Watts area of Los Angeles, and Mound Bayou, Mississippi. The Watts and Mound Bayou clinics were federally funded by the Office of Economic Opportunity, and the West

4.23. Cashion-Horie clinic under construction, West Oakland, California, 1969

Oakland clinic by the U.S. Public Health Service and the Economic Development Administration of the Department of Commerce. The main advantage of these clinics was not their overall economy but their speed of construction. Fig. 4.23 shows how the building components were trucked to the site and prepared for assembly. From site preparation to completion, the average Cashion-Horie clinic required less than half the usual time. The units were shipped from the factory with all fixed equipment in place, ready to be connected to site utility lines. In the case of the West Oakland clinic, a one-story building with thirty thousand square feet of floor space, the on-site assembly of the fifty or so units required two days. The units had a steel frame with wood stud partitions, plywood exterior walls and floors, and metal roof decking.[37]

Marshall Erdman and Associates of Madison, Wisconsin—a firm that in 1970 had built more than a thousand medical buildings in twenty-one years and employed three hundred people in Madison, Dallas, and Princeton, New Jersey—also experimented with the planning and construction of industrialized kit-of-parts clinics and medical office buildings. By 1970 their work reached a high level of refinement: they claimed an economy of 20 to 30 percent over conventionally built clinics comparable in quality.

The key to the success of the Erdman system was the use of uniform building elements in large quantities, thus saving both time and money. Each building was designed on a four-foot module. "Blocks" were then assembled according to a clinic's particular needs. Erdman had a warehouse to store various building components such as hardware, plumbing fixtures, electrical fixtures, and prefab panels, and the firm owned a manufacturing plant that produced window and door frames, millwork, roof trusses, joists, and other building components. The buildings were usually constructed of brick veneer. Erdman was always searching for ways to cut costs and in one instance devised a method to mount doors in the center line of their frame with double hinges so they could be made to swing in either direction.[38] Erdman products continue to be widely used today.

An effort to create an "ideal" modular patient-care environment was developed in the late 1960s at the Texas A&M University College of Architecture, under the sponsorship of the U.S. Public Health Service. This "adaptable building system" was developed for loft-like spaces, intended for use in the then-experimental interstitial building systems. The concept involved the standardization of the patient-room module to make it adaptable to rapid change. The room had four components: a raised floor assembled from panels, a partition panel system, a perforated suspended-ceiling panel, and a one-piece molded Plexiglas "hygiene component." The basic module for all components was sixteen inches, with floor panels of thirty-two inches square, made of wood and a resin-treated paper core. Supported at their corners by leveling jacks, these panels allowed for as much as fourteen inches' clearance for waste lines, water lines, vacuum lines, electricity, and communication lines. The wall panels were two inches thick. Panels could be stacked, or notched and folded to form corners. All components were preassembled, with many made of fiberglass. Shelves and service panels were recessed into the walls. The first installation of this system was at the Presbyterian Hospital in Dallas.[39] Later, similar efforts led to the marketing of prefabricated clinic prototypes, complete with self-contained environmental support systems for electrical, heating, air conditioning, and plumbing systems. These prefabricated buildings also afforded flexibility in terms of wall partition placement and options to create open-plan configurations—for example, in the waiting room (fig. 4.24)—housed within a modular "envelope" (fig 4.25).

A Parade of Medical Technology

Buildings for health care and the equipment within them were visible, tangible expressions of technical innovation. And the new machines were indeed impressive. The world's largest hyperbaric pressure chamber, at Lutheran General Hospital in Park Ridge, Illinois, had a thousand-pound door, strong enough to resist more than four tons of pressure from within. The chambers were interconnected and could hold up to thirty staff and patients for surgery and research.

Another device, the Manikin machine for medical training, duplicated human symptoms and physiological reactions. Aeroject General and the University of Southern California School of Medicine developed the Manikin based on simulation technology used in "nuclear space power systems" (spacecraft support systems), guided missiles, and satellites. Its analog-digital computer allowed the instructor to monitor students' actions and simulated "patient" reactions.

In yet another area, automated central control stations for nurse-patient communications were developed to monitor virtually all aspects of the patient's condition. One particular version monitored arterial pressure, electroencephalogram, pulse, respiration, electrocardiogram data, and body temperature.

At the new medical center for Cologne, West Germany, an automated food-cart system, developed by Gordon Friesen, used a battery of "transferautomats" to convey food through a heat zone at a speed that produced a predetermined degree of cooking (fig. 4.26). Cooked food was then dropped mechanically into hoppers carried along an assembly line, where the food was transferred into disposable plastic dishes, transported to a packaging machine, and sent through a blast-freeze tunnel, terminating in a storage freezer. A robotic device sorted the food, placing it in prelabeled boxes. The entire operation was controlled by a single computer. Sadly, the system, designed by Willi Brunnerkaut of Heidelberg, never worked as its creators intended; it was plagued by chronic breakdowns and unpredictable disruptions.[40]

It was no surprise that the architect had a difficult time keeping up with the rapid rate of change in medical technology in the late 1960s. One leading architectural journal noted:

> Automation . . . systems analysis . . . computers. These magic words, borrowed from the space industry . . . at last are echoing down hospital halls. Now that health care, with its 6 percent slice of the gross national product, has reached the status of an "industry" . . . now that hospital costs are rising at an annual rate of 16 percent . . . the large aerospace corporations (Litton, Lockheed, TRW),

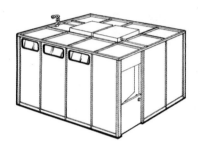

4.24. Open-plan clinic, 1972

4.25. Modular community clinic, Research and Design Institute, 1973

4.26. Transferautomat module, Gordon Friesen, 1967

big electronics firms (GE, RCA, Philco-Ford), and smaller more specialized companies are producing systems and equipment designed to reduce costs and improve service in every medical field from diagnosis to eye surgery. [This] excitement over automation . . . is frequently misguided [because technology] is presented as an apparent panacea for all problems. . . . Material reduction in health care costs is only possible through a basic revision of the whole system of delivering (and paying for) health services in the United States.[41]

Even though leading hospital consultants, including Gordon Friesen and Dr. Louis Block, had been pushing for the all-automated hospital for nearly ten years, by 1970 not a single hospital in the United States was, by their definition, "fully automated" or "fully flexible." Also, by this time critics had begun to question the vast expenditures in health care in general, which seemed to be on a steep upwardly spiraling path. Nevertheless, architects stepped up their race to keep up with high-tech health care.

Interstitialism

From the early 1960s on, architects and medical system planners were under pressure to adopt an anticipatory, proactive stance, rather than a reactive one, to the dilemma of accelerating facility obsolescence. Architects and their clients were already becoming flustered because new facilities were outdated by the time they opened their doors. The concept of interstitial space was proposed in the early 1960s as a way to keep a step ahead of the rapid changes taking place in medicine. The idea had first surfaced in facility-planning circles as early as the mid-1950s. Few, however, were willing to take a chance on such a radical proposition as constructing a complete service floor for building support systems between each pair of occupied floors.

The first health-related building with interstitial service floors was Louis Kahn's Salk Institute of Biological Studies in La Jolla, California (1960–62). Here the interstitial floors were able to accommodate practically any new system needed for high-tech medical research (fig. 4.27). Kahn used interstitial space once again in his Richards Medical Research Laboratory in Philadelphia (1965–67). Before the construction of these buildings, the concept had been applied only in laboratories built by Texas Instruments.

The first acute-care hospitals to adopt the interstitial space concept were the Greenwich Hospital, in London (1963–69), and the McMaster University Health Sciences Center in Hamilton, Ontario (1966–72), designed by Craig, Zeidler, and Strong (fig. 4.28). Soon thereafter the concept was incorporated in a number of Veterans Administration hospitals, notably the hospital in San Diego, by Charles Luckman Associates (1969–71), and Max Urbahn's Lincoln Hospital in the Bronx (1968–72). England's Ministry of Health was a strong early supporter of the idea, in its Best Buy for Hospitals program of new construction in the late 1960s and early 1970s.

In the first article in the U.S. architectural press devoted to this new approach to hospital design, it was stated that the medical profession had made dramatic advances over the past century in keeping patients alive, but now it was racing to prevent the death of the hospital itself: "It is imperative for architects and planners to develop a preventative prescription soon. Too many of our hospitals are already on the critical list by the time they are completed. . . . Scientific, technical, operational, and social [changes] have been occurring too rapidly for anyone to predict what the future needs in hospital facilities will be. . . . This unpredictability only adds to the complexity of designing hospitals." The changing nature of intensive care, the evolving nursing unit, and the influence of "space medicine" were three common justifications for the search for an "infinitely" flexible, and hence non-obsolescent, hospital. But paradoxically, proponents of ever larger, more complex buildings were saying such things as "It seems to be axiomatic that the more complicated a building is the less responsive it is to the needs of the people who work in it. No matter how

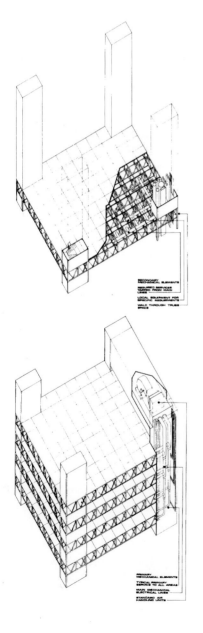

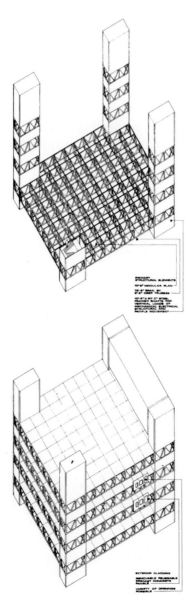

4.27. Salk Institute, La Jolla, California, 1962, interstitial floor

4.28. Interstitial system diagrams, McMaster University Health Sciences Center, Hamilton, Ontario, Canada, 1967

creative and careful a programming job you do, the odds of your being wrong are large, and in the health field, the odds are enormous."[42]

One rationale routinely offered for the situation was that the hospital was unlike most other commissions, such as manufacturing, in which the architect assumes that the clients know something about their specific functional needs and then proposes an architectural solution to comply with those particular requirements. By contrast, doctors, administrators, and hospital boards had become less and less definitive about their needs. They simply did not know what was coming next. Because of the rapid changes in the medical field, the machine hospital, for all its architectural predictability, had become the most complex and *unpredictable* of all building types. The logical response to this dilemma was to attempt to create "infinitely" flexible space.

The notion of infinitely flexible space had been accepted in speculative office buildings and in the manufacturing sector for decades, and since the mid-1950s had been applied to speculative commercial retail buildings, such as the suburban shopping mall. It was argued, however, that the rate of change was far greater in hospitals than in these other settings. Eberhard Zeidler, senior partner of the firm Craig, Zeidler, and Strong, claimed that interstitial space constituted a "fifth dimension" in architecture, which he defined as the rate of change of space-function, itself a function of time.[43]

Interstitial space was initially defined as a series of intermediate levels of a building providing space for mechanical, electrical, and plumbing systems. These floors alternated with floors devoted to "primary"—that is, human—functions. The interstitial floor-to-ceiling height, however, typically only allowed for a worker to stand nearly erect while moving throughout the space. Since the early 1960s many variations of this concept have emerged, yet all are based on a horizontal separation of primary spaces from core service spaces. Hospital designers have also used the terms *interspaces, interfloor services,* and *servo-systems* for this idea. The word *interstitial* was most widely used, because it is also a medical term describing the space within the cellular structure between the layers of the skin in humans and other species.

The benefits of this system included the virtual elimination of obstructions caused by structural columns, mechanical shafts, and waste lines. The minimization of such fixed elements provided unprecedented freedom in planning. Furthermore, it was unnecessary to vacate the floors above and below when changes to the anatomical systems of the building were required. There was no need to enter "primary" floors for routine maintenance or to retrofit any or all of the systems. Larger, unbroken expanses of space were possible, thus allowing for increased social interaction among staff who would have been housed on different floors in a vertically oriented hospital.

These conditions—minimization of fixed vertical obstructions, universal access to building systems, purported social amenity, and large expanses of open floor space—naturally led to the adoption of space-frame and long-span truss systems. These structural systems were also relatively new to architecture, but they had been used for years in bridges, and they allowed building systems to either run parallel to or criss-cross the trusses, which could be exaggerated in scale to function as the interstitial layer. Moreover, Zeidler and others felt that if a building could adapt itself to changes during construction, as occurred at McMaster, then it would probably be able to do so throughout its life.

The earliest criticism of interstitial space was that the added cost of building the extra service layers would not be defrayed by the savings in modifications likely to occur in later years. In response, Zeidler and others claimed, "This new awareness of the costs of a building, for its total lifespan, makes us able to separate the two parts of a building—the permanent parts and the changing parts" (p. 123). They also maintained that the ability to change the mechanical systems was cost effective because these systems constituted a full 60 percent of the total construction budget of the typical modern hospital. The interstitialists therefore asserted that this method resulted in multiple savings: (1) savings in operational costs through simplified maintenance and ease of repairs to building systems; (2) savings in operational costs due to the system's inherent flexibility, as partitions could be moved about with ease; (3) savings because of the shorter construction process, whereby the structural system could be constructed even before all the interior planning was complete, thereby reducing the costs resulting from rising interest rates and inflation in the late 1960s; (4) savings incurred by the system itself, with its minimization of structural components in comparison to conventional structural systems such as poured-in-place concrete; (5) savings due to the ability to bid the project in a number of "bid packages," whereby many contractors could participate in the construction of, say, a $62 million hospital, where one contractor could build the $15 million superstructure and others could be responsible for other components of the building; (6) savings due to the ability to make changes in the design and layout of the primary floors even while the building was in construction; and (7) savings due to timely adaptation through timely recognition of the need for change.

In the United States, interstitialism quickly gained a foothold, as demonstrated by the sectional perspective of the Tufts–New England Medical Center replacement hospital, in Boston, constructed between 1969 and 1971 (fig. 4.29). And the cost-cutting arguments led the U.S. Veterans Administration to require that all its hospitals be built this way, making the VA the leading client of the interstitialists. The VA justified this requirement as the best way to conserve taxpayers' money in the long run. Numerous other governments, notably Canada and England, followed suit to a certain extent.

The interstitialists constantly debated the optimal height of the support floor: the height of the interstitial floors of the Salk Institute—seven feet, six inches—were considered extravagant, although the six-foot interstitial floors of the Greenwich Hospital had already proved too low for easy access. Also debated was whether to construct the floors out of a hard, continuously walkable surface or as a nonstructural, loose membrane. It was soon agreed that the first method was superior.

A third point of contention was the extent to which the system should be applied within a facility. Hospital planners in the 1960s argued that the concept was more necessary in a teaching hospital than in a community hospital because teaching hospitals were more complex and would undoubtedly require greater flexibility in the future.[44] Others argued that the patient-care areas and

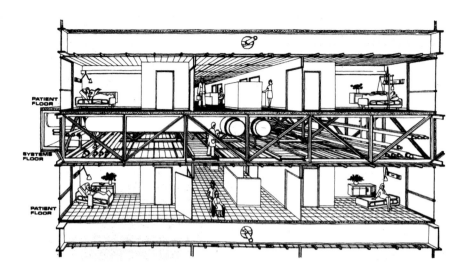

4.29. Tufts–New England Medical Center, Boston, 1969, interstitial system, section

4.30. High-rise interstitial hospital proposal, 1969

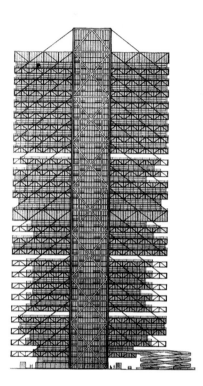

4.31. R. C. Walker (*left*), hospital director, and Dr. John Evans, medical dean, admire a model of McMaster University Health Sciences Center, 1969

office areas did not need interstitial floors. Some others believed that this system should be applied only in the base or podium of a facility and not in the patient tower. The staunchest proponents of the system argued that the concept should be applied to all parts of a hospital because then a patient floor, for example, could be converted to a research floor and the support space for the new infrastructure would already be in place. Subsequent refinements to the concept resulted in cantilevered floor systems, partial-floor interstitial systems where the core or one side of a floor had interstitial space but the other parts of the floor did not, and many other variants.

Meanwhile, in Europe, hospital planners were adapting the American invention of interstitialism to their own needs. A prototype eight-hundred-bed acute-care interstitial skyscraper hospital was proposed by a group of young French architects in 1969 (fig. 4.30). It would have been equivalent in height to a thirty-story building. Its designers justified it as a logical techno-social response to dense urban sites with high land costs. Every floor was to be serviced by an adjoining interstitial floor, and a circular ramp provided access for supplies and emergency vehicles; this artery fed into an elaborate network of transport systems for supplies, machines, materials, and people. Elevators, stairs, mechanical shafts, and related building systems were pulled to the outboard edges of the floor, flanking the sides of the tower. This machine for healing was to contain a combination of four bed wards and semi-private rooms.[45] This unbuilt proposal predated the full-blown high-tech expression of the Centre Pompidou in Paris by Piano and Rogers (1973–77), although it was designed at about the same time. Its bold structural expressiveness might also have been influenced by the early work of British high-tech architect Norman Foster. In fact, the elevation of this French prototype bore an uncanny resemblance to Foster's later Hong Kong and Shanghai Bank (1988–91).

In Canada, a modular system was adopted for the McMaster University Health Sciences Center to allow for vertical as well as horizontal flexibility (fig. 4.31). When McMaster was finally completed in 1972, its reception was lukewarm.[46] Some people said that it looked like a giant factory or prison, with its repetitive towers and uniform, regimented appearance (fig. 4.32). Others considered it an unfriendly Big Brother figure, dwarfing the surrounding community. Still others considered its scale intimidating upon closer encounter and found it difficult to navigate.

In a stinging article in *Architectural Forum* soon after the building's completion, Robert Jensen took its creators and administrators to task for making what in his view were a number of highly questionable assumptions.[47] One was that social tradition can and must be redefined to fit into a utopian vision. Another was that the view of the administration and medical staff was the best moral outlook in an era of high-tech medicine, and that the public therefore should have no input into the healthcare delivery system or the design of the places where care was dispensed.

First, Jensen questioned the sheer bulk of the complex. Each floor covered ten acres, and each exterior facade was 610 feet long. Its eight-story height contained four occupiable floors and four interstitial floors (fig. 4.33). The total floor area was 1.34 million square feet. About one-third of its total area was allocated for research; it housed one nuclear reactor and two nuclear accelerators. Patient-care functions occupied the remaining 51 percent of the building.

Second, he attacked the grim symbolic presence of the huge mechanical systems positioned at intervals along the roofscape and expressed as nodes in the floor plan (figs. 4.34, 4.35, and 4.36), and the ominous visual effect of mechanical ductwork and other building systems throughout the entire interior. Third, the building was criticized as uncompassionate, lacking any degree of human

4.32. McMaster, front elevation, 1972

4.33. McMaster, exposed structural-grid canopy over main entrance, 1972

4.34. McMaster, view showing its overpowering scale in the context of its community, 1972

scale on the interior; Jensen, like many others, felt that McMaster was a cold rather than a caring place. Typically, the outer floor-to-floor dimensions, in buildings that incorporated the interstitial option, had grown to enormous proportions, even in allied building types dedicated to non-acute care, such as the Woodhull Mental and Medical Health Center (1970–72) in Brooklyn (fig. 4.37). At McMaster, the interstitial floors were immense, and the interior design budget was less than one percent of the total construction cost. Jensen concluded:

It is a twentieth century vision, cultural and architectural, that was unknown to any prior era; but however immutable it seems now, it has not always been a "fact." Therefore it is conceivable (just) that it may not always be a fact in the future. But it is certainly fact in today's medical research and tertiary medicine's marvelous instruments, as portrayed by the building. . . . So we should not be surprised that the building represents the research commitments and power structure of North American medicine, or the underlying assumptions of society generally: grounded as they are in affluence . . . the hopefulness and awe with which we view science and technology itself. But that is an awkward reality to accommodate in medicine, for sickness and accidents are messy, personal, all

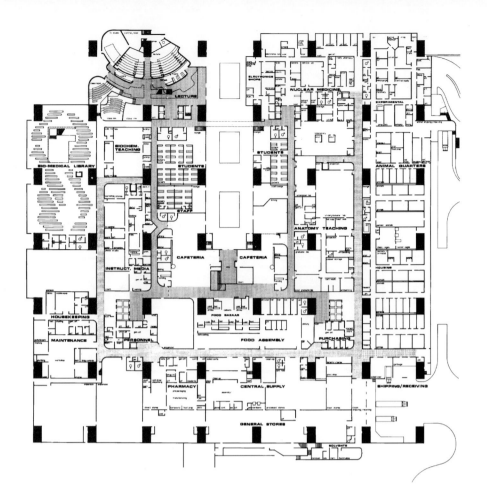

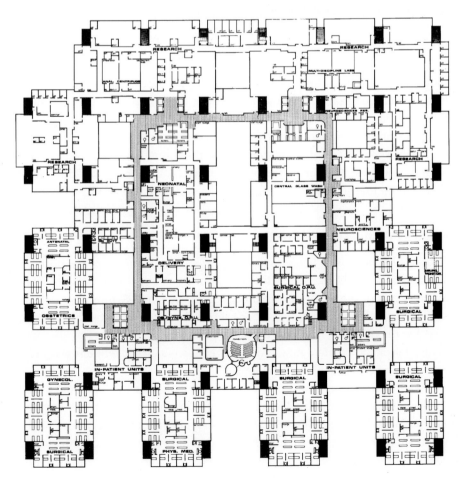

4.35. McMaster, main-floor plan

4.36. McMaster, fourth-floor plan

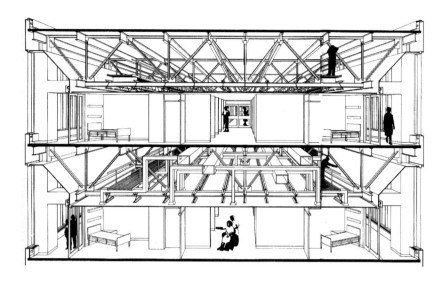

4.37. Woodhull Mental and Medical Health Center, Brooklyn, 1972, typical interstitial and patient-care floors

too human . . . [but] adequate treatment is only sporadically, at great cost, being delivered by the institutions whose images the new patient himself perhaps valued the day before. For the first time it might occur to him that the culture of which he is a part appears to isolate illness from its consciousness, or place it at a safe distance among machines.[48]

In a rebuttal to Jensen, published a few months later, Eberhard Zeidler, the lead architect, and Dr. J. F. Mustard, the administrator of McMaster, sought to defend their work. They claimed that McMaster's physical autonomy from its immediate community was justifiable. It was never intended, architecturally, to fit into Hamilton because of its special mission as a technological response to the demands of high technology.[49] In retrospect, their rebuttal seems vague and unsure. By 1980, with few exceptions, the interstitialist movement was dead, for the most part the victim of high initial building costs and the lack of any evidence that significant savings would result down the road.

Visionary Architecture in Practice

In Robert Kronenburg's book on the history and development of the portable building, he notes that science fiction was a source of inspiration for the visionary architects of the 1960s. Science fiction, like visionary architectural design, is experimental; it challenges preconceptions and seeks out possible alternatives. For the designer, however, the same process involves risk. The visionary architect seeks to create a new order by being iconoclastic while hoping that something new and viable will emerge.

The work of one group, Archigram, and its leaders, Peter Cook, David Greene, Mike Webb, and Ron Herron, sought to extend the tradition of nomadicism advanced in the 1930s by Buckminster Fuller and the creators of the Airstream mobile home.[50] Archigram, founded in 1960, produced writings and visionary proposals for mechanized, movable cities and buildings that

undoubtedly influenced E. Todd Wheeler's visionary hospital proposals and shared Zeidler's rejection of the conventional hospital. Both Wheeler and Zeidler embraced technology as a panacea for society's ills. For Archigram, this attitude was expressed in its fully mechanized Walking City (1964) by Ron Herron (fig. 4.38), the Plug-In City (1964) by Peter Cook (fig. 4.39), and the Blow-Out Village (1966), also by Cook (fig. 4.40).[51] Although Archigram did not put forth any visionary proposals for hospitals per se, the firm, in the opinion of some, did attempt to acknowledge the importance of well-being (in a utopian sense) in the urban milieu through its various proposals.

The spirit of these unbuilt proposals was evident in McMaster, almost as if Zeidler would have built his machine hospital to be plug-in (which it was) and movable (which it was not), if only he had been able to convince someone that such a facility was worth building—that is, cost effective. Similarly, the Atomedic Hospital, with its portability and flexibility, was developed in the same iconoclastic spirit.

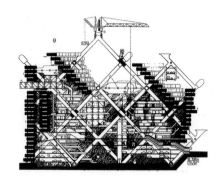

4.38. Walking City, Archigram, 1964

4.39. Plug-In City, Archigram, 1964

In contrast to the private sector, government embraced, and subsequently paid for, interstitialism to a far greater extent. The VA hospitals in the United States had incorporated the modular interstitial system developed in 1968–69 by George Agron of Stone Marraccini Patterson (SMP) of San Francisco. The Houston VA replacement medical center (1983–90) was the largest, most costly interstitial hospital ever built in the United States at the time of its opening. It was planned by the VA's in-house facility-planning staff in Washington, D.C., in consort with SMP and 3D/International of Houston. The interior design was coordinated by SMP, and the exterior architectural design and site planning were completed under the leadership of Norman Hoover, design director of 3D/International. This medical center provided comprehensive outpatient, acute, and long-term care for veterans and their families. In addition, the Houston facility provided psychiatry, treatment for drug and alcohol abuse, a regional spinal-cord treatment center, and a geriatric medicine program.

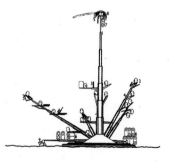

All the programs were housed within a single monolithic building of 1.5 million square feet (fig. 4.41). Earlier interstitial hospitals had been based on a deeper rectangular grid. In Houston a more linear partí (a formal term for the plan configuration and overall composition of a building) was developed, and instead of the square racetrack circulation pattern, a single corridor spine separated triangulated diagnostic and treatment clinics, administrative support, arrival functions, and special-care units on one side of the spine from the general nursing units on the other side. The entire footprint of the building was triangulated to some extent (fig. 4.42). Each triangulated unit was a "service module"; all vertical building-system elements—stairs, columns, mechanical equipment zones—were housed in twelve towers at the outer apexes of the service zones (fig. 4.43). The universal space made possible by these elaborate architectural devices resulted in a massive, sprawling complex: it was the equivalent of a twelve-story building in height, but only six floors of the building were actually occupied. The design of the exterior skin was a major challenge to the architectural design team members, who were often reduced to little more than window dressers. Yet the residentially scaled front arrival structure, which functioned as a bus shelter, the expression of the chapel on an axis

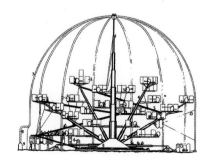

4.40. Blow-Out Village, Archigram, 1966

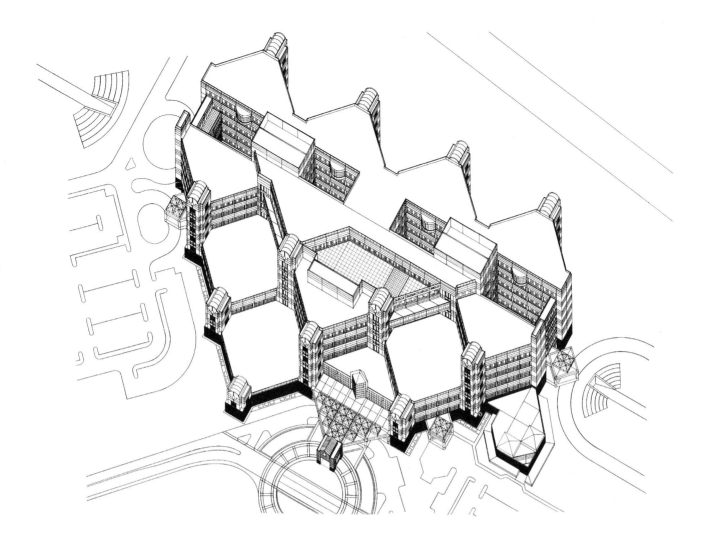

4.41. Veterans Administration
Medical Center (now
Department of Veterans' Affairs
Medical Center), Houston, 1985,
axonometric view

with this "house," a generous porte cochere at the main entrance, the continuous bands of windows in the patient modules, the high-quality materials, and the banding of the exterior base were successful devices to break down its massiveness. All these elements were incorporated relatively late in the planning and design process in an attempt to inject some degree of human scale and attractiveness. As recently as 1994 the architecture was still being rationalized: "The innovative high-tech design solution skillfully controls the movement of people, materials and services within a large complex institution that is both adaptable to change and free to grow in the future. Externally its massiveness is broken up by the undulating plan form and by the elegantly detailed towers. Four large internal landscaped courtyards bring daylight into the patient rooms and the spine corridors. However it is in the clinical areas on the other side of the spine that the interior appears very much at the mercy of the system. Of some 2000 rooms in this densely planned area, more than half are without daylight or external view."[52]

In their zeal to build this 1,044-bed megahospital, the planners and designers failed to recognize that a fundamental shift was taking place—away from highly centralized, overscaled facilities and toward smaller, decentralized facilities. As a result, this "infinitely flexible" hospital was in fact thoroughly anachronistic the day it opened, but for entirely different reasons than those the early interstitialists sought to overcome some twenty years earlier. Nevertheless, this hospital, too, was rooted in the 1960s utopian ideal of the adaptable

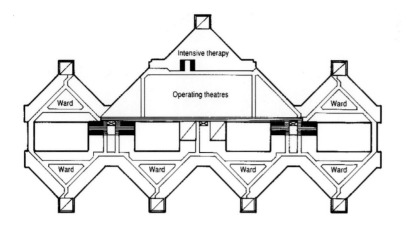

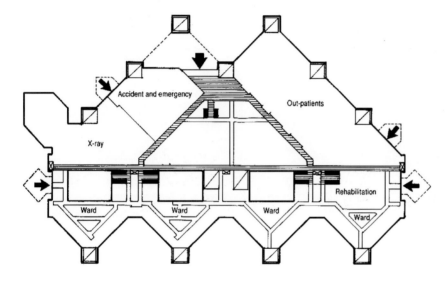

4.42. Department of Veterans' Affairs Medical Center, Houston, plans: (*top*) fifth floor; (*bottom*) ground floor

machine hospital. It was a medical city unto itself, evoking the autonomy of the medieval monastic hospital with its surrounding brick walls and gated entrance. The Houston VA came complete with the present-day corollary of an underground roadway beneath its main linear circulation spine.

In a 1979 essay on the stifling conditions that staff and patients were being exposed to in the modern megahospital, Lord Taylor criticized the architect and the hospital administrator as co-conspirators in the creation of a generation of inhumane buildings.[53] He attacked, among other things, the vast zones of windowless space at the core of these hospitals, their lack of operable windows in the name of efficiency and conservation at the expense of human comfort, their enormous size and lack of human scale, and the loss of neighborhoods destroyed to make way for these edifices. He put forth seven principles for the planning and design of hospitals, which amounted to a call for the total reform of the architecture of the modern hospital.

A second attack, the essay "How Modern Hospitals Got That Way," was written in 1979 by Roslyn Lindheim, an architecture professor at the University of California at Berkeley.[54] It contained a scathing appraisal of the harsh institutionality and oppressiveness of the typical high-tech machine hospital. This critique stands on a par with Jane Jacobs' seminal assessment of the harshness of modern urban architecture, *The Death and Life of Great American Cities*, in

4.43. Department of Veterans'
Affairs Medical Center, Houston,
1990, main entrance

which she condemned the modernist urban movement as lifeless and inhuman in scale.[55] Lindheim, singling out McMaster, attacked a system that she considered out of synch with the realities of everyday life and the needs of everyday users of health facilities:

> Indeed a look at the modern hospital speaks not of human healing but of awe of technological progress, not of caring but of increase in the GNP, not of generating health but of saving jobs and institutions. Despite this, the belief in hospitals is strong today. . . . The problem—the Catch 22—is trying to develop a rational approach to the design and operation of hospitals within the context of an irrational society. . . . With this overriding emphasis on technology and efficiency, the more important concerns of personalized patient care were overlooked. As hospital facilities grew larger and post war medical technology continued, the paramount architectural issue was not the most caring way to accommodate the needs of the sick but how to build flexible forms to house constantly changing medical technology. . . . The facility was obsolete when it opened its doors. Around the world, architects worked to develop systems to plan these hospitals.[56]

Lindheim concluded that the utopian designs of E. Todd Wheeler—the underwater hospital, the inverted pyramid hospital—were no more than "impersonal structures, anticipating 'space age' medicine while neglecting human concerns. . . . While it is possible to laugh at the visionary designs, the reality of the large modern mega-medical center is no laughing matter."[57] Of the megahospital, Lindheim wrote:

> With the advent of Medicare and Medicaid in 1965, reimbursement rates favored development of increasingly more complicated treatments and institutions to house them. Studies preceding the Hill-Burton legislation had anticipated and recommended decentralized medical care in a so-called "coordinated hospital system." Ideally, there would be one large, central hospital and teaching center, several secondary district hospitals, and many small neighborhood clinics providing people with primary care near their homes. Instead, in larger cities, medical facilities began to cluster around more expensive, complex services, and we began to have "Pill Hills" depleting the rest of the city and the outlying areas of available medical care. . . . The larger, more technological hospitals absorbed the smaller ones and resulted in institutions of enormous size, confusion, and complexity.[58]

Lindheim went on to argue that throughout the 1970s, when patients and staff found their immediate environment oppressive and inhumane, the administration usually responded by putting carpet on the floors, painting the walls with supergraphics, and making otherwise cosmetic improvements while ignoring the fundamental underlying flaws of patient and staff disempowerment and the lack of human scale. Clearly, however, health architecture had reached a crossroads and was in need of critical, interdisciplinary rethinking.

PART II **Reconfiguration**

East Jefferson General Hospital,
Metairie, Louisiana, atrium

CHAPTER 5

Reinventing the Hospital

The old idea of one hospital to satisfy all needs is a thing of the past. We need a series of institutions. We'll always need some healthcare factories for efficient, short-term, intensive-care stays, but we'll need others where humanity won't have to overcome the technical apparatus.

—John Thompson, 1976

By 1980 many community hospitals had rechristened themselves "medical centers." As in the past, those with the highest bed capacity, the fewest empty beds, the best-qualified staff, and the most sophisticated procedures were accorded the highest prestige within the industry. One aspect was different from the past, however. New alliances were being formed among networks of providers, and the investor-owned segment of the industry, though viewed skeptically by the voluntary sector, was about to enter a period of immense and sustained expansionism. The federal government, through its Health Care Financing Administration (HCFA), was about to implement a program to yet again transform the health landscape. At the same time, healthcare expenditures were skyrocketing; Medicaid and Medicare had become the most costly federal entitlement programs, and cost containment emerged as a managerial imperative. Now the marketplace figured more prominently in the equation than ever before, and astute providers began to view architecture and interior design as ways to gain an advantage over their competitors. If hospitals had previously been planned (either intentionally or unintentionally) as staff-friendly and staff-focused, the emphasis now would have to be on amenities—attractors—to draw staff and patients through referrals and repeat visits. Renovations and expansions were no longer automatically justifiable. In short, the rules of the game had changed.

Many began to advocate for the architectural reinvention of the medical-center-based hospital. The term *postmodern* describes here two contingents in the healthcare milieu that arrived at roughly the same conclusions at about the same time but from very different viewpoints. The first camp advocated patient-centered care and patient-centered facilities. The second camp consisted of providers concerned primarily with the business of health care. They realized that an attractive, inviting facility could have a positive impact on the bottom line. Both camps can be considered postmodern, denoting a shift away from the traditional architecture of the modern hospital and toward a more pluralistic approach. At first the two groups were separate from one another, but soon their concerns converged. These concerns, and their manifestation in built form, would dominate the period from 1980 to the end of the century.

The resulting changes, at first essentially organizational in nature, were later to be imbued with an aesthetic imperative. There was a shift away from autonomous, highly centralized medical centers toward networks of providers in integrated delivery systems, often with a medical center remaining at the hub but with a significantly increased focus on ambulatory care provided in off-site locations. The hospital, as it had been constituted for nearly five decades, was picked apart, and the pieces that once had composed the highly centralized, autonomous hospital were redistributed. In this way, the hospital was subjected to a fundamental reappraisal and, hence, began to experience a period of accelerated reassessment and heightened scrutiny as a building type. We refer to this process, for purposes of the present discussion, as one of "functional deconstruction," defined as a system-wide redistribution of services to community-based sites and the reconstitution of what would remain in the hospital "mothership." Three overlapping trends led to the functional deconstruction of a given medical center. First was competition in the marketplace, fueled by (and which in turn would fuel) heightened expectations among healthcare consumers. Second, the inexorable forces of cost containment spurred the creation of new revenue-producing services. Third, a postmodern ideology in architecture, and to some extent in health facility planning, emerged, calling for pluralism, in its ideal manifestation, of the most salient attributes of both the premodern and the modern periods of architecture.

Contextualism, one aspect of postmodernism, and defined in the present discussion as "new residentialism," would take root contemporaneously within this pluralist aesthetic climate as a byproduct of the functional deconstruction of the hospital and, in turn, the medical center. This subcurrent was fueled by the newfound freedom, in the postmodern climate, to explore alternative approaches to health architecture, by a reawakened interest in homelike elements arising from the antihospitalism of the 1970s in the healthcare community, and by ever more pervasive cost-containment pressures. As is typically the case in architecture, however, this triad of forces was applied first in "safe" settings—new, small outpatient building types endemic to the new decentralized provider networks—because they were, by comparison with the hospital, small in scale and the relative risk associated with experimentation was minimal. Later, the process of experimentation was extended to larger-scale settings. And even later, the New Residentialism would be incorporated in the planning and design of the fully transformed—deconstructed—hospital and medical center.

It should be noted that the term *deconstruction*, as used in literary theory, should not be confused with functional deconstruction as applied here in the healthcare milieu. Deconstruction in architecture, as it evolved during the 1980s in the work and writings of architectural theorists, was based in the field of literary theory, particularly in the work of Jacques Derrida. The avant-garde in architectural formalism soon became fascinated with the "testing" of this discourse for its utility in the making of a deconstructed architecture. As argued by architectural theorist Mark Wigley, among others, the theory of deconstruction was at its most vulnerable when applied to architecture, and therefore its testing would be of critical importance.[1] Architects enamored with this approach soon unveiled building proposals featuring jagged, sloped roof forms, abrupt diagonalizations, collisions of hallways, walls, and staircases, and otherwise unconventional forms. These proposals were remote from anything being discussed or built in the healthcare mainstream at the time. By contrast, the term *functional deconstruction,* as used here in the context of health architecture, consists of the dissection of existing internal components and their redistribution either within the medical center or elsewhere in the community landscape.

The Origins of Functional Deconstruction: The Megahospital

In the United States, early governmental efforts to stabilize hospital costs included Certificate of Need programs to regulate the number of beds and place controls over other high-cost hospital services. Yet these controls were significantly weakened with the withdrawal of federal funding for health planning under the Health Planning and Resources Development Act of 1974. In the early 1980s, the Reagan administration, with a supportive Congress, enacted legislation to deregulate the industry and spur competition among health providers as a means to control spiraling costs while minimizing governmental intervention. Federal support for Certificate of Need programs was also withdrawn. Subsequently, competition among providers increased to a level never before experienced, ushering in a construction boom. The federal government soon realized that more than unbridled free enterprise would be necessary to rein in upwardly spiraling healthcare expenditures.

In 1983, the passage of the Tax Equity and Fiscal Responsibility Act (TEFRA) mandated the reimbursement of hospital inpatient services provided to Medicare and Medicaid recipients according to "diagnosis-related groups" (DRGS). The DRG system, based on prospective, or "capped," pricing categories instead of the previous fee-for-service system, provided the incentive for a hospital to contain costs—that is, to minimize the length of hospital stays, to avoid unnecessary services, and to treat many more people on an outpatient basis than ever before.

After TEFRA, then, hospitals were faced with a dramatic rise in outpatients, most of whom arrived unaccompanied and who were often overwhelmed by the size and complexity of a facility. With the new consumerism in health care, people were becoming more aware of the choices available to them and were more prepared to assert their own preferences. They expected the same courtesy and consideration as a purchaser of any other commodity or service. Additionally, insurance providers were demanding second and, often, third opinions, and the outpatient clinic was an ideal setting to assess health needs because the patient could be prescreened to determine the level of care appropriate to his or her condition. The obvious benefit of such a system was the emphasis on prevention and abatement of "unnecessary" tests and procedures in the outpatient "gatekeeper" clinics. Medical centers met these challenges either by relocating certain services off site to their newly built outpatient satellite health centers or by relocating and consolidating them in a single on-site center for ambulatory care, often in a renovated portion of the existing facility, such as vacated nursing floors formerly used for inpatient care. Some medical centers also consolidated certain services in healthcare "malls" dedicated to women's care, pediatric care, surgicenters, MRI units, or, later, even birthing centers. In short, the pressure was on to convert to a new mixture of inpatient and outpatient care.[2]

In 1983, when the federally mandated Certificate of Need system was discontinued, states were given authority to enact their own programs, but a number chose not to do so. In these states, then, hospitals could expand and rebuild as they saw fit, spending money only on those capital improvement projects deemed cost-effective. The states that chose to maintain a CON system became more lenient in their review of projects, and when the system was eventually abandoned in the United States altogether, the industry experienced a surge in construction.[3] The rise of ambulatory and community-based care, DRGS, the new consumerism, and new medical technology all gave rise to a new wave of master planning on the premise that an upscale facility would attract more patients and quality staff. Additionally, new technology continued to render the older hospitals functionally obsolete. Such technologies as the MRI, the PET, and the Gamma Knife all had new shielding and electrical requirements, which often conspired to foil any interest in retrofitting older spaces.

The proliferation of health maintenance organizations (HMOs) and preferred provider organizations (PPOs) in the 1980s also transformed the modern hospital. Capitated managed care soon became a formidable force in transforming the hospital from its traditional role as the option of first resort into the option of last resort in this new landscape. By the mid-1980s a few HMOs were actually offering incentive payments to physicians and other specialists to *not* use the hospital for the care of their patients. The impact of this and related policies was profound. As a result, new construction tended to be rechanneled to smaller facilities than in the past. Not surprisingly, the typical patient in the hospital now tended to be more acutely ill than previously.[4] Yet these changes were felt much sooner in the private sector; government-built hospitals were far slower to adapt. In the largest institutions the influence of modernism persisted, although by 1980 many administrators realized that the dictum "bigger is better" no longer applied.

A large, late modernist example in the public sector was the first-stage Walter Reed Army Medical Center (1976–80), in Washington, D.C., designed by Stone, Marraccini, and Patterson of San Francisco. The hospital was, from the exterior, little more than a highly centralized extruded functional-planning diagram (fig. 5.1).[5] Its austerity and clean lines were praised as a clear acknowledgment of the purity of modernism. Its use of pilotís was reminiscent of Le Corbusier's Carpenter Center for the Performing Arts at Harvard University. The result was that the building floated ominously on a pedestal above the entry approach from the plaza. The machine metaphor was applied in both the exterior and the interior; the floor plans looked like an electrical diagram of overlapping circuitry-circulation grids on and between the various levels (fig. 5.2).

The continuing yet waning influence of modernism was by no means exclusively correlated with facility size. A notable example of late modernism in the private sector was the Bronx Developmental Center (1978–80), designed by Richard Meier. This building showcased Meier's internationally known palette of ubiquitous white metal exterior panels and formal minimalism

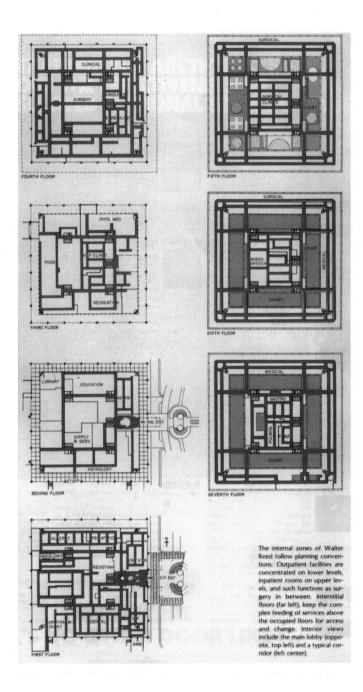

5.1. Walter Reed Army Medical Center, Washington, D.C., 1980

5.2. System flow diagrams, Walter Reed Army Medical Center

The internal zones of Walter Reed follow planning conventions. Outpatient facilities are concentrated on lower levels, inpatient rooms on upper levels, and such functions as surgery in between. Interstitial floors (far left), keep the complex feeding of services above the occupied floors for access and change. Interior views include the main lobby (opposite, top left) and a typical corridor (left center).

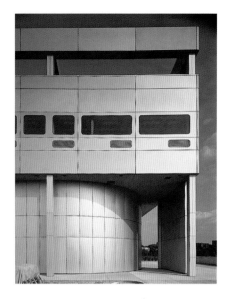

5.3. Bronx Developmental
Center, New York, 1980, exterior

5.4. Bronx Developmental
Center

5.5. Walter C. MacKenzie Health
Sciences Center, Edmonton,
Alberta, Canada, 1984

Opposite:
5.6. Walter C. MacKenzie Health
Sciences Center, interior atrium

(fig. 5.3).[6] To some, however, its exterior emphasized its character as no more than a machine housing machines. Notwithstanding, its balconies provided an intermediary zone between the interior envelope and the city beyond. The overall scale of this facility was small compared to the large federally built facilities (fig. 5.4). Nonetheless, the Bronx Developmental Center would prove noteworthy for two reasons. First, it was one of the few hospitals of the period designed by an internationally established architect who had become widely known for buildings other than hospitals. Second, because it was designed by Meier, it was a building that would influence the work of other architects working on hospitals at the time.

At the other end of the scale, megahospitals, such as the Veterans Administration hospital in Houston (see Chapter 4), carried the late modern approach further, establishing themselves as fully autonomous entities—high-technocracies.[7] The same trend was evident in Europe and in Canada, where governments built megahospitals in urban areas as a means to avoid the "redundancy" of decentralizing services. The Canadian government built some of the largest megahospitals in history. Both the McMaster University Health Sciences Center in Hamilton, Ontario (see Chapter 4), and the Walter C. MacKenzie Health Sciences Center (1980–86), in Edmonton, Alberta, were built on the premise that bigger was indeed better in terms of staffing, equipment, and overall efficiency of resources (because of the high degree of centralization). MacKenzie, like McMaster, was the brainchild of Eberhard Zeidler. It was designed by the Zeidler Roberts Partnership in association with Groves, Hodgson, Palenstein, and Wood Gardner, of Edmonton. Also like McMaster, it was an interstitial hospital, with a service floor interspersed between each pair of occupied floors. From the exterior it was the height of an eleven-story building (fig. 5.5). Interior organizational planning was dominated by a pair of immense atria intended to function as orienting devices (fig. 5.6).[8]

MacKenzie was a city unto itself. Vast patient floors were connected to circulation spines wrapped around each atrium. Connecting "main streets" between the atria enabled socialization and the movement of supplies. By comparison with the interstitial system and the atria, only modest attention was given to patient rooms or the myriad other departments of the mothership. The building was hermetically sealed; that is, most of the windows did not open. Furthermore, the immense scale of the building tended to overpower patients, staff, and visitors alike. In a critique, writer and architect Peter Hemingway asked:

What does this huge pile of precast brick in the middle of the University of Alberta signify? Is it the Mayo Clinic of the North as originally promised . . . or is it an overpriced medical dinosaur as some of its critics charge? . . . Oh! How much easier it was in the past to criticize architecture when buildings could be viewed purely as structures without introducing extraneous social judgments. But this is not the past because current architecture involves the spending of huge amounts of taxpayers' money and each of us now tends to feel personally involved in the success or failure of these huge government megastructures. To evaluate this building, I felt that I must talk to a wide spectrum of people from the planners of the initial program to the end users, the patients and staff. From

my first interview, however, I sensed contradictions . . . as one official succinctly said, "The government expectation of what they were buying, the architect's assessment of what they were building, and the hospital's opinion of what they were responsible for was never really reconciled." . . . And all this for 450 million. There is of course no comparison between the two institutions; the new one is up to date, humanized, high tech reflecting as Eb Zeidler says "a feeling of hope, kindliness, and beauty" while the existing building presumably and again in the architect's own words reflected "pain, desperation and despair." Poetic license aside . . . a building such as this will never again be built because no one can afford it![9]

MacKenzie was conceived during the 1970s, when the oil economy of Alberta was riding high, but by the 1980s the oil boom had gone bust, and Canadians were forced to accept a 13 percent tax increase, largely to pay for soaring medical expenses. This tax was seen as evidence of mismanagement within the healthcare enterprise in Canada. As for the formal attributes of the hospital, Hemingway continued:

> How is it as architecture? To begin with, it is much more successful inside than out. The architect's obsession with exterior horizontality, presumably to offset the sheer size of the place, is pure 1960 design credo. . . . This has resulted in some dubious design decisions. . . . Why did the architect want to create the impression that the hospital was a series of brick sandwich wafers piled on top of each other? Perhaps we shall never know the answer. I certainly cannot accept the argument that it is reminiscent of Georgian detailing. The aesthetic might be appropriate for a garment factory or a Zeppelin works but for an institution devoted to healing individuals, it is simply inappropriate. The Post-Modern movement came just in time to question this type of inhuman design willfulness. Inside though is another matter. The organization of space and the level of detailing is extremely competent; I almost wrote terrifyingly competent because when a highly placed government member first visited the complex, he told me it scared him because it looked "so bloody expensive." He could almost see the brickbats flying as indeed some have since the centre has opened. The truth is that the building is not as opulent as it first appears. Statistics show that it will be more economical to operate on a square meter basis than the old building. The materials are carefully chosen and maintenance free, and the general atmosphere is that of a well-appointed hotel. The main reason for the success of the interior architecture are undoubtedly the two atria. . . . [They] provide a sense of orientation to what would otherwise be an enormous undifferentiated space.[10]

In a predictable rebuttal, echoing his defense of McMaster some years before, Eberhard Zeidler asserted that this critic "swam in confusion."[11]

A few years before MacKenzie was built, petroleum-importing countries had begun to rethink their energy policies because of the oil-pricing strategies of the Organization of Petroleum Exporting Countries (OPEC). Architects joined in this quest for alternatives. Energy conservation courses sprang up in archi-

5.7. Medical Center, Technical University of Aachen, Germany, 1984

5.8. Medical Center, nurses' station

tecture curricula across the United States and in other developed countries, and all building types were scrutinized for ways to reduce energy consumption. The hospital was no exception. Computer programs were written to calculate thermal gains and losses, with cost-benefit ratios calculated of the consequences of various design strategies: patterns of consumption were calculated over twenty-four-hour periods during each day, week, and month of the year.[12]

Megahospitals were found to consume enormous amounts of energy, but this cost was justified by their creators on the grounds that other savings were being achieved. For this reason additional megahospitals were built in the public sector. At about the same time as MacKenzie, one European counterpart was planned and built. The Medical Center of the Technical University of Aachen, Germany (1978–84), by Weber, Brand, and Partners, from a distance looked like an immense auto factory (fig. 5.7). Upon closer inspection, its vast scale and its rooftop tectonic landscape, given over entirely to machines, indeed threatened to overpower passersby, not unlike the effect of the massive Hull Infirmary in England (see Chapter 3). Within, the individual wall and furnishing systems, including staff workstations and nurses' stations, were "plugged in" to the superstructure's main aperture (fig. 5.8). Colin Davies, in his book *High Tech Architecture* (1988), a largely sympathetic treatment of the subject, supplied the following noncommittal description:

> The building, or megastructure, contains lecture theaters, laboratories, cafeterias and other teaching, research, and social facilities, as well as wards, and diagnostic and treatment facilities. Twenty-four towers, 177'/54 m tall, in four rows of six, dominate the composition. These house the vertical circulation and plant. The main structure, of *in situ* and precast concrete, is animated visually by yellow and silver external steel ducts and by red painted cradles, railings, stairs, and canopies. Inside, the metal detailing and strong colours draw attention away from the massive concrete structure. Most of the accommodation is in areas that span between, and are serviced from, parallel bands of structure. There are also large landscaped courtyards. Circulation routes within the build-

ing are organized to encourage casual social and educational encounters. Access is from parking stretched adjacent to the long southern edge of the building. Beyond the entrance foyer are lecture theaters, library, restaurant, cafeteria, and seminar rooms. On the next two floors are the various medical departments with their consulting rooms and treatment facilities. The wards are in narrower wings on the top three floors and look into the courtyards, some of which open only through these three top floors. Others open right down to the entrance floor. Below the entrance floor is another level of storerooms and services.[13]

Even though Davies was an advocate for high tech, his discussion was descriptive rather than insightful in his assessment of this building, the only health facility included among the thirty-seven structures discussed in his book. He did not specifically address its scale, its mechanization, or how its occupants responded to the factory-like appearance.

In some large medical centers, connections had to be coordinated among multiple facilities. In the case of Houston's vast Texas Medical Center, an elaborate network of tunnels and overhead bridges connected parking garages and support services with hospitals and clinics. These devices were necessary to bundle together what by 1991 had become the world's largest medical center, with 667 acres, forty-one member institutions, and 6,549 licensed beds. Formed in 1946 as a 134-acre development, the medical center had expanded about a dozen times. By 1990, the Texas Medical Center had had 3.6 million patient visits, including 618,170 admissions and 3 million outpatient visits.[14]

In the 1980s, many hospitals continued to flee their declining neighborhoods for the greener pastures of suburbia, while others built bigger walls to protect themselves from their inner-city neighborhoods. The partnership created between the City of Phoenix and Good Samaritan Hospital in the late 1970s had been hailed in the field of healthcare administration as a model of how a community and a hospital could work together toward neighborhood redevelopment without causing community dislocation. This arrangement, however, was a new version of the neighborhood "removal" policies of prior years. It involved an ambitious effort to condemn property on behalf of the redevelopment authority set up by the hospital, with the help of the city's powers of eminent domain and the waiver of $100,000 in building permit fees. The city also provided technical assistance in the form of traffic flow analysis and related services. The hospital soon generated much adverse publicity after it relocated 140 families and twelve businesses and demolished more than a hundred structures. The administration defended its policy in 1984 by reporting that census was up and a number of medical-related projects were rising on the cleared land.[15]

At the same time, other hospitals were beginning to downsize to withstand the effects of DRGs and the newly competitive marketplace. To cope, hospitals were developing subacute specialty units in former acute-care, medical-surgical units.[16] Between 1980 and 1988, 445 U.S. acute-care hospitals closed.[17] Texas was, ironically, the state with the most closures. Although many of the hospitals that closed were in rural areas, the expansion of the highly developed, sprawling Texas Medical Center clearly was occurring, to some extent, at the expense of these other institutions. And their rural communities were losing their sole access to community-based hospital care.

High-Tech Romanticism

The megahospitals, because of their immensity, tended to overshadow another type of high-tech hospital. These hospitals were smaller in scale but no less expressive. The best of them extolled the virtues of high technology while making concessions to history, human scale, certain traditional planning concepts, and responses to landscape and local cultural determinants. The Mount Druitt Hospital in Sydney, Australia (1976–78), designed by Lawrence Nield, was an interstitial community hospital configured as a side-by-side platform, with diagnostic, treatment, administrative, and other support functions contiguous to but autonomous from the nursing wards. On the exterior a shiny steel-banded facade gave the building a shiplike appearance (fig. 5.9) or the look of a huge stainless-steel diner. The plan of this hospital was dominated by a set of three triangulated nursing units, each with patient rooms wrapped around a staff support core (fig. 5.10).[18]

Other hospitals—notably St. Joseph Medical Center (1982–86) in Bellingham, Washington, by Kaplan/McLaughlin/Diaz—also employed curvilinear motifs to create distinctive imagery. The top of St. Joseph evoked an art deco 1930s luxury ocean liner (fig. 5.11).[19] Yet the ten years between the construction of Mount Druitt and St. Joseph were telling. In Mount Druitt, applied ornament for the sake of imagery was still eschewed. But in St. Joseph, pluralism justified the invocation of a somewhat more narrative set of associational meanings.

In other cases the hospital took on the attributes of its site or the feel and look of other building types. In the Robert Debré Pediatric Hospital in Paris (1983–85), by Pierre Riboulet, the partí of the hospital echoed the highways that wrapped around it (figs. 5.12 and 5.13).[20] And even into the 1990s the influence of the International Style, albeit transfigured and softened considerably, was evident in newly built medical centers, such as the Rush-Copley Medical Center (1993–95) in Aurora, Illinois, near Chicago, by O'Donnell Wicklund Pigozzi and Peterson. This facility, also similar in appearance to a network of roadway arteries carrying people, supplies, and equipment, was configured in anticipation of new plug-in technology for support components to be changed as needs changed. In response a series of "ports" were created. The ports were similar to the gates of an airport terminal, and the entire hospital, with its curved circulation spine, was eerily reminiscent of an airport (figs. 5.14 and 5.15).[21]

The plan of the patient floor of the Bruck Regional Hospital (1992–95), in Styria, Austria, by Domenig/Eisenkock Architects, snaked across its site with a single corridor winding its way through end to end. At two points it intersected its attached yet largely independent support structure in a side-by-side arrangement (fig. 5.16).[22] In this case the architects dramatized the relationship between building and site by creating a bold, undulating form (the snake). The romanticization of this element was clearly of greater interest to the designers than the monotonous institutional arrangement of the four-bed patient wards. This concept of a central spine or street, though certainly not a recent innovation, drove the entire floor plan.

5.9. Mount Druitt Hospital,
Sydney, Australia, 1978

5.10. Mount Druitt Hospital,
plans: (*top*) second floor;
(*bottom*) main floor

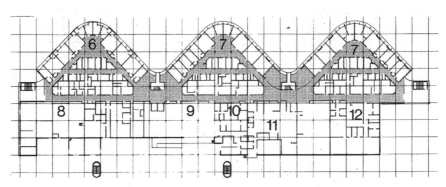

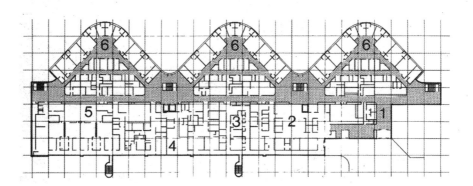

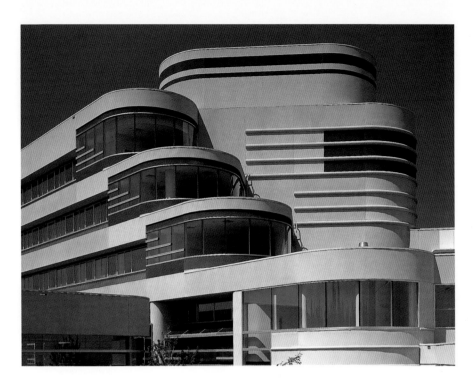

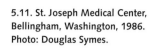
5.11. St. Joseph Medical Center, Bellingham, Washington, 1986. Photo: Douglas Symes.

5.12. Robert Debré Pediatric Hospital, Paris, 1985

5.13. Robert Debré Pediatric Hospital, site plan

Below: 5.14. Rush-Copley Medical Center, Aurora, Illinois, 1995, perspective

Left: 5.15. Rush-Copley Medical Center, interior corridor

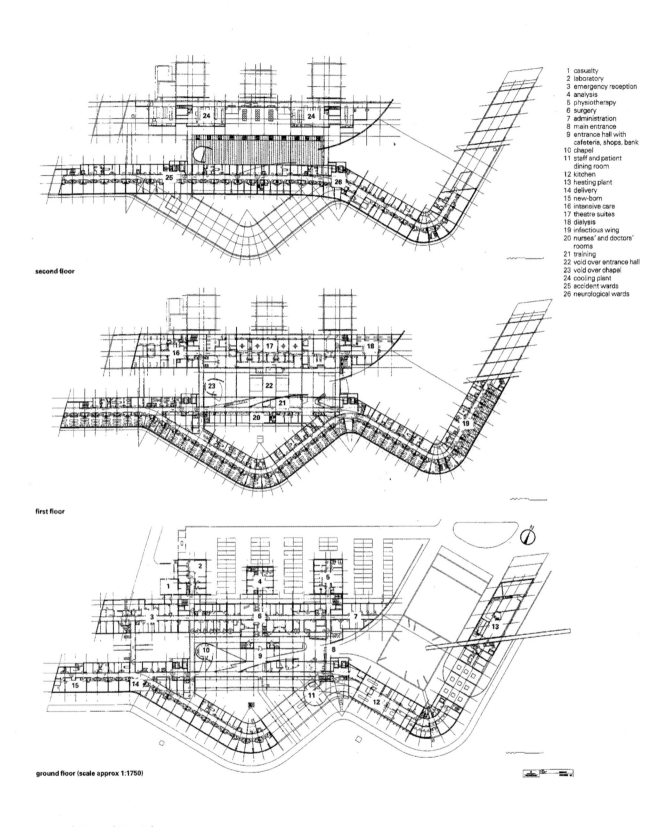

second floor

first floor

ground floor (scale approx 1:1750)

1 casualty
2 laboratory
3 emergency reception
4 analysis
5 physiotherapy
6 surgery
7 administration
8 main entrance
9 entrance hall with
   cafeteria, shops, bank
10 chapel
11 staff and patient
   dining room
12 kitchen
13 heating plant
14 delivery
15 new-born
16 intensive care
17 theatre suites
18 dialysis
19 infectious wing
20 nurses' and doctors'
   rooms
21 training
22 void over entrance hall
23 void over chapel
24 cooling plant
25 accident wards
26 neurological wards

5.16. Bruck Regional Hospital,
Austria, 1995, plans: (top)
second floor; (middle) patient-
care floor; (bottom) ground floor

5.17. Marin General Hospital
addition, California, 1990

In other instances architects would not act on an obsession with a particular form at the expense of other concerns, but would make tempered, less conspicuous references to historical sources. In the Marin General Hospital (1987–90), in Marin County, California, by Kaplan/McLaughlin/Diaz, the obvious reference was to Gothic architecture. The main building had an eclectic composition, with a horizontal emphasis on one side and a more vertical expression on the other (fig. 5.17).[23]

In Japan, a similar attempt to borrow from the past was evident in the courtyard hospital built in Kagoshima. The Tamazato Hospital (1988–90), designed by Takanori Tamura Atelier KAN Architects, was a block that appeared to be scissored into two wings, thereby creating a courtyard. The main atrium entrance functioned as the hinge at the apex of the two wings (figs. 5.18 and 5.19).[24] The courtyard was reminiscent of the European palace hospitals of centuries earlier, particularly St. Thomas's Hospital in London (1693–1709) and the central courtyards of the Maison Nationale de Charenton in Paris (1838–85). A series of walkways crisscrossed the lawn (fig. 5.20), and the patient wards invoked traditional Japanese residences, with their gridded wall and ceiling planes, patterned floors, clerestories in patient rooms, full-height windows, and generous amounts of wood finishes.

In England, a grand attempt to blend elements of the Nightingale hospital with the language of high-tech architecture occurred at Newport, on the Isle of Wight. St. Mary's Hospital (1981–91), designed by Ahrends, Burton, and Koralek, London, was a poetic synthesis of nineteenth- and late twentieth-century planning ideals (fig. 5.21). The architects aimed to create the antithesis of a modern block hospital—a romanticized notion of the hospital-in-a-park (fig. 5.22). Patient units were arrayed as four wings that radiated from a central support building and were connected at two points to each other (fig. 5.23). The outdoor areas between the wings were Nightingale-style courtyards. The wards were laid out rather conventionally, at the ends of the wings. The main entrance had a tensile-structure canopy with expressed-steel tubular framing (fig. 5.24). On the interior a modified interstitial system was employed whereby the ser-

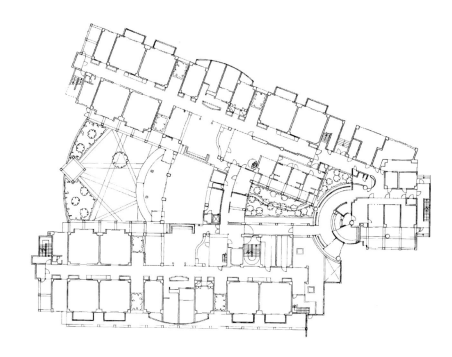

5.18. Tamazato Hospital, Kagoshima, Japan, 1990, first-floor plan

5.19. Tamazato Hospital, axonometric view

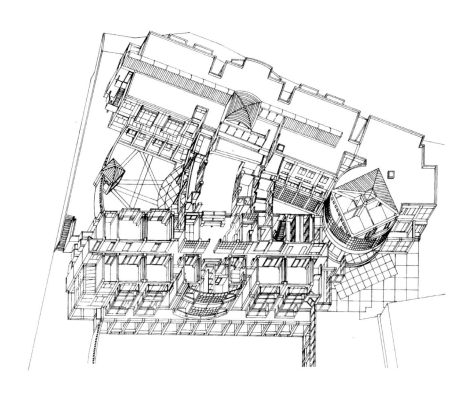

5.20. Tamazato Hospital,
courtyard

5.21. St. Mary's Hospital, Isle of
Wight, England, 1991

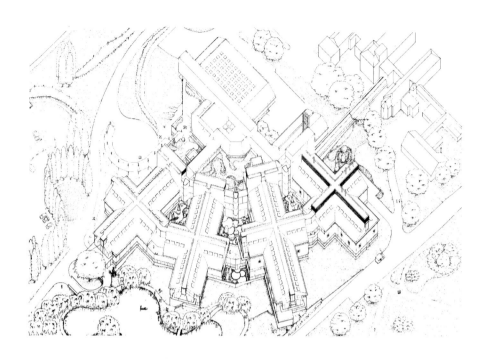

5.22. St. Mary's Hospital,
axonometric view

vice core was situated above the patient rooms in the center space of each wing, paralleling the circulation elements (fig. 5.25). This "floating" service zone was housed in the gabled roofs of the wings, which, from the exterior, contributed to a scaled-down neo-traditional quasi-residentialism fused with the vocabulary of high-tech architecture. One architectural journal contained a provocative account of this institution and the buildings it replaced:

Just across the road, to the north of [a] desolate [prison] complex, is St. Mary's, the island's main hospital, which until recently must have been almost as miserable a place as Parkhurst [Prison]. In this, it was no different to many old National Health Service [NHS] hospitals with their muddle of utilitarian buildings that range from Victorian institutional brick to Welfare State plastic and plywood. Now, the whole atmosphere has been remarkably transformed by a major new addition. Glittering and confident, the huge building offers 191 bed spaces, new out-patients', children's and old people's departments, laboratories, workshops and operating theaters as well as a social centre for the whole of the rambling medical village. Its existence shows that the Conservative Party has not been entirely lying in its claims. . . . St. Mary's is far more than a quantitative achiever. Its architect Richard Burton talks about the way in which he, as a designer, unused to hospital work, was keen to make an efficient healing machine, but one in which patients should be considered not just as objects to be worked on: a place where their needs were as much taken into account as those of the medical and administrative staff. . . . If anything, they [the NHS], have made it [the system] more confused. In a state system it is plainly not appropriate to offer the standard of semi-hotel-like luxury that is provided by those American hospitals that get published in the magazines, or by their often very much less distinguished equivalents in the British healthcare system. On the

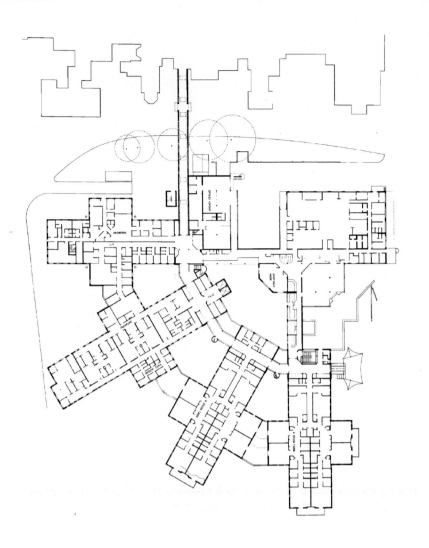

5.23. St. Mary's Hospital, plans:
(*top*) main floor; (*bottom*)
patient-care floor

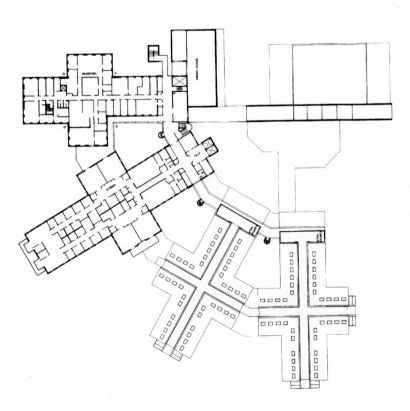

5.24. St. Mary's Hospital, main
entrance

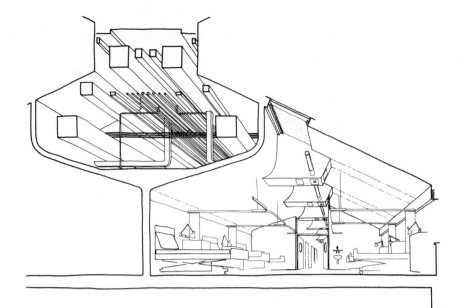

5.25. St. Mary's Hospital, interstitial and daylighting systems (perspective)

other hand, the Florence Nightingale image of rows of beds appropriate for treating large numbers of poor people *en masse* . . . is clearly inappropriate too.

At present, and for the foreseeable future, thoughts are enshrined in Nucleus, a system which imposes a standard structure and cruciform plans on all new NHS hospitals. The figure allows a wide range of ward arrangements toward the outer end of the plan. It gives a diversity of bed arrangements ranging from individual cells for the very sick to larger spaces . . . arranged around a central station. But it must be admitted that Nucleus has some extremely dumb moments. Technically, it can be questioned whether the middle of the plan is the best place for highly complex parts like operating theaters, which undergo a very rapid life cycle. . . . It could perhaps be more sensible to make the pods on the outside, serviced externally [as at Rush-Copley, discussed above]. At a human level, the template makes the approach to the ward area a rather grim and institutional experience. . . . A third problem of Nucleus is that it has a high ratio of surface area to volume. . . . As in nature, this leads to an inefficient organism: one that loses far more energy than it needs to. Burton's response to the inherently energy-wasting harness of Nucleus has been to coalesce a plan form into four spikes radiating from a common hub . . . [and] making it easier than in a longitudinally-planned building to get from place to place.

The account continued:

The upper parts of the webbed fingers that spread out from the base of the hand are service floors. The standard Nucleus concrete frame is topped by a lightweight steel structure which runs longitudinally down the length of the individual fingers. This innovative move gives a large service space between two longitudinal trusses . . . and, because the sloping roofs of the wards below are supported by secondary triangulated trusses at right angles to the main steel structure, large roof lights are possible, bringing daylight into the middle of the top wards. . . . The glittering ribbed stainless-steel cladding is intended to make the most of day and sunlight by inter-reflection. As the sun moves, the whole building changes its aspect, like a gigantic sundial creating endlessly changing abstract patterns. This diurnal sequence is echoed in an annual one, whereby the windows are thrown open in clement weather, which both reduces demands on the air-conditioning system and allows patients contact with the world outside. An apparently simple device—operable windows—makes the hospital both more energy efficient and more humane, and reduces the sometimes sickening human smells of post-operative wards. . . . This holistic approach to organization is reflected in the way in which the trees of the site have been preserved. . . . [The trees] set off a new lake formed to the south of the site. It will be planted to resemble Monet's garden, and will be the termination of a spatial sequence intended to reflect progression in recuperation. Seriously sick patients will of course be confined to their beds . . . but as their health improves, and they become more mobile, patients will be able to visit the conservatories that terminate the tips of the templates and, on fine days, they can go further to the balconies outside. From there, the natural progression will be to the grounds. . . . The passion for water [the lake and fountains in the courtyards between the wings] is continued in the art program within the building. . . . Already, murals, paintings and tapestries are in place; they will be added to as the building is used. . . . Altogether, St. Mary's promises to be a civilized and uninstitutional place, in which the care lavished on provision of a richly layered and integrated environment should bear rewards in a happier life for patients and staff alike.[25]

St. Mary's was, if nothing else, a romanticized modern machine hospital, planned and designed, however interestingly, in the spirit of the late nineteenth-century Nightingale hospital. It was not the first instance of a reprise of Nightingalism in England—the Slough General Hospital of the 1960s (see Chapter 2) was a kindred spirit to St. Mary's in its overall organization and its relation to nature. Yet at St. Mary's, the retention pond and the landscaping of the site added considerably to the overall impression. It stands as a synthesis of modern and postmodern hospital planning and ideals, a benchmark for other government-built hospitals in Britain and other developed nations. Specifically, its use of high technology—for example, partial interstitialism—was tempered with concern for view, access to nature, daylight, and human-scaled rooms within. A conscious effort was made to limit the potentially controlling effect of its high-tech attributes.

Elsewhere in Europe the megahospital was alive and well in the face of valiant but ultimately futile attempts to ameliorate its grand scale and soften its exterior armament. The Berlin-Neukölln Hospital addition in Berlin (1983–88), designed by Josef Paul Kleihues, doggedly embodied megahospitalist principles. Its symmetry was near absolute, and the rhythm of its facades and interior spaces was Baroque in its classical proportions and in terms of finish detailing (fig. 5.26). From a distance it appeared, like McMaster and others, to be a massive factory, perhaps an automobile or aircraft assembly plant (fig. 5.27).[26] In section, the superstructure was a series of layered trusses, and the domed roof of its grand atrium at the center, in cross-section, was reminiscent of a temple or the central spine of a palace hospital (fig. 5.28). The interior of the atrium provided a promenade galleria in the grand European tradition (fig. 5.29). Ultimately, however, this heroic display of high technology, with its sys-

5.26. Berlin-Neukölln Hospital, Berlin, 1988, exterior

5.27. Berlin-Neukölln Hospital, exterior from a distance

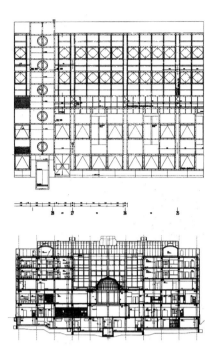

tematized planning concepts and neoclassically scaled atrium, remained problematic for users because of its scale and regimentation.

The strong belief in high technology continued to be held into the 1990s. Many hospital administrators and architects still felt that advanced building technology could ultimately cure all facility-related problems. This attitude was demonstrated in the replacement facility for the Shriners Hospital for Crippled Children Burns Institute (1994–97), in Boston, by Odell Associates of Charlotte, North Carolina. Faced with an obsolete facility, the owner elected to build a total replacement on the *same site* as the existing hospital, without disrupting

5.28. Berlin-Neukölln Hospital: (*top*) partial longitudinal section; (*bottom*) transverse section

5.29. Berlin-Neukölln Hospital, atrium

5.30. Shriners Hospital for Crippled Children Burns Institute, Boston, Massachusetts, phased reconstruction on same site (clockwise starting from top left)

the day-to-day operation of the facility. This strategy was adopted upon the board's conclusion that the site was well located within the community on a valuable parcel of real estate, yet there were no viable opportunities for horizontal expansion. As a result, a new hospital was built on top of the old one. The multi-year phasing strategy masterfully executed by the Barton-Malow construction firm was divided into four parts, starting with the construction of a protective truss above the existing hospital. Next, the new patient tower was constructed around and above this truss, after which the old hospital was demolished and the infill hospital was built in its place on the underside of the new tower (fig. 5.30).[27] A visual story of this remarkable "reinvention-in-place" project was videotaped and aired in 1998 by the Public Broadcasting System.

The Age of the Atrium and the Hospital-Based Ambulatory Care Clinic

The large, theatrical atrium was the hallmark of the late-1980s hospital as providers sought new forms of prestige, new types of patients, and increased market share. In the investor-owned segment of the industry an increasingly competitive marketplace was a compelling rationale for including an atrium. For the tax-exempt hospital, particularly large public institutions, the atrium was seen as recollective of the grand hospital lobbies of the late nineteenth and early twentieth centuries. Stately hotel lobbies of these bygone eras were to be a prime source of inspiration, as shown in the Kleihues hospital in Germany. The atrium lobby of the University Hospital at Sart Tilman in Liège, Belgium (1980–85), by Charles Vandenhove, was a richly ornamented space with ribbed skylights, elaborate floor and wall surfaces, and elegant details and finishes (fig. 5.31). A multi-level atrium was the dominant feature of the exterior.[28]

The enclosed suburban shopping mall or arcade would also provide inspiration for the many atrium hospitals built in the United States during this period. The large public atrium lobby was most prevalent, predictably, among hospitals in cold climates, such as MacKenzie in Canada. In the United States the largest mall-like hospital was built at the Dartmouth-Hitchcock Medical Center

5.31. University Hospital at Sart Tilman, Liège, Belgium, 1985, atrium

(1989–92), in Lebanon, New Hampshire, designed by the Boston firm Shepley, Bulfinch, Richardson, and Abbott (fig. 5.32). At Dartmouth-Hitchcock, a massive atrium rose three levels, running the length of the complex's linear interior pedestrian "street" (by then a common term for a service corridor).[29] The Reily Pavilion atrium of the Tulane University Medical Center's ambulatory care facility (1989–92), designed by Lyons and Hudson Architects of New Orleans and Jones Mah Gaskill Rhodes of Memphis, conveyed a related image of grand hospitality.

The hotel-like lobby of the Columbia/HCA Centennial Medical Center in Nashville (1991–94), by Earl Swensson Associates, was created to unify a series of buildings that had undergone years of part-by-part expansion. The atrium provided a new heart for this large campus by connecting new and existing buildings with a skylit space, reminiscent of the grand lobbies created by architect John Portman in the 1970s and 1980s for the Hyatt Regency hotel chain (fig. 5.33).[30] This aesthetic was also dramatically applied at the Austin Diagnostic Clinic (1992–95), in Austin, Texas, by the Gould Turner Group, also with Earl Swensson Associates. From four upper levels one could overlook open skywalks, hanging plantings, and the hotel-like lobby at ground level. The experience was at once theatrical and informative—many parts of the building could be seen from a single vantage point.

By contrast, other approaches to the hospital atrium were less commodious from the perspective of the healthcare consumer. The neo-brutalist lobby of the Kiryu Kosei General Hospital (1988–90), in Kiryu, Japan, is one example. This hospital, designed by Tohru Funakoshi and Arcom R&D, Architects, employed cast-in-place concrete. The immense height of the ceiling and the heavy concrete beams resulted in a building that hovered over its inhabitants,

5.32. Dartmouth-Hitchcock
Medical Center, Lebanon, New
Hampshire, 1992, atrium

with fixed, rigid seating reminiscent of a train station (fig. 5.34).[31] This same problem was present in the vast main lobby of I. M. Pei's Guggenheim Pavilion at Mount Sinai Medical Center (1989–92), designed by Pei, Cobb, Freed, and Partners, of New York. Mount Sinai was similar to Kiryu Kosei in its grand scale and minimalist aesthetic. Its main lobby, however, opened upward to an eleven-story atrium, with the hospital's three patient towers situated around it, each with a five-level secondary atrium that functioned as a public area and a dayroom for the patient-care towers.[32]

5.33. Columbia/HCA Centennial Medical Center, Nashville, 1994, atrium

5.34. Kiryu Kosei General Hospital, Kiryu, Japan, 1990, atrium

The incorporation of nature, a high-minded goal in and of itself, was taken in some instances to new (and, some would contend, absurd) heights of theatricality in the context of the late twentieth-century atrium hospital. The most dramatic use of water in a community hospital atrium lobby during this period was at the 115-bed Lakeland Medical Center (1983–86), in Athens, Texas, designed by Ellerbe Associates of Minneapolis (fig. 5.35). The water from an adjacent retention pond was designed to appear as if it flowed into the hospital. On the exterior the reflective glass of the minimalist hospital block was contrasted against the water, at times appearing to be a continuation of the pond (fig. 5.36). The site plan indicated how the main hospital was positioned in relation to the water (fig. 5.37).[33]

5.35. Lakeland Medical Center, Athens, Texas, 1986, atrium

5.36. Lakeland Medical Center, retention pond and main entrance

5.37. Lakeland Medical Center, site plan

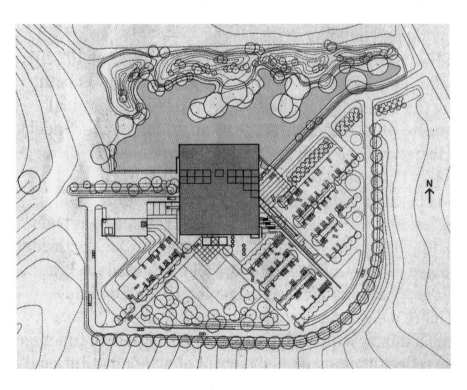

5.38. Ambulatory Services
Building, Brigham and Women's
Hospital, Boston, 1987, atrium

5.39. Brigham and Women's
Hospital, handrail detail

The late twentieth-century grand atrium would be short lived. The hotel and mall-like atria were built between 1983 and 1993. By the mid-1990s, providers, experiencing increasing pressure to contain building costs, targeted the atrium for cutbacks. With the widespread implementation of managed care, there was less incentive to create such grand architectural attractors because the patient had fewer facilities to choose from, and in some cases, no choice but to go to the institution prespecified by the HMO or PPO plan. Architects nevertheless continued to advocate what they considered a key ingredient of the postmodern hospital environment. And the atrium retained its importance for everyday users of the hospital.

Atria continued to be built at the in-house outpatient clinics within medical centers. These ambulatory clinics had emerged as providers either adaptively reused portions of the hospital previously used for inpatient care, or built new architectural attractors for outpatients. The atrium of the Ambulatory Services Building at Boston's Brigham and Women's Hospital (1984–87), designed by Kaplan/McLaughlin/Diaz, was particularly successful in the way it connected new and existing buildings (fig. 5.38). It was flanked by the outpatient clinic and the hospital's main circulation axis, known as The Pike. Skylights, trees, and a hotel- or mall-like ambiance characterized this space.[34] At Brigham and Women's, attention to detail in lighting fixtures, rails, stairs, and interior finishes was unparalleled for a building of this type in the United States (fig. 5.39).

Another significant in-house atrium of this period was the Cedars-Sinai Comprehensive Cancer Center (1985–87) in Los Angeles, by Morphosis with Gruen Associates of Los Angeles. This outpatient treatment center was embedded in a large urban medical center on the edge of Beverly Hills. Its waiting room was below grade, and at its center was a twenty-four-foot-high steel and wood play structure and aquarium; a tree atop this structure symbolically marked the street level above (fig. 5.40). Painstaking drawings, characteristic of the work of Morphosis, documented its "narrative" (fig. 5.41).[35] From the exterior the center resembled, unfortunately, a nondescript crypt-like element within the overall institution (fig. 5.42). In Italy, the Urology Clinic at Rome University (1991–93),

5.40. Cedars-Sinai
Comprehensive Cancer Center,
Los Angeles, 1987, waiting
room

5.41. Cedars-Sinai
Comprehensive Cancer Center,
play structure (conceptual
elevations)

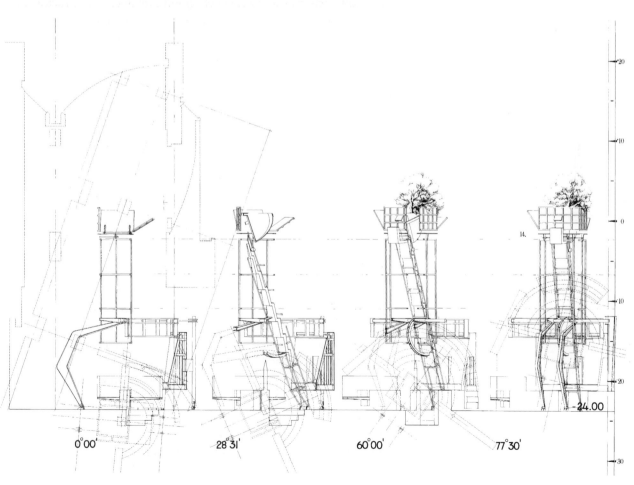

0°00'   28°31'   60°00'   77°30'

5.42. Cedars-Sinai
Comprehensive Cancer Center,
exterior

designed by Guido Gigli, was also built as part of an urban medical center, although it was elevated prominently above the street level. It was in the form of a barrel-vaulted steel-protrusion "wall" on an upper floor. The interior space that this unusual form yielded served as the waiting area of the clinic.[36]

Somewhat later, an atrium was constructed at East Jefferson General Hospital, a publicly owned health facility that opened on its present site in 1971. By 1997 the original 245-bed hospital had grown in four stages to 556 beds. As the market leader in Metairie, Louisiana, East Jefferson experienced rapid growth from 1986 to 1997 and in seven separate projects added more than one million square feet of new outpatient space, including parking for 2,066 cars, a sixty-six-bed ambulatory surgery facility, a cancer center, and two medical office buildings. A design was needed to knit together the pre-existing and new buildings and, at the same time, to create a front door to the entire complex.

The solution, by Sizeler Architects of New Orleans and associated architect Falick/Klein Partnership of Houston, was a two-story entrance atrium connecting the three major structures (see illustration on page 132). East Jefferson made use of an innovative planning paradigm following Disney principles, intended to emphasize the hospital's nationally recognized commitment to hospitality. The design incorporated clear views of and access to the main entrance of the hospital, the gift shop, a central dining facility, the new parking structure, and a medical office building, and featured improved wayfinding for users of the new facilities. The space included a dramatic colonnade that functioned as a point of spatial orientation and reference; a series of seating areas landscaped with full-height trees and planters; and a fountain. The attendant public space incorporated divisible meeting areas available to community organizations. Escalators extended access to an outpatient-inpatient intake and consultation area on the second level.

The ceiling vaults were lit from below at intervals in order to separate areas of activity and transition within the space. Full-height glazing of the two-level atrium facilitated direct views onto an adjacent courtyard and arrival areas for patients and visitors. In sum, this atrium was an example of successful collaboration among owner, architects, interior designers, and contractors. In this way, a 1970s-era hospital was updated to meet the current and future needs of its patients.

Ancillary Attractors

Of the numerous in-house ambulatory care clinics on the campuses of medical centers around the world—including pediatric, dialysis, diet and nutrition, psychiatric, primary care, oncology, wellness, and rehabilitation clinics—perhaps the Magnetic Resonance Imaging (MRI) unit in the United States, initially known as the Nuclear Magnetic Resonance (NMR) clinic, was the most distinctive. Many were added as specialty units in the early 1980s, and by 1990 they were common, not the status symbol they had been eight or ten years earlier. Because the equipment they housed (principally the large magnets) were thought in the earliest generation to require isolation, these units were often grafted onto an older

5.43. The Cleveland Clinic, NMR (MRI) Unit, Ohio, 1985

core of a hospital. An example of a circular MRI unit was the Cleveland Clinic (1983–85), designed by Dalton, Dalton, Newport of Cleveland. In this case the architects used the technical requirements to maximum metaphorical effect, resulting in sweeping curves designed to symbolize the powerful magnetic waves generated by the technical apparatus housed within (fig. 5.43).[37]

Myriad new programs were created by hospitals to fill the void left by unused space resulting from institutional downsizing. One of these, Easy Street, was an extension of rehabilitation treatment in which inpatients and outpatients were able to relearn activities of daily living in a simulated setting within the hospital. The first patented Easy Street in the United States was opened at Phoenix Memorial Hospital in 1985, designed by Guynes Design, with funding primarily from sponsorships. Patients with disabilities including stroke, multiple sclerosis, and paralysis due to spinal cord injury, amputation, or arthritis could learn to negotiate a series of real-life activities, with each setting sponsored by a local entity such as a bank, grocery store, or clothing store. The challenge "course" required the patient to negotiate stairs, ramps, and curbs, walk on a variety of surfaces, shop in a clothing store, go to the bank, drive a car, climb onto a bus, and so on. Following the success of the first program, Easy Streets were subsequently built across the United States.[38]

The medical mall concept also emerged in the mid-1980s as a means to centralize a variety of "retail" medical specialty services on the site of the medical center, at roughly one-half the cost per square foot of building traditional acute-care hospital space. Early examples in the United States were at Providence Hospital (1984–86), in Mobile, Alabama, and the $125 million HealthPark Florida (1984–87), built in Fort Myers, which included a hundred-bed acute-care hospital and a physicians' office building as "anchor stores" for other healthcare tenants.[39]

By 1986 the repeal of many states' Certificate of Need laws fueled a minor yet significant construction boom in residentially based psychiatric and substance-abuse treatment facilities. Many were completely new buildings, but some were created in spaces formerly used for inpatient acute care. The building boom occurred in psychiatric care because that field did not, by comparison with acute-care hospitals, require extensive capital. In addition, the need for medical-surgical beds was dwindling, and psychiatric facilities were an opportune market to generate significant cash flow relatively early in the investment cycle. At first, perceived consumer demand drove many companies to enter the market, flooding it with institutions that, after a while, provided services that were indistinguishable from one another.[40]

The deregulation of hospital capital expenditures had led to an increase in competition among providers and an increase in overall hospital spending, as shown in a 1988 report by the American Hospital Association's State Issues Forum.[41] The industry had clearly wanted the CON laws repealed:

> A new Federal Trade commission study reinforces the need to unshackle the hospital industry from certificate-of-need programs. The sooner the dollar thresholds for CON reviews are altered or eliminated, the healthier hospitals and their patients' pocketbooks will be. . . . The FTC's Bureau of Economics estimates that hospitals would save 1.3 billion if CON thresholds were doubled. The CON process was designed to save consumers money by avoiding duplication of services in the same market. That philosophy made sense in a pricing environment that rewarded excessive services and care. But as cost containment, managed care and prospective pricing became more prevalent, the need for such review was reduced. In fact, we believe the CON process increases hospital costs and decreases competition. Imagine, for example, the pricing freedom enjoyed by the operator of an area's only lithotripter. . . . The industry's competitiveness will do more to thwart overexpansion than filling out forms and hiring expensive lawyers to present a case to regulators. Simply put, the barriers erected by CON are not healthy for healthcare.[42]

During the seven-year period starting from 1983, twelve states dropped their CON programs. On January 1, 1987, the federal law that created CON programs expired, and Congress did not appropriate any money thereafter to fund state healthcare-planning agencies. With deregulation came a construction boom, but not in acute-care hospitals. Few new hospitals were built, and even fewer new beds were added. On top of this, trench warfare had broken out between providers operating in the same market: a provider seeking to expand services in a particular specialty area would be challenged by competitors with claims that the market was already saturated. Opposition from competitors was a primary reason why CON applications were rejected.[43] Excess bed capacity was on the verge of becoming a national embarrassment. By 1990 it was estimated that nearly two hundred thousand hospital beds were vacant each night in the United States, incurring capital costs of $3.1 billion per year.[44] As of 1991, thirty-eight states and the District of Columbia maintained some version of CON programs, but by 1996 eight additional states had dropped their CON laws, with the exception of long-term-care construction.[45]

New Residentialism and Critical Regionalism

Meanwhile, in England physicians, staff, patients, and observers in the popular media were dissatisfied with the sheer brutalism exhibited in health architecture of the 1960s and 1970s. Immense minimalist hospitals and allied institutional building types—including university buildings, elementary schools, prisons, town halls, and even museums—had been under attack for years, and even the Prince of Wales had joined in the criticism.[46] The architectural press, popular press, and everyday users condemned the British healthcare system's extreme bureaucratization. A change was in order, but the question arose: If the hospital was no longer to be expressed as a machine, what should it look like? Modernism seemed to have been exhausted; supposedly new directions were to be found in postmodernism. One postmodernist stream, the "new residentialism," blended elements of home, neighborhood context, and an effort to scale down the institution, with elements of technology. At first such architectural references to other building types or historical periods were applied only on a small scale within the framework of large hospitals, with the introduction of a gabled roof pitch, the use of color, a carpet pattern, a canopy entrance, a balcony off a patient room, or a dayroom with operable windows. Regardless, the hospital mothership remained unyielding in its conservatism, and relatively small-scale vignettes such as these came off as awkward interventions—interruptions of an otherwise thoroughly straightforward, mainstream approach on the larger scale.

In England and other parts of Europe, contextualism in general, and new residentialism in the particular case of the hospital, was evident in, for example, the West Dorset Hospital in Dorchester (1984–87), by the Percy Thomas Partnership. The exterior was given over to elegant masonry patterns, and its roofs were gabled. Window treatments were derived from traditional nineteenth-century architecture, and most windows were operable.[47] The Vrinnevis Hospital, in Norrköping, Sweden (1980–83), designed by Bo Castenfors, had earlier experimented with home-sized dayrooms in the patient units. These smaller-scale transitional elements, connected to the main massing of the facility, had doors that opened onto a landscaped courtyard (fig. 5.44).[48] Both West Dorset and Vrinnevis therefore reflected a sharp break with the standard block hospitals built up to that point.

In the United States, perhaps the earliest example of the new residentialism in a hospital was the Arbour Hospital (1980–83) in Jamaica Plain, Massachusetts, designed by Graham/Meus Architects. It featured gables on the patient floors, wood siding, and operable windows (fig. 5.45), all radical breaks from the modern hospital. Its internal organization, however, adhered to mainstream planning principles and was not nearly as innovative as its exterior expression.[49]

A related example of the new residentialism was the Renfrew Center (1983–85) in Philadelphia, designed by Tony Atkins and Associates of Philadelphia. This psychiatric treatment center was modeled on the nineteenth-century estate hospitals of England, which typically had picturesque rural settings (fig. 5.46). The campus was strung along an axis, its entrance at one end and existing buildings incorporated at the other end. The floor plan of the main inpatient

5.44. Vrinnevis Hospital, Norrköping, Sweden, 1983

5.45. Arbour Hospital, Jamaica Plain, Massachusetts, 1983

facility was reminiscent of a country manor house, with a colonnade on the ground level, views overlooking the landscape, and the overall ambiance of a stately manor house (fig. 5.47). The dayroom was well appointed and inviting (fig. 5.48), in diametric opposition to the stark, monochromatic institutionality of the typical dayroom found in most psychiatric hospitals.[50]

This new approach, though far from widely emulated at the time, attracted considerable attention within the industry and was boldly expressed in the Shenandoah Regional Campus (1989–91) in Manassas, Virginia, designed by Richard Rauh and Associates of Atlanta. Created in the heart of the Manassas historic district, this facility was constructed for inpatient and outpatient rehabilitation of persons with severe head trauma and related injuries. Rauh renovated the main house, a carriage house, and outbuildings of an abandoned late-nineteenth-century estate and added four new freestanding structures. The new buildings were strongly residentialist in character, in keeping with the main house (figs. 5.49 and 5.50). The site plan depicted the cluster of the preexisting main administration building and other buildings on the campus, including three freestanding buildings for inpatients and four independent-living buildings for stabilized patients, connected with covered walkways (figs. 5.51–5.53). Theorists have referred to this way of blending new and old—by responding to a specific place, its history, and its local traditions while remaining cognizant of broader trends—as critical regionalism. Critic Lynn Nesmith stated:

> An example of a [new] specialized building type was commissioned by Londonderry, New Hampshire–based Learning Services Corporation, a six-year-old organization that provides convalescence and rehabilitation for victims of traumatic head injuries. Like any healthcare facility, Shenandoah Center was regulated by strict building codes and life-safety standards. However, as Learning Services President Daniel Donovan explains, "We deliberately disguised the features that would telegraph that message that this is an institution." . . . The facility does not resemble a hospital environment that cushions its occupants. . . . A major part of the treatment [at Shenandoah] is relearning how to function in traditional settings. . . . The context is an established residential neighborhood. . . . Rather than slavishly copying a particular style, Rauh derived a vocabulary based on bungalows, Gustav Stickley's Craftsman houses, and indigent cement structures. Drawing from the proportions, massing, and shed roofs of vernacular farm buildings and materials, the architect created a compound that might have gradually evolved on the edge of a Northern Virginia town at the turn of the century. . . . Masquerading as a barn is the facility's bulkiest new structure, which houses staff offices and therapeutic and educational spaces. To

5.46. The Renfrew Center, Philadelphia, 1985

5.47. The Renfrew Center, plans: (*top*) first floor; (*bottom*) second floor

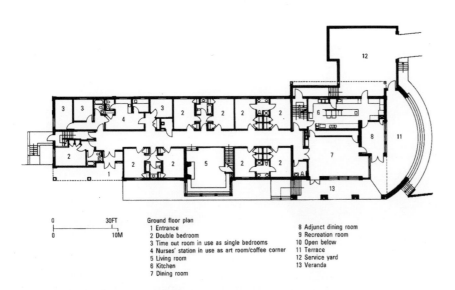

0   30FT
0   10M

Ground floor plan
1 Entrance
2 Double bedroom
3 Time out room in use as single bedrooms
4 Nurses' station in use as art room/coffee corner
5 Living room
6 Kitchen
7 Dining room

8 Adjunct dining room
9 Recreation room
10 Open below
11 Terrace
12 Service yard
13 Veranda

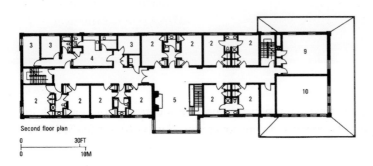

Second floor plan
0   30FT
0   10M

5.48. The Renfrew Center, main room

5.49. Shenandoah Regional Campus, Manassas, Virginia, 1991, main building

5.50. Shenandoah Regional
Campus, Dogwood House

5.51. Shenandoah Regional
Campus, site axonometric

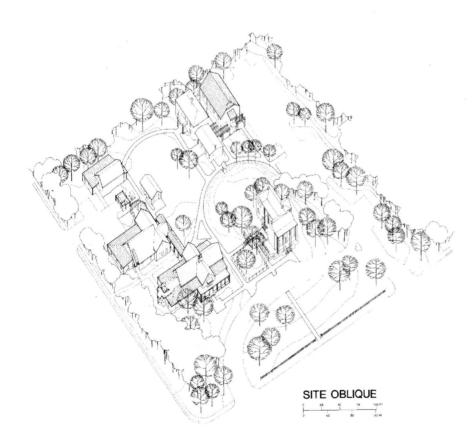

SITE OBLIQUE

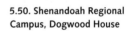

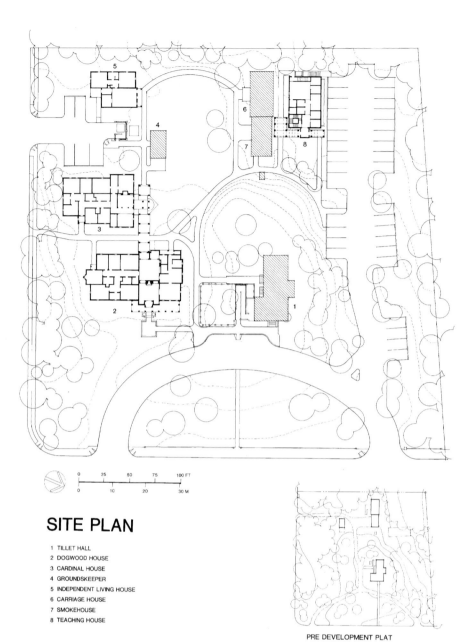

5.52. Shenandoah Regional Campus, site plan

SITE PLAN

1 TILLET HALL
2 DOGWOOD HOUSE
3 CARDINAL HOUSE
4 GROUNDSKEEPER
5 INDEPENDENT LIVING HOUSE
6 CARRIAGE HOUSE
7 SMOKEHOUSE
8 TEACHING HOUSE

PRE DEVELOPMENT PLAT

reduce the apparent mass, Rauh set two stories atop a full basement and tucked the building behind an existing smokehouse and a carriage house; it simply appears as one more ancillary farm structure. . . . [The] 13 bedrooms (both private and shared) were dispersed into three individual "houses" . . . arranged around a central village green, with discreet back yards for recreational activities and a formal front yard. . . . In evoking residential symbols, Rauh borrowed freely from various twentieth century American precedents . . . however, Shenandoah's unapologetic recall of "home" conveys much more than nostalgic imagery.[51]

Urban settings provided equivalent opportunities for new residentialism. In the above-mentioned Brigham and Women's Ambulatory Services Building in Boston (1984–88), designed by Kaplan/McLaughlin/Diaz, the rhythm, scale, and figure-ground relation of the detached row houses directly across the street were carefully reiterated on the building's exterior (fig. 5.54) and were also transposed on the interior of an expansive atrium (see fig. 5.38).[52] From the

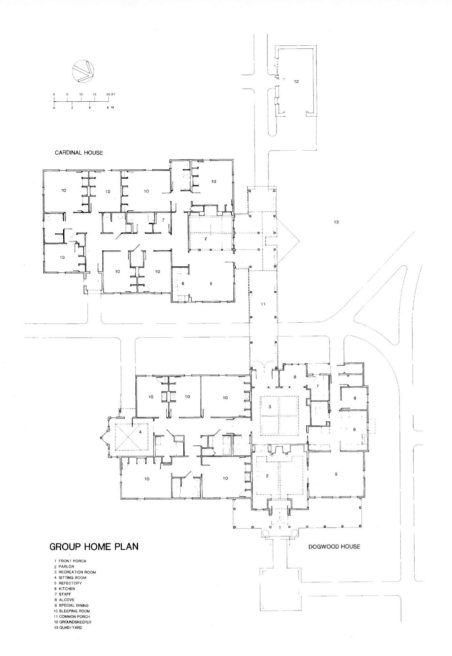

CARDINAL HOUSE

GROUP HOME PLAN

1 FRONT PORCH
2 PARLOR
3 RECREATION ROOM
4 SITTING ROOM
5 REFECTORY
6 KITCHEN
7 STAFF
8 ALCOVE
9 SPECIAL DINING
10 SLEEPING ROOM
11 COMMON PORCH
12 GROUNDSKEEPER
13 QUAD/YARD

DOGWOOD HOUSE

5.53. Shenandoah Regional
Campus, floor plans

street side, the walkup stairs of the houses were expressed in the banded
masonry courses at the sidewalk, and the building's fenestration echoed that of
the houses across the street, successfully achieving a transition in scale from the
homes to a 1970s patient tower in the background.

This new residentialism and associated regional variants in health architecture were traceable to architectural theorist Kenneth Frampton's call, in 1983,
for a critical regionalism.[53] His essay has since become highly influential among
architects because he championed an *appropriate* interpretation of local culture—one that possessed significant cultural meaning and authenticity—as
opposed to the common debasement and erasure of local tradition, which had
been zealously pursued in the case of the modern hospital. In general, critical
regionalism proposed resistance to the homogenization of the built environment resulting from post-1945 standardization of product manufacturing and
construction techniques. Frampton rejected this simplistic caricature and copy-
ing of vernacular motifs, construction techniques, and materials. He took an
alternative theoretical position based on the pre-1940 modern movement, which

in his view had balanced symbolic, technical, and cultural traditions of the immediate region with larger influences from beyond the region. Yet Frampton remained vague on which buildings or building types or architect's work had most genuinely combined these qualities.

Nevertheless, many planners and designers of health facilities in the 1990s followed suit in incorporating elements of the new residentialism, in large part because of the new freedom afforded by the pluralism inherent in postmodernism and one of its major tenets, regional vernacular architecture. The pluralism by now pervasive in health architecture was centered on sanctioned, self-conscious borrowing from a panoply of sources. Traditional design vocabularies, imagery, construction methods, and materials could be incorporated to blend past with present. Not unlike the Renfrew Center or the Shenandoah Regional Campus and built at approximately the same time, the Acadia Hospital (1987–90) in Bangor, Maine, by Cannon Architects of Grand Island, New York, could have easily been mistaken for a long-established resort lodge

5.54. Ambulatory Services Building II, Brigham and Women's Hospital, Boston, 1987, exterior

5.55. Acadia Hospital, Bangor, Maine, 1990

5.56. Acadia Hospital, terrace

(fig. 5.55).[54] The use of local horizontal clapboard siding, gabled roofs, residential windows, porticos, trellised canopies, and landscaping provided a strong dose of indigenous residential influences. This hospital, the Renfrew Center, and Shenandoah were all at least somewhat based in the tradition of Sir Edward Lutyen's country estate residences of the late nineteenth century. At the Acadia Hospital, the obvious reference in its composition and appearance was to New England vernacular, and its outdoor terraces and connections with nature directly recalled both this tradition and Lutyen's masterful attention to nature and the importance of transitional space—in this case, partially enclosed, trellised semi-outdoor patios commonly referred to as outdoor rooms (fig. 5.56).

By this time, many architects whose work was called postmodern by others (few used the word to describe their own work) had become uncomfortable with the label, feeling that it was only a tag hung on the fashion of the moment. No one, it seemed, wished to be called a postmodernist, in part because the movement itself had come under attack. By the mid-1980s, its critics argued that it had already disintegrated into a stylistic conundrum, a dead end subjected to myriad bastardizations in the hands of its lesser-skilled practitioners. And to many it had become a watered-down caricature of its earlier potentialities, as was clearly evident in the countless roadside suburban strip malls with gabled roofs and cupolas, the second-rate office parks, and the high-rise office buildings in downtown areas across the United States and elsewhere. By contrast, to refer to an architect as a critical regionalist (particularly in academia) was not viewed as an insult. Interestingly, in a more populist vein, to refer to a health architect's work as homelike or anti-institutional was viewed as far from an affront.

In the southwestern region of the United States, the Hi-Desert Medical Center (1988–90) was a noteworthy example of critical regionalism far from the East Coast. This facility, in Joshua Tree, California, by Kaplan/McLaughlin/Diaz, confirmed the firm's aesthetic dexterity. Its styles ranged from neo-Gothic (Marin General) to the walk-up Northeast urban rowhouse (Brigham and Women's) to adobe and pueblo influences from the desert Southwest, as in Hi-Desert, a thirty-eight-thousand-square-foot skilled-nursing addition to an existing hospital (fig. 5.57). The building's stucco exterior, massing, scale, colors, deeply recessed windows, and inset tilework all recalled the vernacular architecture of the local culture. Outdoor terraces and walkways were shaded, and a tower element housed the chapel. The hospital was organized around an internal courtyard, with public spaces arranged on the north side to afford views of the desert, and patient rooms to the south in the less public portion of the site. The decision to create wings with central double-loaded corridors allowed for a relatively narrow outer wall-to-wall width. The creation of the courtyard provided the primary vehicle for expression of the region's vernacular. This concept precluded the pushing together of departments and nursing units into large "blocks," which would have resulted in an entirely different planning approach (fig. 5.58). This facility was described as follows:

> Derived from Southwestern missions, the stuccoed building is clearly defined as a cultural landmark in contrast to [anonymous suburbanized] local built form. The context . . . is landscape: the site is located near Joshua Tree National

**5.57. Hi-Desert Medical Center,
Joshua Tree, California,
1988–90, exterior**

**5.58. Hi-Desert Medical Center,
ground-floor plan**

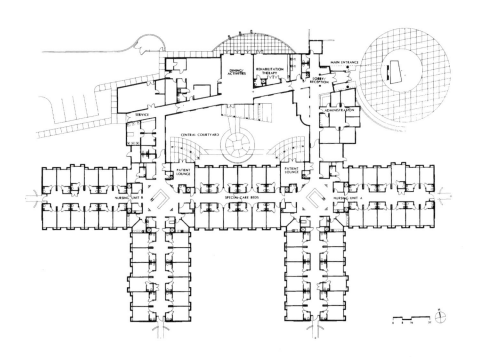

Monument and shares its dramatic setting, which forms the backdrop to the building. On a long slope descending to the North, the building defines the front edge of an artificial plateau, created to divert the violent run-off caused by desert storms. . . . Rendered to nearly match the color of the earth beneath it, the building, anchored by the splayed base of its tower, appears to grow out of the ground. The surrounding pad and slope, much of it still raw, further enhances [this] relationship. Inside . . . two nursing stations are positioned at the intersections of the patient wings. The middle wing can be supervised by either station; when patient numbers are small, one station can be closed. . . . The community is apparently more than pleased with the facility. . . . In fact, the hospital district plans to build future facilities similarly. Such community change represents yet another charge [at] Joshua Tree . . . [which is] the protection of the ill and [an] endangered culture, a view which the Hi-Desert Medical center aptly symbolizes.[55]

Another example of a hospital that attempted to incorporate Native American culture and its vernacular traditions was the Shiprock Comprehensive Health Care Center (1991–94), in Shiprock, New Mexico, designed by Anderson DeBartolo Pan of Tucson, Arizona. Its site plan, including parking areas, was in the shape of a wigwam (that is, circular). At the center of the site the main entrance, a diamond-shaped element referring to indigenous sacred structures, was set against the flatness of the vast building, itself silhouetted against the desert sky.[56]

At the Children's Hospital and Health Center of San Diego (1990–93), by NBBJ of Seattle, the exterior and interior spaces created in a single structure the iconography and feel of a village streetscape. Its exterior was recollective of mission architecture, with its clock tower (church) and plaza (town square), and its interior spaces were divided into individual "buildings," as if a small town had been arranged within a space-planning grid.[57] A somewhat similar approach was taken at the Columbus Regional Hospital (1992–95), in Columbus, Indiana, designed by Robert A. M. Stern Architects of New York with the Falick/Klein Partnership of Houston. At Columbus, a fascination with the midwestern vocabulary, notably the Prairie School vernacular developed by Frank Lloyd Wright in the late nineteenth and early twentieth centuries, was carried throughout the interiors, and to some extent was present on the exterior in terms of its materials, roof lines, and attention to detail—attributes inspired by Prairie School residences. Its lobbies and dining areas were exemplary in their acknowledgment of the architecture of the midwestern prairie (fig. 5.59).[58]

In contrast to the previous examples, a hospital constructed in Alaska nearly a decade earlier—before the shift from mainstream high-tech modernism to a pluralistic critical regionalism—was somewhat less successful. The Yukon-Kuskokwim Delta Regional Hospital (1976–80) in Bethel, Alaska, was a fifty-bed hospital located in southwestern Alaska, sixty miles from the Bering Sea. It was designed by the Houston firm CRSS Commercial Group. Climate had been a strong design determinant, resulting in the orientation of the entrances to the south to avoid snowdrifts, and in triple-glazed twelve-inch-thick windows based on the slit-bone glare-reducing sun glasses worn in the region.

Within, however, high technology dominated this machine for healing perched on stilts on the snow-laden tundra. The emphasis at Bethel had been on a system of lightweight prefabricated components for assembly on site. Although the overall effort was striking, it made little direct response to indigenous building traditions.[59]

By the late 1980s, the critical regionalist and new residentialist movements in health architecture had become increasingly multinational. In Japan, imagery and planning concepts were drawn from traditional Japanese dwellings, farm structures, and ancient landscapes and gardens. This hybridization was evident in the Iwate Rehabilitation Center (1991–93) in Shizukuishi, Japan, by Kyodo Architects and Associates of Tokyo. Vernacular farm structures were woven into a composition centered around an atrium with a gambrel-shaped roof and a cupola to its rear, with such spaces as the physical therapy room housed beneath a large octagonal dome. The main body of the building remained, in contrast, austere and conservative.[60] In the Hijirigaoka Hospital (1987–90) in Tokyo, by ARS Design Associates, the singular reference point for its exterior imagery and interior ornamentation and finishes was American colonial architecture. Columns, pediments, and red brick dominated the exterior. This preoccupation with a vernacular imported from many thousands of miles away was curious, even bizarre. The ambiance and look of this private hospital suggested an upscale "health hotel," which could have as easily, and more appropriately, been built in colonial Williamsburg, Virginia (fig. 5.60).[61]

The Health Village

In the United States, England, and other industrialized countries, vast medical centers continued to be built. Their designers attempted to grapple with the inherent tensions between modernism and postmodernism: bigness versus

5.60. Hijirigaoka Hospital,
Tokyo, 1990

smallness, compactness versus linearity, low- versus mid- or high-rise, and
whether to centralize their facilities or decentralize them in a scattered-site
approach. The health village of the late twentieth century was to be a reprise of
a medieval and, later, a nineteenth-century concept in health architecture. It
had long been widely accepted that for certain types of sickness and for the
treatment of the insane, the self-contained asylum was an optimal model of
care. In the ninth through eleventh centuries, the monastic hospitals of Europe,
such as St. Gall's and the hospital at Cluny, had been cities unto themselves,
built in rural settings, though near cities. And in the asylums built in the eighteenth and nineteenth centuries, isolation of the patient from society was considered essential. Food, supplies, and even equipment were produced on site.
These institutions were based on a decentralized pavilion model of care, with
wards and support buildings scattered across a campus enclosed by a continuous wall or fence.

A few of the new wave of freestanding, new residentialist psychiatric
facilities were reminiscent of certain of these qualities. The Laurel Ridge Psychiatric Hospital (1986–88), by HKS Architects of Dallas, was set at the far edge
of San Antonio on a wooded hilltop in the Texas hill country. It was built initially for two hundred beds, but later the number of patient beds would diminish to nearly half that amount. At Laurel Ridge the main entrance was built on
an axis with a campanile—a landmark visible at a distance from the campus,
not unlike the watchtowers of the monastic hospitals (fig. 5.61). The buildings
were set in cloister-like clusters, each pavilion a freestanding building connected with the others via walkways (fig. 5.62). Each of the five residential
pavilions was configured around a central open dayroom, with a cathedral ceil-

5.61. Laurel Ridge Psychiatric Hospital, San Antonio, Texas, 1988

ing of exposed laminated wood trusses and skylights; each dayroom opened onto a patio. Administration and support buildings were set apart from the residential domain. Many of the buildings had colonnades that provided shade from the sun. Vehicular traffic was separated from pedestrian movement on the campus. The buildings were of white stucco with red tile roofs, in keeping with the regional vernacular. The arched walls were thickened to accentuate the influence of traditional construction methods (fig. 5.63). A vocabulary of critical regionalism fused with historicist precedent from medieval infirmaries was pervasive throughout the campus.[62]

The campus of Vista Hill Hospital (1986–88) in Chula Vista (San Diego), by Kaplan/McLaughlin/Diaz, was configured as a courtyard hospital. The buildings were set around a triangular court, fronted on one side by a one-level undulating band of single-loaded patient rooms with staff and patient support spaces across a hallway.[63] The health village metaphor was also applied in a replacement facility plan for the New Life Center at DePaul Hospital (1989–90; unbuilt) in New Orleans, by R-2ARCH/New Orleans and Los Angeles. At DePaul, which was also a psychiatric substance-abuse facility, the provider, Hospital Corporation of America (now Columbia/HCA), requested a residential inpatient-outpatient treatment program to center on a village streetscape, not unlike those in adjacent historic uptown neighborhoods of New Orleans. In response, activity buildings, such as the creative arts therapy center, and social spaces were set in small-scale residences at the center of a courtyard (fig. 5.64). The courtyard opened onto a large Olmsted-designed park and golf course, continuing the rhythm set by the homes that fronted along the park. The entrance was capped with a domed skylight, and structures were of materials matching those of the neighboring houses. Like Vista Hill, DePaul was planned and designed using a critical regionalist approach:

its small-scale courtyard buildings were residentialist in character, scale, and overall appearance.[64]

The residentialist village concept was also applied on a larger scale. The massive Freeport Health Care Village (first phase 1986–89) in Kitchener, Ontario, by the NORR Partnership with McMurrich and Oxley Architects, was the first massive North American effort to centralize health services on a single site in a decentralized cluster of structures. Freeport was to symbolize rejection of the ultra-centralized approach of the McMaster megahospital built at Hamilton, Ontario, some fifteen years earlier. At Freeport, the various buildings were situated around a central courtyard plaza. The campus buildings were of red brick, the fenestration patterns were those found in multi-family

5.63. Laurel Ridge, typical patient-care pavilion

5.64. DePaul Hospital New Life Center (proposal), New Orleans, 1989

housing, and the roofscapes and massing reflected an attempt to make a single entity appear like many separate entities (fig. 5.65). The campus was composed of five interconnected buildings: administration, three patient buildings, and an auditorium (fig. 5.66). Heights varied from five levels to two levels, and the network of enclosed walkways between buildings countered the winter weather:

> While other hospitals work to further trim patient stays already cut to less than a week, chronic-care facilities such as the 350-bed Freeport Hospital expect to house their patients for an average of six months, and in some cases for many years. Variety, stimulation, personal relationships—the ingredients of normal life—become paramount. . . . The NORR Partnership capitalized on the hospital's ambitious 313,000 square-foot expansion program by translating its diverse requirements into discrete elements suggesting a small tightly-knit village. The heart of the village is a "town square" anchored by a new "government" building containing administrative offices on the West and, opposite it, an auditorium that serves as the community's town hall. Closing the sides, two four-story nursing units, designed to read as a cluster of individual buildings, employ a "living-over-the-store" arrangement of special treatment facilities and activity rooms (library, game room, café, laundry) on the ground floor and patients' rooms above.
>
> Street-level spaces are prefaced and linked around the central open space by the "verandah," a glass-walled arcade that offers a ready reference point as well as outdoor access. By gently controlling circulation beyond the inner ring of public areas, it also allows ambulatory patients . . . to move freely and securely about the complex. A small "gateway" pavilion between the new complex and a renovated existing [structure] affords visitors direct entry to the court from the main parking lot. . . . By dispersing its components, both recreational and therapeutic, while tying them together via the verandah and courtyard, the architects have transformed an ordinary space program into a lively and diverse environment. . . . The zoning of public and private realms continues through semipublic house living rooms to the patients' bedrooms, which share small attached sunrooms. Within the bedrooms, furnishings may be arranged as residents please, providing another measure of privacy and autonomy.[65]

The health village concept was also incorporated in residentially based environments for the terminally ill. The new residentialism had been an intrinsic ingredient of hospices for decades, and it continued to be so through the 1980s and into the 1990s. At the Evergreen Hospice Center (1989–91) in Kirkland, Washington, designed by Mahlum and Nordfors of Seattle, a courtyard became the focal point for a series of cottages. Each cluster of cottages consisted of individual small, semi-detached houses, each with gabled roofs and exterior wood shingles, appearing thoroughly residential, both singly and collectively.[66] In the 1990s numerous hospice facilities for AIDS patients were built or established in adapted, renovated buildings. Two other notable examples of a successful synthesis between home and the support and surveillance afforded by a twenty-four-hour-care facility were the Institute for Immunological Disorders (1984–86) in Houston and the Bailey-Boushay House (1990–92) in Seattle.[67]

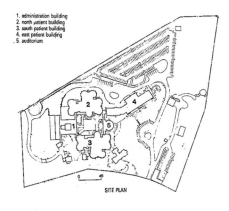

1. administration building
2. north patient building
3. south patient building
4. east patient building
5. auditorium

SITE PLAN

5.65. Freeport Health Care Village, Kitchener, Ontario, Canada, 1989

5.66. Freeport Health Care Village, site plan

One of the most ambitious new freestanding hospice facilities built in the United States in the 1990s was in Houston. The Hospice at the Texas Medical Center (1992–95), designed by Graham Luhn, Architects, of Houston, was a twenty-five-bed acute-care hospice. Most of its patients, as in most hospices, were cared for through an extensive home care program. The facility, part new and part old, was built on the grounds of the mansion of a former mayor of Houston, Oscar Holcomb, who had donated his home and grounds to the adjacent Texas Medical Center. From the provider's perspective, this hospice was made possible through the combined effort of all member institutions in the Texas Medical Center. Hospice care had gained acceptance by the mainstream medical community only through a slow, laborious process. Eight different architectural schemes were developed before one was accepted and built. The main building, the former residence (1927), was adapted to house the administration and home care program. New structures on the grounds consisted of a chapel and a three-level care wing designed in a Tudor style to match the original residence. The generous $11 million construction budget allowed for a forty-car parking tier to be built below the new residential care wing. Two of the hospice's most significant amenities for residents, staff, and families were the intricately planned and detailed garden designed by landscape architect Pat Fleming, and the children's garden designed by Herbert Pickworth. Both were exemplary in their use of existing and new landscape elements, in their scale, and in the creation of places of refuge and solitude. The "writing wall" in the children's garden was particularly well received.

Laurel Ridge, Vista Hill, the DePaul proposal, Freeport, the Evergreen hospice, and the hospice in Houston all shared a basic site-planning concept: a decentralized cluster of buildings around a single unifying space. These six North American examples were all highly residentialist in their cognizance of critical regionalism and vernacular traditions. If residentialism had become a trend in the United States and Canada by this time, however, it would be erroneous to claim it as an original trend. In Scandinavia residentialism had been incorporated in health facilities for many decades, and the health architecture of Scandinavia influenced the work of some U.S. architects. By the mid-1990s variants of residentialism were in evidence in many other parts of the world as well.

For example, the Kaedi Regional Hospital (1984–87) in Kaedi, Mauritania, designed by Fabrizio Carola/ADUA (Association for the Natural Development of African Architecture and Urbanism), incorporated indigenous influences in a series of interconnected domed circular buildings housing patient wards, and other buildings that housed administrative and various diagnostic and treatment functions (fig. 5.67 and 5.68). The buildings were set in a pattern suggestive of the anthropomorphism and leaf-like patterns in traditional thatched dwellings (fig. 5.69). A pair of rectangular support buildings, housing central administration and central supplies, were connected to this branch-like cluster of structures. The building materials, colors, and details, and the ribbed barrel vaults of the connecting walkways, were taken from the traditional architecture of the region. This hospital received an Aga Khan Award for design excellence in 1995.[68]

5.67. Kaedi Regional Hospital,
Kaedi, Mauritania, 1987, typical
circulation corridor connecting
domed patient-care pavilions

5.68. Kaedi Regional Hospital,
exterior view

5.69. Kaedi Regional Hospital,
site plan

Functional Deconstruction and the Contemporary Hospital

New residentialism, critical regionalism, and the health village were by no means the only set of forces shaping health architecture. By the 1990s the hospital was being transformed by broader forces. In theoretical circles the debate in architecture was becoming not one of modernist versus postmodernist ideology but one of the merits of the transposition of deconstructivism and its legitimacy as the displacer of postmodernism. Deconstructivism, or theoretical deconstruction (as mentioned earlier), was essentially a literary theory promulgated years earlier by theorists including Jacques Derrida and Roland Barthes and expropriated in the writings, and later the built work, of Peter Eisenman, Bernard Tschumi, Frank Gehry, Zaha Hadid, and Daniel Libeskind, among others. This avant-garde had focused its efforts on building types other than health care. The wheels of change turn slowly in the milieu of institutional building types, and in health architecture the effects of new paradigmatic approaches in the twentieth century had been particularly slow to gain acceptance, with the notable exception of change brought on by the necessities of war. This conservativism, when added to the preoccupations of providers—the unbundling and redefinition of the outpatient community health clinic, ambulatory surgery center, freestanding diagnostic clinic, mobile services, and so on—gave rise not to an aesthetically driven expression of deconstruction per se but to a functionally driven expression. Here, the constituent "parts of speech" were thrown out of equilibrium: departments and services were being reconceptualized and recast, within and without. The hospital, by the late 1990s subjected to widespread functional deconstruction of its internal components, was faced with downsizing to a flexible, less costly, yet more intensive rapid-response entity, leading to dramatic changes in its scope and mission. In 1996, Lester B. Knight, a leading healthcare executive, remarked: "It used to be that hospitals wanted to fill as many beds as possible, that's how they made money. The incentive now is to keep beds empty. When the bed is empty, the patient is not using up resources. That mentality change is a big change for the industry. It's exciting to me."[69]

In the case of Columbia/HCA, which by 1996 had 350 hospitals and revenues of $22 billion (although it would downsize significantly within three years as an indirect result of governmental investigations), the corporation maintained its aggressive agenda of acquisitions, new construction, and the functional deconstruction of its acute-care hospitals.[70] In the 1990s it had embarked on building acute-care hospitals with as few as thirty-five beds. These beds would be filled with patients sicker than in the past, owing to the many community- and home-based outpatient-care alternatives available within the Columbia/HCA network. The prototype mini-hospital built by Columbia/HCA was the Pine Lake Medical Center (1991–93) in Mayfield, Kentucky, designed by Earl Swensson Associates of Nashville.[71] Their standardized hospital template by the late 1990s had between thirty-two and forty beds.[72] Columbia/HCA, and other investor-owned providers, had realized early on that the patients in the hospital of the future would be sicker than before, and pressures to contain costs would result in fewer but larger patient rooms, all of which would be convertible to a de facto critical care unit (CCU). This would eliminate the need to construct costly single-function ICU and other traditionally autonomous special-care units elsewhere within the building.

In the second-generation version of this prototype, and in similar new templates, the hospital would more accurately be referred to as the critical care center (CCC). Functional deconstruction involved reappraisal of each component of every hospital in order to determine how to provide a service in the most cost-effective manner. This analysis formed the basis of regional strategic plans, on the assumption that hospital networks could demonstrate cost savings resulting from the pooling of resources within and across regions. Instead of four accounting departments in four hospitals, one would now be sufficient. Unlike in the past, perhaps only one out of four hospitals would house the dialysis unit, only one the fixed-base MRI, and so on. In the end, the marketplace had, in a quiet revolution, supplanted the failed CON program through this pattern of reappraisal and reconceptualization of the essential functions of a "hospital."

Yet, for the most part, health architects were interested in the strategic-planning (or organizational-spatial) nuances of this change in approach far more than in any aesthetic ramifications of deconstruction, or, for that matter, postmodernism. Mainstream hospital planners listened passively to the "big picture" debates of their provider-clients and attempted to interpret optimum functionality through identifying the best room adjacencies, size, service mix, and layout of the hospital; these planners often chose to remain indifferent (or at most neutral) to any large-scale rethinking of the core assumptions of their field. Regardless, such innovations as bedside computerization made an impact on the design of the nursing unit.

Humanists who embraced the new residentialism and its focus on the architectural ramifications of patient-centered care would often reject classification of their efforts as postmodern. By contrast, deconstruction, as a design language, was, according to its proponents, grounded in the dislocation of accepted formal relationships within buildings and in a questioning of deeper societal issues. To humanists this constituted a subversion of the notion of well-being: was it now to be appropriate for health architecture to express the chaos, inherent dislocational nature, and "discomfort" of contemporary culture and society rather than to promote health and wellness through a "comforting" architecture? More-

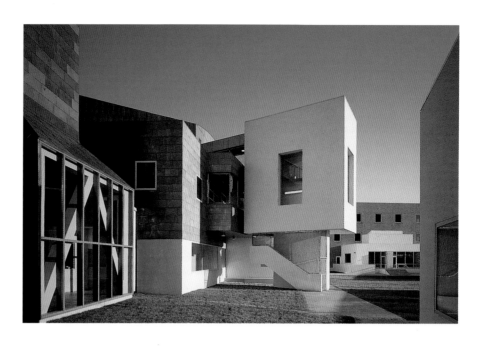

5.70. Yale Psychiatric Institute,
New Haven, Connecticut, 1990

over, one might assume that the notion of a fully deconstructed health architecture, in both functional and formal-aesthetic terms, would be virtually antithetical to the notion of health architecture as a therapeutic, life-supportive modality.

Regardless, an infinitesimal but influential fraction of the vast landscape of health architecture began to be influenced by the formal-aesthetic aspects of deconstruction. Perhaps the most well-known example was the Yale Psychiatric Institute (1987–90) in New Haven, by Frank Gehry. On a tight urban site, a replacement facility was designed as a campus composed of an assemblage of smaller parts that were skewed, twisted, and distended to form a seemingly randomized, informal composition around a courtyard (fig. 5.70). Materials and forms were juxtaposed, with particular emphasis on the orchestration of stairs and vertical circulation. In a postoccupancy evaluation of this complex a few years later, it was found that some retrofitting had been necessary to make the facility more fully functional. Overall, however, the building proved to work relatively well for the purpose for which it was initially designed.[73]

At the Charles-Foix Hospital (1988–90) in France, a residential treatment center for the aged by André Bruyère, the roofs were perforated, undulating above a series of otherwise conventional rectangular boxes set in clusters on the campus (fig. 5.71). Some of the roofs had overhangs that nearly scraped the ground, while other overhangs appeared to float blissfully above the buildings.[74] This aesthetic was carried into the design of interior furnishings and fixtures, with dramatic effect.

At the Central Washington Hospital (1989–92) in Wenatchee, Washington, by NBBJ Architects of Seattle, a series of brightly colored frontispiece architectural elements created a new image for the existing medical center. Various planes were pulled away from the main volume of the hospital and treated in different bright colors as distinct components—an arch, a porte cochere, a threshold—with perforations and projecting canopies evoking the spare, minimalist work of Mexican architect Luis Barragán (fig. 5.72):

> The Central Washington Hospital, serving the apple-belt community of Wenatchee, is a place where patients arrive for treatment wearing cowboy hats. This maverick spirit is captured in a bold new design by NBBJ of Seattle, a firm

that has added new wings to the hospital since 1978. Since its completion in 1964, the locally designed institution had evolved to form a rambling, 200,000 square-foot complex with an obscure entrance. . . . [The] assignment was to enhance the main entrance, expand the emergency room, add a day surgery center, and establish a sophisticated identity for a major hospital serving a four-county area. The designers . . . sought to site the new additions against the strong presence of the Cascades' Eastern foothills. The scheme focuses on three, 34-foot-high, stucco "screen walls" that clearly mark the entrances. . . . Colored to match the fruit grown in irrigated orchards along the nearby Columbia River Valley, the billboardlike grids [are] juxtaposed against the surrounding landscape [like] dramatic Western paintings. . . . The sweeping walls were "not exactly warmly embraced." In fact, the walls were initially greeted with some hostility, although [the administrator] maintains the community has come to appreciate the colorful elements, if not for their abstraction, as entrance markers that tie the rambling complex together. To the locals, the walls are as one headline writer described them for the town's newspaper. . . . "Not Art, Just Color Coding."[75]

5.71. Charles-Foix Hospital, Ivry, France, 1990

5.72. Central Washington Hospital, Wenatchee, Washington, 1992

Would Yale Psychiatric, Charles-Foix, and Central Washington serve as the bellwethers of a shift from a mainstream postmodern position to a tentative position of deconstruction in both functional and aesthetic terms? In each, the underlying organizational and aesthetic premise had been questioned, and although the purely functional aspects of each might not have been radically deconstructed, their aesthetic vocabularies provided some evidence of a search for balance between functional dislocation, aesthetic dislocation, and genuine therapeutic support.

The health architecture of the ubiquitous, everyday American landscape was far removed from such experiments, however. The three most often imitated types—the single-family detached house, the roadside hotel, and the suburban shopping mall—had been widely accepted by American culture in the late twentieth century, and all were premised on a common purpose: convenience in the name of comfort. The first type—the home—remained unquestionably at the heart of the notion of community. Second, the hotel, and later the roadside motel, had once shared a certain grandiosity with the urban hospital: the lobbies of downtown hospitals built between the late nineteenth century and World War II—such as the Cullen Pavilion at Hermann Hospital in Houston (1923–25)—were often opulent in scale and appointments, conveying a strong, confident sense of self and place and reinforcing the dignity of the guest. After 1945, both the hotel and the hospital lobby greatly diminished in size and importance as more and more space was devoted to high technology. As for the suburban mall, it was marketed as a convenient, weatherproof alternative to traditional main streets. One could shop, see others, and be seen in a hermetically controlled environment. This condition, too, was considered worthwhile and appropriate for a contemporary hospital setting.

Apart from issues of lifestyle, aesthetics, or their specific relation to the reconstituted hospital and medical center, the field of health architecture had not fostered a tradition of research. Through the years, important decisions of spatial organization and design had been made on the basis of anecdotal evidence and a limited realm of cumulative personal experience. As a result, scant empirical work was available to examine the effect of the profound transformations taking place in the healthcare milieu. Gradually, research emerged identifying the hospital environment as a cause of undue and chronic environmental stress. Behavioral research on the effects of the modern hospital had, by and large, focused on the difficulty of patients and other visitors to navigate within its confines, on the overly institutional ambiance of the patient room and the restrictiveness of the typical medical-surgical nursing unit, on the deleterious effect of the lack of privacy for patients and staff, and on the problem of excessive noise. These variables were typically conceptualized by researchers in terms of a cause-effect relationship, with the environment viewed as a series of stressors acting to cause a decrease (or increase) in well-being on the part of the patient. Janet Carpman and Myron Grant's review of this literature, and their own investigations at the University of Michigan Hospitals, had the goal of furthering the understanding of the patient and visitor experience, as part of a comprehensive replacement hospital project.[76]

Nevertheless, no study had directly compared the effect (in terms of user well-being or satisfaction) of the modern hospital center with that of a functionally deconstructed medical center. The scant prior research on user perceptions of the modern hospital had had a discernible but minor impact, especially in comparison to the well-funded financial, competitor, and market analyses that had fueled the reshaping of the industry. In short, providers had routinely based costly, long-term facility-related decisions on a subset of information, without systematic knowledge of consumer preferences and the effect of the healthcare environment on health and well-being. Hospital administrators and their mainstream healthcare firms instead sought commercial success in their institutions, and residentialism, the health mall, and the grand atrium were often seized upon as the ideal attractors of business. (fig. 5.73) And these amenities aptly projected the desired image of an open, caring, friendly environment, but was this enough?[77] Many health architects still considered it reckless to justify design decisions on any terms other than "form follows function"—a credo that had guided hospital architects since Florence Nightingale.

Sociologist Robert Gutman has argued that the tendency of architects to be preoccupied with external image has been a hindrance because it has tended to reduce the architect to the role of image-maker. A second, related concern has been the excessive willingness of architects to work in teams, with the designer assigned the position of window dresser for the exterior of a building whose layout is essentially designed by health facility planners or by non-architectural professionals:

> There are many explanations for the willingness of architectural firms to collaborate with offices of a different stripe or accept control by clients and developers. For example, in terms of the theory of architecture, it has become easier for architects to accommodate themselves to a more confined role because of the spread of the modernist doctrine in the arts which argues that the esthetic dimension is autonomous. Architecture resisted this doctrine longer than the other arts, because architecture, unlike painting or literature, seemed to have a connection to building function and use which was impossible to sever. However, contemporary efficiencies in the system of building production and construction technology . . . [have] now liberated architects along with other artists.[78]

It is particularly telling that many of the most significant, innovative small-scale health buildings of the 1980s and 1990s were designed by firms that did not specialize in health architecture. Judging from these buildings, the outsider status of the "non-health" firms presumably allowed clients the freedom to break away from the standard solutions being offered by mainstream health-based architectural firms. Also, the small scale of these buildings—such as primary care centers, surgicenters, kidney dialysis clinics, women's health centers, and outpatient rehabilitation facilities—indicative of the deconstructed hospital mainframe, required significantly less dexterity in space planning and were of a less complex technical nature than when they had been intertwined with the full-scale medical center.

By 1996, it was clear that spending on healthcare construction was headed in two directions at once. According to figures compiled by the F. W. Dodge Division of the McGraw-Hill Companies, the value of construction contract awards for hospitals in the United States steadily decreased from $6.784 billion in 1992 to $5.281 billion in 1996. The amount of hospital construction paralleled this, going from 37.0 million square feet in 1992 to 23.1 million square feet in 1996. By contrast, the construction of health facilities other than hospitals increased rather significantly, rising from $4.076 billion (39.8 million square feet) in 1992 to $5.570 billion (52.7 million square feet) in 1996.[79] Therefore, whereas the overall cost of all health facilities built was nearly constant during this period—$10.860 billion in 1992 compared with $10.851 billion in 1996—the *mix* of buildings being built had shifted dramatically. The experts continued to call for smaller, more community-based facilities, which were cheaper to build and operate than the modernist megahospitals. And the wave of mergers, consolidations, and hospital closures continued, showing no sign of slowing as the twenty-first century approached. By the mid-1990s other countries were seeking out the expertise of American architectural firms on a widespread basis. For the U.S. architects and planners such exports were seen as little different from any other industry's efforts to expand its economic base internationally. For health architecture more broadly construed, such transfers risked the denigration of critical regionalism, as had occurred with the International Style during the postwar decades.

In 1980 the hospital was a highly centralized, relatively autonomous organizational and physical entity, but by the late 1990s it had been subjected to profound transformation. The late-twentieth-century megahospital, the high-tech romanticist hospital, new residentialist hospitals and hospitals whose appearance and form were based to varying degrees on critical regionalism, and the emergence of the health village as an alternative to the mainframe hospital superstructure all proliferated during the final fifteen years of the century. This pluralism was the result of four events that occurred at precisely the same time: a new freedom made possible by the rise of postmodernism, the acknowledged failure of the autonomous modern megahospital, new medical technologies permitting more services to be provided on an outpatient basis, and competitive pressures. Hospital reformist and futurist Wanda J. Jones wrote the following manifesto in 1993, summarizing the rationale for this new order:

> Health insurance is not the only part of the healthcare system that should be reformed. The organization and structure of the hospital are in need of a complete overhaul. Over the next two decades, architects are likely to find clients on the cusp of change, for whom a new building may be a great opportunity to create a new environment for healthcare work. But healthcare providers aren't in the business of building hospitals all the time. Most will be involved in designing a new building only once or twice in their entire careers. So it is no wonder that they want to build a hospital that looks like the one they presently manage. That is, an imposing structure with patient beds in towers and diagnostic and treatment services on lower floors. But this model causes patients to move to services, fostering inefficiency.

In hospitals designed around the needs of the patient, routine diagnosis and treatment—70 percent of all services—are decentralized to the patient floor, suite, or room. Lab tests in this patient-focused arrangement require seven minutes to process, instead of the current two hours. Clinical pharmacies are located on the patient floor, as are radiology, labs and operating suites. Such decentralization produces savings for the whole hospital. In fact, some departments, such as admitting and discharge planning, disappear as nursing staff and program administrators on each floor take responsibility for the care management of their patients through bedside computing. Hospital interiors will need to accommodate these changes by providing space for a professional and support core on each floor. Wherever site permits, broad structures should replace tall, slim buildings. Outpatient services should be organized adjacent to the hospital; they may also take over much of the area originally designated as diagnostic and treatment spaces for inpatients.

The hospital of the future must also make site-related changes. The current megacampus paradigm implies certain assumptions: that all patients, no matter how well or ill, should come to the same place because that is where the doctors are; they should come only when they are ill, rather than when they want help in not becoming ill; they should arrive by automobiles or bus, rather than on foot; and they should merely look at the green, unbuilt part of the campus, rather than make use of it. All of these assumptions are wrong, and they lead to an unfortunate alienation of the urban hospital from its surrounding community.

To make hospitals more hospitable, the edges of their campuses should be like live coral reefs—full of energy and activity, pulling neighborhood residents in rather than shutting them out . . . so in addition to offering traditional treatment, healthcare providers in the city have a public health role to play. Community based planning should be utilized to produce hospital programs and services that address what ails the community, and not merely what physicians and healthcare administrators know how to do. It is clear that, in the future, hospitals will no longer be healthcare's "main event." The main event will be outpatient services and associated case management systems for patients with chronic illnesses. What an opportunity for architects! They can help their clients to design delivery systems, not just hospitals; community services networks, not just campuses; and new patient-focused operating systems, not just sets of rooms and spaces for equipment. The patient-focused concept is a powerful idea . . . now we need a breakthrough for the hospital site itself. Architects who are prepared to offer this kind of visionary leadership will produce something much more meaningful than a beautiful building.[80]

Jones stopped short of using the term *postmodern* to describe her ideas. However, her prognostications were indeed well grounded in functional deconstruction, human scale, contextualism, residentialism, and in the virtue of extolling the uniqueness of place. In the significantly downsized, transformed, and reconfigured hospital, destined to be rechristened the critical care center, core functions would remain, but by 2000 its patients were, on average, much sicker than those of 1980, not to mention those of 1965. The survival of these intensive acute-care and treatment settings would depend more than ever on their transformability and adaptability to a sicker patient population than at any time since the Middle Ages.

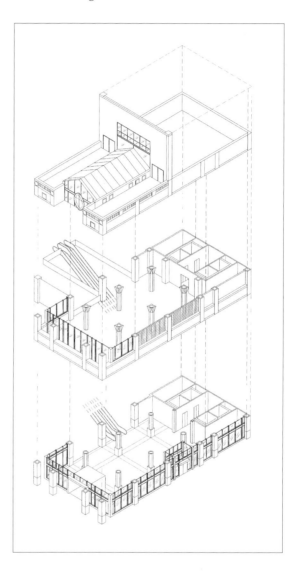

5.73. Reily Pavilion Atrium, Tulane University Hospital and Clinic, 1991, exploded axonometric

CHAPTER 6

Reinventing the Patient Room

Throughout history the experience of the patient has been accepted as dislocational—set apart from everyday life—but justified as necessary in order to provide effective care for the sick. And from Florence Nightingale on, succeeding generations of healthcare planners have routinely rejected the status quo in favor of the latest innovation. For the patient, however, the unfamiliarity of the hospital setting, coupled with the sense of confinement, loss of privacy, and detachment from friends and loved ones, often gave rise to particularly acute emotional distress. In the United States, providers believed by the mid-1960s that the all-private-room hospital was the logical answer. But too often such inpatient facilities only exacerbated the patient's sense of alienation, dislocation, and fear.

After 1945 in the United States, the single most significant change in hospital planning with respect to the patient room was the dramatic shift away from the open ward. From then on, facility and equipment expenditures were pursued fervently, with, by comparison, only minor improvements introduced into the basic configuration of the nursing unit and patient room. Apart from experiments with radial and triangular nursing units in the 1950s and 1960s, until the mid-1970s the furnishings within the room continued to evolve without major impact on the size, amenities, or ambiance of the room itself. Layout, furnishings, orientation, and even the aesthetic experience of the patient room tended to be chronically overshadowed by what might be termed a bigness syndrome, with highest status accorded the hospital with the highest total bed count. The patient room, therefore, was the victim of benign neglect resulting from the inordinate amount of attention devoted to other parts of the hospital, specifically, the highly specialized diagnostic and treatment units being expanded in zones remote from the nursing unit.

This chapter concerns the shift away from Nightingale wards to semi-private and, later, all-private-room arrangements in the late-twentieth-century hospital and the shift from the modern to the postmodern patient room and nursing unit. (Here, as before, *postmodern* is an umbrella term used to denote an attitudinal shift away from the modernist sensibility and is employed only secondarily as a stylistic label.) Whereas the first of these developments occurred in a period of escalating expansionism, the second occurred in the context of a significantly downsized and reconfigured acute-care hospital.

The Triumph of the Private Room

The evolution of the modern nursing unit mirrored the monumental debate during the 1950s and 1960s over the merits of the open ward versus the private or semi-private patient room. The Nightingale ward, it was generally agreed, was a dying template, yet it continued to be viewed by its staunchest advocates as the heart and soul of the hospital. In the early 1970s, John Thompson and Grace Golden concluded:

> After reading widely in the American literature of the past century about privacy [the private room,] we conclude that: (1) it is still an open question; (2) arguments for either side come close to canceling each other out; and (3) therefore, no strong preference for or against privacy should be stated as an axiom. A patient pays more for privacy; no way has yet been found to controvert this fact. Not all patients, even of the upper classes, want privacy. . . . Privacy means and will always mean a sacrifice of continuous supervision. As for ensuring a sanitary environment, no experiment yet undertaken has proven that a patient's recovery or relapse was determined by his degree of privacy in [the] hospital. A steady trend toward more privacy in every aspect of twentieth-century life accounts in part for an overemphasis on the single room in hospitals.[1]

Nightingale had been against the private room as well as the restrictiveness of small-scale wards. Using the simple principle that ease of supervision and spaciousness superseded all else, she argued that a higher quality of nursing care was achievable if forty patients were grouped in one large open ward than if there were four wards of ten patients each or, worse, forty rooms of one patient each. In eschewing small wards of six to ten patients, she reasoned that the benefits of efficiency and its outcome—increased health status—outweighed the need for individual privacy, and that well-run institutions had devised ways to "counterbalance what unavoidable evil there is in having patients together."[2] On the issue of infection control, isolation rooms on the unit were deemed essential. Such isolation rooms had been first used in St. Thomas Hospital in London, which had opened in 1871, with each of its thirty-bed wards equipped with two isolation rooms adjacent to the nurses' station.[3]

Thompson and Golden, as Nightingale sympathists, drew their conclusion in large part in reaction to such hospital planners of the 1960s as Gordon Friesen, who had boldly proclaimed that the time had come for *every* patient to have a private room. By this point, the all-private-room argument was being waged on largely cultural grounds, in the sense that it symbolized societal progress, rather than on the basis of strictly rationalized medical justifications.

Nevertheless, by 1970 some hospital planners began to argue for a middle ground whereby the modern hospital would offer several variants on the typical medical-surgical nursing unit, consisting of a mixture of private rooms, double-occupancy rooms, and small wards of up to six beds. The term *semi-private* had already been in use for decades; in the 1920s S. S. Goldwater had advocated for the rich and the sickest poor to be assigned to private rooms; additionally, the middle class who could pay could have private rooms, and the lower middle classes would be housed in small wards of up to six patients each.[4]

The United States was one of the first countries to disavow the ward concept (and remains virtually the only country to have done so). This shift began after 1945 and was nearly complete by 1972, with some notable exceptions, such as urban charity hospitals and large state-run institutions. Wards housing up to six patients continue to find medical, religious, economic, social, and cultural rationales in many other countries, based as much on long-established cultural norms as on healthcare economics. In Europe, hospitals that were otherwise deemed to have the latest amenities continued to be built with a mix of open wards and private rooms. In the case of the Porte de Choissy Medical and Surgical Center (1962–64) in Paris, designed by Stainov and Orième Architects with Delacroix and Schischmanoff, the rooms in the staff housing tower foreshadowed the trend toward the privatization not only of staff quarters but of patient quarters as well. Amenities in the private rooms at Choissy included a swivel chair, a bedside desk, and a wood-veneer headboard for the bed, with an incandescent light mounted on the wall above the headboard (fig. 6.1). The corridors and the exterior of the tower were modeled on the standard Le Corbusian high-rise block: the building was rectilinear in its overall floor plan, with a flat roof and uniform horizontal ribbon windows.[5] Its significance rested in, first, this dualism between the public and private realms of the institution—the openness of the ward versus the personal amenity of the private rooms—and, second, the level of design attention accorded the private rooms.

Concurrently, experiments with sawtooth, radial, and triangular nursing units took place. Although leading-edge hospital planners were once preoccupied with radial nursing units, by the early 1980s the radial concept fell out of favor because of its inherent staffing inefficiencies, awkward residual spaces at the center of the unit, and irregularly shaped patient rooms. The triangle was presented as the new, much more efficient alternative and eventually supplanted the standard Hill-Burton rectangular racetrack concept. Architects had always experimented with variations on the Hill-Burton model, however. At the West Haldimand Hospital in Hagersville, Ontario (1962–64), Shore and Moffat and Partners had devised a staggered arrangement for each patient room (fig. 6.2). The two-level building was rectangular in plan, with a racetrack circulation loop around a central support core. Each floor housed a mix of one-bed rooms and two-bed, three-bed, and four-bed wards. Its sawtooth exterior walls were justified on the grounds that they afforded more window area and provided each patient direct access to a view. Such efforts to reconfigure the shape of the room and the relationship between the patient's bed and the view from the window occurred on a near-constant basis, although in terms of the level of technology incorporated, the room itself became increasingly reductivist and mechanized.[6] The use of a freestanding dresser, for example, had in many cases given way to a built-in recessed dresser and coat closet. The sink also was recessed, with modular panels for electrical and gas supply. Systems of support became centralized and often mounted above the patient's head, and

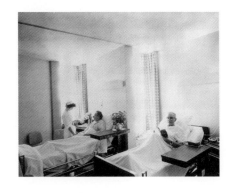

6.1. Porte de Choissy Medical and Surgical Center, Paris, 1964, private room

6.2. West Haldimand Hospital, Hagersville, Ontario, Canada, 1964, semi-private patient room

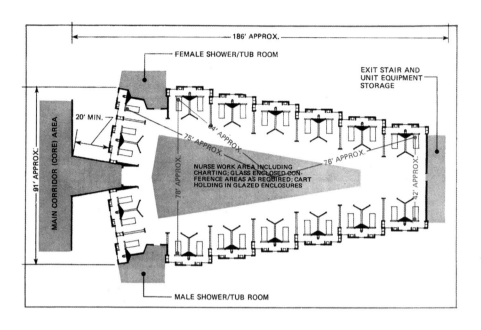

186' APPROX.

FEMALE SHOWER/TUB ROOM

EXIT STAIR AND
UNIT EQUIPMENT
STORAGE

91' APPROX.

MAIN CORRIDOR (CORE) AREA

20' MIN.

84' APPROX.

75' APPROX.

78' APPROX.

76' APPROX.

42' APPROX.

NURSE WORK AREA INCLUDING
CHARTING; GLASS ENCLOSED CON-
FERENCE AREAS AS REQUIRED; CART
HOLDING IN GLAZED ENCLOSURES

MALE SHOWER/TUB ROOM

6.3. Hartman and Malino ward
prototype, 1975

all lighting was provided by fluorescent fixtures mounted on the ceiling or above the patient's headboard.

In the 1970s the debate over the semi-private ward continued. By this point the U.S. General Accounting Office had come out against the open ward on the grounds that single-occupancy rooms provided the most cost efficiency in terms of day-to-day operations and initial construction. It appeared that the all-private-room hospital, a concept introduced early in the century for the benefit of the wealthy, was finally to become the new standard.[7] The minimum size of the private room was squeezed down to 120 square feet, with no lineal dimensions less than ten feet. It was on this policy change that the claim of lower construction was based. Unfortunately, the *minimum* architectural and space-planning criteria standards often became the maximum in terms of what was built.

In the mid-1970s a report was published by Robert Hartman, an architect, and Emily Malino, an interior designer, on a wedge-shaped variation of an open ward. Their concept was described as combining the best aspects of the private patient room and the traditional ward (fig. 6.3). A thirty-bed prototype unit was proposed, with wedge-shaped partitions between each two-bed cluster. Hartman and Malino cited the drawbacks of the traditional open ward and attempted to rectify the problems of image, technology, scale, appearance, and light. At the center of their unit, a glassed-in nurses' work area contained the nurses' station and support. The ward was to be joined to a central spine via a connecting stem. Its overall shape was telescopic, in that its narrowest point was furthest from the connecting corridor spine. Although this prototype was in violation of then-current codes, the authors argued that their concept would yield increased staffing and cost efficiencies, would easily accommodate advanced medical technology, and would result in increased patient satisfaction. Its most

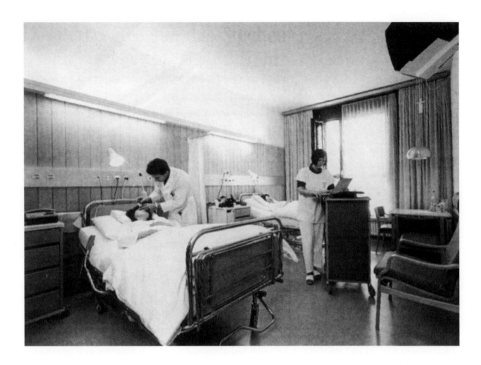

6.4. University Hospital, Zurich, 1994, patient ward

obvious drawbacks included the use of a half-height patient headwall, blocking views outward, and a dressing area and shared toilet situated along the entire outboard side of the unit. Mainstream hospital planners in the United States immediately dismissed the concept as impractical, costly, and socially unacceptable. Interestingly, these critics made little specific mention of major staffing- or technology-related objections to the telescopic ward proposal.[8]

This concept, and others like it, continued to find a far more receptive audience in Europe than in the United States, primarily because of the enduring cultural correctness of the open ward, and a greater social acceptance of limited personal privacy during hospitalization. In the University Hospital in Zurich (1986–94), designed by Haessig and Partners, the typical sixty-bed nursing floor was composed of eight one-bed rooms, twenty two-bed rooms, and three four-bed wards, for a total of sixty beds. The flow pattern was that of a racetrack with vertical circulation core at the center, straddled by two atrium light wells. The typical semi-private room, however, remained virtually unchanged from the standard box design of the previous twenty-five years (fig. 6.4). And the block form itself remained fundamentally unchanged from decades earlier.[9]

If the block plan for the hospital continued to hold currency in the eyes of hospital planners, particularly those schooled in the postwar International Style, subsequent efforts explored ways to vary the base-with-tower box. Although the language of modernism continued to hold sway among mainstream hospital administrators and their boards well into the 1980s, one effort in particular stood out as a marriage of the block-hospital platform base, and interstitialism on the lower floors, with the by-then-accepted triangulation of the nursing unit positioned above the support base: I. M. Pei's design for the

Guggenheim Pavilion at Mount Sinai Medical Center in New York (1989–92). The lower-level base contained various support functions, administration offices, and diagnostic and treatment departments, with these realms separated by interstitial service floors. On the upper floors were three independent towers, each housing seven floors of medical-surgical nursing units. The two endpoint towers had independent vertical circulation cores; the nursing units in the center tower were positioned back to back, forming a diamond in plan. Each tower was connected horizontally via a corridor stem to a central spine running the length of the back side.[10]

The building, striking in silhouette, possessed crisp shadow lines formed by the patient housing towers. Yet, in comparison to the civic prominence of its site and the move toward well-appointed, homelike interior amenities—natural wood trim and wall paneling—a certain level of inattention was accorded individual patient rooms in terms of their basic properties, such as size, shape, and window orientation. Architectural emphasis (and fiscal resources) was seemingly placed elsewhere in the hospital. Early on, for instance, it had been decided to locate all the patient-room washrooms inboard, thereby opening up opportunities for interesting window-wall configurations on the outer perimeter wall. These opportunities were not exploited, however, resulting in a monolithic appearance exacerbated through the use of "punched windows" in a uniform grid, far removed from the interesting sawtooth experiments by Rex Whitaker Allen and others in hospitals on the West Coast built in the early 1960s, such as Mary's Help Hospital in Daly City, California (see figs. 2.18 and 2.19). Pei's decision against a stepped or banded window-wall pattern created dark corners surrounding the window aperture on the outer perimeter wall of the patient room.

Mount Sinai was a late twentieth-century reprise of the seventeenth-century "derived plan," although not in the strictest sense, as in the case of the palace hospitals of Europe, when the plan and the exterior proportions were considered worthy of appropriation nearly verbatim from the estates and palaces of the nobility. In the case of the Guggenheim Pavilion, the plan of the patient towers symbolized a hybrid of the widely accepted triangulated nursing unit and a signature motif in Pei's oeuvre: the sharp triangulated corners dramatically expressed in a widely praised earlier work, the East Wing of the National Gallery of Art (1967–71) in Washington, D.C., and later in the triangulated arrival building on the main plaza level of the Louvre (1983–93) in Paris.

By the 1980s, postmodern classicism had found its way into hospital and nursing unit design, as expressed in the proposal for the Maison de Curé Sainte-Perrine, near Paris (1980–82), designed by Alexandre and Sandoz. Here a symmetrical undulating band of all-private patient rooms was wrapped around a courtyard and garden, the center of which was occupied by an early nineteenth-century residence converted into an administration building. The source of inspiration was clearly the picturesque European palace hospitals and retreats of the seventeenth through nineteenth centuries. The plan was a curious hybrid of a triangulated nursing unit concept, variations of which were detectable in Pei's Mount Sinai, within the context of synthesis with contextual postmodern sensibilities.[11]

Horizontalism

The adoption of the all-private-room hospital occurred at a time when the benefits of premodern and Nightingale horizontal hospitals were being rediscovered as a reaction to inefficiencies caused by excessive vertical movement between floors, the difficulty of expanding either the bottom platform or the bed towers or both, and basic changes in the overall service mix of the contemporary hospital. An appealing, logical alternative was a plan configuration in which a support base would be positioned beside the patient towers, with the two domains connected by a service spine. This arrangement allowed for expansion of either side as future needs dictated. Many acute-care and specialty hospitals of this type, different from the base-top configuration of Pei's hospital, were built during the 1980s, when many institutions were continuing their modernization and expansion programs with the momentum generated by comprehensive master plans, sometimes from years earlier. Examples of this horizontalism included the Southeast Memorial Hospital (1983–85) in Houston, designed by the Falick/Klein Partnership, and the H. Lee Moffit Cancer Center and Research Institute (1981–83) at the University of South Florida in Tampa, designed by Heery and Heery with Stuart L. Bentler.

6.5. Moffit Cancer Center, Tampa, Florida, 1983, axonometric view

Southeast Memorial was significant for its possibilities for expansion: on each floor of the support side, growth could occur horizontally on the roof of the level below, as the four levels were stepped back like a pyramid. The twin bed towers to the rear were constructed to a height of four floors initially, with the capacity for adding an additional three floors to each tower. The entire hospital was symmetrical, with the two sides flanking a central atrium core. At the Moffit Cancer Center, the support platform was similarly symmetrical, with twin towers placed on the back side of the main diagnostic and treatment building (fig. 6.5).[12] Therefore, both hospitals had a similar side-by-side template, with a main public entry axis at a right angle to a service axis connected to the twin towers. Patient-room bathrooms were on the outboard side. In both hospitals this gave the nursing units an interesting zigzag appearance from the exterior, affording shadow lines absent in the large, monotonous exterior walls of such facilities as Mount Sinai. Further, the banded colors of the exterior and the elevation of the nursing units on "legs" (structural columns) at the Moffit Center were in bold contrast to the typically massive volumes of hospitals. Moreover, the level of attention devoted to the undulation and clustering of the patient rooms in these and similar hospitals of the period was impressive. Nonetheless, functionalism prevailed, because these configurations arose from intense pressures to reduce travel distances and improve the supervision of the patient. But had these same arguments not been raised to justify nearly every type of nursing unit: open wards of various sizes, rectangular racetracks, radials, L-shaped units, and earlier versions of the triangulated nursing unit?

Clustering

The clustered nursing units of Southeast Memorial and the Moffit Center were reminiscent of a hospital built in Boston nearly a decade earlier. The cluster-bed nursing unit had been first introduced in the Somerville Hospital (1974–77),

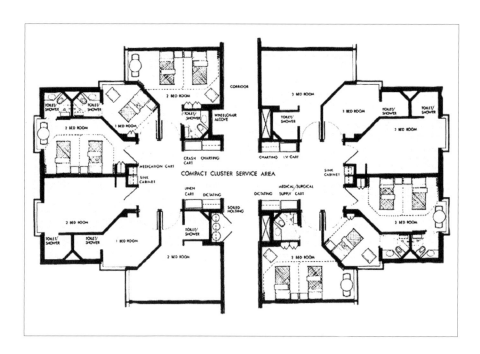

The labels visible in the floor plan include: CORRIDOR, 2 BED ROOM, TOILET/SHOWER, 1 BED ROOM, WHEELCHAIR ALCOVE, MEDICATION CART, SINK CABINET, CRASH CART, CHARTING, IV CART, COMPACT CLUSTER SERVICE AREA, LINEN CART, DICTATING, MEDICAL/SURGICAL SUPPLY CART, SORTED HOLDING.

6.6. Somerville Hospital, Massachusetts, 1974, cluster nursing-unit plan

located in suburban Boston (fig. 6.6). The new building contained two sixty-bed cluster floors, with support space on the ground level below. The new facility replaced an older 121-bed building, although the hospital continued to use a building planned by Friesen in 1964 for its other nursing units. A third building, dating from 1891, had been demolished to make way for the new construction. This concept had been justified, predictably, as an innovative way to minimize the amount of walking for nurses during their routine shifts and to bring them closer to more patients. In a description of events leading to this idea, Normand E. Girard, one of the originators of the concept, wrote:

> The compact cluster as it is used at Somerville was designed by Herbert Bienstock, AIA, and myself in cooperation with the medical and nursing staff. Mr. Bienstock is with Zachary Rosenfield & Partners, Architects, New York. My own interest in the cluster concept was a direct result of my participation in the Yale Traffic Index research project while a graduate student [of John Thompson]. The index, developed in the late 1950s, measures the efficiency of nursing units in terms of walking distance. The compact cluster design deliberately brings together key elements of efficient nursing unit design that have been developing in random fashion during the past twenty years: reduction of staff walking distances; elimination of the nurses' station and provision of drugs and supplies at the point of use; and maximum patient-staff visibility. Somerville's nursing unit achieves these goals by grouping 20 patients in 12 rooms into two six-room clusters across from each other. In the hallway that joins each double cluster are a staff work area with patient charts, a linen cart, a supply cart, a medication cart, a "crash" cart, and external communications for the nurses. . . . Each 20-bed grouping is assigned a nursing team. During the day, the 60-bed floors have one clinical leader each, six RNS/LPNS, three nurses' aides, and one clerk at the con-

trol center, for a total of 11 staff members on each floor. . . . [The units] are connected by an intersecting corridor to a fourth area where the service core is located.[13]

The Yale Index was applied to assess the performance of the new Somerville facility during its initial year of operation, in a series of what would later become known in the health architecture milieu as post-occupancy evaluations (POEs) of buildings-in-use. Through the application of the Yale indices (patient-to-patient distance, nurse-station-to-patient distance, and so on) it was found the cluster unit minimized the most critical "link distances," eliminated others entirely, and removed superfluous links between the patient room and nurses' station and between the unit and other areas of the hospital. After a year of use, the compact cluster floors delivered a higher level of care than the traditional linear unit with only 3.1–3.4 nursing hours per patient day. The staffing level was 14 percent less than that required in the five conventional nursing floors the new building replaced.[14] Girard and other proponents of this performance-based nursing unit took to task the Friesen alternative being widely promoted at the time:

> Hospital consultant Gordon A. Friesen, designer of Somerville's [existing] north building, has over the years been the advocate of elimination of the nurses station and provision of supplies at point of use. Mr. Friesen's supply solution, however, is to provide a supply closet, or nurseserver outside each room. . . . The new building's compact clusters avoid this costly redundancy [of long corridors]. . . . All ten patients in a single cluster are visible from two points in the corridor five feet apart. Patients feel they get a great deal more attention. Complaints of lack of privacy have been voiced by a few patients, but these are easily satisfied by drawing a bedside curtain or closing the door. Some physicians have also complained, on occasion, of not being able to see a patient without being spotted by other patients they don't want to visit at the time. Both complaints, however, serve to prove the effectiveness of the arrangement. . . . More than any other general nursing floor plan, the compact cluster has made possible effective care of the most seriously ill—the all-intensive hospital. Given a national goal of reducing beds and hospitalization, hospitals of the future could be fewer with fewer beds but serving more outpatients if they adopted the clustered system.[15]

Girard's prognostication would prove to be correct. However, when the cluster-bed unit was first conceived, healthcare costs were fully reimbursable and limited pressure existed to contain them. Thus there was little reason to seriously question the continued reliance on the rectilinear straight-corridor nursing unit, and the patient room continued to be thought best configured as a simple, rectangular box. The introduction of clustering fostered rooms of many different shapes: L-shaped rooms, rooms with narrow ends and wide centers, and diagonally shaped rooms, some with walls at forty-five-degree angles. In retrospect, clustering would represent a midpoint between the austerity of the cube room strung along racetrack corridors, as in Friesen's 1964 building at

Somerville, and the residentialism to be experimented with later. During the 1980s, further successes with clustering were reported, as in the case of the Link Pavilion at Hackensack Medical Center in New Jersey.[16] With the advent of cost containment, hospitals large and small sought new ways to reconfigure their nursing units to avoid shutting them down outright.

In spite of the growing popularity of the private room and the cluster concept in the United States, the ward, albeit a smaller version than before, continued to dominate mainstream European hospital planning. When the American innovation of clustering spread to Europe, it was applied to modified ward configurations, as represented in the Bezirksspital (1981–88) in Schwarzenburg, Switzerland, designed by Atelier 5 of Bern. This specialized community hospital for women was built as a reaction to the large government-owned hospitals dominant in the previous decade. It was two levels in height and from the exterior resembled an apartment complex. Landscaping was used to enhance its residentialism and to blend it into its surrounding context. The plan was a cruciform, open to the level below at the center, with decentralized nurses' stations (fig. 6.7). Beds were clustered in a combination of private rooms, two-bed rooms, and four-bed wards. The wards were variants on the traditional four-bed open ward, although provisions were made to increase the privacy of each patient and to situate each bed adjacent to a full-height window with a direct view. The rooms were spare by U.S. standards, though rather well appointed by European standards (fig. 6.8). Corridors were broken by planters positioned at certain room entrances, and by windows situated between the corridor and the patient rooms—a Scandinavian innovation that later would appear in Europe, Japan, and the United States.[17]

In the United States, the all-private-room nursing unit would prove uniquely well-suited to clustering. St. Michael's Hospital (1991–94) in Texarkana, Texas, by Watkins, Carter, Hamilton of Houston, was an outwardly residentialist second-generation cluster-bed hospital. Its gabled roofs gave the appearance of oversized townhouses, in large part the result of an early decision to cluster patient rooms and to relate the building composition to the surrounding residential area. The side-by-side template was similar to those of Southeast Memorial and the Moffit Cancer Center. The plan of St. Michael's was nearly symmetrical, with its twin patient "towers" fanning out from the central service spine in a Y configuration. Rooms were arranged as four-room suites, with the two inboard washrooms along the corridor and the outer two rooms' washrooms on the outboard side (fig. 6.9).[18] The net effect, spatially and in image, was part residentialist, part hotel-like. The clustered design would also prove amenable to miniaturized diagnostic, monitoring, and testing machines, the portable apparatus that would lead to bedside computerization and continuous patient monitoring from the nursing station.

The St. Michael's design had been developed in part as a result of a symposium called Unit 2000, held in Houston in March 1990.[19] The organizers had wanted feedback and ideas from users concerning the design of the nursing unit and the patient room. A series of simulation workshops were held over a three-day period on the premise that each of the numerous teams in the workshop was to develop an "ideal" nursing unit configuration. The results were

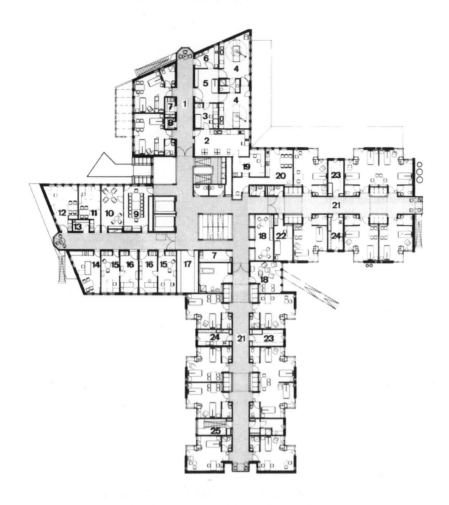

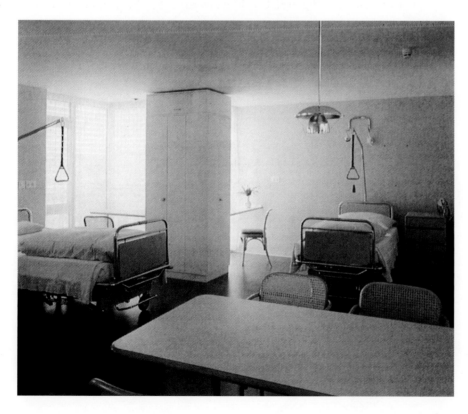

6.7. Bezirksspital,
Schwarzenburg, Switzerland,
1988, second-floor plan

6.8. Bezirksspital, patient ward

6.9. St. Michael's Hospital,
Texarkana, Texas, 1993, cluster
nursing-unit plan

discussed among all participants. In addition, a number of specialists made presentations to the entire group on the topics of room furnishings, bedside computing, the optimal size of the patient room, and anticipated trends in nursing unit and room design in the 1990s. The report that documented the symposium concluded with a series of case studies on recent projects by Watkins, Carter, Hamilton, the sponsoring firm. Among the case studies, one in particular symbolized then-current thinking on flexible cluster-bed pods in large-scale medical-surgical units. This variation on the Somerville concept was soon to be applied in a new fourteen-level patient tower for Hermann Hospital in Houston (1995–97; fig. 6.10). The entire perimeter of each bed floor was devoted to patient rooms. Patient support services were decentralized in an effort to establish a more human-scaled nursing unit as an alternative to the immense scale of the traditional nursing unit of thirty or more beds. The various floors were subdivided into six-bed pods, with four-bed pods for labor-delivery-recovery units and twelve-bed pods for the neonatal intensive care unit. There were nine pods per floor. Each pod included a nurses' station and amenities for charting, data entry and retrieval, dictation, clean and soiled utilities, and medication prepa-

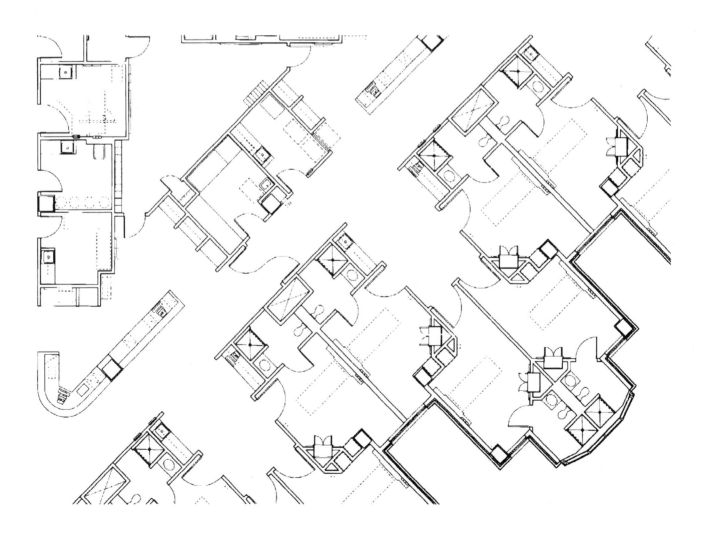

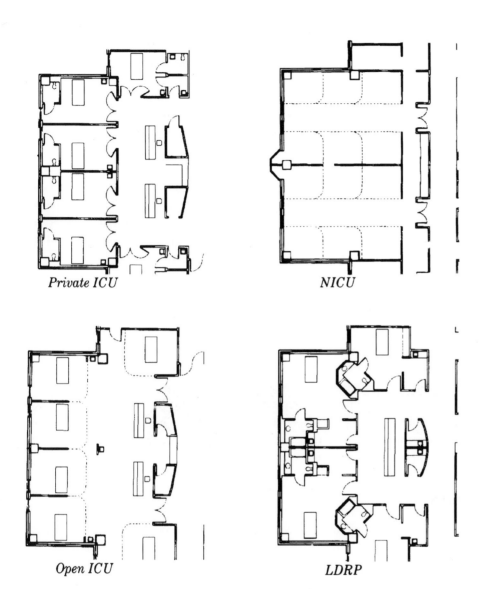

Private ICU

NICU

Open ICU

LDRP

6.10. Hermann Hospital,
Houston, 1993, nursing "pod"
configurations

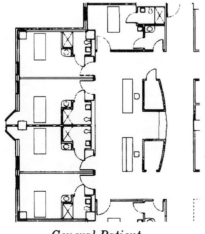

General Patient

ration and nourishment. The pods were essentially independent from one another, with certain shared support functions, such as a staff lounge shared by two pods. With each patient floor approximately 51,000 square feet in area, the tower became a block in plan, with the pods expressed on the exterior to enliven its massive scale somewhat. The exterior of the building was designed in the contextual vein of postmodernism, in a conscious attempt to recollect the ornate, eclectic Spanish-Moroccan style of the original main building (1922–25), the first building of the now immense Texas Medical Center.[20] If the driving force behind experiments with radials, triangles, and most recently cluster-bed units had been the need for direct supervision of the patient with the fewest possible staff, the obsession in the 1990s was one of achieving balance between those kinds of needs and the patient's personal autonomy, privacy, and the unprecedented possibilities resulting from bedside monitorization.

The Transformation of Room Furnishings

There have been few more reliable bellwethers of change in the healthcare industry than the product manufacturers. The firms that provide the beds, lighting fixtures, furnishings, and technical equipment necessary in the patient room have developed new products through a process of continual, diligent collaboration with nurses, physicians, patients and their families, administrators, architects, equipment specifiers, engineers, and interior designers. Consequently, the design, function, and appearance of patient room furnishings and equipment have closely tracked the evolution of the patient room itself: once machine-like in appearance, the equipment and furnishings later took on a softer, quasi-residentialist look, with many items designed to be relocated, concealed, or dismantled when not in use.

If the nursing unit has revolved around the patient room, the patient room has historically revolved around the patient bed and its immediate environs. Before the 1930s, hospital wards were equipped with inflexible metal beds. In 1933 William A. Hillenbrand, the founder of Hill-Rom of Batesville, Indiana, the most prominent manufacturer in the industry, introduced the first adjustable crank double-pedestal overbed table as an accompaniment to the standard hospital bed. Its goal was to reduce the nurse's difficulty in attending to the patient. With a bed that could be adjusted at the headboard, and with such later additions as adjustable siderails, more convenient control was afforded the nursing staff. From 1933 to the mid-1960s, Hill-Rom introduced many new products, which paralleled changes taking place in the hospital.[21] The pediatric bed introduced in 1962 was higher than previous beds and had new safety features to prevent injury (fig. 6.11). The retractable bed introduced in 1964 made it possible to reduce the size of the patient room slightly (fig. 6.12). On the rationale that rising construction costs were forcing hospitals to plan smaller private rooms for patients, the "Enviro-care" prefabricated retractable bed and furniture system was marketed in the mid-1970s as a means to capture an additional sixteen inches of floor space at the foot of the bed (fig. 6.13).

By the 1980s Hill-Rom had earned nearly 90 percent of the market for hospital-room equipment. Its "systems approach"—a marketing strategy whereby

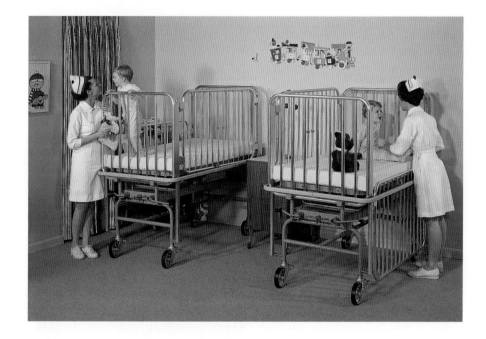

6.11. Hill-Rom Model 49-6
Infant Bed, 1961

the bed and related support equipment were promoted as a package—yielded a variety of high-tech products for the high-tech patient room: integrated head-walls (the wall unit at the head of the bed, consisting of electronic control panels and utilities) and freestanding power columns, remote nurse-patient communications systems, patient-controlled telephones and intercoms mounted on the bed siderail, ergonomic beds for patients with special needs, such as the obese and those with severe physical disabilities, and by the 1990s, computerized systems empowering the patient to control virtually the entire room electronically, including screens, lighting, bed position, and such audio-visual devices as the television and stereo.[22] Hill-Rom product innovation even extended to sleep surfaces designed to avoid pressure sores for the patient confined to a supine position. Over time, the advent of such innovative technology in the patient room, in the form of increasingly high-tech equipment and furnishings, led to the reconsideration of many aspects of room design, such as bed positioning, ceiling height, room lighting, floor and wall surfaces, vanities, closets, window positioning, and the overall size of the room. Beyond this, furnishing systems with freestanding components allowed for more flexibility than fixed furnishings, such as cabinets. Additionally, it became possible to enhance the profitability of a hospital through investment in flexible, patient-focused room and bed technologies that were popular with both patients and caregivers, as demonstrated by extensive survey research.

The Postmodern Nursing Unit

As we have seen, attitudes toward the hospital had undergone considerable reappraisal in the postwar years. The nursing unit and the patient room, however, were not at center stage. Even though attitudes toward the nursing unit

Now your patient can go from this...

Here your patient is in a sleeping position, on the revolutionary new Hill-Rom Retractable Hilow Bed described inside. She is operating the handy control lever that will lift her into a sitting position.

6.12. Hill-Rom Retractable Patient Bed, 1964: "More reasons why the model 70 is the best buy"

to this...

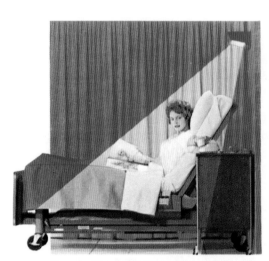

Here she has moved into a sitting position, but—lo and behold!—she **has not** moved forward, out of the reading light and out of reach of the bedside cabinet. In addition, the knee section has automatically risen, to keep her from slumping toward the foot of the bed.

instead of this...

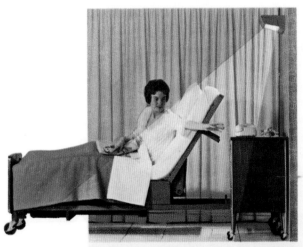

Had she been in any other bed, the head section would have moved her forward as it lifted her up. She would now have to call the nurse, to adjust her reading light and move the bedside cabinet.

6.13. Hill-Rom Enviro-Care
System, 1975: a modular system
of patient-room services and
furnishings

were changing gradually throughout the second half of the twentieth century, administrators' attention was chronically diverted elsewhere in the hospital. In the worst-case scenario the hospital administrator was racing to obtain the best and the latest machines, and the departments that housed these new necessities received priority within the political, economic, and spatial hierarchy. Thus change in new-construction projects occurred at a rapid pace, but in older facilities advancements in nursing-unit design occurred only incrementally (if at all) until Planetree, a nonprofit, consumer-oriented healthcare organization, was founded in San Francisco in 1978. Its goal was to envision and then realize an "ideal" healing environment by approaching hospital care in a manner that maximized the involvement and participation of the patient and family. The idea was simple: patients who were well informed about their condition and who were able to participate in medical decisions were likely to become well sooner than patients cared for in the typical staff-focused setting. Planetree emphasized cooperation with progressive organizations and institutions to create models of a more patient- and consumer-oriented approach to healthcare delivery. Its mission was broad: to restructure the system through improved education, personalization, and the demystification of illness.

Among the group's first projects was the establishment of the Planetree Health Resource Center in San Francisco. This center was created for patients, families, and other nonspecialists who were interested in learning about illness, diagnosis, and various mainstream and alternative health-related topics. And in June 1985 a Planetree unit opened at the Pacific Presbyterian Medical Center in San Francisco. The first medical-surgical unit of its type in the United States, it was a 13-bed unit within the facility of a 310-bed specialty hospital (fig. 6.14). Funding was provided by the Henry J. Kaiser Family Foundation. The first account of this unit in the U.S. architectural press stated:

> In a small section of a moderately sized hospital in San Francisco, a quiet revolution is taking place. Gone is the typical sanitized hospital decor—cold alu-

6.14. Planetree Unit, Pacific Presbyterian Medical Center, San Francisco, 1985, open nurses' station

minum and stainless steel, and linoleum, fluorescent lights, and hard, painted surfaces. Instead, the design esthetic is comfort and hominess: wood, carpet, and incandescent lights. Gone, too, is care that often can be best characterized as dehumanizing, depersonalizing, frightening. In its place are friendly congeniality and highly personalized attention. . . . So far, it has been a resounding success, one in which the physical environment and the patient care work in tandem to create a non-institutional ambiance. The seed for Planetree was planted 10 years ago when Angelica Theiriot, environmentalist and health-care advocate, was hospitalized with a mysterious, life-threatening virus. "That was a nightmare," she recalls. "I was shocked by the bungling and the constantly changing staff. At one point, I was left slumped over in a wheelchair outside X-ray for 45 minutes with a fever of 107 degrees. Later I thought to myself, 'I'm basically young and strong. What happens to people who are less sturdy, less capable of making demands?'" Theiriot's experience and that of other family members led to her realization that "things had to be done differently," she says. "Many of the most important moments of people's lives are spent in hospitals. Yet, for the most part, they are the coldest and ugliest places on the earth."[23]

Theiriot had invited Roslyn Lindheim, an architect and professor at the University of California at Berkeley, and other prominent healthcare professionals in the Bay Area to assist her in launching the prototype Planetree nursing unit. Lindheim, long a critic of the modern hospital, eagerly offered her support and expertise.[24] With a three-year demonstration project grant from the Kaiser Foundation, the first demonstration was established in a renovated nursing unit at Pacific Presbyterian. A second, twenty-five-bed Planetree unit opened at San Jose Medical Center in San Jose, California, in 1989:[25] "We researched everything . . . from the environment to nursing care, to food and the role of arts in healing. . . . Most modern health professionals will readily admit that the patient's state of mind is a major factor in the success of the treatment, yet nothing in the design and operation of the modern hospital reflects this knowledge. Planetree determined that the most crucial social, emotional, and esthetic needs denied routinely to hospitalized persons were supportive human relationships, physical comfort, independence, as much pleasure as is possible under the specific circumstances of a hospital stay, and a sense of autonomy and dignity."[26]

The initial thirteen-bed unit at Pacific Presbyterian housed a mixture of patients, including those with AIDS, cancer, and kidney failure. The two-thousand-square-foot unit was renovated at a cost of $175,000. At first, only twelve physicians agreed to refer patients to the unit; some months later the number had jumped to sixty-two. The basic layout of the unit was a racetrack, as its prior incarnation had been, because this "alternative" unit was restricted by the template of the existing facility. However, the entire staff core at the center was removed and redesigned with a radically different function and ambiance (see fig. 6.14). The traditional nurses' station was replaced with an oak work counter. The windows looked out onto the patient lounge and library. The central staff work area was transformed into a patient lounge and kitchen, to bring a sense of residentialism to the unit. The core spaces of the unit, which had formerly housed staff-only functions, had now been given over to patients. The remaining renovation budget was devoted to making comparatively minor additions to the rooms: curtains, plants, bookshelves, and carpet. The existing hospital beds and bedside furnishings remained, however. Lindheim regretted that limited funds had precluded new furnishings, varied wall treatments, varied room·sizes, or an outdoor terrace or solarium. To break the hospital's ubiquitous right angles, Lindheim modified two of the corner walls to diagonals; room-to-room and room-to-hall windows were created throughout the reconstituted center core.

Obvious influences on the Planetree concept were the hospice movement and the birthing movement of the 1970s and 1980s, with their strong emphasis on patient empowerment, touching therapy, music, patient-family involvement, and the use of appropriate technology. By the late 1990s, dozens of Planetree units were in operation in hospitals across the United States.

At the same time as the early Planetree experiment, hospitals in other parts of the United States were experimenting with new ways to break out of their modernist "box" nursing units. Among the most notable early examples of the "picturesque" appropriation of postmodernism and its visual impact on patient-centered care was the pediatric nursing-unit "streetscape" created at the Mercy Memorial Medical Center in St. Joseph, Michigan (1984–86), designed by Hansen, Lind, Meyer Architects. At Mercy, innovations included a color palette evoking a neighborhood streetscape, a residentialist vocabulary with personalized "front entries" and "doorways" established via banded carpeting, color-coded front "house" facades with gabled soffits, incandescent lighting, side rails that evoked window planters, reinforcement of differences between the "houses," room-to-corridor windows, and a window in the door

6.15. Mercy Memorial Medical Center, St. Joseph, Michigan, 1986, pediatric nursing wing

to each patient's room (fig. 6.15).[27] This project was similar to the first Planetree unit in the patient rooms' sense of openness onto the hallway, although at Mercy the interpretation of home was more aesthetically self-conscious, insofar as it was inspired by the surface imagery common in representational postmodernism of the period. The designers of the Mercy unit, however, did not question the core layout of the unit or the basic design of the nursing station to the extent of their counterparts at Pacific Presbyterian. If the Planetree units were postmodern in underlying ideology but somewhat less so in formal terms, the unit at Mercy, and at other similar hospitals where surface modifications predominated, was moderately postmodern in its synthesis of the patient-focused ideology, but this outlook was secondary to its emphasis on the formal attributes of the genre.

The Transformational Room

Transformational rooms were experimented with as a means to combine elements of residentialism with the tectonics of the hospital environment. One way to distinguish a transformational from a traditional room is to assess its adaptability. Transformational rooms are of two types: first, single-function rooms that can completely convert and then revert to their initial state of use, and second, rooms that possess more than one function in their initial state of use and whose functions are alterable in terms of their hierarchical amenity, or use, across time. The length of time in question in both cases is highly variable, ranging from a matter of minutes to a period of weeks or months in a given state, or mode, of use by the staff, patient, or family member. One type of space, the birthing room, was particularly suited to such transformational experimentation. The birthing suite, an innovation of the 1980s, was created to bring together the traditional qualities of home birthing with the technology and support available in the acute-care hospital. The appearance of these rooms symbolized an acknowledgment by the hospital that the status quo had become unacceptable in the age of antihospitalism, consumerism, cost containment, and women's self-empowerment.

The history and design of the maternity hospital demonstrate how distinctions of gender, race, and class were encoded formally in the healthcare milieu. Maternity hospitals were established in the nineteenth century as urban-based charity asylums to serve the poor, homeless, and the working classes. Sponsored by businessmen, clergy, and philanthropists, these hospitals functioned as institutions offering both medical treatment and social rehabilitation. Many of the expectant mothers in the maternity hospital were servants of wealthy families or were unwed. The maternity hospital provided the patient with a simulated home delivery and a two-month stay, one month before and one month after childbirth. This environment was thought to be best not only for the administration of effective medical treatment but also for teaching women to be "respectable" members of the community. Sometimes the patients even worked to keep the hospital clean. During the Victorian era, what physicians learned through maternity care of the poor and "fallen" women was used to treat "respectable" women at home. A major turning point came when the American Medical Association banned midwives from medical practice in the early twentieth century. As policy, hospital deliveries were from that point promoted over home deliveries. With the advent of medical technology, the birthing process became fully mechanized and institutionalized and was no longer seen as natural or domestic.[28]

In many ways the hospital-based birthing centers created in the 1980s were a reprise of the maternity hospitals and obstetric wards that began to proliferate in the U.S. hospitals built in the 1920s. The best of these had been designed as homelike, almost vacation-like settings. Porches, open-air verandahs, and bright, cheerful colors disguised the institutional quality of the hospital. And conscious efforts were made to maximize personal privacy and individuality.

In the post-1945 maternity wards, private phones, silent nurse-call systems, attractive window treatments, and adjustable beds were introduced. Separate wards for women whose babies had died and special sleeping and waiting quarters for fathers (though these were often down the hall or in an adjacent building) provided humane touches. Once again, however, the degree of innovation was restricted by the dictates posed by the template of the hospital superstructure. In other words, the process usually was one of renovation rather than revolution.[29] As for the function of gender, "If giving birth was the ultimate in femininity, controlling it was quintessentially masculine, and the obstetrician's workplace was designed accordingly."[30] Like factories, hospital-based maternity wards continued to be spatially organized for operational efficiency of the staff. Workers performing specialized tasks were separated in assembly-line fashion, fragmenting both the process of childbirth and the space in which it occurred. Birthing was divided into three components: the labor-and-delivery suite, the newborn nursery, and the postpartum nursing unit. In many hospitals these functions were housed on different floors. Hospitals lacking space often placed the mother in group labor rooms. Because of this, women often became frightened and demoralized by other women's discomfort.[31]

6.16. Center for Women's Health, Cottonwood Hospital, Murray, Utah, 1986

6.17. Center for Women's Health, transformed birthing suite

6.18. Center for Women's Health, exterior

Not until the 1980s, when birthing suites were added to the traditional regimen of spaces in the maternity unit, were couples once again able to experience natural childbirth within the hospital. In order to create a comfortable setting, the suites were designed to be transformational. This planning concept called for the room or suite to be homelike or residentialist one moment and hospitalist the next. The most notable early example was built at the Center for Women's Health at Cottonwood Hospital (1984–86) in Murray, Utah, designed by Kaplan/McLaughlin/Diaz. At one moment the room would be devoid of any obvious medical equipment (fig. 6.16). At the next instant the room would be transformed into a full-fledged labor, delivery, and recovery suite, with all necessary medical equipment brought out from various compartments and concealments along the perimeters of the room (fig. 6.17).[32] The exterior was highly residential, evoking a series of ranch houses along a placid suburban street (fig. 6.18).

At Cottonwood and many other places, space was provided for family and for overnight stays. These transformable birthing rooms eliminated "labor in one place with one set of monitors; a wheeled dash down the hall for delivery by a new corps of attendants; and a brief interlude in a recovery area."[33] Instead, in a single setting a coordinated care team provided labor, delivery, and recovery (LDR) care and a few hours of postpartum recuperative (LDRP) care. Care was brought to the patient rather than vice versa. At first, however, many birthing rooms sat unused in hospitals because of resistance from the medical staff. Also, some women were deemed unable to use these rooms for medical reasons. Regardless, the birthing suite both epitomized and facilitated the shift from the modern (staff-centered) to the postmodern (patient-centered) patient room. Its residentialist furnishings, natural lighting, size (typically one-third larger than the average medical-surgical patient room), attention to ceiling and wall surfaces, and carpet or natural wood floors with area rugs, set these rooms apart from other patient rooms of the era. And such manufacturers as Hill-Rom introduced new products for this new room type, including their Genesis Bed.[34]

The trend toward birthing suites coincided with changing attitudes toward the patient room. Once considered an ancillary space, it became a central element in the downsized, functionally deconstructed hospital of the 1990s. Such providers as Columbia/HCA began to design templates for hospitals of between thirty-two and forty beds that entirely eliminated ICU beds and other special-care units, and in turn expanded each patient room by about 25 percent and enabled nearly every one of them to be potentially used either as a miniature ICU or for somewhat less acutely sick patients. But because patients in these new hospitals were in general sicker than in the past, the patient room had been thoroughly transformed from its role and status of merely ten years before.[35]

Windowness

By the 1980s, the patient room and nursing unit had become the subject of discussion and architectural research on the impact of windows on the well-being of patients and staff. The relationship between the patient and the window and its view had been defined as transactional in nature, denoting a process whereby the window, view, orientation, size, and so on, influence the individual and, conversely, the individual's degree of exposure via the use of curtains, distance from the aperture, decision to open the window or leave it closed, and so on, have a bearing on the setting itself.[36] The quality of the view had been shown to have a bearing on health status; the ability of the patient to experience the view through physical proximity to the window, and more important, the ability to view nature, were found to be instrumental. The term *windowness* was developed to define this quality, and in an empirical study, patients' degree of windowness in six rehabilitation hospitals was found to have a bearing on patient outcome (well-being). Persons low in windowness—distant from the window, in windowless rooms for much of the day, or in rooms with a poor view—experienced a lower level of well-being on the basis of assessments by staff. Moreover, a minor but noticeable negative impact was detected for staff exposed to the same settings.[37] In one well-known study of patients recovering from surgery, it was found that those whose rooms overlooked a small strand of trees had more favorable outcomes than those whose views were of a brick wall.[38]

In most industrialized countries, the ward or room is required by law to have a window. But problems arose in the modern hospital when the window area was minimized either for the sake of aesthetics or to reduce the cost of heating and cooling the building. In other instances the window was placed at an awkward or distant angle from the in-bed viewing station of the patient. At Prentiss Women's Hospital (1971–73) in Chicago, by Bertrand Goldberg, the circular windows were found to be disorienting (see Chapter 3).

The window and its "view amenity" therefore warranted reconsideration as an important design element in the patient room. Opportunities had always existed to establish direct visual connections between indoors and outdoors, dating from the ancient Asclepia in Greece. In contemporary settings, such possibilities included doors opening onto a patio adjacent to the patient room, or full-height glass doors opening onto a balcony. The patient rooms at the Maison de Retraite La Bartavelle, St.-Jean, in Maurienne, France (1991–94), designed

6.19. Charles Canu Hospice at Centre Hospitalier, Vire, France, 1994, patient room

by Brut d'architecture (Jean-Paul Bach, Jean Brucy, and Pascal Fontaine), were oriented to provide maximum views for the patient. Each semi-private room was subdivided into two zones, separated by wooden, partially see-through, open-grid partitions. The windows overlooked an adjacent park. Each room had a door leading to a balcony.[39] At the Charles Canu hospice at the Centre Hospitalier in Vire, France (1991–94), designed by Yann Brunel, the two-tiered windows provided views from a supine position in bed to the ground level of this three-floor residential hospice. The room was large enough for the bed to be repositioned according to the patient's preference (fig. 6.19).[40] In a somewhat similar case, the full-height corner windows of the rooms of the skilled-nursing facility and assisted-living wing at the Bern-Wittigkofen Hospital, in Bern, Switzerland (1988–89), designed by Atelier 5 of Bern, afford equal access by each patient to the view and daylight (fig. 6.20; see also Chapter 7).[41] In all three of these facilities, operable windows allowed natural ventilation into the rooms—a postmodern hospital innovation in its own right.

In the United States, the patient rooms at the Children's Hospital and Health Center of San Diego (1991–93), designed by NBBJ of Seattle, established a direct connection between the indoors and the outdoors. The ground-level rooms opened onto terraces, and each room had a private door and full-height window. One of the window frames was scaled to the height of a child.[42] Other U.S. strategies included the creation of an "executive" patient room, as in the wood-paneled, boardroom-like rooms at Beth Israel Hospital's Reisman Building (1988–90) in Boston, by Rothman Rothman Heineman Architects, with the interiors designed by Crissman and Solomon Architects. The rooms included built-in bookcases and a storage-seating niche.[43] A strongly symbolic as well as functional expression of the transition from the modern to the postmodern patient room occurred at the Greater Baltimore Medical Center (1988–91) in Baltimore, designed by RTKL Architects (fig. 6.21).[44] There, residentialist furnishings, appropriate lighting, wall alcoves, carpet, artwork, and bedside computerization technology gave the rooms an inviting residential ambiance while avoiding a bland caricature of home, hotel, or hospital. Additionally, the windows afforded full-height views unencumbered by furnishings or equipment.

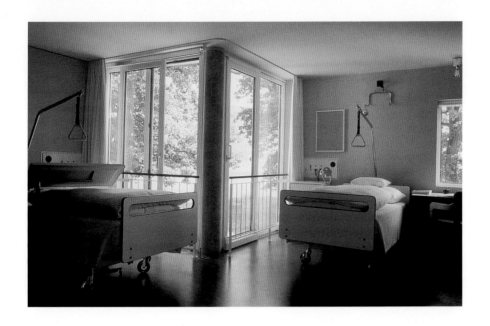

6.20. Bern-Wittigkofen Hospital, Bern, Switzerland, 1989, semi-private patient room

6.21. Greater Baltimore Medical Center, Baltimore, Maryland, 1991, private patient room. Photo © Maxwell Mackenzie.

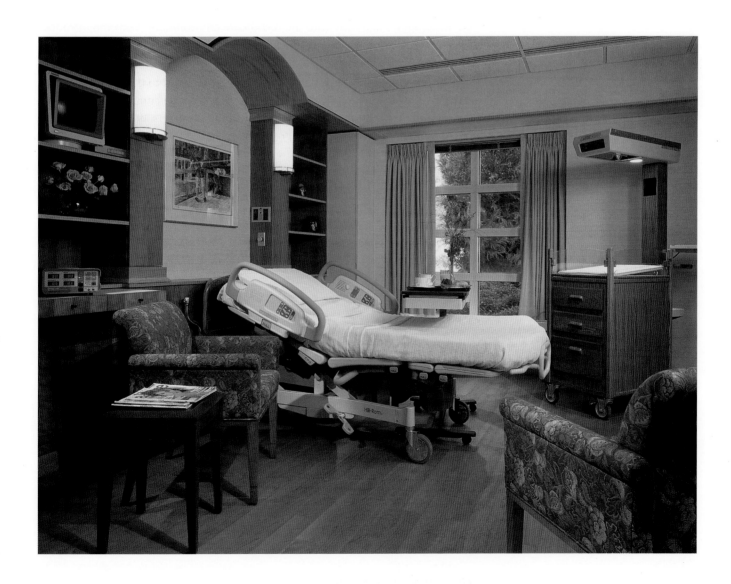

Bedside Computerization and Beyond

During the 1980s the first bedside stand-alone computerization systems were developed, such as the MedTake system, which enabled nurses to input patient-care data into a terminal at the patient's bedside. These systems made medical data immediately available to the patient, prompted patients' and nurses' reporting of routine care, and were found to save about twenty-five minutes per patient per eight-hour shift.[45] In these "point-of-care" systems, the flow of information within a networked hospital revolved around the patient room and the nursing station, from which emanated requests for medication, testing, scheduling, and other aspects of care.

Manufacturers scrambled to capture a portion of this new market. First they had to convince administrators and direct-care providers of the merits of these new data input and management systems. They met with resistance at first.[46] For one thing, the patient room had to be expanded in size to provide space for the computer workstation and peripheral equipment. Administrators were not willing to do this unless cost effectiveness could be clearly demonstrated. By 1990, however, the industry had embraced the concept of bringing the information age fully into the healthcare environment, with the introduction of point-of-care systems by IBM and other major manufacturers.[47] This trend provided a strong impetus for the rise of the critical care center in lieu of the typical modern hospital, because in the critical care center every patient room would have to function as a miniature intensive-care suite when needs dictated. Bedside computerization would play an important role in this scenario. More important, the critical care center's patient room was conceived as a self-contained entity. In the past the patient room had been, for the most part, a dormitory room, and the patient had to be moved elsewhere for most procedures. The new scenario would attempt to turn this pattern around: now the services would be brought to the patient.

Whereas in the 1960s the hospital's armament of machines was considered the lifeblood of its reputation and prestige, along with the quality of its staff, by the 1990s the patient room had, in many ways, assumed a status not seen since the era of Florence Nightingale. Providers had previously tended to focus on regions of the hospital other than the patient room and nursing unit. In the 1990s they realized, however, that attention and resources were well spent when invested in reinventing the nursing unit and the patient room. The single most significant innovation of the 1970s had been the cluster-bed concept. Before clustering, the patient room had been little more than a container for a passive occupant. With clustering, rooms began to appear in a variety of irregular shapes and sizes. The cluster represented a bridge between stark, austere rooms and the more commodious, residentialist postmodern patient room and nursing unit. Then, in the years of cost containment, the transformational patient room supported a decreased range of sickness on the part of the patient. The average patient stay was now shorter and more acutely intensive, with hospitals—CCCs—now designed for the most seriously ill patients. As a result, in the all-private-room hospital of the end of the century, the patient room had grown by about 25 percent to accommodate the additional equipment to be periodically stationed in the room, including bedside computerization apparatus. This growth opened up new space-planning possibilities, including clusters of decentralized micro-units, or pods, within larger medical-surgical or special-care units. The patient was now in a position to reap the benefits of a reinvented patient-care environment. Accordingly, product manufacturers developed furnishings and equipment centered on empowerment of the patient. Whereas the Planetree prototypes were revolutionary in their rejection of the modern nursing unit, it would remain to be seen whether postmodernism, insofar as it affected the nursing unit and the patient room, would live up to the lofty claims of the proponents of the "new humanism" and "patient-centered care" movements in health architecture and, more specifically, whether a reinvented patient housing milieu would translate into quantifiable, positive therapeutic effects on patient well-being.

CHAPTER 7

Architectural Environments for the Aged, 1965–2000

By the mid-1960s the nursing home had come to symbolize the negative aspects of aging and the inevitability of death. In the United States, even the best nursing homes were referred to as "gilded cages," as the popular press uncovered one scandal after another involving mistreatment of the aged, their despair, and the outright greed of profiteers in the nursing-home industry.[1] Yet, fueled by the enactment of Medicare in 1965, between 1965 and 1975 the number of people living in nursing homes in the United States approximately tripled, reaching nearly one million. This figure represented slightly less than 5 percent of all persons over age sixty-five at the time, and the percentage of institutionalized aged has held fairly constant since then.

This chapter summarizes developments since 1965 in architecture for the aged, traces the roots of these developments, examines the role of health facilities and planned communities designed and built for the aged, and attempts to link these communities with the transactional empowerment-disempowerment construct defined in Chapter 1. These trends and countertrends across the health landscape for the aged are also extended across cultural and national boundaries. Note, however, that the many residential retirement communities built across the United States in the post–World War II era, such as the highly popularized Sun City, Arizona, are considered beyond the scope of this discussion because they are first and foremost residential communities rather than healthcare environments. By contrast, the continuing care retirement community is included, because it has a distinct, sustained healthcare component on site.

Precursors of the Contemporary Nursing Home

By the mid-1960s it was a widely held assumption that regardless of cultural, political, or economic factors in a particular country, a certain percentage of the elderly population would be in need of a continuous level of healthcare services most efficiently provided within a long-term institutional setting. The roots of care for the aged in Western culture can be traced as far back as *gerocomia,* the buildings in ancient Rome that housed the elderly. Owing to advances in providing clean (though probably lead-based) water and in sewage disposal methods, the life span of Romans was lengthened considerably, and the literature of this period indicates that four distinct periods of life were recognized: infancy, youth, adulthood, and old age. The practice of medicine was concerned mainly with the treatment of the aged.[2]

The writings of a Roman aristocrat named Pliny the Younger (c. A.D. 61–113) provide insight into the process of aging in Roman culture 1,900 years ago and reveal its many parallels to the late twentieth-century aging process.[3] Shortly after the beginning of the second century, Pliny the Younger made one of his frequent visits to the region of Tuscany. The impressions that he wrote to a friend upon his return might apply equally well to a contemporary retirement community in California: "The summer is wonderfully temperate, for there is always some movement in the air, more often a breeze than a real wind. Hence the number of elderly people living there—you can see the grandfathers and great grandfathers of people who have reached their own manhood, and hear old stories and tales of the past, so that a visit here is like a return to another age."[4] About one-fifth of the population of the Late Roman Empire survived to age fifty-five, a remarkable statistic given that Western life spans did not increase significantly beyond that until the eighteenth century.[5]

After the fall of the Roman Empire in the fourth century, the care for the aged became primarily a charitable deed of Christians. Convents and monasteries, staffed by monks and attendants providing medical care, were constructed throughout Europe. In many of these facilities a separate dormitory ward was created for the aged and infirm. In some areas almshouses or workhouses were built, and in others, hospitals. The church is still closely associated with long-term care in many countries, including Italy and the United States.

The first known almshouse in England opened in A.D. 939. Almshouses, at first provided by the church, were freestanding residences typically configured around a central courtyard, adjacent to church structures. Additional almshouses were constructed during the eleventh and twelfth centuries. During the Reformation of the sixteenth century, when the role of the church diminished significantly, almshouses continued to appear but were funded by wealthy philanthropists. Accommodation was often provided in exchange for a gift of coal. Because of the nearly total lack of organized medical care and poor housing conditions in the emerging factory cities of the Industrial Revolution, survival beyond age sixty-five was an unusual feat. Not until the beginning of the twentieth century did the British government, through the *Royal Commission on the Poor Law of 1909,* officially acknowledge and recommend the provision of special housing for the aged, and no specialty hospitals for the aged existed up to this time.[6] One hundred years earlier, in 1806, the absence of specialized health care for the aged had been noted in a report of the Dundee Royal Infirmary, which stated that physicians had been inappropriately referring to patients in the infirmary as elderly patients who were not "proper objects" and who should instead be referred to the workhouse or almshouse.[7]

Gradually, specialized geriatric hospitals for the aged were established in England and in other countries as a response to the needs of the sick and infirm elderly. In England the absence of a system of facilities for the aged poor in need of long-term care became a recognized problem in the years preceding and during World War II, and as a result the care of the aged became a prime responsibility of the National Health Service (NHS) when it was established in 1948. At first, local authorities were left responsible for the care of the frail aged and the NHS became responsible for the care of the chronically sick aged. At this time, the field of geriatric medicine was formulated and buttressed to care for this second class of patients.

The National Health Service took over all hospitals, whether voluntary, nonprofit, or public, and the standard template for these facilities became a modified version of the Nightingale open ward with its communal lavatories and bathing facilities. Single rooms were provided, as before, for the upper classes, although even these rooms did not have private bathrooms. In these hospitals the aged were treated as undesirable patients who took up valuable bed space—space the medical staff deemed would be better used for younger acute-care patients and returning veterans. Soon thereafter, obsolete acute-care hospitals in England and in other countries, including the United States, were given over to geriatric medical care. These vacated institutions had typically been used for the treatment of infectious diseases, particularly smallpox and tuberculosis. With advances in the treatment of these illnesses, fewer acute-care facilities were necessary for this purpose. Peter Millard summarizes this period:

> In the ensuing thirty years most attention has been concentrated in upgrading accommodation and improving treatment services. In the chronic sick wards provided by local authorities, beds were close together, some even touching, walls were brown and there were no chairs or day rooms. Gradually beds have been taken down, curtains, lockers and day rooms provided, and in some units the wards have been subdivided into four- to six-bedded bays. In the infectious disease hospitals there was more space between beds. . . . Although much has been done in England to improve the standards of medical and nursing care of the aged sick, little attention has been paid to the environmental needs. Fundamentally the English attitude remains that if you are sick you are better off observed at all times and that this is best done in open wards.[8]

By the late twentieth century the aged would be broadly classified by gerontologists in three distinct subgroups: the young elderly (ages 65–74), the mid-elderly (ages 75–84), and the old elderly (age 85 and older). They were further classified according to level of functional abilities as the active elderly, the moderately active elderly, and the inactive elderly. This breakdown was needed largely because of advances in medical science, which gave rise to the expansion of the elderly population in many parts of the world. This, in turn, forced a redefinition of the concept of aging itself.[9]

The first wave of newly built institutions in the post–World War II period would become known as *nursing homes,* a term borrowed from the need for continuous nursing care and from the notion of home in the traditional almshouse system. Yet this anachronistic term, which evoked its precursors' benign societal neglect of the aged and chronically infirm, failed to describe its environment and its patients accurately. The facilities themselves were widely perceived as drab, dehumanizing places, environments of neglect and disposal.

The quality of life was low. Sociologists and gerontologists were among the first to signal the alarm, turning their attention to the rigid institutionality of nursing homes fifteen years before the first critically based architectural treatment of the subject, Joseph A. Koncelik's *Designing the Open Nursing Home*, appeared in 1976. Such work eventually centered on the culture of benign neglect that characterized many nursing institutions during the rapid expansionism of the 1960s and 1970s. A related dimension to this study of the sociology of institutionalization was efforts to learn about the physiology of aging, and the captive audience of the nursing institution proved invaluable to researchers in this respect.[10]

In the postwar era the nursing home increasingly resembled and functioned as a miniaturized acute-care hospital. New, freestanding long-term care facilities proliferated during this period (1945–1960). Architecturally, the aesthetic and functional vocabulary of the International Style was sweeping through developed and developing nations alike. France and other European countries, in particular, were testing grounds for a series of publicly built and operated modernist geriatric hospitals and housing projects for "old people."

In France the institutionalization of long-term-care patients had begun at the start of the eighteenth century, when a special medical service for the aged, *gerocomié*, was established. The result was a certain stature accorded this area of medicine, and in time this led to the creation of three distinct networks of facilities built and operated by the government: acute-care facilities, medium-care facilities, and long-term, semi-independent-care facilities. This system precluded the possibility of the patient's remaining in the same facility for any significant length of time, for as one's needs changed, one was relocated. Unlike England, where the determination of acceptance to a facility was made by the physician, in France the determination was made by the social service agency.[11]

In terms of architecture, by the 1960s the approach in France was to follow the principles established by Le Corbusier in his visionary urban plans of the 1920s and, later, in his Unité d'Habitation in Marseilles (1947–52). The institutions for the care of the aged that were conceived and built on this model, however, were not nearly as inspired as Le Corbusier's vertical "neighborhoods" intended to be built in park-like settings. Le Corbusier's concepts, when watered down by myriad technical criteria and budget constraints and entrusted to the hands of architects considerably less talented, resulted in little more than vertical warehouses for old people, with little or no connection afforded between the patient and the external environment. In the most extreme cases, results were not at all like the ideas advocated by Le Corbusier in his initial proposals decades before. By the mid-1960s this was particularly so in situations where the justification for the height, configuration, and overall appearance of a nursing home was more economic than ideological.

An ambitious example of the 1960s period of the International Style was the residence for the aged built at the International Center for Gerontology in Bagnolet, France (1968–71), designed by Jean Timmel. This rationalist project was straightforward in its orthogonal partí and site-planning principles. All support services were housed in a base beneath a residential tower (fig. 7.1). Reinforced concrete was the primary building material. The facility contained units for eighteen couples and ninety-nine private rooms for individuals. The skilled-nursing floor housed twenty-two private rooms along with four semi-private rooms for couples. Most of the units had small outdoor balconies; the units for couples included an adjoining sitting room. Residents had access to a terrace situated on the roof of the attached support building. In section, the uniformity of the partí was evident: a single double-loaded corridor was straddled with units on either side. The interiors were characteristically austere, in keeping with the principle of simplicity in surface ornamentation, and the proportions of the major elements of the complex were loosely based on proportioning systems incorporated in Le Corbusier's Unité d'Habitation.[12]

A second key example of this period was the Residence for the Aged in Waiblingen, Germany (1971–73), designed by Hans Kammerer and Walter Belz. This building was also designed in the International Style. It was constructed of reinforced concrete and set apart by a stepped podium containing support functions, with residential units on the upper four floors (fig. 7.2). The most significant difference between this facility and the earlier project by Timmel was not its exterior aesthetic composition but the manner in which the modernist legacy of Le Corbusier was integrated: the Waiblingen facility boasted a strong relation between the building and its graduated sloping site and between the indoor and adjoining exterior spaces. Further, the various parts of the building were sited as individual elements, each expressive of a specialized level of care or support function. The main building contained semi-independent residences for seventy-four individuals, with three units set aside for couples. A separate building housed thirty-five patients in need of intensive, skilled nursing care. Parking areas were strung along the site, corresponding to the contours of the sloping site, and a separate building housed administrative functions. The exterior spaces featured expansive terraces for residents and patients in the nursing home. These spaces, some cantilevered, one on the roof of the dining area, contained furniture and plants and were logical extensions of the pure functionalism of the complex. A racetrack circulation configuration was incorporated on the residential floors, which stepped down the site in a thoughtful interplay

7.1. International Center for Gerontology, Bagnolet, France, 1971

7.2. Residence for the Aged, Waiblingen, Germany, 1973

between terrain and building. In this respect the building was a departure from the clichéd approach of setting the residential tower atop a support-administrative base.[13]

In contrast to these minimalist French and German nursing homes, state-of-the-art Scandinavian facilities for the aged were quite different. The highly residentialist nursing homes that evolved in Sweden, Finland, and Denmark stemmed from the talents of individual architects and clients, a profound sense of critical regionalism, and a certain isolation of geography and language. This early work began to receive widespread recognition in English-speaking countries in the 1980 book *Housing for the Elderly: New Trends in Europe,* by the American architect Leon Goldberger. In addition to the two French facilities cited above, this book contained such unusual projects as the honeycombed plan of the White City Estate in London (1974–76), by Noel and Alina Moffett—where each resident occupied an individual cell, as if in a beehive—and the highly residentialist Solgaven Nursing Home (1971–73) in Farum, Denmark, by Palle Svensons Tegnestue A/S. These progressive facilities and the progressive government-client policies they reflected predated the massive assisted-living movement in the United States by more than twenty years.[14]

In the United States and many other industrialized nations, the end of World War II signaled the beginning of the end of the three-generational household. The modern nursing home became a derivative of the modern hospital, and the influence of the "old people's homes" of the past was suppressed by the nursing home's increasing bureaucratization. The architecture of these facilities can be described as a continuum of institutionality, with the International Style that was clearly favored among high-style architects and government-agency sponsors in France representing one pole, and the more subdued residentialism of Denmark and Finland, and to a lesser extent England, representing the other pole. In the United States homes for the aged moved toward one or the other pole: nursing homes increasingly became hospitalist, while congregate housing or assisted living increasingly became residentialist. In Pittsburgh, the Forbes Pavilion Nursing Home, designed by Tasso Katselas (1965–67), was similar in external appearance to its European counterparts. The six-level 100-bed facility was built of reinforced concrete and was symmetrical, punctuated only by a main entrance at the center of the ground floor. From the exterior it could easily have been mistaken for an acute-care hospital (fig. 7.3). Its planning principles were characteristic of hospitals of the era: it had a support base below and patient tower above. The second level housed support services and verandahs. The plan of the four patient floors, however, differed a bit from the acute-care hospitals of the period in the creation of two clusters of rooms, each pair with a common dayroom at the center of the floor. The building was praised at the time for these clusters, which were described as providing a needed sense of individual and group identity.[15] Regardless, the guiding planning ideology of the facility had led to the creating of uninteresting, repetitive spaces.

The geriatrics building of Middletown State Hospital in Middletown, New York (1962–64), designed by Ketchum, Giná, and Sharp, used the structurally expressive vocabulary of Mies van der Rohe, as in the Rehabilitation Institute of Chicago (see Chapter 3). The geriatric facility at Middletown

housed 210 mentally ill, aged inpatients. It was a one-level building, absolute in its orthogonality, with flat roofs and wings situated to create a series of court-yards (fig. 7.4). The building contained four "dormitory" units in two H-shaped wings connected to a core, with patios adjacent to the patients' rooms. The dor-mitories were open in plan, not unlike an open Nightingale ward. The sleeping spaces were subdivided into clusters of six beds with floating partitions that did not reach the ceiling. The nurses' station was panoptical, situated for staff convenience and the maximum observation of patients. A communal wash-room and shower facility, three small bedrooms for the ill, and storage space for personal artifacts and clothing were in the crossbar support area connected to semi-open-plan wards. The rigid daily regimen of patient care was matched with the regimentation of the architecture.[16]

Not all architects were strict adherents to the standard postwar modernist zeitgeist. Some experiments attempted to break away from the work of Le Cor-busier and Mies van der Rohe. Alternate approaches received little serious attention, however. One manifestation of this countermovement, an inversion of the Miesian modernism of the period, was based in the geometry of natural forms. Cellular geometry, made popular by the writings and projects of Buck-minster Fuller, was adapted to health architecture with varying degrees of suc-cess. A nursing home and retirement housing complex in Spiez-Faulensee, Switzerland (1970–71), designed by Fritz Reist, was absolute in its symmetry and appropriation of cell-like honeycombed forms. The exterior had pitched roofs, with residentialist fenestration and exterior materials (fig. 7.5). The floor plan indicates a pattern of cell-like forms and the placement of residents' rooms around a central courtyard (fig. 7.6). The bedrooms were irregularly shaped,

7.3. Forbes Pavilion Nursing Home, Pittsburgh, 1967

7.4. Geriatrics Building, Middletown State Hospital, New York, 1964

7.5. Nursing home, Spiez-
Faulensee, Switzerland, 1971

7.6. Nursing home, Spiez-
Faulensee, plan

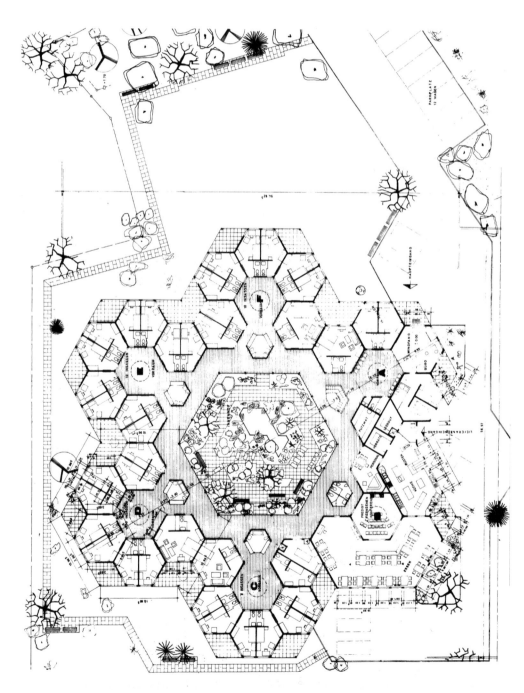

with diagonally sloping walls, and were clustered into pods, each with a nursing station.[17]

A second example of the reaction against modernism was a nursing home and retreat built at Wangen, Germany (1970–72), designed by Wilfried Beck-Erlang. This facility, built in a rural community, sprawled across its site in a far more informal manner than was common of the period. The buildings were connected via a network of covered walkways, and the arrangement of buildings is of interest for the variety of irregular shapes, the views the structures afforded, and the outdoor courtyards (fig. 7.7).[18] The site plan, as shown in a model, conveyed an intent to break from the status quo and thereby established a precedent in health architecture nearly equal to that of the neo-Nightingale low-rise hospitals built in England in the 1960s, such as the one at Slough (see Chapter 2). The irregularity of the site plan and the buildings themselves foreshadowed to some extent the randomness and organized chaos in the work of the deconstructionists two decades later.

7.7. Nursing home, Wangen, Germany, 1972

Utopian Visions for the Aged

By 1965 a few architects were beginning to attempt to extend high-style modernism in a futurist orientation. One project in particular stood out as a visionary scheme for the aged: William N. Breger's proposed building for the Research Institute for the Care of Prolonged Illness (1964) in Warsaw, Indiana, based on Mies van der Rohe's concept of universal space—that is, the principle of flexible volumes able to facilitate and anticipate indeterminate uses, unrestricted by fixed walls and other spatial delimiters, unadorned and abstract in appearance (fig. 7.8). It was a two-level scheme with offices, classrooms, and various support services on the first floor, and a column-free second floor with a Vierendeel frame (later to be referred to as an interstitial floor in hospitals) above to allow experimental, changeable floor plans in various skilled-nursing-unit configurations. The large open expanse was shown in three configurations: semi-open plan, single rooms, and a radial nursing unit. Yet, in light of the residentialist aesthetic in housing that had evolved in Scandinavia and on the U.S. West Coast in the postwar era, in all probability this building would have been a failure had it been built because of its adherence to the modernist machine aesthetic and its interior universal space that had been so fervently championed by Miesian proponents.[19] The project was begun as part of an expansion of the campus of the Murphy Medical Center but was halted for lack of funds during construction in the early 1970s. Subsequently, the partly completed building was demolished, as was the rest of the medical center. A replacement facility, the Koscuisko Community Hospital, was built nearby, but the research center for the aged was never rebuilt. In comparison to the numerous visionary acute-care-hospital proposals during this period, utopian visions of care for the aged were rarely put forth.

As for what actually *was* built, an excellent review of this period's architecture for the aged was presented in Noverre Musson and Helan Heusinkveld's *Buildings for the Elderly,* published in 1963.[20] This book captured the dual influences of the emerging residentialism, which in the United States was largely a West Coast phenomenon, and the austere institutionality of the hospital on mainstream nursing-home architecture. Dozens of "progressive" examples representing varying styles and planning approaches were included as case studies in the second half of the book. These included early examples of residentialism (Sessions Village, Columbus Ohio, 1926, by Miller and Reeves; the Actor's Fund of America Retirement Home, Englewood, New Jersey, 1961, by Moon and Iwatsu; and the Sequoias, discussed below), as well as examples clearly influenced by the International Style (Bayview Manor, Seattle, Washington, 1960, by John Graham and Company; Rockwood Manor, Spokane, Washington, 1960, by Culler, Gale, Martell, Norrie, and Davis; and the postwar West Coast modernist precedent set at Wesley Gardens, Des Moines, Washington, 1956, by William J. Bain and Harrison Overturf). The first half of the book presented an overview of prevailing trends in the United States, with a call for a "non-hospital" image and ambiance. Notably, throughout the book the term *congregate housing* was used instead of *nursing home,* a change in terminology indicative of the significantly less medically intensive nature of congregate housing care compared with the hospital-based model of care provided in the nursing home. A detailed demographic analysis of the elderly and a compendium of key site-planning and design guidelines were capped by a seminal essay titled "How Homes for the Aged May Be De-Institutionalized," by the

7.8. Research Institute for the Care of Prolonged Illness (proposal), Warsaw, Indiana, 1964

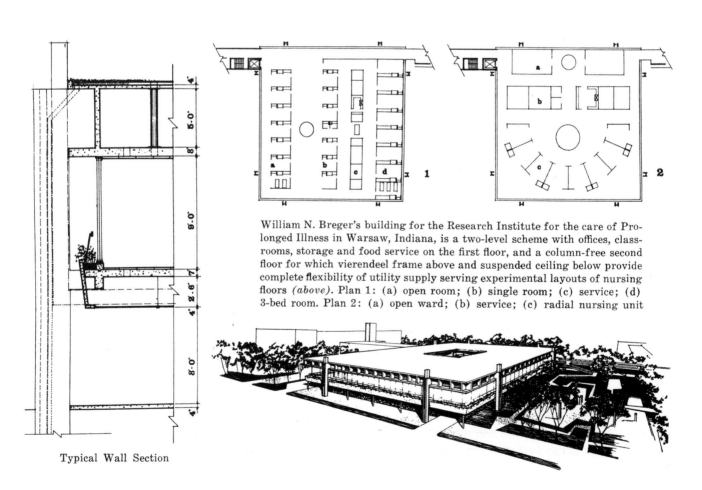

Typical Wall Section

William N. Breger's building for the Research Institute for the care of Prolonged Illness in Warsaw, Indiana, is a two-level scheme with offices, classrooms, storage and food service on the first floor, and a column-free second floor for which vierendeel frame above and suspended ceiling below provide complete flexibility of utility supply serving experimental layouts of nursing floors *(above)*. Plan 1: (a) open room; (b) single room; (c) service; (d) 3-bed room. Plan 2: (a) open ward; (b) service; (c) radial nursing unit

7.9. Capistrano-by-the-Sea nursing home, Dana Point, California, 1967

Swedish architect Bo Boustedt. This essay, and the entire book, constituted a landmark review of the buildings of the period and captured key tenets of Scandinavian residentialist architecture, which would much later influence the planning and design of facilities for the aged (and allied health building types) in other countries.

In the United States, the earliest innovations in postwar nursing homes or congregate housing were built in California. One such facility, Capistrano-by-the-Sea in Dana Point, California (1965–67), designed by Ramberg and Lowrey, was a residentialist resort and nursing home built on a dramatic oceanside site, with strong connections between interior and exterior spaces (fig. 7.9). The building was one level in height, and all rooms opened onto patios with panoramic views of the ocean. The plan was a cruciform with the nurses' station located to the side of a garden in the atrium (fig. 7.10). Three wings housed patients, and the fourth housed support functions and the main living room (fig. 7.11). According to a journal account at the time:

> Ocean, trees and rolling hills are everywhere visible—from the private patios, from the three solarium-terraces, from the large windows in the group living area at the ends of the three bedroom wing corridors. The corridors also feature skylights which create a light and airy effect; and the nurses station, main lounge, and dining areas are treated with exposed woods and stone to further the country atmosphere. Exterior building materials compliment the softness of the setting [with] the low-pitch gable roof. . . . The single rooms, complete with private water closet, storage and patio facilities, assure each patient the luxury of privacy. . . . The solarium terrace at the end of each wing is ideal.[21]

One of the earliest nursing homes to break away from the appearance of a hospital was the Sequoia Health Center's nursing home in Portola Valley, California (1965–67), designed by Rex Whitaker Allen and Associates and John S.

Bolles. It provided extended care services for an existing clinic as well as conventional nursing-home care as required in a 230-apartment community for the aged. The nursing facility had 30 bedrooms, most of them semi-private and each with a washroom; the rooms were situated around a racetrack circulation path. The plan was cruciform, with a centralized nurses' station at the center, and the adjacent buildings on the site were accessible via a covered walkway.[22] This facility was a precursor of the continuing care retirement community (CCRC) movement in the United States two decades later, and was one of the earliest prototypes for the "aging-in-place" model of later care.

Another prototype of the aging-in-place model was the Otterbein Home in Lebanon, Ohio (1972–74), designed by Samborn, Steketee, Otis, and Evans of Toledo. This facility was praised upon its opening as a unique place where residents could live at their highest possible level of independence. The campus consisted of housing for independent living, "residence halls" (an early version of the assisted-living concept) for the semi-independent, and skilled-nursing units for those requiring continuous skilled-nursing care. By mid-1974, 350 residents lived on site, and this figure represented only 8 percent of all applicants.

7.10. Capistrano-by-the-Sea, main social activity room

7.11. Capistrano-by-the-Sea, floor plan

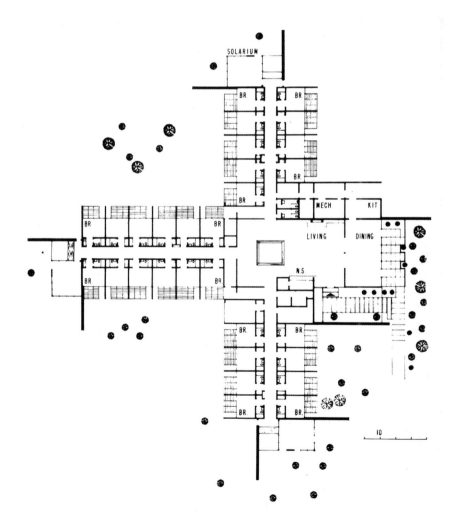

Otterbein had been established in 1913 on the site of a former Shaker village, and its campus included a number of the old Shaker buildings intermingled with newer structures. These new structures, on the cusp of the historic preservation movement in the United States as well as the emerging emphasis on contextualism in architecture in the 1970s, were consciously designed to blend in with the natural amenities of the 116-acre campus. A three-level skilled- and intermediate-care facility, boat-like in plan, was rationalized by the architects as maximizing the viewing angles of staff from the nurses' station into patients' rooms, as a means to avoid excessive circulation space, and as a device to make the building look less massive on the exterior. Various support functions were situated in an attached wing. The "village" portion of the campus, designed by Alvin C. Voorhis of Mason, Ohio, was a community of eighty-four ranch-style duplexes for independent living, which proved immensely popular. In 1974 the medical director observed: "When we first decided to combine housing and medical care we were told we shouldn't do it. We were advised to stay in housing or care but not both. Since then things have changed, and the attitude is now positive. Everything points to the fact that there will be more facilities of this type in the future."[23]

Otterbein borrowed certain features—room size, general layout, overall ambiance, and comfortable scale—from the Osmond Plan of the Weiss pavilion constructed four years earlier at the Philadelphia Geriatric Center, with some of these features reprised in the 1980s at the Corrinne Dolan Center in Ohio (see below). At this time most other providers of long-term care did not have the same awareness or appreciation of historic buildings on their campuses, nor were they cognizant of the deleterious consequences of indiscriminately adapting Le Corbusier's high-rise template to institutions for the aged. An example of such a template was the fourteen-level replacement nursing home built at the Isabella Geriatric Center in New York (1971–73), designed by Joseph Weiss. A seventeen-level apartment building was constructed next door. The apartment building, which had first been proposed in 1964, was also used for nursing-home care until the fourteen-level nursing facility was completed. By 1974, 772 residents were cared for on site in the new nursing home, which contained 315 skilled-nursing, 207 intermediate-care, and 132 residential-care beds (fig. 7.12). The passerby would find it difficult to discern whether it was a health facility or a public housing project, whereas in reality it was grounded in both precursors. The building was touted as a vertical city. Yet because of the scarcity of land, an ornate 1899 facility (fig. 7.13) had been demolished to clear a site for the new nursing home. During the planning stage, patients were asked about desirable interior amenities, color preferences, the design of washrooms, and so on. Notably, however, few were asked whether they wanted to live in a high rise or whether they wished to see the historic buildings on the site demolished.[24]

7.12. Isabella Geriatric Center, New York City, 1973

7.13. Original Isabella facility (1899), later demolished to make way for the 1973 replacement facility

The Critique

The contemporary nursing home evolved from a number of custodial-care building types, most of which were designed to serve the pauper. Most almshouses, orphanages, poor farms, and mental asylums constructed to house the aged operated through either private subsidies or state support, and until the late 1960s very few elderly in the United States lived in state-supported institutions.[25] Many resided in charitable, privately sponsored "old people's homes," forerunners of the hospital-like nursing home.[26] In 1930, however, more people over sixty-five had resided in mental hospitals than in the almshouses and private homes combined.[27] The gradual institutionalization of the privately operated old people's home began with the Social Security Act of 1935 and was fueled by later policy changes allowing for reimbursement for nursing care in institutions.[28] Although Social Security could not be used for almshouses, it could be used for private homes. The Hill-Burton Act of 1946 was a further catalyst for the proliferation of nursing homes.[29] Colleen Johnson and Leslie Grant stated:

> Up to World War II, few facilities serving the elderly population provided more than token nursing care; the elderly with health problems were treated in hospitals. Until late in the nineteenth century, hospitals functioned as a sanctuary for the chronic patients. . . . When hospitals became increasingly specialized treatment centers for acute illnesses . . . the needs of the chronic patients were incompatible. . . . They took up expensive beds, and the chronicity of their conditions was less interesting to treat. The long-term care institution, as it is known today, emerged in the 1960s. With the transfer of patients from acute care hospitals, many features of the medical model of care were also transferred. . . . The Hill-Burton Act provided federal aid to build nursing homes [and] imposed criteria derived from the medical acute care setting. Medicare and Medicaid legislation also favored higher standards of acute care, so it is not surprising that, to comply, these institutions took on many of the characteristics of hospitals.[30]

In 1967 Congress established the Intermediate Care Facility (ICF) as a distinct facility type in the hope of providing a less expensive alternative to skilled-nursing care. Soon thereafter, however, it was found that these facilities housed patients who were considerably sicker than those for whom the buildings were designed. Further fuel for the construction boom of the 1960s was the deinstitutionalization of elderly patients from mental hospitals. Private mental hospitals, and particularly large state-run asylums, claimed to lack space to address the needs of the aged, who as a consequence were often treated in awful "back wards" while the staff concentrated their efforts on younger patients. Because of newly instituted federal regulations mandating certain staff-patient ratios and minimum standards of care while at the same time increasing federal assistance and thereby greater access to the system, by 1970 the nursing-home population had increased significantly, to 72 percent of all institutionalized aged. Meanwhile, the population of aged patients remaining in mental institutions had declined precipitously, to 10 percent.[31]

The contemporary sociological critique of nursing homes as total institutions, a critique followed a few years later by a few architects' calls for reform, dates from sociologist Erving Goffman's essay "On the Characteristics of Total Institutions," in his seminal book *Asylums* (1961).[32] Another important book published around the same time was Jules Henry's study of three institutions for the aged, *Culture Against Man* (1963).[33] Goffman defined total institutions as places where all elements of daily life occur in a single place under a single authority. In a summary of Goffman's thesis, Lee H. Bowker wrote:

> An individual in a total institution does everything with a group of other institutional residents, all of whom are doing the same thing at the same time under a tight schedule imposed by some higher authority. All activities are rationally organized in the service of the institution's goals rather than the goals or needs of the residents. . . . Residents are induced through a complex organization of privileges and punishments to conform to the house rules. . . . They react to these pressures in four ways: 1. withdrawal from the situation, 2. adoption of an intransigent line, 3. colonization, and 4. conversion to the staff's world view. Staff-client relations in total institutions tend toward the caste model of social stratification, which implies considerable social distance between the two groups as well as reciprocal negative stereotypes.[34]

In *Culture Against Man,* Henry described the impact of "human obsolescence" at three nursing homes in the early 1960s: a publicly operated sanitarium and two private for-profit institutions with different degrees of funding. He described the public sanitarium as follows: "So they feel they're not human, and from this comes anguish that expresses itself in clinging. But silence is not the only form of dehumanizing communication to which these people are exposed. Empty walls, rows of beds close together, the dreariness of their fellow inmates, the bed pans, the odors, the routinization, all tell them they have become junk. Capping it all is the hostility of the patients to one another and the arbitrary movement from place to place like empty boxes in a storeroom. At the end is a degraded death."[35] In Rosemont, the poorly funded private institution, the elderly were nearly completely isolated, victims of indifference on the part of their relatives, the staff, and the government. The third facility, the Tower nursing home, served patients in the upper middle class and above. There, the facility was clean, odorless, and well staffed, and the physical—and, to a large extent, emotional—needs of the patients were clearly being met. Even in this setting, however, the patients became increasingly enfeebled from long bedridden periods.[36]

Henry's work indicated that although the best of these institutions met the physical needs of the patients, other aspects of the setting might have a debilitating effect, leading to a sense of disempowerment. In the end, the sense of failure felt by the patient was profoundly systemic and pervasive.[37] As early as 1967, critics were calling for a new type of nursing home. Rex Allen was among the few architects who argued for a less institutional alternative to the typical modernist nursing home and to the monotony of large, obsolescent, state-run institutions:

> The tragedy of nursing homes has been that too often they are nothing more than custodial facilities—places where society shucks off its responsibility and washes its collective hands of the nuisance of caring for the disabled, the infirm, the aged and the senile. Except that it may be closer to home, there is very little

difference in social function and philosophy between such a custodial nursing home and the mammoth state mental hospital—an institution which is fortunately ceasing to be an accepted solution to the care of the mentally ill. So too, it could be hoped, the nursing home will give way to a new type of facility, an "extended care" facility which has an active treatment program and may have a close affiliation with a center of medical care. Such a facility is less complex than an acute hospital but provides a program of care centered on the concept of rehabilitation, of restoring patients to vital roles in the community.[38]

Allen, then, rejected the total institutionality so forcefully described by Goffman and other sociologists, and he advocated a new model of care based on the positive abilities of each resident-patient, the creation of a sense of community, and direct access to medical care if and when needed.

The U.S. nursing home had been conceived of as a group home but had later been recast as a quasi-acute-care hospital as it had evolved into a medically based model of care. As this occurred, gerontologists began to argue that social and psychological aspects of care had been given low priority compared with strictly medical aspects of patient care, and that their lack of input often contributed to numerous missed opportunities for advancements in care. In response to this complaint, an integrative team approach emerged in the 1970s, premised on a continuum of care that ultimately would evolve into the widely popularized aging-in-place model.

The Nursing-Home Machine

Through the 1980s and 1990s, the nursing home continued to cling, though somewhat less tightly, to the core elements found in acute-care hospitals. Paradoxically, the public seemed to want the nursing home to continue to look as it did, perhaps as an expression of the strong belief in the power of advanced medical technology. The institution-based hospitalist model was the medically "correct" approach to providing health care to the aged. This view was generally reinforced by building codes and accreditation standards which assumed that the design of nursing homes was not to be questioned—if the modernist aesthetic was suitable for the acute-care hospital, then it was suitable for the aged as well. A photograph of a patient being escorted in the courtyard of a municipal nursing home designed by Frank Krayenbuhl in Witikon, an area of Zurich, Switzerland (1981–83), conveyed this incongruity: a monolithic, scaleless building dwarfed a less-than-fully-empowered patient in a wheelchair (fig. 7.14).[39]

More recently, nursing homes in Europe continued the modernist aesthetic vocabulary, yet the best of them achieved a stronger synthesis with human scale. The strongest examples fused the modernist tradition with low-rise construction and a direct relation between building massing and the creation of exterior usable spaces, which afforded more amenity than the block towers of the 1960s and 1970s. Yet in terms of outward appearance and internal planning principles, these facilities did not necessarily reference—that is, make use of—the residentialism of Scandinavia and its parallels that emerged in the healthcare milieu in the United States during this period (see Chapters 5 and

7.14. Nursing home, Zurich, Switzerland, 1983

6). Two buildings illustrate the continued perceived viability of high-style modernism combined with attributes of what by the 1980s had come to be known in the United States as an "assisted-living" facility. Assisted living is a model of care based on allowing the resident (not "patient") the maximum possible degree of functional, social, and day-to-day independence and autonomy in a setting that provides non-intrusive nursing and medical care only as needed. Meals, however, are provided in a central dining room in most facilities. One example of such institutions, the Bern-Wittigkofen Hospital in Bern, Switzerland (1988–89), designed by Atelier 5 of Bern, housed 120 patients in a combination of assisted living and long-term care for the chronically ill. The building, three levels in height, was configured as two wings connected by a central spine housing support functions, with a main level devoted to activities, dining, administrative areas, and recreational areas. A retention pond was created next to the building. Patient rooms were diagonal L-shaped semi-private spaces, half of which overlooked the adjacent pond (fig. 7.15). The nursing-care units were triangulated, as in some U.S. hospitals of the 1980s (fig. 7.16). The washrooms in the patient rooms were inboard, and the windows in the outer walls were operable and functioned as a buffer between the beds, which were situated at right angles to one another. The exterior skin, an inset concrete panel system, was reminiscent of the British school of high-tech architecture of Grimshaw and Partners and Norman Foster.[40]

Second, in a reprise of 1930s classic modernism, a nursing home and residential facility in Campdevanol, Girona, Italy, designed by Jose Luis Mateo and Jaume Avellaneda (1992–95), was strikingly austere, in sharp contrast with 1990s residentialist approaches. The building was set in a dramatic mountainous rural region, and its partí was bar-shaped. The building, appearing diagrammatic in plan, section, and elevation, was raised on pilotís in response to its irregular site, thus allowing light to enter the ground-level activity rooms. General technical support spaces were on the lower level, services for residents and visitors were on the first floor, and the top two levels housed private and semi-private rooms. A pair of outdoor shaded terraces functioned as dayrooms; these spaces relieved the repetitious interior corridors. The form of the building resembled a ship, in the spirit of Le Corbusier's buildings and writings six decades earlier. Patients were not provided with usable spaces on the flat roof. The palette of materials, primarily masonry block and glass, was minimal. The siting of the building, its shiplike presence as an abstraction against the dramatic landscape, its platonic relationship with the immediate site, and its stark materials, combined to render this an intriguing formal statement in the context of modern classicism, yet an uninviting place to live. Nevertheless, it was deemed worthy of praise in the European architectural press and is noteworthy for its revivalism.[41]

New Residentialism in Long-Term Care

By the early 1980s the modernist hospital-based nursing home had been rejected by a growing number of architects and long-term-care administrators as inappropriate and antithetical to the call for more homelike settings. Skilled-

7.15. Bern-Wittigkofen Hospital, Bern, Switzerland, 1989

7.16. Bern-Wittigkofen Hospital, plan of typical patient-care floor: (1) private (one-bed) room, (2) semi-private (two-bed) room, (3) semi-private (four-bed) suite, (4) observation room, (5) observation room, (6) staff support, (7) restroom, (8) staff support, (9) nurses' station, (10) kitchen, (11) conference/staff, (12) terrace (outdoor), (13) supplies, (14) restroom, (15) central supplies, (16) restroom

nursing facilities were seen as being in great demand in future years within the continuum-of-care and aging-in-place models. Administrators and architects searched for alternatives and were able to learn much from residentialist approaches in a period when pluralism in architecture was the norm for those seeking to break out of modern minimalism.

A landmark project in this vein, designed by Herman Hertzberger and built in Almere, in the Netherlands, was a highly humane yet aesthetically sophisticated effort to fuse modernist, residentialist, and social concerns. The

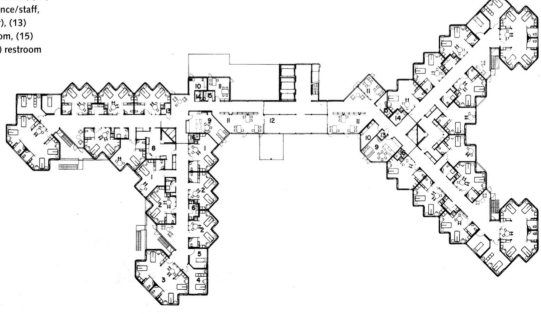

De Overloop at Almere-Haven (1980–84) contained assisted-living and congregate retirement housing for eighty-four individual units and eight double-occupancy units, twenty apartments for independent living, and twenty-one skilled-nursing beds housed in an infirmary.

In this building, Hertzberger appropriated the imagery of a ship beached at the edge of Almere, a new town for twenty-five thousand inhabitants built on reclaimed seabed (see also Chapter 8). Its architecture was significant in terms of its aesthetics, functional planning, and symbolic importance as a civic landmark: in its siting, in the building program, and in the remarkable degree of "give and take" in its formal language and partí. In terms of program and type, the building was vaguely analogous to a steamer or a monastery, and to the phalanstery that Le Corbusier had employed in his Venice City Hospital proposal, where life played itself out in individual cells and social communication was confined to the collective spaces. Hertzberger's steamer recalled the nautical imagery of the pioneering buildings of the modern movement:

> In the "new town" of Almere, Herman Hertzberger once again faces the theme of an old people's home, previously encountered in his exemplary project "De Drie Hoven" in Amsterdam (1964–1974). Although the building's [De Overloop's] internal organization is concentrated on the relations between the individual and collective spaces, its exemplary characteristic lies in the solution of a difficult site already occupied in part by a school and a garage . . . without giving way to formalistic temptations. If the functional issues continue to provide a central role for Hertzberger's design, the question of form cannot be reduced to mechanical deduction of commonplace functionalism. In this sense Team Ten's still relevant tradition [regarding Team Ten's work, see Chapter 3] is continued, by attempting to establish an ideal continuity with the architecture of the "founding fathers" of the Dutch Modern Movement like Duiker, Van der Vlugt or Brinkman, to whom this building makes homage through a subtle game of quotations.[42]

The building faced a dam at the water's edge and was constructed of reinforced concrete, with infill panes of concrete block, windows and bow-window frames in timber, with metal framing throughout (fig. 7.17). The floor plan shows the three main dwelling types: single rooms (in dark gray), small two-bedroom apartments (in medium gray), and semi-autonomous houses (not shaded) (fig. 7.18). The specifics of the three unit types (one-person, two-person, and expanded apartment for two or three people) indicated their various sizes (fig. 7.19). The shiplike upper levels dominated the exterior composition and imagery, and the lower portions in the exterior elevations were composed largely of the balconies and the large windows that overlooked the courtyards (fig. 7.20). The sense of spaciousness was carried throughout the interior circulation spaces (fig. 7.21). De Overloop at Almere-Haven was deliberately more "finished" than Hertzberger's earlier project De Drie Hoven, because there the residents had been challenged to complete the rough finishes of the building themselves. Although in retrospect this experiment seems to have worked, the building at Almere was much more subtle and refined and less manifesto-like in its assertiveness. In another review of the building, it was written:

7.17. De Overloop, Almere-
Haven, the Netherlands, 1984

The forms and function are completely apt to the new building. Here the curved forms shelter (for some perhaps curiously drawing attention to) an aspect of old age homes that is usually treated with circumspection, if not downright embarrassment. Old age homes inevitably have frequent deaths. Usually the bodies are spirited away to a basement and later carted out through a service yard almost like refuse. Hertzberger . . . rejected such a solution as undignified and quite unsatisfactory for those wishing to pay their last respects. So he has made proper provision for the coffin to rest in a place . . . where relatives and friends may meet. For fellow residents, too, to say good-bye properly is important. . . . While below the semicircular room is a lounge whose projecting eaves emphasize the panoramic views. . . . De Overloop realizes many notions of community. By various strategies it attempts to draw people out of themselves and to encourage spontaneous social interaction. . . . People feel at home and are also encouraged to colonize the building and make it their own. . . . De Overloop is not just a testament to Hertzberger's increasing maturity as a designer but also of the continuing and deepening humanity that has always fired his explorations and commitment to architecture.[43]

In a similar modernist-residentialist hybrid in Japan, a mixed-use building housing a *Kofuen* (Japanese for "nursing home") and elderly day service center, built in Kawasaki, Kanagawa Province, Japan (1985–87), represented an alternative approach in aesthetic and functional terms. Designed by Yuzuru Tominaga and Form System Institute, this circular building (fig. 7.22) was set in a dense urban fabric rich with neighborhood stores, including an open-air food market. It was located on an irregularly shaped industrial site formerly used as an ironworks foundry. The new three-level building was dominated by a courtyard and a continuous spiral ramp useful for circulation and as a balcony, with

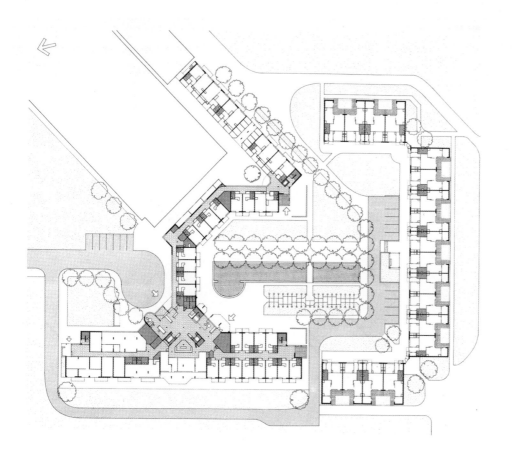

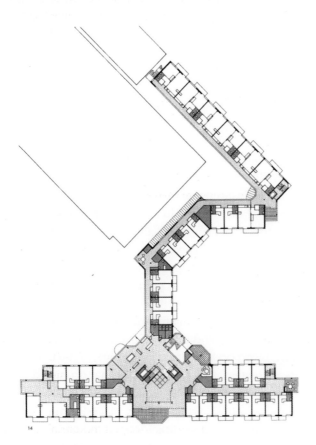

7.18. De Overloop, plans:
(*top*) ground floor; (*bottom*)
second floor

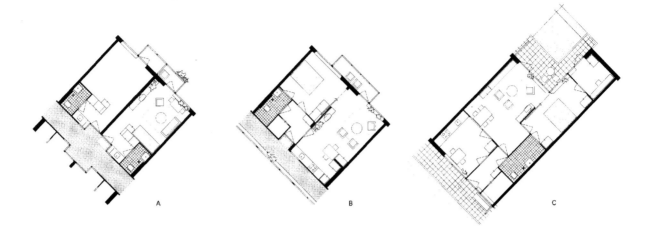

A   B   C

7.19. De Overloop, unit plan types: (*A*) single-person unit; (*B*) two-person unit; (*C*) expanded apartment

entrances situated at intervals along the ramp. The courtyard, used for social activities and contact with the outdoors, served as the focal point, with all spaces literally revolving around its threaded spiral circulation core (fig. 7.23).

On the interior, the first level housed the day service center; the second and third levels housed a nursing home with a total capacity of sixty beds. The day service center was open to all elderly residents of the neighborhood, not only residents of the facility. It included a bathing service, accommodation for short-time non-overnight stays, and a home healthcare program. The inpatient resident rooms on the upper levels opened onto the courtyard, and the exterior perimeter windows afforded views of the working-class neighborhood and the surrounding city. The fan-shaped rooms were configured to provide each patient with at least some privacy and personal space, and with a larger window area than would exist in a conventional square-shaped bedroom (figs. 7.24 and 7.25). Bathrooms were inboard, with the nurses' station situated near the stairs. In his account of the design, the architect likened this feature to the petals of a flower arrayed around its center. This building represented a conscious attempt on his part to avoid both an overtly institutional look and a literally homelike one: "I think that the shape of a public building should be impressive from the city's viewpoint as well as show its function. I hope that this building arouses the interest of the neighbors . . . a cylindrically shaped building. A simple and strong structure was required in a site full of miscellaneous, featureless things. Rarely is a nursing home built in the center of a city; so I intended to make it conform to the active environment instead of hiding it as an isolated, lonely place."[44]

This building contributed to the renewal of its inner urban neighborhood, reaffirmed the importance and place of its elderly residents within their long-time community, incorporated nature in the form of its courtyard, and afforded a pleasant internal-external spatial sequence that promoted a sense of human scale and informal social contact. This and related examples of specialized long-term-care facilities emerged as alternatives that addressed both the needs of a particular type of patient and shifting ideology in care philosophies and architecture. Inpatients as well as outpatients could be cared for depending on community needs and available funding, and the mission of the special-care facility

7.20. De Overloop, balconies facing semi-courtyard

7.21. De Overloop, view of corridor

7.22. Kofuen and Day Service
Center, Kawasaki, Japan, 1987

7.23. Kofuen and Day Service
Center, ramp in courtyard

now was to provide a more patient-centered level of care tailored to the unique nature of each patient's condition. In this regard the special-care facility was now an integral element in the emerging models of care. Note, however, that the term *special-care facility* is defined broadly here to include any freestanding, long-term care program that in the past would have been provided within an acute-care geriatric hospital setting. Thus this repositioning of services away from the nursing home represented its functional deconstruction, parallel to that of the acute-care hospital, which was taking place at the same time. As such, efforts to deinstitutionalize persons not needing costly, continuous nursing care gave rise to new care settings. One such setting was an intriguing synthesis of a geriatric hospital, outpatient community clinic, and country estate retreat. Another was a blend of a twentieth-century architectural master's style with residentialist sensibilities. Both these examples of antihospitalist and antinursing-home settings will be explored in more detail.

In Great Britain, the National Health Service had commissioned the construction of many geriatric hospitals in the years following the end of World War II, and these later acted as lightning rods for the attacks of critics. One facility in particular, the Lambeth Community Care Centre in Lambeth, England (1981–85), though not a nursing home by strict definition, stood apart as a particularly innovative continuum-of-care setting (fig. 7.26). This facility, designed by Edward Cullinan Architects of London, was both a community inpatient-care center for geriatric medicine, devoting twenty inpatient beds to this purpose, and an outpatient elderly day program for rehabilitation, providing space for thirty-five patients.

Historically, the term *community hospital* had been used in the Oxford region to describe a local hospital in a rural area, and many smaller "cottage

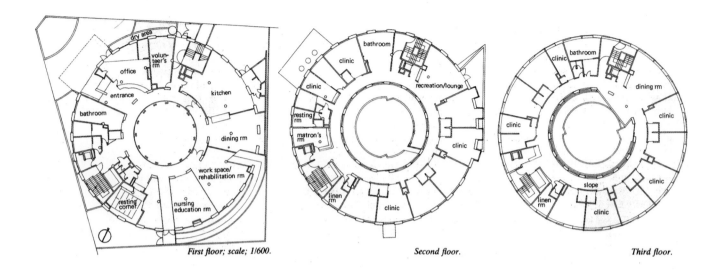

First floor; scale; 1/600.   *Second floor.*   *Third floor.*

hospitals" had been constructed during the late nineteenth century to provide a combination of medical care, daily activities of living, support services such as laundry and food service, and elements of what is now generally known as assisted living. Although these had proved popular with patients, most were closed when the network of government-sponsored district general hospitals, which included geriatric hospitals, were built. The cottage hospitals were considered too inefficient because of their small scale and their obsolete, unsophisticated level of technical support.[45] By contrast, the Lambeth Centre was regarded as perhaps the best "neo-cottage hospital" special-care facility, intended to be an economic alternative to the high-tech district general hospital, in this case St. Thomas's. Also, just as Slough General Hospital had revived old ideas (such as Nightingale planning principles and a horizontal composition on the grounds) in a new package (see Chapter 2), at Lambeth a twenty-bed ward with double-occupancy rooms was situated on a second floor above an outpatient treatment program. In a sectional drawing of the facility the residentialist scale of the spaces and varied ceiling heights were apparent (fig. 7.27), and the floor plans indicated a continuum of space from interior to exterior (fig. 7.28). The facility provided a modicum of post-acute care for longer-term stays than would have been warranted in the hospital in the present era of cost containment, combined with respite care for the aged and a terminal-care program. Inpatients were housed either in one of the four four-bed rooms or in one of the four private rooms (fig. 7.29). The program also included a home care hospice program as well as occupational and physical therapy, chiropody (chiropractic), and dentistry services.

The facility had been conceived in response to the public outcry against the closing of a nearby obsolescent geriatric hospital. The architects had worked closely with representatives of the Community Health Council to create a patient-centered building, and the remarkable degree of collaboration achieved between architect and building users has been well documented in the literature. The building has been praised for its shattering of the myth that user

7.24. Kofuen and Day Service Center, floor plans

7.25. Kofuen and Day Service Center, semi-private residence

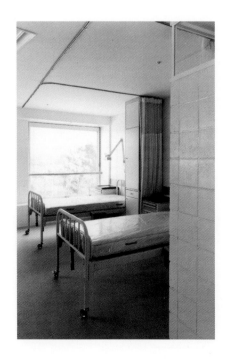

7.26. Lambeth Community Care
Centre, England, 1985

7.27. Lambeth Community Care
Centre, drawing

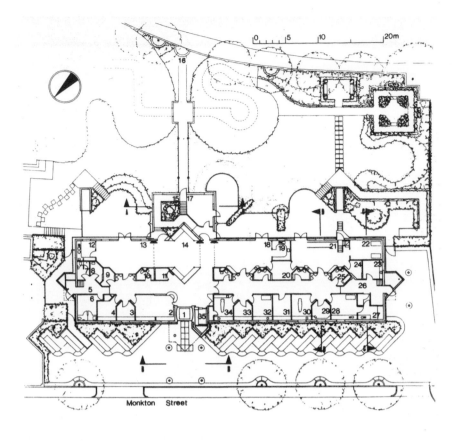

Monkton Street

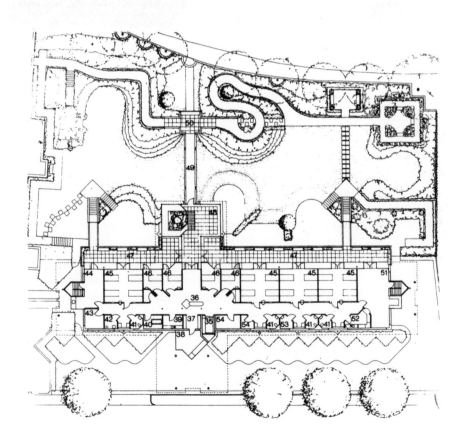

7.28. Lambeth Community Care Centre, plans: (*top*) first floor; (*bottom*) second floor. *Key:* (1) draft lobby, (2) reception, records, and general administration, (3) community link worker, (4) administrator and evaluator, (5) staff lobby and stairs to staff room, (6) female changing room, (7) male changing room, (8) cleaner's storage, (9) storage for wheelchairs and frames, (10) client's restroom, (11) cloakroom, (12) servery and preparation of drinks, (13) dining room, (14) sitting room, (15) lower conservatory, (16) back gate to Gilbert Road, (17) seminar room, (18) occupational therapy, (19) assessment kitchen, (20) assessment bedroom, (21) physiotherapy, (22) passive physiotherapy, (23) workshop, (24) physiotherapy storage, (25) bathroom, (26) delivery and disposal lobby and staff stairs to sitting room, (27) dirty utility and laundry, (28) clean utility and treatment room, (29) hairdresser, (30) chiropodist, (31) staff office, (32) speech therapy (33) social worker, (34) dentist, (35) elevator, (36) nurses' station, (37) clean utility, (38) sister's office, (39) dirty utility, (40) bathroom, (41) client's restroom, (42) cleaner's room, (43) boiler room, (44) staff room, (45) four-bed ward, (46) single-bed room, (47) upper terrace, (48) upper conservatory and sun room, (49) bridge, (50) belvedere, (51) sitting and dining room, (52) servery, (53) shower, (54) storage.

7.29. Lambeth Community Care
Centre, typical patient room

involvement in design must invariably lead to buildings of low aesthetic quality or ones that are otherwise removed from the formalist vanguard. It incorporated the appearance and feel of a large country house, with its terraces, abundant daylight, courtyards, residential imagery, and such small-scale details as window seats. Fluorescent lighting was eschewed, and the ambiance of tempered institutional residentialism symbolized a thorough rejection of the total institutionality of its nearby acute-care hospital, St. Thomas's.[46]

The second example of the new directions taken in the design of antihospitalist long-term-care settings was a landmark special-care facility for the treatment of Alzheimer's disease victims built in the United States in the late 1980s. The Corrinne Dolan Alzheimer Center at Heather Hill (1987–89), designed by Taliesin Associated Architects, was constructed on the grounds of a 150-acre nursing home and health facility located in Chardon, Ohio. In 1987 the Dolan Family Foundation, one of the most extensive research programs in the world on the origins and treatment of Alzheimer's disease, awarded Heather Hill a $2.5 million grant to design and build an experimental inpatient-care research prototype. Opened in 1989, the center housed a twenty-four-bed residential program for persons in the early and middle stages of the disease (fig. 7.30). Although not a licensed nursing home per se, the Dolan Center was adjacent to the Heather Hill health facilities, which included a skilled-nursing facility on site.[47]

The exterior emphasized the horizontality found in the Prairie school of architecture promulgated in the writings and work of Frank Lloyd Wright, and his followers such as Dwight Perkins, in the early to mid-twentieth century (fig. 7.31). The plan of the patient floor was a modified triangle with truncated cor-

ners at the two most distant ends. The center housed support services and an irregularly shaped "interior street" angled to cue patients to subtle spatial and sensory variations along the interior hallways (fig. 7.32). The residential character of the nursing unit was enhanced by residentialist design features and finish materials (fig. 7.33). The idea of sloping the corridors inward in plan was not new, however, as it had been incorporated elsewhere in Ohio, specifically in the Otterbein Home nursing facility of the early 1970s. An account of the project related:

> In developing the design, Heather Hill turned to Taliesin Associated Architects of Scottsdale, Arizona, with whom they had previously worked to develop a master plan. Heather Hill president Robert Harr had become familiar with Frank Lloyd Wright's legacy at Taliesin on a visit to the Southwest in the 1970s and felt that his organic approach to architecture, emulated by the Taliesin architects, was appropriate to the Dolan project. Taliesin architect Steve Nemtin worked closely with the Heather Hill research team. . . . The [goal] is to find ways in which the environment might mediate some of the disorientation associated with the disease by providing various sensory cues. . . . The low, sprawling Dolan center has a contemporary, somewhat southwestern feel in contrast with the traditional or colonial imagery usually associated with old-age facilities. As might be expected, one sees everywhere the unmistakable influence, if not the genius, of Wright's imagery and design approach. Wrightian touches include low ceilings and light coves at the building entry, low overhanging eaves, and the curvilinear motif of the fenestration. The references to Wright can become a bit reverential and obsessive. Nevertheless, they do tend to create an environment that is unique in every aspect and not likely to confuse the

7.30. Corrine Dolan Alzheimer Center at Heather Hill, Chardon, Ohio, 1989

7.31. Corrine Dolan Center, exterior view

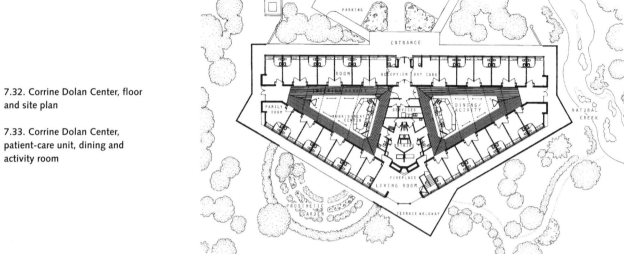
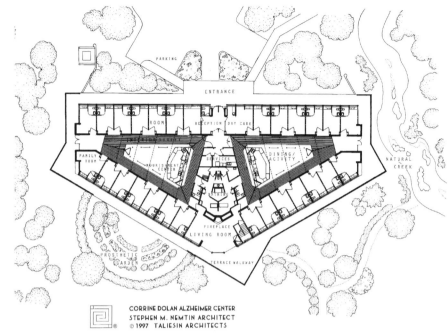

CORRINE DOLAN ALZHEIMER CENTER
STEPHEN M. NEMTIN ARCHITECT
© 1997 TALIESIN ARCHITECTS

7.32. Corrine Dolan Center, floor
and site plan

7.33. Corrine Dolan Center,
patient-care unit, dining and
activity room

patients. . . . The materials are, by and large, natural and simple: wood and brick with rounded or chamfered corners. The exterior is finished in adobe-colored stucco. Warm earth tones throughout help to create a relaxed and comfortable setting that feels more like a resort or lodge than a healthcare facility.[48]

Residents were allowed a great deal of independence, and such devices as a glass-enclosed display case for personal artifacts were intended to trigger cognitive recollections. This facility has been the subject of widespread publications in the long-term-care literature, and since its opening in 1989 had received more than two hundred visitors from Japan alone by the end of 1992. The central activity space has not been replicated widely, as it was found to lack flexibility in terms of programmatic use by staff and residents. Nevertheless, patients, staff, and families considered the facility a success in bridging the distance between home and institution in an architecturally non-threatening manner. The Dolan Family Foundation soon began planning two additional centers based on the success of the Dolan Center.

The Continuing Care Retirement Community Movement

The continuing care retirement community (CCRC) movement of the 1980s and 1990s in the United States was rooted in religious organizations' initiation of the concept of self-insurance in order to provide a stable financial foundation for the provision of care to its aged and disabled members. In many cases, individuals had willed their entire estates to the church in return for the guarantee of continuous care in their remaining years of life. By the late 1980s there were approximately seven hundred "sanctioned" CCRCs in forty states with an average of about three hundred residents each.[49] The basic concept provided a full spectrum of on-site care in accord with need, from independent living to skilled-nursing care. In the 1970s and 1980s, CCRCs generally had guaranteed total access to long-term care for the duration of the resident's lifetime, but by the 1990s fewer facilities offered such extensive or unlimited coverage at the time of entry.[50] Instead, the trend became one of offering refundable entry fees and in effect becoming more rental-oriented. This occurred as a result of changes in the federal tax structure, regulatory agencies' increasingly complex task of monitoring nursing homes, and the general aging of the population. By 1989 the American people were spending an estimated $42 billion for care for the elderly at home and in nursing homes. Of this amount, 82 percent ($34 billion) went for nursing homes, with nearly 57 percent ($24 billion) paid directly to providers by residents or their families.[51] As of the mid-1990s no clear, comprehensive financing policy for long-term care was yet in place even though by this time four distinct architectural CCRC types had emerged: the pastoral "campus" type, the denser "suburban" type, the "new urbanist" village type, and the "urban high-rise" type of aging-in-place retirement community.

Precursors to the contemporary CCRC in the United States were traceable to the British system of almshouses, some of which were still in use as sheltered housing for the aged as recently as the mid-1980s. Walpole Court (1982–86), a part-new, part-old community in the village of Puddletown in Dorset, England,

7.34. Walpole Court,
Puddletown, Dorset, England,
1986

7.35. Pomperaug Woods,
Southbury, Connecticut, 1990,
aerial view

carried this deeply rooted tradition forward through a site plan centered around a large courtyard (a main feature of the most enduring almshouses in history) flanked by rowhouse residences (fig. 7.34). Designed by Sidell Gibson Partnership, Walpole Court was developed in two phases. Phase 1 involved the conversion of existing stables and cottages dating from the mid-nineteenth century. Phase 2, completed a year later, consisted of new courtyard housing echoing the scale and architectural imagery of the adapted historic buildings. Walpole Court therefore was a combination of a derived and a designed community. The cottages and apartments were made available to residents via long-term leases. The local village was within walking distance, each unit had its own garage, and many had private patios. Each dwelling had a first level for use by the resident and an upper-level ancillary living quarters available for use by a relative or live-in nurse when needed. Although the facility did not include the most intensive level of skilled-nursing care, a full-service nursing home was located nearby in the village.[52]

An American counterpart to the British model typified in Walpole Court, the Quadrangle, in Haverford, Pennsylvania (1987–89), was designed by Wallace Roberts Todd of Philadelphia and was one of the first ventures undertaken by the life-care division of Marriott Corporation. The architects had adopted a somewhat similar plan developed a decade earlier by a local Quaker group, which

called for a commons building and campanile to be situated at the center of a campus. The 309 apartments were connected to the commons area via an enclosed walkway, and thirty-six assisted-living units were similarly linked to a forty-three-bed skilled-nursing facility. The walkways, however, were counter to the Quaker philosophy, which called for maximum contact of the individual with the exterior natural environment. The campus plan recalled that of the nearby Haverford College, and the plan of the skilled-nursing building and the attached commons was curious insofar as it symbolized a somewhat unusual juxtaposition of these functions. As at Walpole Court, the residential units had two bedrooms, but at the Quadrangle the two-bedroom units were entirely on one level.[53]

A variation of the courtyard campus of the Quadrangle was employed at Pomperaug Woods in Southbury, Connecticut (1988–90), designed by Engelbrecht and Griffin Architects. Unfortunately, its absolute symmetry recalled the totalitarianism of the immense state-operated panopticon institutions of the seventeenth and eighteenth centuries, with the large center court functioning as the symbolic center—the control point—of this CCRC campus (fig. 7.35).[54]

A notable example of the second of the four basic CCRC architectural types, the suburban community, was the White Horse Village in Edgmont Township, Pennsylvania (1987–90), designed by Bower Lewis Thrower/Architects of Philadelphia. This community packed its eighty-four-acre site with a mid-rise medical building that housed 57 skilled-nursing beds and 40 assisted-care units, a one-level commons building attached to T-shaped apartment clusters housing a total of 102 two-bedroom, one-bedroom, and studio units, and four clusters of garden apartments with 80 one-bedroom units. This overall plan was denser than most and more formal in its arrangement of units, to the point where an aerial view revealed the simplistic diagram of the continuum of care, with the most independent residents at one end and the most dependent on the other (fig. 7.36). Many of the apartment "villas" had attached carports (fig. 7.37). The overall effect was of a caricaturized suburban neighborhood.[55]

The third architectural type, the new urbanist retirement village, was expressed in the small-town planning concepts evident in Crab Creek, a combi-

7.36. White Horse Village, Edgmont Township, Pennsylvania, 1990 (in construction)

7.37. White Horse Village, villa units with attached carports

nation CCRC and active adult community near Annapolis, Maryland (1989–95), designed and planned by Cochran, Stephenson, and Donkervoet of Baltimore. The town plan reflected the increasing density of these communities, along with the CCRC's newfound source of inspiration: the classic American small town of the early twentieth century as reinterpreted through such successful upscale new towns as Seaside, Florida. At Crab Creek, the adult community was on one side of a winding street and the CCRC was on the other side. The two domains were envisioned as separate but equal elements on the 110-acre site, and residents of both shared the town center where a beauty parlor, doctor's offices, a post office, and so on, were treated as storefronts along a main square with apartments above. The health center, with its 120 skilled-nursing beds, was set apart in a configuration reflective of prevailing marketing realities: active residents needed the reassuring presence of the nursing home, but they did not want to be reminded of its perceived negative connotations each day. One difficulty encountered by the developers was the archaic zoning restrictions, which precluded the type of dense, mixed-use community envisioned for Crab Creek. Typically, in the new urbanist developments of the 1980s and 1990s the developer had to submit a master plan and "internal zoning" criteria to local zoning officials for approval, requiring, often, a set of zoning variances prerequisite to the start of construction. This would prove to be a sporadic yet persistent challenge across the United States, particularly in the case of postwar suburban communities, whose residents did not always favor the introduction of a CCRC for fear of depreciation of local property values, traffic congestion, and the persistently negative image of the modern nursing home. Often, the community would reject a proposed development largely on the basis of the "not in my backyard," or NIMBY, syndrome.[56]

The fourth type, the urban high-rise CCRC, was evident in the partí of the Marriott Jefferson in Arlington, Virginia (1990–92), also designed by Cochran, Stephenson, and Donkervoet and located on a dense 1.5-acre site between two new office buildings. The Jefferson stacked 325 one- and two-bedroom apartments above 57 assisted-living units and 31 skilled-nursing units, together with the usual congregate facilities, above three levels of underground parking (fig. 7.38). The symmetrical plan (fig. 7.39) included a large atrium on the first and second floors, and the building looked like an upscale hotel. Eventually, projects such as the Virginia Marriott would fuel a debate in the 1990s between the merits of high-rise (and other highly centralized) CCRCs and low-rise campus-type decentralized CCRCs. By this time, the first *American Association of Homes for the Aging* statistics on this subject had been released, suggesting that highly centralized high-rise CCRCs were more conducive to the notion of aging in place than the traditional decentralized campus where residents were typically moved at least once yet remained on the same site. The centralized urban high-rise type, however, confronted administrators and architects with health and safety concerns ranging from whether the apartment elevators should bypass nursing floors to residents' virtual absence of routine contact with fresh air and the natural environment. The centralized CCRC facility was seen by its critics as little more than a modified high-rise nursing home in new garb—that is, stepped levels of care in an institutional setting.[57]

Many CCRCs in the United States, particularly the urban high rises, were labeled by critics as little more than havens for the affluent elderly, because of their high buy-in fees. This and related critiques were aimed at the large developers of office buildings and the major hotel chains that had entered the industry in the 1990s. In the 1970s the typical CCRC was a rural campus; by the late 1990s, denser, more urban or suburban sites were seen as more marketable and more desirable because the inhabitants could remain closer to their children and their children's families. Also, because the initial investment in land and infrastructure costs for a horizontally master-planned CCRC was increasingly

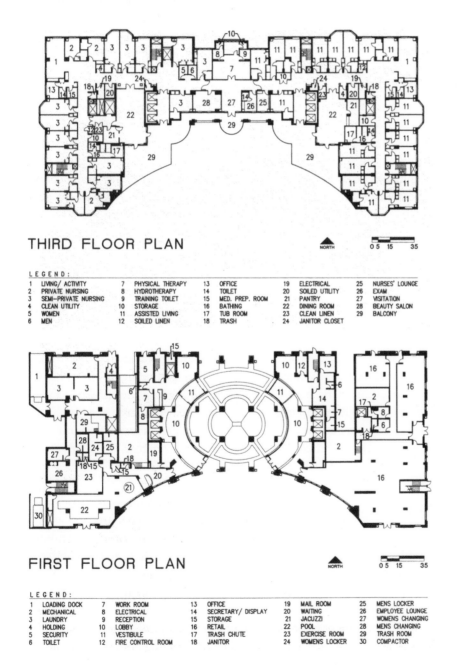

THIRD FLOOR PLAN

NORTH 0 5 15 35

7.38. The Marriott Jefferson, Arlington, Virginia, 1992

7.39. The Marriott Jefferson, floor plans

LEGEND:

1	LIVING/ ACTIVITY	7	PHYSICAL THERAPY	13	OFFICE	19	ELECTRICAL	25	NURSES' LOUNGE
2	PRIVATE NURSING	8	HYDROTHERAPY	14	TOILET	20	SOILED UTILITY	26	EXAM
3	SEMI-PRIVATE NURSING	9	TRAINING TOILET	15	MED. PREP. ROOM	21	PANTRY	27	VISITATION
4	CLEAN UTILITY	10	STORAGE	16	BATHING	22	DINING ROOM	28	BEAUTY SALON
5	WOMEN	11	ASSISTED LIVING	17	TUB ROOM	23	CLEAN LINEN	29	BALCONY
6	MEN	12	SOILED LINEN	18	TRASH	24	JANITOR CLOSET		

FIRST FLOOR PLAN

NORTH 0 5 15 35

LEGEND:

1	LOADING DOCK	7	WORK ROOM	13	OFFICE	19	MAIL ROOM	25	MENS LOCKER
2	MECHANICAL	8	ELECTRICAL	14	SECRETARY/ DISPLAY	20	WAITING	26	EMPLOYEE LOUNGE
3	LAUNDRY	9	RECEPTION	15	STORAGE	21	JACUZZI	27	WOMENS CHANGING
4	HOLDING	10	LOBBY	16	RETAIL	22	POOL	28	MENS CHANGING
5	SECURITY	11	VESTIBULE	17	TRASH CHUTE	23	EXERCISE ROOM	29	TRASH ROOM
6	TOILET	12	FIRE CONTROL ROOM	18	JANITOR	24	WOMENS LOCKER	30	COMPACTOR

high, larger up-front buy-in fees became necessary. As often became the norm, Quadrangle and Crab Creek had targeted upscale alumni and former faculty from an array of nearby colleges, whereas their urban counterparts, now calling themselves "assisted-living communities," touted their constituents' ties to their longtime neighbors. In 1989 it was first reported that CCRC residents lived about 20 percent longer than the elderly population at large, and the lifestyle and services they experienced had by that time become the accepted standard by which all forms of health care and housing for the elderly were typically judged. Yet only about 2 percent of the elderly lived in CCRCs at that time. It had become clear to critics and caregivers alike that the perception of the tranquil, picturesque retirement community in a natural setting was at odds with the reality of the places where most retirees resided. This reality was promulgated by the for-profit private developers because the "ideal" was attainable only for a small segment of the market.[58]

In addition, by 1990 the CCRC movement had become the victim of its own success in the form of rising start-up costs, rising buy-in costs, the CCRC's failure to be all things to all people, and the appearance of more cost-effective competitors in the accelerating assisted-living milieu. The first three factors were also inhibiting the development of new towns in the United States, despite strong evidence of the benefits of multigenerationality and planned communities: "The stumbling block that has prevented the real revival of small towns in suburban America likewise lurks in life care. Contemporary codes rarely permit the complex mix of functions that is the very essence of small town life. . . . Thus regulations conspire to keep the elderly isolated, in spite of substantial research that urges the opposite. And yet the notion of integrating life care communities into their communities continues to win advocates. . . . Here, beyond both health care and hospitality, lies the leading edge of life care."[59] Certainly, CCRCs and their offspring, the assisted-living community, had evolved into complex institutions. They had become a hybrid of long-term-care insurer, restaurant, apartment complex, social service agency, health spa, real estate entity, health maintenance organization, primary care clinic, home care program, and nursing home. Naive providers did not comprehend the depth of these complexities, and many would fall into bankruptcy at a time when the early enthusiasm garnered by the CCRC movement was cooling significantly. A cheaper, more cost-effective alternative was emerging, with broad appeal among the aged and their families.[60]

The Assisted-Living Movement

The CCRC movement's initial strength had been its pluralism—the mixture of multiple care and building types in a single, multifaceted campus entity. One of its components, the assisted-living unit, had functioned successfully as a midpoint between on-site congregate apartment housing and the on-site skilled-nursing facility in many CCRCs. From the standpoint of building codes and zoning, however, the hybrid nature of the typical full-service CCRC had been the source of confusion for years. Partly as a result of such confusion, the assisted-living unit emerged, albeit slowly and without fanfare, as an autonomous entity, or outgrowth, within the larger framework of the CCRC. Yet in the 1980s providers did not place much emphasis on assisted living as a stand-alone model of care because it was not considered nearly as profitable as skilled-nursing care. Thus most early assisted-living units were located as elements within CCRC campuses. Soon, however, more and more providers realized the potential of developing freestanding assisted-living facilities in older suburban and urban neighborhoods, just as freestanding nursing homes had been established apart from acute-care hospitals years before. But, to complicate matters, during the 1980s the definition of "assisted living" itself was evolving. Because of demographic shifts, new economic realities, and shifts in the health status of patients, with more residents living longer and thus becoming sicker than before, the assisted-living unit assumed a new prominence in the 1990s. For purposes of clarification, Victor Regnier, an architect cross-trained in gerontology and a leading proponent of this type of care, defined assisted living as a "long term care alternative which involves the delivery of professionally managed personal and health care services in a group setting that is residential in character and appearance in ways that optimize the physical and psychological independence of residents."[61]

The freestanding assisted-living facility was neither an invention of the CCRC nor a particularly heavily promoted component of it. In fact, the assisted-living facility was an offshoot of other building types, including board and care facilities and personal-care facilities. This background accounted for its residential, antihospitalist appearance. Yet the assisted-living unit was held in close check by stringent code requirements when any part of the complex was directly connected either to a skilled-nursing unit or to congregate housing or independent-living apartments. Gradually, assisted living emerged as a less costly community-based alternative to nursing-home care. But providers, often acting in their own interest, traditionally connected the skilled-nursing unit to all other components. By providing slightly larger rooms and carpeting, they were able to call any part of their facility a skilled-nursing unit when the demographics changed. This practice, however, proved to be a disservice to residents on the assisted-living unit, who required less intensive care. Only when a assisted-living facility was freestanding did the vagueness and, often, the absence of codes allow it to take on a residential character and scale.

One of the first architecturally notable examples of what would eventually be referred to as an assisted-living facility was the Annie Maxim House in Rochester, Massachusetts (1983–85), designed by KJA Architects of Cambridge, Massachusetts. This project consisted of twelve one-bedroom apartments, each with entry porch, eat-in kitchen, courtyard, library, living room, dining area, and laundry (fig. 7.40). The exterior resembled a large country manor or nineteenth-century resort spa (fig. 7.41). This facility was difficult to categorize at the time of its opening because of its innovativeness: was this hybrid fundamentally a health facility or apartments? In fact it was both. The same firm had previously designed the Captain Eldridge Congregate House in Hyannis, Massachusetts (1979–81), which combined new construction with adaptive use in an innovative manner considered a seminal precedent, and which was featured on the cover of *Progressive Architecture* (August 1980). Captain Eldridge also influ-

7.40. Annie Maxim House, Rochester, Massachusetts, 1985

7.41. Annie Maxim House, exterior

7.42. Annie Maxim House, main social activity room

enced the design of Elder-Homestead in Minneapolis, which was built soon thereafter.[62]

Located at the edge of a large wooded site next to a pond, the Annie Maxim House was vigorously symmetrical, with the common spaces at the center and units arrayed along the two adjoining wings (figs. 7.42 and 7.43). A large wrap-around porch connected all units to an elliptical central courtyard. The forms were dominated by a large roof articulated with a skylight and gables. Interior common spaces as well as semi-private individual alcoves that adjoined these units were available for residents' use. The connecting porch was the main

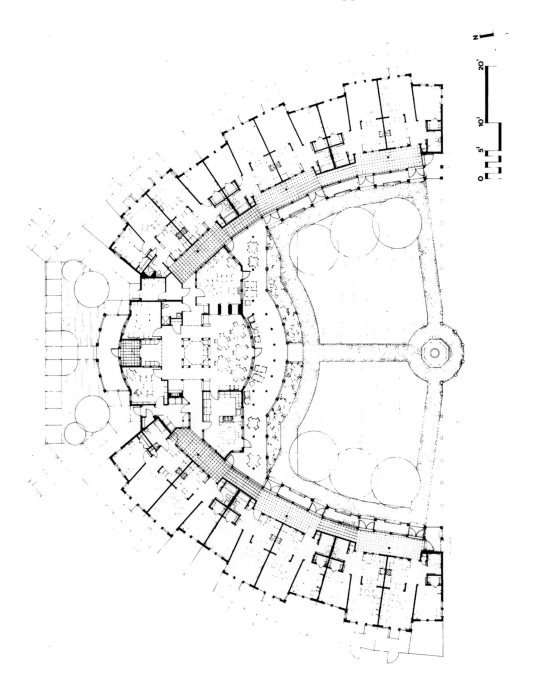

7.44. Woodside Place, Oakmont, Pennsylvania, 1991

7.45. Woodside Place, combined floor plan and site plan

circulation path. Rooms were equipped with pull cords, residents had access to nursing care on an on-call basis, and the design itself was found to promote a sense of community among residents and staff. It was built for independent and semi-independent elderly persons. Technically, however, it should be emphasized that at the time neither the Annie Maxim House nor Captain Eldridge was considered an assisted-living facility in the strictest sense. Instead, Annie Maxim was described as follows: "KJA's Annie Maxim House is not anti-institutional; but it is noninstitutional, drawing upon a vocabulary that is readily

7.46. Woodside Place, aerial view

7.47. Woodside Place, axonometric view of typical room

associated with country inns and restaurants. . . . [It] is a complete unit, both architecturally and socially."[63]

The paradigmatic shift to the new residentialism of Captain Eldridge House and Annie Maxim House was pushed and defined much further in Woodside Place, built in Oakmont, Pennsylvania (1989–91), designed by David Hoglund with Perkins Geddis Eastman, Architects and Planners, New York. This assisted-living facility was created for thirty-six mentally frail persons. Features similar to those at the Maxim House, such as covered porches and pronounced roof gables, were incorporated (fig. 7.44). The residential units were configured in three wings, which projected out from a support core (fig. 7.45). The units provided a hierarchy of spaces, with "redundant" cueing devices—multisensory information such as a flashing light in consort with an audio instruction for emergency exit routes in the event of fire, or the use of distinct colors as well as shapes for the entry doors of each unit—to provide spatial and cognitive orientation to residents (figs. 7.46 and 7.47). The facility received national recognition for its non-institutionality: "The design concept involves the use of three small 'houses,' of twelve residents each, linked to one another and to common services through an enclosed wandering pathway. Thus the intimacy of a small group is achieved, while economics of scale are sufficient enough to support a self contained kitchen and a variety of common spaces. . . . Designed to look like a Shaker commune from the outside, the juxtaposition of outdoor areas for view . . . with an interior that accommodates wandering and informal socializing are among the project's most compelling features."[64]

Woodside Place was also innovative because a participatory design process was used, with the state licensing agency as an integral part of the design review team. This arrangement made it possible to test new interpretations of the codes and regulations a priori in a collaborative manner. A post-occupancy evaluation conducted some years later indicated the following: the staffing ratios on the twelve-bed units had to be increased beyond initial expectations; 80 percent of all rooms had been converted to private rooms; the setting was deemed attractive and functional by its occupants; common kitchen areas had been adapted

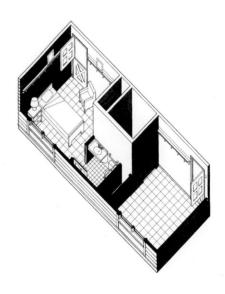

to staff conference areas; residents tended to use their own personal kitchens instead of the communal kitchen; the allotment of six hundred square feet per resident was deemed too generous from a cost-management standpoint, and therefore density was recommended to be somewhat increased in future efforts elsewhere; the views of the courtyards were as popular as those out onto parking and arrival areas; most residents spent much time in main entry and arrival areas; and additional fine-tuning by the management had been necessary to maximize the functional as well as aesthetic amenity of the facility and its site environs.[65] While Captain Eldridge and the Annie Maxim facilities captured attention in the architectural press, Woodside Place, along with the Dolan Center, were regarded by most research-based design specialists in the field of environment and aging as the two most seminal facilities built in the 1980s. Yet similar facilities had been built years earlier in Europe.

A new wave of assisted-living facilities soon appeared across the United States. The St. Clement Health Center in St. Louis, Missouri (1987–89), designed by the Pearce Corporation of St. Louis, was primarily an assisted-living facility but also accommodated residents in need of more intensive nursing care. The facility exerted a striking presence, with its deep red brick and vertical windows. Although it housed only thirty beds, its plan consisted of three wings radiating from a core containing the central nurses' station and a chapel. The repetitive residential units were individualized by varied window patterns. St. Clement was significant for its assertive, nonresidentialist architectural vocabulary, largely the result of its location on the campus of a monastery. This architectural approach was widely replicated.[66]

In a larger sense, the search for an appropriate vocabulary for assisted-living facilities was something of a struggle for architects. In its rejection of the nursing home's institutionality, the countertrend resulted too often in a "soft-focus" or "homey" brand of residentialism, stemming, at best, from the goal of creating homelike buildings or, at worst, from a profit-fueled compulsion to capitulate to the level of nondescript speculative architecture. In many cases, such as St. Catherine's Village in Madison, Mississippi (1986–88), designed by Cooke, Douglass, and Farr Architects, the net result was caricature, in this case of an entire village.[67] Critics labeled this design approach superficial or, condescendingly, "warm and fuzzy," something quite apart from the ideals of critical regionalism or from thoughtful postmodernist approaches to the creation of a sense of place and symbolism in architecture. Too often, the final product lacked substance. The ultimate effect was a watered-down regional vernacular, and such overtly "user friendly" design approaches ran the risk of being interpreted as condescension or even arrogance on the part of the provider, if not the architect. This was especially the case in situations where both the providers and the designers assumed that the aged consumer would reject more challenging design approaches.

At St. Catherine's and similar places, the dilemma was determining aesthetic appropriateness. By contrast, when the architectural vocabulary was locally based, the possibilities of critical regionalism could be more successfully mined. Such was the case with Heritage House in Kankakee, Illinois (1993–95), designed by O'Donnell Wicklund Pigozzi and Peterson Architects of Chicago,

HERITAGE HOUSE   OVP&P · ARCHITECTS

Illinois. As at the Corrine Dolan Center in Ohio, the Prairie School of Frank Lloyd Wright and his followers was a strong influence on the exterior of this twenty-six-unit freestanding assisted-living residence (fig. 7.48). The building was set on a flat, open, windswept site. The Prairie School style, characterized by sweeping horizontality punctuated with vertical flourishes, natural materials (notably face brick), and masonry ornamentation, was carried throughout the interior (fig. 7.49). The public and social areas were at the center, including reception, living and dining areas, and an "interior street" widened and paved with decorative tile. Within this street, activity and support rooms were placed at even intervals (fig. 7.50a). The arrangement of the residential units was characteristic of the cluster concept endemic to nursing-unit design in this period. The kitchen and living area, which had bay windows with curtains, were nearest the interior street. The bedrooms were at the outer perimeter, adjacent to a patio shared with the neighboring residence (fig. 7.50b).

The National Association of Assisted Living, based in Washington, D.C., experienced a tenfold increase in its membership between 1990 and 1994. Ninety percent of this increase was due to the proliferation of investor-owned providers. These providers were of two types. First, large corporations, including such national hotel chains as Marriott, entered the market in the late 1980s. In 1996, Marriott asserted that this market was going to be a major focus of its operations for the next five to ten years because demand far exceeded supply. Its typical approach was to construct multiple facilities within a market, such as the northern Atlanta suburbs. This technique enabled multiple sites to be regionally managed and coordinated and to share resources, thus maximizing efficiency.

Second, some states allowed virtually anyone to open an assisted-living residence; in a few states, the facility could hold as few as six residents.[68] This trend captured a key segment of the market. Meanwhile, the CCRC struggled to capture the endpoints as well as the mid-ranges of the continuum of care for the aging. By the mid-1990s, the concept of aging in place had arrived at a crossroads: should the facility be flexible in its design in order to avoid relocation and possible post-relocation trauma on the part of the resident, or should multiple "types" of living units be provided on the same site? As a result, the

7.48. Heritage House, Kankakee, Illinois, 1995

7.49. Heritage House, Meadowview Lodge

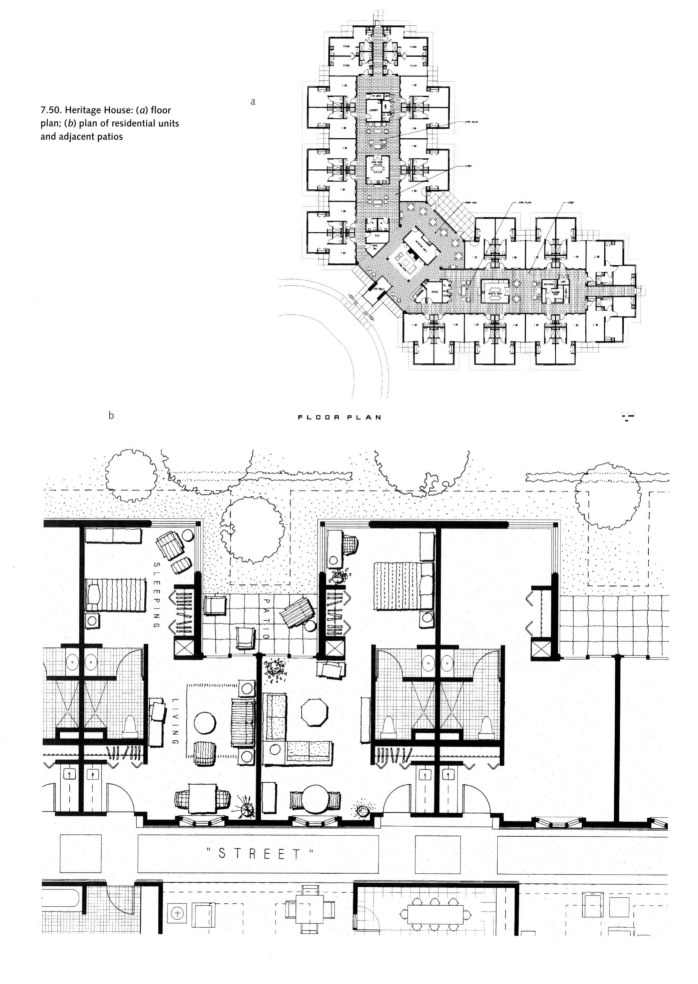

7.50. Heritage House: (*a*) floor plan; (*b*) plan of residential units and adjacent patios

a

b

FLOOR PLAN

SLEEPING

PATIO

LIVING

"STREET"

most progressive assisted-living centers, particularly among freestanding CCRC and assisted-living facilities, were those in which the living unit and central activity areas were adaptable to a changing, reduced level of physical and cognitive ability on the part of the resident. This flexibility responded to the reality that the typical resident would stay only three to four years and would experience reduced physical and cognitive abilities. Regardless, few bona fide assisted-living facilities would allow themselves to be overtly marketed as analogous to a nursing home, whether or not their facility was consciously designed for this type of "step-up" care.[69]

The American Association of Homes and Services for the Aging, working with architects and developers in the private sector, actively promoted the expansion of the CCRC and assisted-living movements in the 1990s. These efforts included a program begun in 1994 through a subsidiary of the AAHSA, Collaborative Innovations, to develop turnkey facilities throughout the United States. This program was established by a group of experts in geriatrics and long-term care who had admired the best CCRCs for their comprehensiveness of care and their high level of resident satisfaction. By the late 1990s, however, critics were calling for tighter accreditation and licensing standards and more comprehensive federal reimbursement policies to at once more generously fund and establish controls over this rapidly growing and changing domain of the health landscape.[70]

Landmark Research in Environment and Aging

The research literature on housing and healthcare settings for the elderly is, by comparison to the other domains of the health landscape addressed in this book, vast, including articles in architectural journals, awards programs and summary reviews, healthcare administration literature, and published research in such refereed journals as the *Gerontologist*. Environment and aging research emerged around 1970 in response to the total institutionality, as defined by Goffman and others, of the nursing home of the 1950s and 1960s. Early studies of the deleterious effects of forced relocation stand as a milestone.[71] These studies were followed by efforts of gerontologists to develop theories of environment and aging, with perhaps the most widely disseminated theory having been developed by M. Powell Lawton and colleagues at the Philadelphia Geriatric Center.[72] The work by Leon Pastalan on the empathic model represented one of the first efforts to sensitize designers to the particular limitations and difficulties encountered by the sensory impaired and physically frail elderly person.[73] Later research on wayfinding by Gerald Wiesman, Lorraine Hiatt, and others led to the call for buildings for the aged that would be more legible and interesting from the standpoint of visual variation, layout, colors, scale, and imagery.[74] Thomas Byerts was, in the mid-1970s, a leading proponent of the field of environment and aging research, having established the Environment and Aging Section within the Gerontological Society of America. His efforts brought focus to the area and resulted in at least six books and research monographs. Additionally, the work of Sandra Howell, particularly her book *Designing for Aging*, won awards and stimulated an entire generation of architectural students. Sociologist John Zeisel and colleagues published a book on low-rise housing for the aged, and were the main influence on the design of the Captain Eldridge facility and numerous assisted-living-care settings since. Victor Regnier and Jon Pynoos's edited volume on housing for the aged assembled the work of twenty researchers in the field. Wiesman's work with Uriel Cohen on the design of special-care units for Alzheimer's patients extended this earlier research into the long-term-care setting in a useful format for both providers and architects.[75]

Starting even earlier, Rudolph Moos and colleagues had developed environmental assessment scales to measure the relative institutionality of a long-term-care facility along a series of empirically prevalidated rating scales.[76] With respect to assisted living, Regnier had made a significant contribution by undertaking surveys of providers and case studies in the United States and in Europe, using a method similar to that used by Goldberger in the late 1970s.[77] Beyond this, interior designers with an appreciation of environment and aging research, notably Jain Malkin, endeavored in the 1990s to bring environment and aging research into a broader interior design and architectural mainstream.[78]

Such design innovations as the room-to-room (or, in this case, room-to-corridor) window in the Musquodoboit Valley Home for Special Care in Halifax, Nova Scotia (1989–91), were influenced by research that called for the deinstitutionalization of the corridor. Designed by William Nycum Architects, Ltd., of Halifax, Musquodoboit Valley had a residential ambiance on the interior (fig. 7.51), as opposed to the traditional austere, hospital-like nursing-home corridor.[79] Earlier, however, Zeisel had been instrumental in incorporating this feature in nursing-home design, and in Europe, Herman Hertzberger had introduced the concept even earlier.

Typically, architectural firms, if they did any research at all, hired consultant specialists in design and aging or conducted their own limited work in house. In the design of the Joseph L. Morse Geriatric Center in West Palm Beach, Florida (1989–91), Perkins, Geddis, and Eastman Architects, New York, rejected the traditional semi-private room after a series of consultations with residents and staff. Instead, they adopted a semi-private room with individual privacy zones for each patient.[80]

Research has been conducted on the role of nature in the long-term-care experience, and many providers responded by incorporating gardens and wandering paths for patients and residents. Some of these have received widespread attention, such as the garden at the Mountain Trace Nursing Center in Sylva, North Carolina.[81] The gardens at the Motion Picture Country House, near Los Angeles, created two "ecologies" via two independent wandering paths. Claire Cooper Narcus and Marni Barnes conducted a series of case studies of the uses and therapeutic benefits of gardens in healthcare settings, although most examples were of acute-care medical centers.[82]

Meanwhile, formalist architects proposed schemes for housing the aged. In 1991, prototypes for a "round room" and a "rectangular room" in a long-term-care unit were developed by French architect Jean Marc Gauthier. In the round room, a semi-circular movable screen mediated the space between the bed area and an adjacent alcove or living room off the corridor. Gauthier's rec-

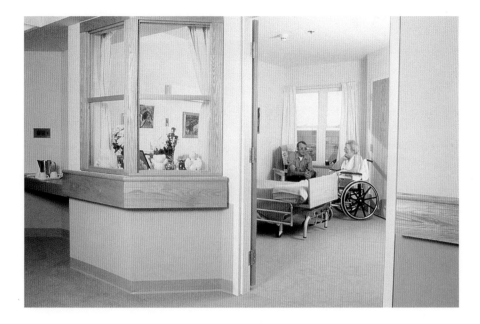

7.51. Musquodoboit Valley
Home for Special Care, Halifax,
Nova Scotia, Canada, 1989–91,
typical room-to-corridor window

tangular room employed a similar, though linear, intermediary space adjacent
to the bed area, with a slit window to the hall. This approach was limited, however, because it was indicative of a reductive, deterministic attitude in design.
Such proposals reflected a simplistic, overly formal conception of the behavioral and spiritual dimensions of the aging experience.[83]

Other visionary efforts included the ambitious, speculative Synergenial
Healthcare Community proposals for a CCRC (1990–91) by Earl. S. Swensson and
Associates of Nashville, Tennessee. This proposal called for a completely self-contained "city" for the aged, with elaborate internal infrastructural support systems.
The overall impression conveyed by the color rendering was of a futuristic village, with inhabitants moving blissfully about.[84] The impact of this and other
architectural visions for the elderly in the new century remains to be seen.

The Search for a Viable Aesthetic Language: International
Residentialism

In the boom years of nursing-home construction in the 1960s and 1970s, little
thought was given to historic preservation or the adaptive use of older buildings. By the 1980s, however, healthcare providers realized the possibilities of
restoring and adapting old buildings for new functions. One example was the
conversion of an old convent, located in McKee's Rocks, Pennsylvania, into the
Xavier Residential Care Facility (1984–86), a twenty-four-bed licensed personal-
care facility. Convents were chosen for conversion into long-term-care facilities
by the provider, Schneider Health Services, because of their natural tie-ins to
the existing parish. Parishioners tended to strongly support the rebirth of what
was, to them, an extremely important civic building. In this instance, a close
working relationship with local code officials ensured that such hand-crafted
features as the ornate main door and entrance could remain intact.[85]

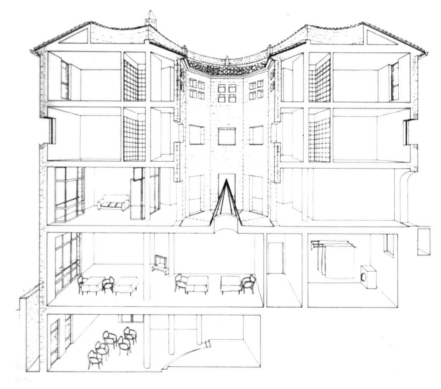

7.52. Casa di Accoglienza
Anziani a Montecchio, Terni,
Italy, 1987

7.53. Casa di Accoglienza
Anziani a Montecchio, sectional
perspective

In other situations, a new building was inserted into a historic context. In the case of the Casa di Accoglienza Anziani a Montecchio, in Terni, Italy (1986–88), an assisted-living twenty-four-hour care facility was constructed in the center of an old city on a hillside site (fig. 7.52). This building, designed by Clara Garcia La Fuente and Mariolina Monge, was five floors in height with three floors above grade. The spaces were arrayed around a central octagonal courtyard, with the two lower floors functioning as a base set into the site (fig. 7.53). Adjacent to the new building was an old agricultural shed converted into the chapel. The administrative, dining, social activity, and staff support functions were housed in the base, and the roof was terraced for residents' recreational use. The architect provided the following account:

The living rooms, subdivided into the traditionally medium-sized spaces familiar to the local people, face onto the pathway round the octagonal courtyard-fulcrum. . . . The wall of the central living room is in fact glazed, to provide visual transparencies between interior and exterior. As soon as you enter the building you can see the courtyard and catch a glimpse, through the central living room, of the valley below. . . . On the top two floors the corridor ring is smaller and develops to form a St. Andrew's cross with four stretches leading to the rooms, while the pillars, with the waste outlet pipes built into them, are incorporated in the perimeter walls of the bathrooms. Every floor has ten rooms, each with two beds and bath. The roof plays on the geometric elements of the ground plan, a small pitch covering the corridor ring and leaving the central inner courtyard open, while the ring terrace with vista is built into the pavilion roof. . . . The perimeter walls and those of the octagonal courtyard are in unfaced stone called "sponga." The blocks cut in this calcareous stone, much loved by Ridolfi and similar to travertine in color and consistency but porous like corral, measure 30 × 24 × 8 cm. . . . The shutters are set [deep] into the walls so as not to superimpose the stone facade when opened. A special inlet, in the form of a glass cone resting on the center of the courtyard, sends a shaft of light down to the dining room below; whilst the basement receives light from the air space.[86]

This assisted-living facility, having been derived from a historic context, was in the contextual vein of postmodernism. A contrasting yet equally invigorated, thoughtful approach was expressed in the Mount Pleasant Lane Nursing Home (1982–84), designed by Anthony Richardson and Partners, London (fig. 7.54). This project was described as follows: "Anthony Richardson & Partners have responded to an inner city site surrounded by a nondescript estate of middle rise flats by providing a clear contrast. The use of exterior materials, when viewed in the general context of the site and its environs, certainly has the effect of giving a lift to the area and has become a landmark to the local community. Residents also like the fact that it does not look like 'an old people's home,' but rather 'a posh hotel.'"[87]

Finland, like France and other industrialized countries, was confronted in the 1990s with the need to house a population living longer than ever before. Finnish health architecture had stemmed from the seminal influence of Alvar Aalto and his followers, dating from his humanist sanitarium hospital project, the Paimio Sanatorium in Paimio, Finland (1929–33), and from the broader Scandinavian tradition of deinstitutional facilities that characterized a sizable portion of its health architecture in succeeding decades. A sheltered housing complex in Kiuruvesi, Finland (1990–92), designed by NVØ, embodied numerous residentialist characteristics, inviting comparison with the many late-modernist projects for the aged that were being built in France. The complex made full use of the facility's "privileged site," on the edge of a lake, and its floor plan was simple and well articulated (figs. 7.55 and 7.56). To avoid flooding, the center was located on the highest portion of the site, and the lakeside was treated as "natural parkland." Clusters of four two-person units were linked together by a spine connected with central administrative and related support services. The further clustering of approximately fifty living units into bands, or wings,

7.54. Mount Pleasant Lane
Nursing Home, London,
1982–84

enabled the creation of a village scale, with the central support and circulation spine running its length. The overall architecture was unconventional, while making use of variety and surprise. Treatment of the residential units was deliberately neutral in order to leave room for residents' self-expression. The facility was composed of concrete, metal, and treated exposed plywood (fig. 7.57). Its architectural language refused to fall into a reprise of the past or into nondescript suburbanism.[88]

A fifth example of residentialism, and the only one of the five built in the United States, was the iconoclastic Colton Palms retirement village in Colton, California (1990–92), designed by Joseph Valerio and Associates of Chicago. The client, Co-Operative Services, of Oak Park, Michigan, called for housing and associated social, recreational, administrative, and ancillary nursing and personal-care support functions in a hundred-unit facility. This program defied classification in relation to widely accepted definitions of long-term-care building types. It was part independent-living facility and part congregate housing, resulting in a mixed-use, intergenerational community (fig. 7.58). The units were designed to accommodate a live-in nurse or aide. The kitchen and bathrooms in all units included a pull cord monitored by a twenty-four-hour nursing service off site. The complex's deconstructed elements—unusual tilted roofs and wall planes, columns, jutting balconies, diagonals, juxtaposition, and unex-

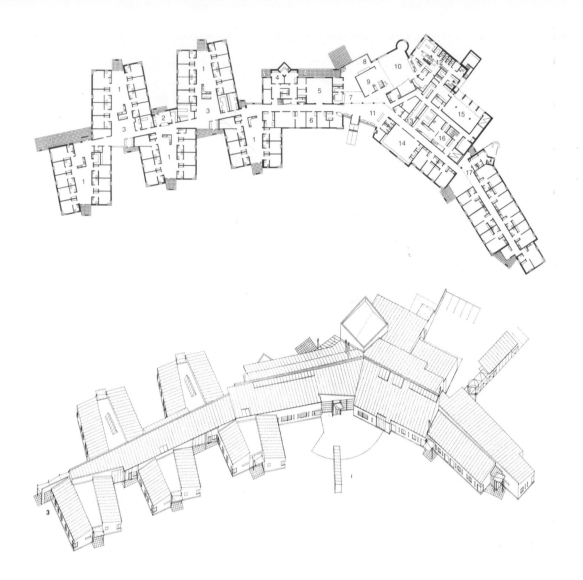

7.55. Sheltered housing for the aged, Kiuruvesi, Finland, 1992, floor plan

7.56. Sheltered housing for the aged, axonometric view

7.57. Sheltered housing for the aged, exterior view depicting unusual palette of materials

pected accent colors—were at odds with the status quo (figs. 7.59 and 7.60). Its architectural vocabulary was aesthetically provocative, albeit well grounded in the daily needs of its users:

> The site is at the center of the City of Colton—Hub of industry: a town that is on the edge of Los Angeles. Single family homes seemingly inspired by Irving Gill or, in other cases, by the Greene brothers dominate the area. The fabric and scale of the city is recalled by the [Palms'] structures and objects. . . . The premiated design was chosen from 137 entries in a national competition. The overall organization is based on a nine square; each is a three story cluster of ten to twelve apartments, with the center square removed for the green. . . . At many places on the site, the pattern of apartment clusters makes room for landmark "public" buildings—meeting hall, library, crafts pavilion and the entry buildings. . . . Each object "spins" off from its origins. . . . Purposely lost are any specific meanings of a [traditional] architectural language, purposely embraced are the ambiguities of modern times—encouraging individual and unpredictable interpretations of the architecture.[89]

7.58. Colton Palms Apartments, California, 1992, axonometric view

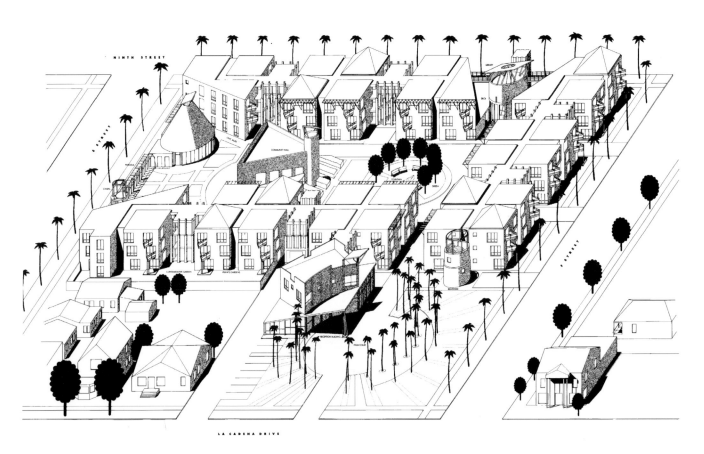

7.59. Colton Palms, exterior
view of courtyard

7.60. Colton Palms, partial floor
plans

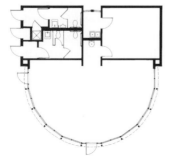

All five of these examples broke with the status quo, each in response to site-specific sociocultural conditions, their programs, their administrations, and the ideological predilections of their architects. Although the only common ingredient among them was their break with the commonplace, the claim might be made that they all reflected, in general, "high-style" values and as such were bound to be rejected by their users in light of populist "soft-architecture" predilections. But this assumption was not necessarily borne out by evidence.

On the modern nursing home's expansionist years, Joseph Koncelik stated in 1976:

> In the late 1950s and through to the mid-1960s, for about a decade, there was an incredible push to construct. . . . The determination to build superseded the knowledge of what to build. Ollie Randall, the noted gerontologist, said it best when she reflected a few years ago, "We built in ignorance, but we had to build." Unfortunately, this country is left with the legacy of mistakes and ignorance in brick and mortar—difficult to live with but equally difficult to find the motivation to change. . . . The sad truth is the boom in institutional building took place without a coherent body of knowledge having been assembled . . . within the framework of the human factors of aging. . . . It is not feasible to demolish what has been built and not possible to turn back the clock. There will not be the great boom of the 1950s and 1960s, but there will be steady new development and a great deal of refurbishing and conversion.[90]

Koncelik was inaccurate in his prognostication with respect to the level of construction activity for care settings for the elderly but accurate in asserting that the rush to build tended to surpass adequate knowledge of *what to build*. Fortunately, in comparison to other domains of the health landscape, a wealth of information was available by the mid-1990s that was applicable to the spectrum of health building types for the aged. Unfortunately, too few providers and their architects availed themselves of this knowledge. The late-century wave of building activity resulted, more often than not, in the homogenization of this segment of the healthcare industry. Many providers were eager to build blindly in the rush to attain market share. In the worst cases, architecture pandered to the lowest common denominator, at times resulting in high-rise warehouses for the aged, such as the Asbury Home in Gaithersburg, Maryland (1988–91), designed by CHK Architects and Planners of Silver Spring, Maryland (fig. 7.61). Such designs represented little more than a reprise of the high-rise public assistance housing schemes in the United States in the 1950s and 1960s, many of which were being demolished by the late 1990s.

All in all, it remained to be seen whether more sophisticated architectural ideologies would be accepted by the better-educated baby boomer generation in the United States as they reached their own retirement age in the twenty-first century. Roslyn Lindheim, writing in 1975 on the need for humane, human-scaled environments for the elderly, concluded: "The key problems in building environments for the elderly in the future are learning how to plan our lives so that there is an opportunity for intergenerational living and dying,

and for work opportunities, play and recreation interspersed—so that access, supervision, and interdependence become a way of life. If we are serious about looking toward future-oriented design for the 1990s and beyond, we can't settle for finding out how to design better concentration camps for the elderly."[91]

This chapter has attempted to make some sense of an expansive body of built and written work in the realm of aging and the architectural environment in the years since the advent of Medicaid and Medicare. The demographic trends indicating the aging of society-at-large have become an indisputable reality. And high-quality research in this realm of health architecture undoubtedly outweighs that in any other realm within the health landscape. Yet, in the end, the extensive body of empirical information in this domain has received only minimal use, given its potential impact on the huge volume of construction in health architecture and housing alternatives for the aged that has taken place and is anticipated to continue in the new millennium.

In the time of Pliny the Younger, the elderly were revered and esteemed for their insight, experience, and wisdom. This attitude has much to offer the generations of the twenty-first century. The possibilities now exist for a well-grounded ideology of care for the aged, expressed as a hybrid of the strongest attributes of modernism and the strongest attributes of postmodernism. Such a synthesis, which might be appropriately termed "international residentialism," would be premised on an architectural language based in the present space and time, as opposed to condescending revivalist approaches. This aesthetic language, however, must be thoroughly grounded in humanism in order to be fully successful. Architectural mistakes in providing care settings for the aged are not predestined for repetition, for they can occur only as the result of ignorance, haste, fear, greed, or sheer indifference.

7.61. Asbury Home,
Gaithersburg, Maryland, 1991

CHAPTER 8

The Community Care Clinic

Two periods have dominated the architecture of the contemporary community health clinic in the United States. The first is defined by the Hill-Burton years, from 1947 to 1983, and the second by the managed-care movement from 1983 onward, whereby the proliferation of the community-based outpatient clinic coincided with the functional deconstruction of the acute-care hospital, as discussed in Chapter 5. In the years between 1947 and 1983, federal funds were available on a fairly consistent basis to construct community-based health centers and clinics. Much of this money flowed to the states through the Hill-Burton program. Funds were available for public as well as private not-for-profit institutions and state health agencies. Hundreds of community health clinics were built across the United States, with many still in operation at this writing, though essentially obsolete. The first federal healthcare cost-containment legislation, in the early 1980s, signaled the end of the Hill-Burton era and a surge of construction of ambulatory care centers in medical centers and in freestanding settings. With reimbursement limitations resulting from diagnosis-related groups or population management incentives arising from managed care, providers were motivated to redistribute, decentralize, and overhaul the delivery of outpatient care. A new ethos of "wellness" and preventive care had great impact.

By the 1980s, particularly in the United States, architects and allied designers found themselves attempting to determine how new care-delivery and payment systems would affect the design of hospitals, outpatient clinics, and other health facilities.[1] Administrators, for their part, were going through the same process, in a period when turnover of executives was high. Small hospitals were faced with the choice of downsizing even further, merging, or closing.[2] As a result, coordinated healthcare networks began to dominate the health landscape, using their size, capital resources, and sophisticated, pooled management expertise to provide a full spectrum of services at multiple yet coordinated access points. During this time, annual capital construction expenditures increased steadily: existing hospitals needed to upgrade their aging facilities, and cost-containment legislation gave rise to a new period of growth in satellite outpatient health centers. This restructuring of the healthcare industry led to new urban-suburban-rural interorganizational linkages of hospitals with multiple satellites, resulting in a minor construction boom in the United States. In 1989 Jeff Goldsmith adroitly noted the profound dislocations resulting from the failures of the modern hospital, new economic realities, and the transformations in medical technology:

> Ambulatory services are the fastest growing part of the hospital; already, ambulatory visits outnumber inpatient admissions in some smaller facilities by as much as 10 to 1. And yet at most hospitals, outpatient diagnostic and surgical services remain stepchildren. . . . They are scattered like anemones in a coral reef. In a teaching hospital, a cancer patient on a treatment visit may be obliged to walk more than a mile through a maze of corridors to reach the admission, laboratory, and radiology stations and an examination room. Ambulatory services are located where it is convenient for the inpatient-focused bureaucracy, not for the outpatients or the people dealing with them. . . . Increasingly, treatment paths for complex illnesses are bypassing the hospital. Whole surgical disciplines have disappeared from inpatient suites, and often from the hospital altogether. These include ophthalmology and plastic surgery, as well as major segments of gynecologic surgery, general surgery, and orthopedics. . . . New, noninvasive or minimally invasive diagnostic tools, like Doppler ultrasound and flexible, fiber-optic scopes, are changing the way physicians practice internal medicine. Gastroenterology and cardiology are migrating into outpatient and non-hospital settings.[3]

Hospitals took a series of steps to respond to these trends. First, they relocated their outpatient services into new wings on their campuses, away from inpatient areas, or established subacute specialty units in areas formerly used for acute care. Some hospitals built freestanding, integrated campuses, often called Professional Office Buildings, which combined outpatient and diagnostic and treatment services with doctors' office space. Meanwhile, the hospital continued to provide inpatient and critical care. Coordinated networks of satellite clinics and integrated campuses, with one or more specialized hospitals at the hub, were the norm by the mid-1990s. The largest providers created regional and even national networks. These networks of primary care centers, outpatient surgery centers, medical office buildings, and hospitals were differentiated yet unified in their emphasis: to provide a full spectrum of health care.[4]

The Modern Clinic and Its Legacy

The modernist clinics built in Europe during the 1930s were seminal to the development of the postwar modernist box clinic and to the postmodern residentialist community care clinics of the 1980s and 1990s. These prewar clinics were most notable for their minimalism, for their simplicity in plan and scale, and for the heroic aspirations of their builders to provide a civic symbol of progress in heightening the level of public health. In the years before World War II, a number of experimental outpatient clinics were built, particularly in England and France. The most architecturally significant of these was the Finsbury

Health Centre (1935–38), designed by Berthold Lubetkin and Tecton (fig. 8.1).
This clinic, built in one of the poorest sections of London, was a radical though
welcomed intervention. Lubetkin was a Russian-born architect who had undertaken his studies right around the time of the Russian Revolution of 1917. He
had left Russia in 1921 for Berlin, where he began his practice. After spending a
few years in Vienna, he relocated to Paris in 1925, where he was heavily influenced by members of the Paris avant-garde, including the French Cubist painters
Fernand Léger, Georges Braque, and Juan Gris. In 1931 he moved to London and
was a founder of the Tecton group, which began as a collective largely composed
of graduates of the Architectural Association (an influential London-based
school of architecture), and by 1935 his practice was well established. In 1934, he
and Tecton had received worldwide acclaim for their widely published design of
the Penguin Pool at the London Zoo. Lubetkin had by this time forged a clear
ideological conception of the ultimate purpose of modernism, which to him was
about the expression of the machine age but about more than strict functionalism
per se. In his words, such a reductivist approach as pure functionalism was "the
best way to divest architecture of that living richness and complexity that has
throughout history given it significance and purpose."[5]

The Finsbury Health Centre is regarded as the venerable progenitor of a
tradition of community-based health architecture, and its fiftieth anniversary,
in 1988, was an appropriate occasion to reflect on its significance:

> If you had to select a single building from the 1930s which most aptly embodied
> the idea of "caring" in architecture, you would be hard-pressed to find a more
> cogent example than Lubetkin and Tecton's Finsbury Health Centre. . . . It seems
> to me that this building owes its significance and reputation to being the prod-
> uct of one of those rare moments of synchronicity, when under the fertile con-
> ditions of committed patronage and architectural vision, a radical social
> programme finds its expression in a radical design solution. . . . [A single] prin-
> ciple permeated the entire project. . . . This might be termed the principle of
> causality, which in this case related to a shared and unqualified belief in the
> potentiality of architecture as an agent of social improvement.[6]

Lubetkin's political convictions were directly connected to his architecture. In large measure because of his well-known powers of persuasion, his ideals were adopted by public health officials in the borough of Finsbury, who subsequently hired Tecton to develop a comprehensive social and physical survey of the borough as the first step in a multifaceted Finsbury Plan. This was envisioned as a master plan encompassing the entire infrastructure of the community: housing, health care, education, transportation, and recreational amenities. The advent of World War II precluded its implementation, however, with the exception of two housing projects and the Finsbury Health Centre, which was the only project built during the 1930s.

The Finsbury Health Centre was planned before the establishment of the National Health Service, a period during which the provision of care remained a haphazard quilt of public and private providers:

> The first requirement of the brief, developed in conjunction with Dr. Chuni Katial, Chairman of the Public Health Committee, and Dr. Nicholas Dunscombe, Medical Officer of Health, was to amalgamate and standardize the various services and facilities that had accumulated piecemeal in different parts of the borough. At the same time it was clear that provision must be made for adaptation and the development of new clinical programs, for although the catalogue of maladies faced by inner-urban boroughs like Finsbury—tuberculosis, pneumonia, bronchitis, vitamin deficiency, rickets, infestation and malnutrition—perforce meant that the primary clinical effort must be devoted to diagnosis and treatment, nevertheless there was an equal concern to pursue the new concepts of health education and preventive medicine. . . . This presented the fascinating problem of establishing the typology of a building for which there was really no modern precedent or pattern. Clearly it would be larger and more diversified than a doctor's practice, but it would also be smaller and less specialist than a hospital. It must in fact establish a scale and identity of its own, being neither wholly domestic nor wholly institutional.[7]

In the initial discussions with the client, the building was conceived as an "open-access club," with an inviting ambiance and imagery, and therefore no reception desk was planned in the main foyer. This idea was later rejected as impractical, but in analyzing this building, architect and critic John Allen viewed the plan as an attempt to reconcile formality with friendliness, breaking ranks dramatically with the implied "us-versus-them" mentality of the hospital. The initial range of services included physicians' and dentists' outpatient surgical suites, a women's clinic, radiology and tuberculosis clinics, a solarium and laboratories, a mortuary, and a meat room containing confiscated food samples to be tested for contamination, along with various administrative and clinical support functions. Also included were an emergency shelter for a small number of evacuated families, a roof terrace, and a seventy-seat auditorium.

The resolution of this eclectic mixture of programmatic requirements was achieved in an H-shaped axial plan with a central zone for arrival and support functions and two narrow wings, one to each side, housing the other functions. It was perhaps the first modern clinic to be designed with no interior load-bearing columns or other elements, thereby rendering the interior space completely flexible and adaptable to changing needs. The success of this arrangement was proved repeatedly across fifty years of renovations. The architects also developed a series of explanatory diagrams for laypersons on the building's various features, including descriptions of its structural, heating, and organizational innovations (fig. 8.2). The staff, it was claimed, could thereby become simply an adjunct to (or extension of) the building's inherent therapeutic attributes.

Allen, in support of the tempered and, in retrospect, humanist, modernist approach of Lubetkin, simultaneously attacked the movement toward, in his view, the watered-down residentialism exhibited in community clinic architecture in England in the 1980s:

> The implied paternalism of caring shades into simple democracy . . . [in] the rumpled Neo-vernacular community centres that fill the pages of the Brick Bulletin. It seems to me however that democracy is not necessarily achieved by being casual or folksy, or indeed even by masking the social classifications needed to achieve specific tasks. Democracy—in this as in other spheres—is surely to do with freedom of information, or, architecturally speaking, about legibility of organization, explicitness of intention. . . . Finsbury Health Centre is saturated with such ideals. The entrance is unmistakable, surmounted by its municipal crest like a seal of guarantee—pro bono publico.[8]

The features of the building that Allen considered especially supportive of these democratic ideals were the arrival ramp at the main entrance, the waiting areas, the circulation patterns designed to facilitate wayfinding, and the adornment of interior walls, most notably the dramatic, colorful murals created by Gordon Cullen in the main foyer, proclaiming such public-health truths as "Chest diseases are preventable and curable," as if, in Allen's words, "to eradicate any lingering superstition that the cause of such affliction was a divine mystery" (fig. 8.3).[9]

The clinic stood in glowing contrast to its Victorian-era surroundings, with its main arrival axis and central core flanked by a pair of wings. The administrative and clinic areas were planned in anticipation of future adaptations, whereas the lecture hall, arrival, and waiting areas were intended to have a greater level of permanence. In writing of the building's significance, Peter Coe and Malcolm Reading concluded:

> The building stands out as a "megaphone for health" with the wings splayed out from the central axis. The central element is a framed concrete structure with the ground floor freed to produce a spacious waiting hall. To each side is a stair, providing the access to the angled wings. A constructional system which fully exploited the potential flexibility was employed in the wings. Horizontal channel sections support the slabs of floor and roof, with regularly spaced mullions acting as edge columns. Both end walls are monolithic and act as bracing, stabilizing the structure against wind deflection. This produces: flexibility within a structure of possible arrangements—increments of the module (not an infinite choice)—freedom within defined limits.[10]

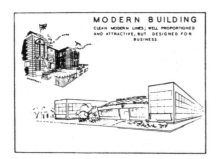

MODERN BUILDING
CLEAN MODERN LINES; WELL PROPORTIONED AND ATTRACTIVE, BUT DESIGNED FOR BUSINESS.

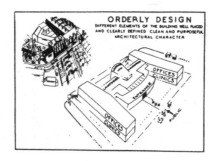

ORDERLY DESIGN
DIFFERENT ELEMENTS OF THE BUILDING WELL PLACED AND CLEARLY DEFINED CLEAN AND PURPOSEFUL ARCHITECTURAL CHARACTER

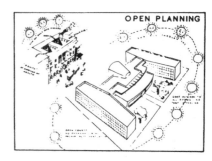

OPEN PLANNING

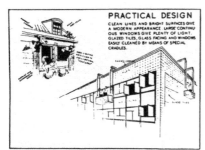

PRACTICAL DESIGN
CLEAN LINES AND BRIGHT SURFACES GIVE A MODERN APPEARANCE. LARGE CONTINUOUS WINDOWS GIVE PLENTY OF LIGHT. GLAZED TILES, GLASS FACING AND WINDOWS EASILY CLEANED BY MEANS OF SPECIAL CRADLES.

CHEERFUL ATMOSPHERE
ENTRANCE HALL FLOODED WITH LIGHT THROUGH WALL OF GLASS BRICKS CLEAN SURFACES AND BRIGHT COLOURS PRODUCE CHEERFUL EFFECT AIR OF EFFICIENCY GIVES CONFIDENCE TO THE PATIENTS

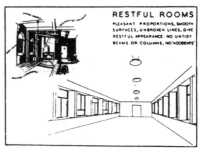

RESTFUL ROOMS
PLEASANT PROPORTIONS, SMOOTH SURFACES, UNBROKEN LINES, GIVE RESTFUL APPEARANCE. NO UNTIDY BEAMS OR COLUMNS, NO 'ACCIDENTS'

WELL LIT ROOMS
LARGE CONTINUOUS WINDOWS AND SHALLOW ROOMS GIVE AMPLE LIGHT IN ALL PARTS OF THE BUILDING . BLINDS EASILY FITTED WHERE NECESSARY

OPEN LOBBIES
WELL LIT CHEERFUL LOBBIES INSTEAD OF 'CORRIDORS'.

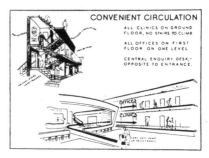

CONVENIENT CIRCULATION
ALL CLINICS ON GROUND FLOOR, NO STAIRS TO CLIMB

ALL OFFICES ON FIRST FLOOR ON ONE LEVEL

CENTRAL ENQUIRY DESK, OPPOSITE TO ENTRANCE.

CONSISTENT STYLE
EVERY DETAIL DESIGNED WITH THE SAME ARCHITECTURAL CHARACTER

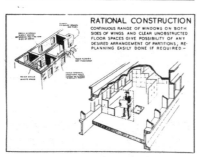

RATIONAL CONSTRUCTION
CONTINUOUS RANGE OF WINDOWS ON BOTH SIDES OF WINGS AND CLEAR UNOBSTRUCTED FLOOR SPACES GIVE POSSIBILITY OF ANY DESIRED ARRANGEMENT OF PARTITIONS, RE-PLANNING EASILY DONE IF REQUIRED -

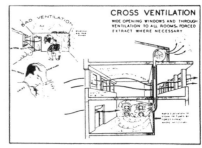

CROSS VENTILATION
WIDE OPENING WINDOWS AND THROUGH VENTILATION TO ALL ROOMS. FORCED EXTRACT WHERE NECESSARY

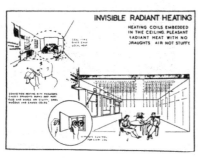

INVISIBLE RADIANT HEATING
HEATING COILS EMBEDDED IN THE CEILING. PLEASANT RADIANT HEAT WITH NO DRAUGHTS AIR NOT STUFFY

DUCTS FOR PLUMBING
ALL PLUMBING PIPES TAKEN IN CONCEALED DUCTS; EASILY AND QUICKLY ACCESSIBLE THROUGH REMOVABLE PANELS FOR CONNECTING ADDITIONAL FITTINGS.

DUCTS FOR POWER WIRING
ALL WIRING FOR ELECTRIC FITTINGS TAKEN IN NEAT REMOVABLE SKIRTING - DUCTS. REPAIRS AND ADDITIONS QUICKLY & CHEAPLY MADE. ALL CLINICAL EQUIPMENT EASILY CONNECTED

8.2. Finsbury Health Centre,
explanatory design-process
diagrams

8.3. Finsbury Health Centre, mural in main lobby

The Finsbury Health Centre, though perhaps not the most architecturally significant work of its architects, has stood the test of time as an expression of the belief that architecture can be an agent for human betterment. The entire building has been called a "propaganda machine" that would give the citizens of Finsbury a new outlook. With its clean geometry and fresh, bright appearance, it was indeed a beacon in dowdy Finsbury. Like earlier work at the London Zoo and in the Highpoint One and Highpoint Two housing projects, the Finsbury Health Centre captured much public attention. Many favorable reviews appeared in medical journals and architectural journals, and the popular press acclaimed the fit between the imagery of the building and its social purpose. The high level of communication between architect, client sponsor, and the layperson was aided greatly through the series of explanatory diagrams that were prepared and published in the popular press and in leaflets upon the building's opening (see fig. 8.2). These annotated diagrams stand, in the milieu of health architecture, as one of the very few instances where the architect provided supplemental explanatory—or, in this case, somewhat propagandist—information to the building's users.[11]

Unfortunately, the ideals of Finsbury were to be all but lost in the postwar period. Architecturally, many clinics would be based to some extent on the precedent set at Finsbury, with most planned and executed in accord with the principles of the International Style. The Hill-Burton minimalist, flat-roofed "box clinics" built during the 1950s and 1960s were intended to fill in a gap in care at the community level, particularly in rural areas underserved by hospitals. The legacy of the modern movement, and its preoccupation with the expression of technology, continued to influence the architecture of small community-based outpatient clinics during this second boom. In the larger sense, their mission was similar to that of all outpatient clinics, but the specific forces that led to the Hill-Burton clinics were quite different from those that would fuel the third boom in construction, especially in the non-governmental sector during the 1980s and 1990s in the United States.

Sometimes, the obsession with technology was elevated to the level of fetish. A notable example of this was the Kinoshita "capsule clinic" by Yoh Design Office (1978–80), designed to look like a capsular dose of medication. This late modernist "pill," built at Hakota Bay near Fukuoka City, Japan, was technically innovative for its concept, materials, and striking imagery (fig. 8.4). Though identified as a health clinic by a sign on a cruciform anchor, its entry-

8.4. Kinoshita "capsule clinic," Hakota Bay, Japan, 1980

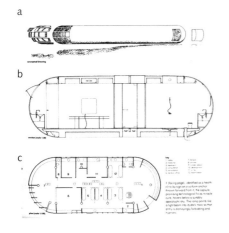

8.5. Kinoshita "capsule clinic":
(*a*) drawing of exterior;
(*b*) section; (*c*) floor plan

8.6. Kinoshita "capsule clinic," interior corridor

way was rather forbidding. The striking structure was made of concrete, and support systems were integrated into the structural frame. In plan and in section it was unabashedly a machine for care, which could be interpreted metaphorically as a space capsule (fig. 8.5). The interior was austere and somewhat alienating for the patient, with stark white or glass walls and minimalist built-in furnishings (fig. 8.6). In an account of this building, a British journal's critique was characteristically blunt:

> Architecture is not the only profession in which reliance on the specialist and on sophisticated technology has proved alienating. So perhaps the Kinoshita Clinic, designed by Yoh Design office, and hovering like an invader from outer space above the coast of Hakata Bay near Fukuoka City, Japan, is most apt as a metaphor for modern medicine. It is an intimidating capsule indigestible to its surroundings. . . . The image seems not to be a product of functional and constructional necessity, but rather to disorient and mystify users into a bewildered passivity. Approached by a ramping path to an unelaborated doorway, entry is neither sheltered nor reassuring. Inside is even more disconcerting. Walls bulge away from one or are merely cold and insubstantial sheets of glass. Between waiting and examination rooms only minimal privacy is afforded by a paint-sprayed strip revealing legs and dropped underwear below. Between examination rooms there is no privacy at all. The partition is clear glass (as is the rather unnerving desk) and stops far short of the external wall so that there is no acoustic privacy either. If not dismayed and disoriented by all this then one will be by nightfall when the lights come on—they shine up through the floor illuminating nurses' legs but little else.[12]

Other efforts at the time were centered on the continued attempt to apply industrialized building techniques, including the use of modular systems. This view had emerged in utopianist health architecture circles in the 1960s (see Chapter 4). The Middle East Modules (1978–81), by Derek Stow and Partners, were a second-generation attempt to employ advanced building systems concepts developed by that firm with the British Modular Building Consortium. This prefabricated manufacturing system was developed for Saudi Arabia, where the intense sun and arid climate called for a high-quality system that could be quickly erected. Each module was independently constructed and transported to the site (fig. 8.7). There the modules were to be plugged in to one another, with all infrastructure systems contained in each segment. Plumbing and pilings would be laid out, the modules stacked, services connected, and sunshades fitted, and the facility would be ready to open.

This system could be assembled in many ways, ranging from a single-unit clinic to a three-level hospital for a community of sixty thousand. One clinic of twenty-five module units, for example, was configured as a racetrack (fig. 8.8). This concept was significantly different from conventional modular systems of the time because a range of capsule types were created. Capsules were interchangeable and long lasting. Rather than rework a capsule, it could simply be unplugged and replaced.[13]

After developing this system, Stow built a health center in London's East End using most of the same principles. This facility, the South Poplar Health Centre (1979–81), was to test the capsules and show them in action to potential buyers. First, a prototype outpatient facility was to be assembled for the local health authority. But because of regulations of the Department of Health and Social Security and their policy that the building could not be an exception to their competitive bidding rules, Stow was forced to abandon the capsules. In the end, he "stuck to a modular system of identical dimension, and as close as possible in principle to the capsule system. This was both to retain the advantages of relocatability, but also because he finds that simplifying the design of specific buildings to the selection of and arrangement of a range of encapsulated functional components greatly speeds up the briefing and design process. . . . So though the modules . . . are completely fabricated on site, rather than in a factory, each contains a functional unit of accommodation similar to that in the range of capsules, and each is constructionally independent and so relocatable."[14]

The clinic was composed of sixteen modules configured as a square, with the waiting area in the center two modules. The bright, shiny red box clinic looked like a trailer: stationary but capable of moving at any moment. The assembly connections were made less obvious through use of black cladding strips. The interior spaces were above the standard quality for prefabricated systems at the time.

Other experiments with modular approaches during the early 1980s used fixed-feature components, without the option of relocatability. A noteworthy example was the Detroit HMO Clinic (1981–83), by Smith, Hinchman, and Grylls Associates of Detroit. This circular clinic, described in the healthcare administration literature as "space age" in appearance, had a roof that looked like a series of four tents supported by masts, and a tentlike canopy at the main entrance (fig. 8.9). The plan was configured as a series of concentric rings, with the main waiting area at the center, a control area in the second ring, a series of modular clinics housing exam, treatment, and consultation rooms, along with the administration area, in the third ring, and various diagnostic and treatment

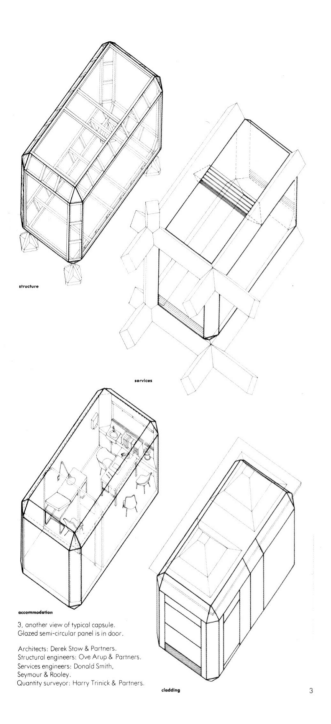

structure

services

accommodation

3, another view of typical capsule.
Glazed semi-circular panel is in door.

Architects: Derek Stow & Partners.
Structural engineers: Ove Arup & Partners.
Services engineers: Donald Smith,
Seymour & Rooley.
Quantity surveyor: Harry Trinick & Partners.

cladding

3

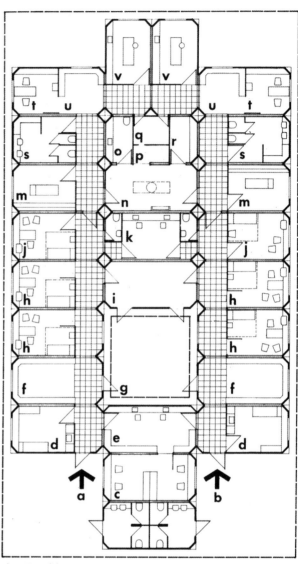

plan: 25-module unit

key

a, male entrance
b, female entrance
c, records/reception/dispensary
d, overnight stay
e, pharmacy
f, waiting
g, courtyard
h, consulting/examination
i, health education
j, treatment
k, laboratory
m, patient preparation/recovery
n, minor operation
o, dirty
p, mobile x-ray
q, dark room
r, clean
s, staff
t, dental reception
u, waiting
v, dental surgery

Above: **8.7. Modular Hospital for the Middle East, prototype, London, 1978. Courtesy of Derek Stow & Partners, London, England, Architects, Planners, Designers.**

Right: **8.8. Modular Hospital, twenty-five-unit clinic variant. Courtesy of Derek Stow & Partners, London, England, Architects, Planners, Designers.**

support functions in the outermost ring. In the initial building, a zone was set aside for future expansion of one or more rings, thereby completing the rings. The novel design was said by its administrators to attract a surge in walk-in enrollments immediately after its opening.[15] Many features of this clinic were strikingly reminiscent of the Atomedic Hospital prototypes of the early 1960s (see Chapter 4).

One of the main limitations of modular systems of the time was the repetitive use of a single building element. This tended to result in visual monotony unless particular care was devoted to a signature feature or attribute, such as an unusual color, unique window pattern, or distinctive roof shape. The Scripps Clinic (1986–88) in Carmel Mountain Ranch, California, by the Austin Hansen Fehlman Group, Architects, made artful use of tilt-up concrete slab casting in a manner that was both aesthetically attractive and cost effective. The clinic was built near La Jolla with a construction technique that had been used by the architects on a number of office and warehouse buildings. Their familiarity with tilt-up casting and with its application to an interlocking system of modular elements, and their interest in stretching its design possibilities, resulted in a composition of many smaller interlocking units. They worked in tandem with the concrete subcontractor to cast many three-story panels, and a standard casting grid was developed for ease of assembly and integration with structural framing and support systems. The simplicity of the process belied the partí— the complex formal composition of the completed building.[16]

Nomadic Clinics

The recreational vehicle (RV) industry contributed to the evolution of the outpatient health center in the last third of the century. These nomadic clinics-on-wheels were cousins to the campers that had initially fueled the growth of the RV industry. The movement toward vehicular outpatient health clinics dated from the late 1940s, when the first mobile tuberculosis testing units were put in service in municipalities across the United States. By the 1960s, these "buildings on wheels" were used for immunizations and blood donor programs. In the 1970s they were adopted for use as mobile clinics housing sophisticated

8.9. HMO Clinic, aerial view, Detroit, 1983

diagnostic tools, including the first mobile computed axial tomography brain scan unit in the United States.[17] Later the vehicle-as-portable-building would be adapted for use as nomadic MRI clinics. By the 1980s such mobile units were a regular attraction at the local shopping mall, housing everything from dental care to mammography. It was estimated that two hundred mobile mammography units were on the road in the United States by 1990.[18] In the 1990s, such mobile units were increasingly used as an adjunct to the established occupational health programs of large employers in the United States.

Some mobile units were docked alongside conventional hospitals to provide ad hoc support space. One hospital in Iowa borrowed some "deployable medical systems shelters," or depmeds, from the army for use during one of the hospital's renovation projects. These same units had been used in Saudi Arabia during the 1991 Gulf War.[19] Such relations between mobile and fixed facilities had the benefit of permitting expensive diagnostic equipment to be shared by several hospitals in the same area.

By the 1990s four major U.S. manufacturers had emerged: MOEX, Medicoach (which later merged with MOEX), Winnebago, and Perspective Enterprises. The typical nomadic health unit was used for community health and education, and included immunization programs, nutritional education, and primary care. These units were 35–40 feet long, and by the late 1990s they were equipped with sophisticated wireless data-processing systems for "curbside computerization" (the corollary of bedside computerization), relatively comfortable interiors, and with flexible floor plans. Many states operated mobile health facilities by the late 1990s. In Louisiana, six units were purchased in 1995 for dissemination of community public health care in localities remote from fixed-site clinics. Each was linked to a fixed-site clinic in its region, from which it was deployed to the field each day. On-board electronic capabilities included video telemedicine conferencing, audio tapes for training and education, a cellular phone link with the home base, and portable laptop computers for data entry and case management. In a review of nomadic buildings it was predicted that more such facilities would be on the road in the next millennium.[20]

The two basic plan types of these units were the side corridor and the center double-loaded corridor. The basic chassis and engine were provided by an automobile maker, such as General Motors, and the bodies and interiors were made to order.[21] Therefore, these were classic examples of a derived plan, adopted from its initial purpose for use as a health facility.

Yet the trend toward mobile units, however convenient for the provider, was to its critics symptomatic of a betrayal of the ideals of architecture as a means of providing commodity, firmness, and delight. The substitution of a mobile unit for a fixed building was viewed as a means of subverting the ideals of modernism and, more significantly, of removing the "sense of place entitlement" and continuity with a community endemic to a fixed-site building. To these critics, nomadic clinics were seen as expedient machines whereby all remaining vestiges of architecture—and the expensive up-front investment they required—could now be stripped away in the name of cost effectiveness in an age of reduced fiscal resources and diminished societal confidence in the proposition of architecture as a valued long-term investment.

Neoexpressionist Clinics

In Europe, in particular, the International Style continued to influence the design of clinics during the 1980s, although it was by then reduced to one of many styles at the disposal of the architect. Architect Sandro Giulianelli saw fit to expropriate this style for a clinic in the small Umbrian city of Terni. The Day Hospital at Terni (1981–84) was a curious mixture, at once oppositional and sympathetic to the traditional vernacular architecture of the region, while in keeping with modernist buildings built there earlier in the century. Its formal language was minimalist, and cubist in composition. The back side was dominated by two large cutouts in an otherwise sparse white wall, each revealing an internal realm of the building. The duality of the facility was acknowledged in a critique: "Anxious to get away from the narrow restraints of a provincial architecture which luckily nobody today would dare any longer to whitewash as a minority culture, Giulianelli has felt the need to go farther afield by looking at more international and 'out of context' experiences. . . . The day hospital, among Giulianelli's most mature works, manages to elude the narrow logic of the functional machine to become a more sober element in the recomposition and restitching of a previously existing order . . . and this quest for deep roots alludes to those of the infancy of modern architecture."[22]

Other clinics in this late modern tradition included the celebrated architect Arata Isozaki's Etoh Clinic (1981–83), in Japan,[23] and Dutch architect Wiel Arets' Medical Center in Weert, Holland (1984–86).[24] Both buildings expressed a highly cultivated and radical minimalism, both subtly drew from local vernacular traditions, and both strayed little from the canon of purist modernism. The Etoh Clinic, with specialized obstetric-gynecological functions, was a new building type for the region, built across the bay from Isozaki's home town. The building was a fusion of simple, layered planes, bold colors, and a humane, inviting imagery.

A third example of this tradition was the S. G. C. Health Center (1985–87) by Jo Coenen, built in Eindhoven, the Netherlands. Its shiplike imagery, patterned masonry, horizontally banded windows, human scale, and stepped flat roofs continued this tradition. At first glance it could be mistaken for a 1950s health building, with materials, details, and horizontal composition drawn from the many industrial buildings constructed by Philips Electrical Corporation in Eindhoven during the 1950s.[25]

The language of modernism, therefore, continued to have potential as a valid approach shown to transcend cultural and geographic boundaries. This tradition of humane rationality dates from Finsbury (1935–38), whose main waiting area and interior spaces were a prototype of the modernist outpatient health clinic. A thread of continuity existed between the heroism of Finsbury as a humane machine for care and reinterpretations of modernism decades later. Aesthetics aside, even the aforementioned nomadic vehicular clinics that proliferated at the end of the century shared a functional straightforwardness with Finsbury and its successors.

In fixed-site health clinics, by the 1980s this ideal became somewhat obscured with architects' interest in high-tech expressionism. A notable example was the Crowndale Health Centre (1987–89) by Rock Townsend, Architects, built

8.10. Crowndale Health Centre, North London, 1989 (identifiable by its arched roof), amid neighboring buildings

8.11. Crowndale Health Centre, atrium

in Camden Town in North London.[26] The exterior walls of an old post office were incorporated in the design, thereby weaving the new building into the fabric of its site (fig. 8.10). Its interior plan was dominated by a large atrium, common for the period in hotels, malls, and later, hospitals. The mechanical ductwork was expressed as vertical limbs that appeared to dangle from above, flanked by a boldly expressed structural system of floor plates and columns, reminiscent of spider legs about to descend at any second (fig. 8.11). Moreover, the height of the space created a sense of impersonality and uncaring that the other parts of the clinic would have to work hard to overcome. Despite the building's successful historical adaptation, the atrium was a disappointment. Though a strong focal point, it lacked the intimacy of the best of its predecessors.

In stark contrast to the above-mentioned work, a new type of clinic was emerging in Japan. During the last two decades of the century, young Japanese architects designed a number of health clinics with striking—at times shocking—imagery. The earliest of this new "neoexpressionist" wave was the Ark dental clinic (1981–83) in Kyoto, by Shin Takamatsu. The Ark was situated on a tight urban site adjacent to a railway station. It looked like a large machine or steam engine poised to roll down its "tracks" (figs. 8.12 and 8.13). The three-level structure, of concrete and steel, housed a futuristic dental suite on the top floor.[27]

A second clinic in Kyoto by Takamatsu, dubbed the Pharaoh (1981–83), was somewhat less anti-contextual in its form, materiality, and relation to its surroundings (specifically, the nearby train station). It appeared like a machine on its corner site (fig. 8.14). The first floor was a dental clinic, and the two floors above were residential, in keeping with the Japanese tradition of the physician's combination residence-clinic. The curved port at the corner of the site was the waiting room, and the area above was the entrance hall to the living areas. The mechanical atmosphere of the exterior elements—the concrete molding, the three towers, and the slotted and circular window penetrations—concealed the interior functions. The south facade contained the screened, shielded entrance to the residence (fig. 8.15).[28] In an interpretation of these buildings, Sally Wood-bridge, an American architectural journalist, noted:

> In American cities, we have come to see context as an important determinant of form. In modern Japan, where codes for height and sunlight access are strict, architectural etiquette is a low priority. Those designers who choose to make a public statement occasionally give their buildings bizarre or shocking imagery, which American architects are more likely to consign to the theme park and the strip. One wonders how, in a country of social conformity [Japan], such mischief can go on. . . . Much of the time sites are so small that structures must be shoe-horned into them. Buildings are even locked inside city blocks, and architects must find ways of signaling their existence. . . . The Japanese also respect artistic integrity and demand as high a level of craftsmanship for follies as for corporate headquarters. In conservative Kyoto, Shin Takamatsu designs building-size puns that are alternatively witty and sinister . . . yet his buildings are not throw-away one-liners. Instead of cheap construction, they reveal a concern for finish and detail that is mind-boggling.[29]

Of her first encounter with the Ark and the Pharaoh, Woodbridge wrote:

> Your train stops at the station, and upon exiting you see, over the fence, an over-sized concrete and metal steam engine immobilized on the adjacent site. Is this a transportation facility? No . . . [but] everyone in the neighborhood knows the building. . . . In another suburb of Kyoto, your taxi turns the corner into a non-descript intersection and there, sitting right at the edge of the street pavement, is another dental clinic, called Pharaoh, that looks like a machine of undetermined

8.12. The Ark, Kyoto, Japan, 1982, profile view of locomotive imagery

8.13. The Ark, building set against urban context

8.14. Pharaoh, Kyoto, Japan,
1983, view from intersection

8.15. Pharaoh, exterior view

use devised by a mad scientist. Alas, there is no easy explanation for the imagery of these buildings. Nor do the names signify anything conventional. . . . The buildings have an armored quality. Porthole windows, for example, look as though they were designed to seal the interior and to protect its occupants from an alien world. As for their creator, Takamatsu has been described as an architectural sorcerer; he has described himself as a "Blade Runner." The wonder of it all is that not only do his follies get built, but their designer is also taken seriously and rewarded with opportunities to do more.[30]

British critic Chris Fawcett described the Pharaoh as the architect's oddest building to date, with its "fabulous realism": "Three skinny, up reaching, spiked-metal light-towers and black granite verticals interbuild with the complications in plan. Steel braces . . . which ought to be restraining the building's menace, actually contribute to it through their sharp metal protrusions. My first reading of the thing was a suicide machine." Fawcett referred to an "excessive expressionism" in various interior details and materials, which conveyed violent connotations. He declared that the building would be suitable for a new classification system of "unfocused-focus building," an amalgamation of vestiges of great buildings of the past into the Ultimate Building. He claimed that this and other work by Takamatsu would be contenders for this New Order, with the Pharaoh as its "morgue or crypt."[31]

A contemporary of Takamatsu, Team Zoo, produced equally shocking buildings, with dark imagery and unusual interpretations of ancient Japanese spiritual motifs. These included striking juxtapositions of ancient ornamentation and contemporary building technologies, premised on the extensive use of cast-in-place concrete. One of their most well known buildings of this period was the combination pediatric medical clinic, day hospital, and doctor's residence, the Kazura Clinic (1980–82) in Chiba, Japan. The building broke ranks with conventional health architecture in nearly every way. Its forms were almost animal-like in silhouette (fig. 8.16). The roof rolled down the side of the building, evoking the slope of a mountainside and its own sloping site. A domed roof was truncated at the end to create a roof terrace for the residence. The lower two levels housed the clinic, which was arranged around a small center court, with twelve patient beds at one end. This box was injected with an egg-shaped entry foyer and similarly curved staircase. In section, the various levels, the sloping site, and the interplay of site topography and the roof forms were visible. The forms took on at once a playfulness and a sinister air, like a giant mechanized reptile on the verge of striking.[32] This building foreshadowed a trend anticipated in the new millennium: the shift from single-function, or uni-programmed, health buildings to multi-functional, or transprogrammed, buildings. Ideally, a truly transprogrammed building's many functions would become indistinguishable from one another.

Other Japanese clinics built around the same time were more orthodox in appearance and image without compromising their designers' devotion to the principles of modern architecture. Among these, the clinic-residence in Hadano, Japan (1988–89), by Hajime Yatsuka/UPM Architects, was noteworthy for adhering to modernist formal dictates without becoming subservient to this tradition (fig. 8.17). A hemodialysis clinic was housed on the first three levels, with the residence on the fourth level. The building was essentially an articulated white box, with various projections and incisions introduced in a platonic form. In this sense it was a highly mannered, restrained response to the period, and a commentary on the relation between the clinic and the hospital, which were viewed as allied yet distinct types. In the architect's account of this building he sought to react to the "showy play of forms" that had recently proliferated in Japan. While sympathetic to the ideals of the machine aesthetic, he had ultimately rejected it, turning to a synthesis that, by his own account, straddled the line between modernism and postmodernism.[33]

The issue of aesthetics, of course, is directly correlated with what a client is willing to build. In Japan very few facilities exist solely for public health and

8.16. Kazura Clinic, Chiba, Japan, 1982

8.17. Clinic-residence, Hadano, Japan, 1989

social welfare. The Himeji City Health and Welfare Center (1992–94), by Kisho Kurokawa, was built near a national treasure, the Himeji Castle. Kurokawa had been a member of the internationally known Metabolist group of architect-urbanists in the 1960s and 1970s. Metabolism had gained notoriety as a movement sympathetic to late modernism, which sought to make use of advanced technology in a synthesis with organic principles in nature and science.[34] Kurokawa became the most prolific builder and writer of this group, and his ideas have been influential in Japan and beyond. At times these preoccupations crossed with social ideals, and to this end the clinic in Himeji also housed welfare offices. In the center of the five-level building, a tension structure canopy hovered over a wedge-shaped stairway that extended to the building's second level. This stairway was interrupted by a conical skylight, which appeared like a pointed knife edge or sharpened pencil point, penetrating upward through the stairs from below. Its prime function, ostensibly, was to bring natural daylight to a lounge on the lower level (fig. 8.18). The overall building was a box split into three fragments; these elements corresponded to the major parts of the functional space program (fig. 8.19). The glass roof was equipped with a retractable lighting grid, which could be lowered so that the stair and landing could be used as an outdoor theater. Precast panels, made by embedding ninety-nine different shapes of cut stone to make sixteen patterns, clad the exterior walls. The window openings were oriented to yield full views of the nearby castle.[35]

If the pointed skylight of the Himeji clinic could be interpreted as a metaphor for a surgical tool—or, more cynically, for a pencil-pushing social bureaucracy—a far less poetic metaphor of the act of surgery (or bureaucracy), perhaps symbolic of the implements of the physician, was conveyed in the razor-sharp projection of the canopy of the Hirayama Clinic (1985–87), by Yasumitsu Matsunaga with SKM Architects and Planners. The projection hovered aggressively over patients arriving at the clinic. Like many high-tech clinics in Japan, this residence-clinic was a tour-de-force, though sedate next to the Ark or Pharaoh clinics. By comparison with those buildings, it blended much more into its neighborhood.[36] A bold example of Japanese late modern neoexpressionism in health architecture, and perhaps only slightly less assertive in form than the Ark and the Pharaoh, was the Matsushita Pediatric Clinic (1988–90) in Nagasaki, by Shoei Yoh. This suspended bridge-clinic, with parking below and a two-level

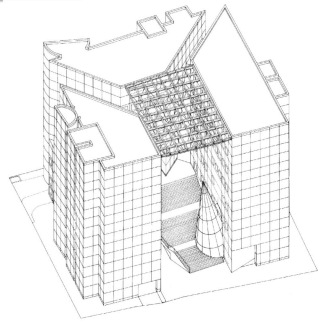

8.18. City Health and Welfare
Center, Himeji, Japan, 1994

8.19. City Health and Welfare
Center, axonometric view

clinic above, was sandwiched between two streets on an extremely narrow site. The building hovered precariously like a robotic device poised for hostile deployment (fig. 8.20). Inside, the examination room and support spaces were housed in a sloping-glass wedge volume tapering in plan, with floor-to-ceiling glass and views only minimally screened, if at all, from passersby (fig. 8.21). Tension cables were employed to support the floor loads of this cantilevered "bridge building." Although the building is impressive, it is difficult to imagine children, or anyone for that matter, finding this an inviting place.[37]

Yet another neoexpressionist clinic-residence built in Japan in the 1980s crossed the legacy of the machine with the curvilinearity of the art nouveau period of the early decades of the twentieth century. The Sugai Clinic (1984–86) by Itsuko Hasegawa, in Matsuyama, could have been a project of Antonio Gaudí (1852–1926), had he practiced a century later. This six-level, mixed-use building was perched above the city on a wooded hillside site, serving as a landmark. The striped facade was decorated with abstract symbols of playing

8.20. Matsushita Pediatric Clinic, Nagasaki, Japan, 1990

8.21. Matsushita Pediatric Clinic, examination room on the second floor

cards (fig. 8.22). The building was banded with alternating patterns of glass block, small square porcelain tiles, and perforated aluminum panel screens. The three lower levels housed the clinic. The two uppermost levels housed the residence, with a child's room on the sixth level in a composition of curved, animated forms, completely sheathed in the brightly colored tiles. The plan was essentially a cube with vertical circulation centered along an outer perimeter wall. The building was approached on one side via a steep stairway and on the other side via a ramped footbridge. The balconies of the various levels, which undulated in wavelike forms, provided outdoor spaces for the clinic and residence (fig. 8.23). The undulating, curved balconies were reminiscent of Gaudí's

8.22. Sugai Clinic, Matsuyama, Japan, 1986

8.23. Sugai Clinic, detail of exterior tile ornamentation and undulating balconies

Casa Mila apartment building in Barcelona (1905–7). The extensive use of applied surface ornamentation set this clinic apart from the other avant-garde clinics built in Japan during this period, which tended to be either cast-in-place concrete or high-tech buildings with boldly expressed structural systems and components.[38]

During this period, bold, curvilinear shapes were incorporated not only in wall surfaces but also in roofs. The RYU Clinic (1991–93) in Zentsuji, by Yoshiaki Tada, made use of a curved galvanized metal roof to create a distinctive image for this clinic located in a dense urban site. In other respects, such as scale and materials, it was not unlike its neighboring buildings. This building, and the other aforementioned neoexpressionist projects in Japan, were indicative of the many approaches found acceptable to clients in Japan.[39] Indeed, many Japanese clients considered themselves patrons of their architect. In the United States, however, the architect of outpatient clinics has not had such latitude.

Avant-garde neoexpressionist clinics built in Japan and elsewhere outside the United States were far more daring in terms of their aesthetic aims, geometry, and imagery than the earlier generation of clinics. An example from Europe was an orthodontist's practice built in Almere, the Netherlands (1991–93), by the Dutch firm Meyer and van Schooten. Almere was a town built on newly reclaimed land outside Amsterdam. It lacked cohesive urban-planning concepts, and therefore entire districts were built in an ad hoc manner. One such zone was chosen for the site of the clinic. In response to the nondescript character of the area and its automobile-dominated scale of suburban development, the building's roof was sloped downward on the side facing the street, with the main entrance on the street side as well (fig. 8.24). Beneath the lowest zone of the roof was the waiting room, its scale intended to "comfort" children, who composed the bulk of patients. On the highest (opposite) side was a suite of four dental treatment stations, with support spaces to the sides (fig. 8.25a). The

8.24. Orthodontist clinic, Almere-Haven, the Netherlands, 1993

8.25. Orthodontist clinic: (*a*) floor plan; (*b*) section

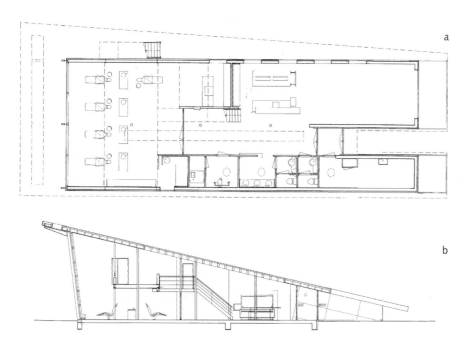

a

b

patient had a full-height view to the outdoors through the outward-sloped glass wall. Support and administrative space was in a loft directly above the dental suite. In profile, the building appeared to be sinking like an abandoned ship (fig. 8.25b); in reality the building was entirely on grade with no basement. Journalist Arthur Wortman assessed its didactic nature:

> Their [the architects'] building keeps itself to itself. In an unmistakable metaphor, they sunk the facade into the ground. It can not be denied that the roof, which is consequently experienced in a very physical way—especially as you enter the building, when its surface splits open to leave the way clear for you—comes off as rather ponderous in this confrontation. Like an ostrich with its head in the sand forgetting that its ugly rump is still on display, the front is buried into the polder [site] leaving the backside of the building facing the surroundings. . . . Inside, it becomes clear that the sloping roof line is not purely a reaction to the surroundings, but also has to do with functional considerations. . . . What visual greenery is to the flat-dweller, the ceiling is to the dental patient. . . . As you lie with your jaw wedged open, the more open perspective offers a little visual compensation for the dentist's sardonic visage. The waiting room is at the low end of the building. . . . Inside, there is little [that is] introverted.[40]

Wortman concluded that the building was a mixed success in that it did not effectively deal with its site, although the interior afforded the patient a functional, aesthetically pleasing experience.

In this same vein a series of seven "pyramid" clinics were built by USAID in and around Cairo, Egypt, between 1980 and 1984. These clinics were stepped back from their ground level to the third floor, like miniaturized pyramids. The seven clinics were nearly identical and thus conveyed a puzzling, if evocative, image to staff and patients.

The previous examples of expressionist clinics are self-assured in the use of bold geometries, and assert themselves on their site and in their immediate contexts. In so doing, in the extreme (particularly the Pharaoh and Ark clinics) each reacts against its context and even against itself.

Postmodern Neoclassicist Clinics

Of the postmodern community clinics built in the United States, perhaps none quoted neoclassicist planning and proportional concepts more overtly than the Kaiser/Rockwood Medical Office Complex (1983–85), built in Portland, Oregon, by BOOR/A Architects. This building was absolute in its symmetry and outward imagery, with a central drive leading to the main entrance, flanked by two wings of nearly identical proportion (fig. 8.26). The building conveyed an image similar to that of the palace hospitals, particularly the Julius Hospital, built four centuries earlier (1576–85) in Würzburg, Germany (fig. 8.27).[41] From the point of arrival the effect was nearly identical, although from then on the situation differed markedly. At the Julius Hospital, the narrow finger-wards and support functions were situated around a courtyard; at Kaiser/Rockwood, by contrast, the front of

the building contained the administration and support, and the rear of this box housed two pavilion wings (fig. 8.28). The ground-floor and second-floor plans were similar to one another, and the building was by and large hospitalist in appearance, with its symmetry, wings, and connective circulation spine.

The term *wings* is loosely applied here, however, because from the exterior the scale and height implied something entirely different from what actually occurred within. From the exterior rear, these two appendages appeared as open ward pavilions, with historical proportions and siting and a light court connecting in between. The net effect, nonetheless, was only an indirect reference to the open-ward concept. In reality, the interior of each wing was a highly compartmentalized collection of examination rooms and staff support spaces. The pavilion concept was in evidence, but expressed elsewhere, in the atrium and the large clerestories on the second level above the nurses' stations. The full-

8.26. Kaiser/Rockwood Clinic, Portland, Oregon, 1985

8.27. Julius Hospital, Würzburg, Germany, 1576–85

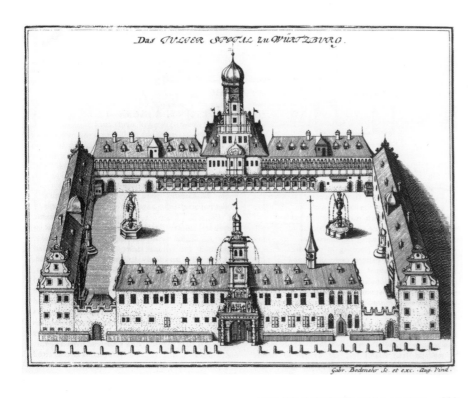

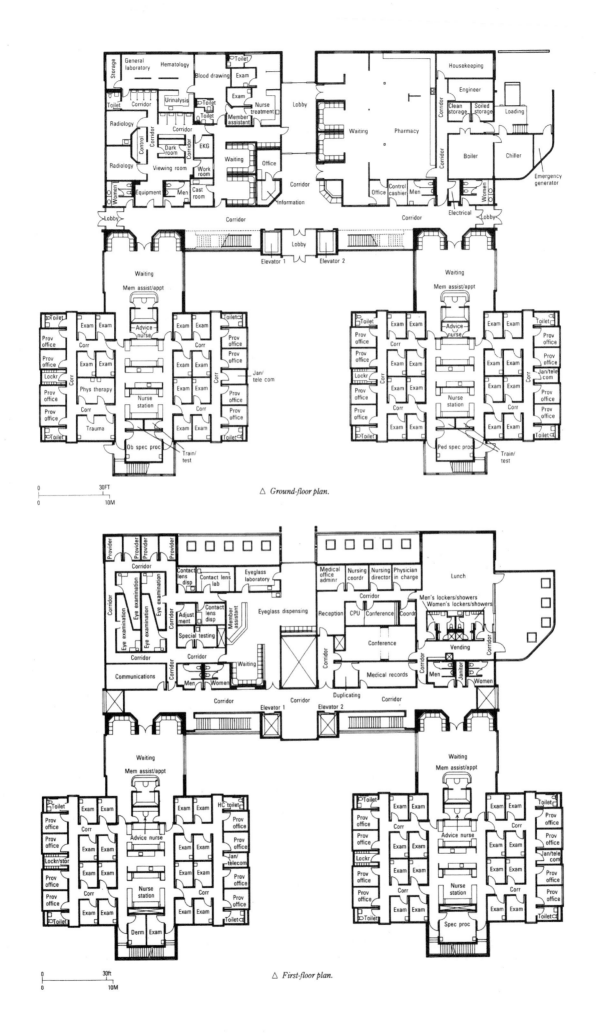

△ Ground-floor plan.

△ First-floor plan.

height windows at the end of each wing, suggesting from the exterior an indoor dayroom reminiscent of the solariums of hospitals and sanitariums built early in the century, were anticlimactic from the patient's perspective. Actually, the end-points of the wings housed clinicians' rooms, and a stairway connecting the two levels at this point greatly reduced the amenity for the occupants of the clinic.

Yet the spacious main lobby-atrium, with laminated wood beams and expansive windows, was a success. The wood beams spanned the entire atrium, giving it the ambiance of a Cascade mountain lodge (fig. 8.29). In the public spaces, the patient was made to feel important and welcomed; this was a requirement of the provider organization, which saw Kaiser/Rockwood as a prototype outpatient clinic for its expanding HMO organization. A post-occupancy evaluation indicated satisfaction on the part of staff and patients. This clinic was widely published and quickly became a symbol of postmodern, patient-centered health architecture in the United States.[42]

Other architects and healthcare providers, particularly in European countries experiencing the disintegration of the Soviet Union and its satellites, sought to synthesize architectural traditions with the pluralism and new freedoms inherent in postmodernism. Such was the case in the design of an outpatient pediatric clinic in a residential neighborhood of Prague (1984–87), in what is now the Czech Republic, by Design Architecture (D.A.) Studio, Prague. This design-build firm enlisted the skills of artists, industrial designers, and artisans as part of the total construction process. This project and other work of the firm during this period symbolized a break from the austere socialist *Stavoprojekt* state-sponsored architecture of the postwar modern era. The anticipation of a new era of aesthetic freedom proved inspiring in the pursuit of a looser yet ordered aesthetic.

8.30. Children's clinic, Prague, 1987, view from street

The clinic was housed in a transformed modernist structure of the 1920s that was rebuilt, expanded, and raised an additional floor in height. The building presented a formal image from the street, with its wall and axial path leading to the entrance (fig. 8.30). On the opposite side, a walkway bridge, suspended over a play yard below, also led to a formal entrance. The waiting room was designed as a playroom with a large mural; toys were encased along the walls, and an interactive wall was provided for children to compose their own mural. The plan of the clinic was governed by a strong central axis anchored to flanking streets (fig. 8.31). A series of steel grids painted white were introduced on the exterior and interior, as were Georgian doors and windows and brightly color-coded objects in the rooms and outdoors. The loose yet highly orchestrated arrangement of objects was a counterpoint to an otherwise nondescript box-shaped building (fig. 8.32). This clinic hinted at the expansive range of sources that could now be quoted by architects in an era dominated by pluralism.[43]

New Residentialism, Critical Regionalism, and the Community Clinic

The movement toward residentialism in outpatient health architecture generally has been a number of steps ahead of the movement toward residentialism in the acute-care and specialty hospitals. This is logical for two reasons. First, the scale of the community clinic is diminutive compared to that of the typical hospital and the clinic is often far less complex, so innovations can then be implemented more readily, without the cumbersome ripple effects associated with hospital-based capital improvements. As a result, less capital investment is needed per square foot. Second, the clinic has been more naturally able to take on attributes of its surroundings, growing out of them rather than existing in opposition to them, as has often been the case with hospitals. Many extreme cases, such as inner-urban storefront advocacy clinics, have existed solely on shoestring community resources and have been housed ad hoc for years in substandard quarters on crowded city streets.

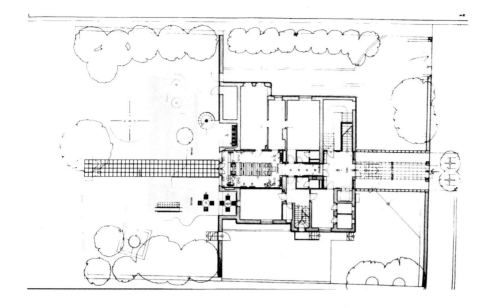

8.31. Children's clinic, main-floor plan

8.32. Children's clinic: (*top*) axonometric toward north; (*bottom*) axonometric toward south

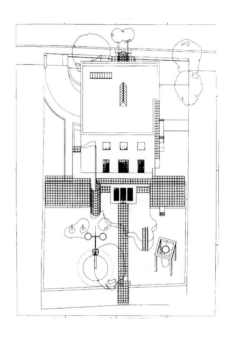

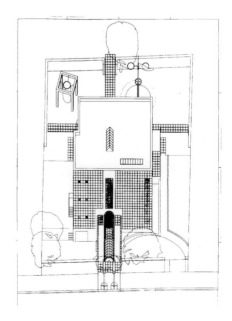

An early, seminal example of residentialism in the postwar years was built in Denmark. The Medical Center (1968–71) in Store Heddinge, Stevns, designed by Karsten Vibild with Finn Sonderbaek and Bent Falk, was a community care clinic built in the center of a small city. It was sited to become part of the new town square, adjacent to a new town hall, and therefore assumed the status of a key civic building. But because no public funding was available, it was funded privately. Its exterior looked like a house, with face brick and a tile roof, and on the interior the visitor would encounter a timber-framed central hall (fig. 8.33). The plan was a square, with four quadrants situated around a small landscaped courtyard (fig. 8.34). The clusters of waiting areas at the center looked out onto the courtyard (fig. 8.35). The traditional vernacular materials, furnishings, and natural wood used throughout were residentialist in nearly every respect. This pedestrian-scaled walk-up clinic was an example of the influence of critical regionalism, which was manifested in a synthesis between local building traditions and a self-conscious filtered incorporation of external, broader technological influences (see Chapter 5). The residentialist, regionalist vocabulary of the Medical Center at Store Heddinge was ahead of its time. It was a benchmark for later residentialist community health clinics and was particularly antithetical to the overt modernism of the Finsbury Health Centre and the many successors it spawned in the period between 1940 and 1970.

A later yet equally seminal example of residentialism crossed with critical regionalism was the Kensington Health Centre (1981–83), in Melbourne, Australia, by Ian McDougall. Like the Medical Center in Denmark, it was a walk-up clinic. This rather avuncular collection of interconnected structures, loosely fitted to its site, was created in an established residential area. It incorporated an existing bungalow and a second existing old house, with new in-fill construction. The new portion was made to look like the older attached dwellings in terms of color, materials, composition, scale, and trim (fig. 8.36). The complex was irregularly shaped, with services scattered across its constituent parts. A review of the clinic stated:

> McDougall gathered together specific elements from his locality, in this case an older inner suburb, to make up his building—a process he likens to collecting bits and pieces at a flea market. He was concerned that the Health Centre

8.33. Medical Center, Store
Heddinge, Denmark, 1971

8.34. Medical Center, ground-
floor plan

8.35. Medical Center, interior
view to courtyard

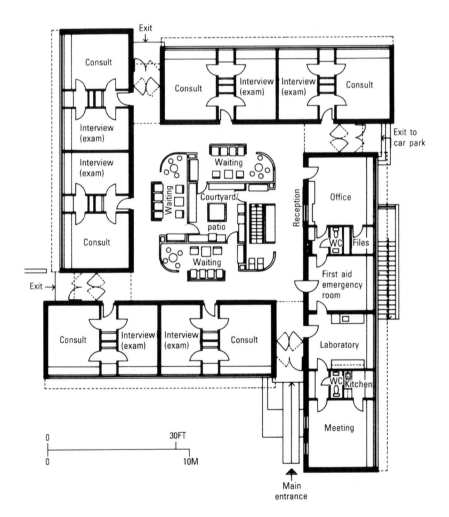

should be approachable. To this end, he incorporated imitation sash windows which are really top-hung, a gable and a hipped roof echoing ones in the same street, 1950s-style railings inspired by the existing bungalow next door and even a floor from one of the soulless prefabricated public housing blocks nearby, dropped onto the roof as a clerestory to the transverse corridor. The building, according to McDougall, "miniaturizes the urban soup of its location." . . . On the interior, as on the exterior, there is an impression of a motley collection of old buildings, crudely cobbled together, when in reality the building is largely new. . . . Much effort . . . went into choosing a highly decorated "grandma's carpet" that was assured to epitomize the taste of the locals.[45]

8.36. Kensington Health Centre, Melbourne, Australia, 1983

8.37. Bethnal Green Health Centre (foreground), London, 1988

The reviewer mentioned the positive theoretical influence of Robert Venturi and his call for a messy, ambiguous, contradictory, and hence vital architecture, but in writing of the specifics of the Health Centre he missed the main point: that this was a place created in the indigenous vernacular of its neighborhood and reflecting the aspirations of its inhabitants, not an entity extemporaneously established by an external structure imposing the requirements of an indifferent, off-site bureaucratic provider.

A similar attitude, though not nearly as extreme, was in evidence in the Highgate Group Practice clinic (1984–86) in London, by Douglas Stephen and Partners. This outpatient surgical center was built in a dense neighborhood with a rich historic context, including Lubetkin and Tecton's Highpoint housing and adjacent eighteenth-century Victorian cottages.[46] In response, the clinic was a mixture of high technology, contextualism, and residentialism. The partially exposed steel frame and the gabled clerestory window on the front of the

8.38. Bethnal Green Health Centre, main waiting area

8.39. Bethnal Green Health Centre, exploded axonometric view

building were gestures aimed to strike a balance between historic context and avant-garde trends in British architecture. The clinic had two levels, with examination rooms and waiting areas on both, with the waiting areas at the center. This clinic was an exemplary attempt to blend in without mimicking or, worse, homogenizing its immediate surroundings or cultural context.

Other clinics built at about this same time sought to expropriate forms and images from domestic architecture for the purposes of abstraction, superimposition, and synthesis with the relatively simple functional requirements of community health care (as opposed to those of the typical hospital). One clinic in particular was conceived and executed in the socially empathic tradition of the Finsbury Health Centre. The Bethnal Green Health Centre (1985–88), by Avanti Architects, was, like Finsbury, built in one of the poorest parts of London. The architects were faced with the task of creating an impressionable, important civic statement in a public building for a diverse local constituency. A symmetrical building was chosen as the most logical site-planning response to the three main program requirements, which called for two physicians' group practices and the local health authority public- and primary-health clinic. The site was long and narrow, facing onto an open, neglected field. The building's domesticity was achieved by stretching it from end to end on the site. From the exterior, the clinic looked like two smaller buildings in collision (fig. 8.37). The entrance was positioned at the midpoint, and the patient had a sense of its quasi-residential scale because of the narrow depth of building at the point of arrival. Two wings and

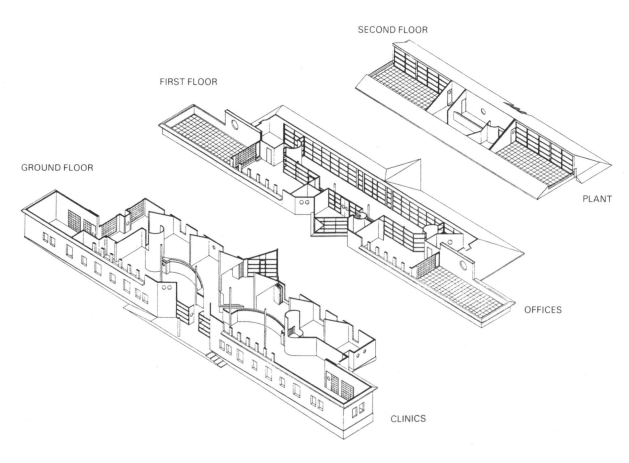

SECOND FLOOR

FIRST FLOOR

GROUND FLOOR

PLANT

OFFICES

CLINICS

their circulation paths emanated from three distinct reception desks—one for each clinic—with waiting rooms to the center (fig. 8.38). Ceilings sloped and interlocked above, creating a series of dynamic spaces. The considerable civic stature of the building was achieved through its symmetry, its siting, its length, and the decision to place staff offices on the second level, above the entrance (fig. 8.39). The external imagery of the clinic was criticized at the time for being overtly postmodern, but the architects, who had developed seven schemes before finalizing the design, defended their concept as simply a means to create a civic building. This clinic has since been praised in the British architectural press as a late-century successor to the heroic tradition established at Finsbury.[47]

Another clinic by Avanti Architects borrowed more literally from the formal imagery of the single-family detached dwelling. The Church End Medical Centre (1992–93), in London, was a square in plan, with a two-level gabled roof, front to rear (fig. 8.40). The interior was dominated by a large open room with a skylight at its center. This space housed the waiting area; the seating was curvilinear, consisting of elements fixed to a sweeping wall that doubled as a visual buffer between the various clinic rooms that surrounded it on three sides (figs. 8.41 and 8.42). The structure was residentialist in scale, exterior appearance, and the scale of its interior spaces housing various clinic functions. Critic Peter Scher wrote:

8.40. Church End Medical Centre, London, 1993

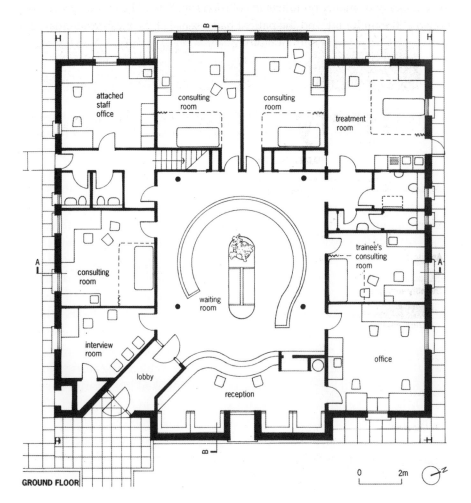

GROUND FLOOR

0   2m

8.41. Church End Medical Centre, ground-floor plan

8.42. Church End Medical Centre, main waiting area

8.43. Shindo Children's Clinic,
Fukuoka, Japan, 1989

8.44. Shindo Children's Clinic,
section showing clinic-residence

This building is a small architectural gem set in a deceptively bland-looking London suburb. It is also a model project in cost and operational terms, though that model may no longer fit a health service reformed to suit the enterprise culture. The accommodation can and should be on one level (as here), but the significance of the building within its community demands something of a higher stature. This is achieved at Church End with an almost perfectly square plan under a pitched roof, a decision of elegant simplicity that embodies many architectural virtues. . . . By using the gable end for its front elevation, facing onto the axis of the road into the estate [subdivision], the building reflects its community purpose.[48]

This clinic was no more than a house among houses, and its expropriation of the suburban tract house was seen as its main virtue, together with its simple interior spaces and layout. The Shindo Children's Clinic (1988–89), in Fukuoka, Japan, by the Architectural Laboratory for Systems Environment Development, similarly aspired to project a quiet, reassuring, yet symbolically forceful presence in its suburban milieu. The front of the clinic resembled a single-family residence, with the entrance at the center and a gabled roof (fig. 8.43). In section, however, it is revealed as a gabled two-level structure housing the clinic and the residence in a series of interlocking spaces. As in many of the Japanese clinic-residences, the physician's residence was situated on the upper floor, with the clinic on the ground level below (fig. 8.44).[49]

In the United States, many freestanding community care clinics were built to blend in contextually with their surroundings. The interest in contextualism first arose in the 1970s in cities and accompanied the rise of the historic preservation movement, but it also coincided with the residentialist impulses of clients and their designers, whose aim was to have their community health clinic be as nonthreatening to the patient as possible, and certainly far more amenable than if it were housed at a distant medical center. The language of the suburban house was widely borrowed in clinics operated by both private for-profit providers and governmental nonprofit providers. One example of a public community health clinic was the West Ouachita Parish Health Center (1982–84), in Monroe, Louisiana, by R-2ARCH with Hugh Parker Architects. In this case, the imagery and materials of the single-family detached house were incorporated literally, in a synthesis with local warehouse and agricultural equipment structures prevalent in the region and immediate environs, while the residentialist imagery of the house was abstracted. The resultant building, therefore, was a hybrid of the regional vernacular of residential forms and imagery and industrial forms and imagery. The exterior of the building was of gray-blue wood-simulated siding, and the roof was gabled. The abstracted residentialist motif of the examination rooms, which looked like a series of small, semi-detached "health houses" extruded from the main body of the building (fig. 8.45), set this apart from earlier clinics, with their inboard cell-like examination rooms. At West Ouachita, each examination room was conceived as a semi-autonomous entity, with its own countertop testing and diagnostic equipment, yet each remained in immediate proximity to its essential support functions.[50] This prototype clinic was the result of a coordinated research-based

8.45. West Ouachita Parish Health Center, West Monroe, Louisiana, 1994

initiative begun in Louisiana in 1990, which resulted in dozens of new and renovated clinics.[51]

By the 1990s, residentialism had crossed paths not only with strains of critical regionalism in community clinic architecture but also with the desire for an ethnic community to express itself and its aspirations through its local clinic's architecture. A notable example was the East Austin Multipurpose Center (1990–91) in Austin, Texas, by Coffee, Crier, and Schenck, Architects (fig. 8.46). Although small-scale community health clinics had become commonplace, few were as warmly embraced by their community. In addition to an outpatient clinic, the facility included a multipurpose neighborhood activity center that, as the administration and the architects had anticipated, soon hosted gatherings ranging from community meetings to bridal showers, and also provided office space for many local advocacy and arts groups. The outdoor spaces of the center functioned as informal social attractors for children and their caregivers (fig. 8.47). This proprietary attitude on the part of the long-established Chicano community in East Austin stemmed from their participation as of the earliest planning and design phases, and their wish that the building reflect their Mexican heritage. As a result the building drew from culturally resonant forms, materials, and motifs. Soon after the opening of the facility, neighborhood artists painted, on a facing building, a large-scale, colorful mural that celebrated, in part, the fundamental role of health care in the community. The mural conveyed the same spirit as Gordon Cullen's work at the Finsbury Clinic in London nearly sixty years earlier. Clad in brick and striped stucco, with a roof of red tiles, the building—and by extension, the mural—immediately became a civic icon—a symbol of a community's pride and self-determination through its civic buildings.[52]

Similar culturally sensitive approaches were being used in Latin America. The vernacular traditions of Bolivia were the primary inspiration for three clinics designed by Argentinean architect Miguel Angel Roca and built in La

8.46. East Austin Multipurpose Center, Austin, Texas, 1990–91

8.47. East Austin Multipurpose Center, entry colonnade

Paz between 1988 and 1991. Like the "pyramid" clinics built in Cairo, all three shared the same program, which in this case consisted of a community hall, a community health clinic, and a pharmacy. In each building, these elements were expressed as three color-coded elemental shapes: triangle, circle, and square. Taking cues from local dwellings, the buildings assumed, and aspired to transcend, the appearance and attributes of an archaic urbanism. They responded to a newly established governmental policy, which extended to social services and cultural institutions, to decentralize in order to relocate services to local districts. A fundamental characteristic of these clinics was their assertive, symbolic presence in their communities as a means to reaffirm the history and dignity of the local residents.

At one of these clinics, the Cotahuma District Center and Health Center in La Paz, Bolivia (1988–91), the massing reflected a synthesis of the architect's knowledge of the International Style and local vernacular traditions in architecture. The massing was abstracted in response to this dualism. Its scale and presence were low key. Its white exterior and subtle colors conveyed the public nature of the building, and its protrusions along the edges of the site had the effect of establishing a connection with its environs. The General Health Centers, also in La Paz (1989–91), followed these same principles, although on a much smaller scale. It was, because of its dominant site overlooking the community, a strong visual and symbolic presence; it also quickly became a landmark of the town and lent visual cohesion to the entire district. These buildings were widely published in the international architectural press.[53] Yet, to those most in need of health care—the working poor and the desperately poor in these locations—the sheer presence of these clinics was what really mattered. Architectural context or aesthetic quality were, of course, of less importance. In these settings the mere existence of a clinic of *any* type was the paramount concern.

The Storefront Clinic

Before 1990, community health clinics, whether designed by architects or not, were, with few exceptions, considered of minimal theoretical value by a dismissive architectural press. Yet the storefront clinics that appeared in the late 1960s had been the most neglected of all health-related building types. True, the structures that housed these clinics were very seldom built initially as health clinics, but this accounts for only a portion of historians' lack of interest. Often the grassroots efforts of local ad hoc steering committees and volunteers had strong roots in inner urban neighborhoods inhabited by largely minority or underclass populations, as in La Paz and Austin. But unlike those architect-designed facilities, storefront clinics were typically established in makeshift storefront operations, or sometimes even former private residences. A 1971 commentary on the East Palo Alto Health Center, a temporary clinic set up to serve twenty-three thousand people, stated:

> Bringing health care to the people [is] surer than getting them to the health facility. And when the health facility is large and formidable, and across town, it may not be what their particular needs require. For poor people, the pressing need in

health is for the accessible, the familiar, the personal; and these spell the neighborhood health center. There is nothing new about the neighborhood health center concept; the problem is that there are so few of them. . . . The reasons are many, largely lack of funds for operating the centers, and lack of personnel to staff them. But also there has been a lack of funds to construct new centers, so that for the most part they have existed in empty stores, old houses, anything available and convenient to the people to be served. Almost never does the storefront clinic have the benefit of even the most modest architectural help in organizing its functions in the space it has to use. An exception is the temporary location of the East Palo Alto/East Menlo Park Health Center, situated on a busy commercial street in a largely black community near San Francisco. . . . [The architects] remodeled a library for administrative offices, and a onetime store across the street for the clinic, giving the two units organization and order, and a pleasant sense of unity. Even such minimal architectural assistance and treatment is rare, however. Most neighborhood health centers operate with sheets to separate examining rooms and interview areas, in a general atmosphere of chaos.[54]

The challenge of providing care for indigent patients in the inner cities of America did not diminish in the final years of the century. Storefront clinics such as the one described above continued to exist in a hand-to-mouth manner. Assistance centers, run mostly by volunteers, had been set up to provide a safety net of architectural, urban planning, and urban design services to assist these neighborhoods. But the first wave of these Community Design Centers, established by activist architects, allied designers, and builders in many U.S. cities, had all but disappeared by 1980.

A parallel phenomenon in the United States, the community mental health center, grew rapidly, beginning with the first federal funding in 1963 for the construction of a network of new community-based treatment centers. In order to offset increasing reliance on inpatient treatment in the system of state-operated mental hospitals, the federal program created a highly decentralized system of care, based on community "catchment areas." By the early 1970s, more than 450 of these areas, varying in population from 75,000 to 250,000 persons, had developed the prerequisite menu of healthcare services required by the government and were designated Community Mental Health Centers, a moniker that was accorded a clinic and its local catchment area. The five mandated or essential services were inpatient care, outpatient care, partial hospitalization, emergency and consultation, and education.[55]

Satellite mental health facilities were located in storefronts, converted homes, office buildings, or even mobile units, and in some communities were supplemented by halfway houses and boarding houses. In time, the phrase "not in my backyard" was coined to describe the dilemma of where to locate these centers. By the 1990s, the situation had not changed dramatically. Outpatient clinics for persons discharged from mental institutions, and for persons undergoing treatment for drug and alcohol abuse, continued to be considered negative social influences in the community.

By 1991, 550 community rural and migrant clinics for public health or mental health served 6 million patients at 1,400 sites in the United States. These health centers received appropriated federal funds of $585 million, and their total budgets were $1.4 billion. They occupied a central role in providing medical needs to chronically underserved minority communities. This preventive and primary care was mandated by federal legislation, and care was provided regardless of ability to pay. Architecturally, the clinics assumed a nondescript, low-budget approach to health facility design and construction: the typical clinic might be in a prefabricated steel building or an adapted school building.[56]

Residential Birthing Centers

In contrast to the neighborhood mental health center, with its persistent negative associations, freestanding birthing centers emerged as a socially acceptable building type. By the mid-1990s, in the United States and in other parts of the world, hundreds of such centers were providing birthing services on an outpatient basis, with patients spending minimal time in residence. These facilities were viewed as an empowering alternative for women, compared with conventional labor, delivery, and recovery (LDR) units in hospitals. Birthing centers, fueled by what many in the U.S. feminist movement viewed as the failure of the hospital to provide an appropriate environment for the birthing process, set up shop in adapted former residences, some of which became mixed-use facilities not unlike the combination clinic-residences in Japan.

With the movement toward birthing centers, history was in the process of repeating itself. Midwifery dated from antiquity and had been an important aspect of virtually all ancient cultures. Home birthing was the sole domain of the midwife until the rise of the medical establishment in the early nineteenth century. But as women rejected the impersonal scale of the large hospital, many alternatives, focused on birthing centers, arose in the late 1960s and in the 1970s to fulfill the specialized needs of pregnant women. Thus these centers, some of which were actually converted homes, were a contributing factor in the functional deconstruction of the hospital (see Chapter 5). In 1983, there were more than one hundred birthing centers in the United States. One year later, three hundred more were in the planning stages. Yet during the 1980s, soaring rates for liability insurance for maternity care put many plans on hold. By 1989, the National Association of Childbearing Centers reported that 130 birth centers were in operation in the United States.[57]

Birthing centers were a low-cost, consumer-controlled, and community-based alternative. The more formal examples were generally licensed by state health departments. Certified nurse-midwives, consulting physicians, registered nurses and dietitians, and other ancillary medical professionals provided care. The centers offered programs for pregnant women and their families in such areas as physical fitness, childbirth, family health and nutrition, and parenting. Women were carefully screened for potential complications during pregnancy and delivery, and only low-risk mothers anticipating normal childbirth were typically accepted. This characteristic would have profound impact on the architectural environment because it was possible to do without many of the clinical accoutrements of the high-tech hospital and to relax somewhat the stringent code requirements of medical-center-based birthing centers. Also, far fewer specialized rooms were needed, compared with the hospital LDR units, which tended to isolate different stages of the birthing process in compartmentalized zones of the labor-and-delivery suite.

The birthing center combined clinical, educational, and residential elements in two distinct spatial realms: prenatal and birthing. The prenatal realm comprised examination rooms, classroom-fitness rooms, interview rooms, reception and administration, reference and library, restrooms, and play areas for children. In some centers an income-producing shop or workspace was included. The best of these centers provided direct access to nature: a quiet garden, an atrium or greenhouse, generously sized windows, water, natural light, and full views of the outdoor environs. By the date of actual childbirth, the center would already be a familiar setting to an expectant mother and her family. Once in the birthing space, the midwife was usually considered a guest. The suite typically consisted of a bedroom, family gathering room, kitchen and eating area, and a full bath-shower room. Couples were encouraged to bring in artifacts to personalize their space. Typically, a family left the center with their newborn within eight to twelve hours after the delivery.[58]

A third birthing option available to women, in addition to birth at the hospital or the birthing center, was home birth. Advocates claimed that it was safer in many instances, and a far more humane architectural environment, than the hospital. In response, hospitals in the 1990s began to establish freestanding outpatient specialty birthing centers in the spirit of the old maternity hospitals, and they restructured their in-house LDR units to meet the needs of this growing market (see Chapter 6). Nevertheless, the architecture of birthing continued to be directly related to the political and economic ideologies that defined the medical profession. Its paternalistic attitude toward birthing continued through the late 1990s. Mainstream providers exerted control over the outpatient-care boom by keeping LDR units near, or on the grounds of, the medical center. This was said to be essential in order to maintain close links with the resources of the hospital. Second, it was deemed a cost-effective strategy.[59]

The Boom Years

By the late 1980s, primary care centers, freestanding diagnostic imaging centers, and surgicenters were proliferating in the United States. In 1988, hospital systems and independent providers operated 2,085 ambulatory care centers, an 18.2 percent increase from just the year before. Independent providers operated 358 of the centers.[60] By 1993, the total number had increased to 5,492, with the number of freestanding centers reaching 2,530.[61]

An important trend was the rise of "mall medicine." Providers, noting the phenomenal success of shopping malls, developed medical shopping malls, which combined a wide range of specialty shops and clinics under one roof. One could now walk past the podiatrist and the optometrist on the way to the primary care clinic to obtain immunizations.[62] The HMO movement quickly took to the mall concept, opening clinics in malls across the United States, and some shopping malls were even converted to health malls, while others added new wings devoted to this purpose.[63]

Hotels related to medical centers reappeared during these years. This building type was for patients recovering from outpatient surgery whose condition was not acute enough to justify admittance to the hospital but who needed a place to stay overnight.[64] Other providers opened freestanding hotels for the relatives of patients in their acute-care hospital. This concept had been previously explored in the late 1960s by the firm of Ludwig Mies van der Rohe, which was hired to develop a prototype step-down hospital–residential facility for construction alongside acute-care hospitals. The principal function of this building type would be to serve as the midpoint between the hospital and the freestanding outpatient clinic. The prototype, however, was never built.[65] Nevertheless, the concept was decades ahead of its time, while somewhat reminiscent of the overnight hostel sleeping quarters for the less than acutely ill that had been provided in the monastic hospitals of Europe and the Middle East a thousand years earlier.

The Clinic as Rediscovered Civic Symbol

Residentialism, as much an attitude as an architectural style, was embraced by providers, architects, and the public as a valid expression of emerging philosophies of patient-centered care. Yet residentialism, particularly when crossed with postmodern classicist geometry and ornament, was not universally admired. To some, it was seen as little more than a cost-driven recentering of the industry, as more patient care was being provided away from the hospital. The community care clinic, ostensibly looking more friendly and less overtly clinical than before, by the 1990s often fell victim to excessively tight design and construction budgets. Therefore, many low-budget clinics were little more than watered-down caricatures of a historical style, resulting in buildings that were pseudo-Victorian, pseudo-Georgian, and so on. Eventually, as is so often the case in architecture, high ideals disintegrated as they wound their way through to the mainstream.

Where vision did prevail, fueled by adequate funding for construction, clinics were built to rival such civic symbols as the local community library and other cultural institutions. By the 1990s, the New Age health movement began to influence outpatient health facilities. The widespread focus on wellness, as opposed to illness, led to explorations into organic architecture, which took its inspiration from nature. An example was the Holistic Health Center (1990–93) by Donald Hopper, built in Hemet, California (fig. 8.48). The center housed administrative and physicians' offices, a multipurpose room, an auditorium, and a clinic. The floor plan was radial, with an open courtyard and a fountain at the center (fig. 8.49). The site had once been part of a ranch belonging to famed movie producer Louis Mayer. Situated a hundred miles southeast of Los Angeles in semi-arid terrain, the one-level center was perched in the foothills of the San Jacinto mountains. The architect's narrative accompanying the publication of his building ran as follows:

> The program of the competition which has given birth to this complex called for
> an architecture that would express the principles of holistic medicine and unite

8.48. Holistic Health Center, Hemet, California, 1993

8.49. Holistic Health Center, floor plan

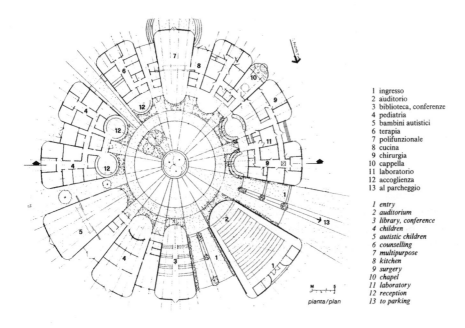

1	ingresso
2	auditorio
3	biblioteca, conferenze
4	pediatria
5	bambini autistici
6	terapia
7	polifunzionale
8	cucina
9	chirurgia
10	cappella
11	laboratorio
12	accoglienza
13	al parcheggio

1	entry
2	auditorium
3	library, conference
4	children
5	autistic children
6	counselling
7	multipurpose
8	kitchen
9	surgery
10	chapel
11	laboratory
12	reception
13	to parking

pianta/plan

the disciplines of alternative medicine: homeopathy, allopathy, naturopathy, acupuncture, psychology and other therapies. Design expansion and flexibility were required to adapt to future needs and development. . . . Shaded garden areas for patients to relax were also provided. The solution was a plan of modular units radiating from a central garden court. Growth can expand asymmetrically to suit future needs. Modules are linked by curving corridors that follow the topography of the site. Their dropped ceilings contain lighting and the air conditioning ducts. Avoiding the standard catalog ceiling, these are individually designed, of cedar wood strips and fiberglass translucent panels. The form of the light fixtures—diamond, circle, or triangle—expresses the identity of each module. Natural materials are used. The exterior brick walls keep the interior cool during the day and release heat at night. The adobe brick was made in a Mexican village across the border. . . . Organic architecture, growing out of the landscape, with its intimate human scale, demonstrates that there is an alternative to the dehumanized, sterile modern hospital. . . . Holistic healing shares a common root with organic architecture: the emphasis on synthesis rather than analysis and the conviction that "the part is to the whole as the whole is to the part."[66]

Meanwhile, large mainstream medical centers were rushing to build out-patient wellness centers on or near their campuses, often using time-proven, conservative architectural styles. One such high-tech example, antithetical to the organic architecture of the Holistic Health Center, was the Northwest Community Hospital Wellness Center (1994–96), in Arlington Heights, Illinois, by O'Donnell Wicklund Pigozzi and Peterson. The center had a decidedly industrial, quasi-corporate aesthetic, a bowed roof, expanses of windows above a collection of recreational activity areas, a sports medicine and cardiac rehabilitation clinic, and a children's activity area, café, library, and community meeting rooms. This 80,000-square-foot facility was indicative of the persistence of "top-down" corporate initiatives that were antithetical to the grassroots approach used with the clinic in Austin. Such top-down methods had been applied previously in the design of the hospital, and medical-center administrators and their architects seemed willing to reflexively continue to use them or derivatives of them.

Others had quite different views of the challenge of giving physical shape to community health facilities. In Melbourne, Australia, the Northcote Community Health Centre (1988–90), by Greg Burgess, was a modestly scaled attempt to fuse the functional requirements of a primary care clinic and a dental clinic, using the language of organic architecture. Its site was adjacent to the main library of a Melbourne suburb. Its plan appeared random, with spaces flowing into one another. From the exterior its attributes were unremarkable, with the exception of a bulbous roof line curving around the corner above the main entrance. On the interior, by contrast, the spaces flowed in a pattern of nearly continuous wavy walls and angular corridors, with walls and ceilings turning and falling away. One had the sense of being within a vessel, or even inside a human body, as one moved through the clinic. This sensation was reinforced by the undulating skylight above the main circulation artery, which traced the ribbed structural pattern of the roof. The ceiling of the waiting room was marked with irregularly spaced expressive wood-beam ribbed trusses placed in a relatively free-form exoskeletal pattern. The unique ambiance of the facility was described as follows:

> The ribs that curve upwards and outwards from the central support of this delicate and gentle space terminate in clerestory windows, so that daylight is brought down into the middle of the plan and, usually, sunlight too, for the sinuous path of the main artery and its subsidiaries allows for sun penetration at almost any time of the day. The device of using a curved ribbed covering for the main public space might on first hearing be thought to be too osseous, too skeletal to be appropriate for a building for the treatment of the sick. In fact, the effect is far more like the organic structure of flowers, reaching up to the light and bringing it in.[67]

It remains to be seen whether this organic approach to clinic design will be widely emulated. The serpentine plan of the single band of patient rooms at the Vista Hill Psychiatric Hospital (1984–86; closed 1994), in Chula Vista, California, by Kaplan/McLaughlin/Diaz, was influenced by a related set of principles, but this influence was not carried to the same extent as at the Holistic Health Center or the Northcote Health Centre.

8.50. Health clinic, Almere-Haven, the Netherlands, 1992

8.51. Almere-Haven, town plan indicating location of health clinic

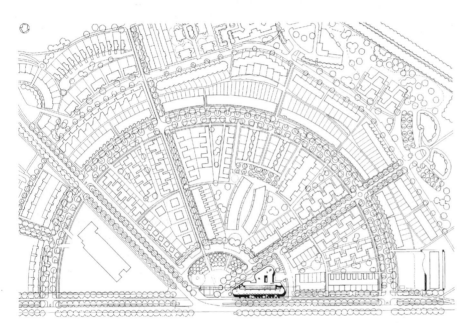

In many instances the community health center was given a site of importance in the community. Such sites—at the center of the village, or overlooking the town, or at the heart of a new town plan—would at one time have been reserved for the hospital. In at least one case an entire new community was planned around the health clinic. The new town of Almere, the Netherlands, established in 1976, was also the site of the De Overloop assisted-living facility by Herman Hertzberger (see Chapter 7). The Almere health clinic (1990–92), was designed by Julyan Wickham of A. and H. van Eyck and Partners. It occupied a central site, fronting a large paved plaza at the center of a radially configured town plan (figs. 8.50 and 8.51). The street grid fanned out from the civic center of the town. Residences, stores, and various institutions were interspersed along the streetscapes in a quasi-urban tapestry, and the streets were, curiously, named after film stars (Orson Wellesstraat, for example, was the name of one street). The clinic, not unlike Dutch architecture in general, was viewed by its architects and the town planners as a catalyst for social change, and therefore the building housed community rooms as well as the clinic. Bold colors and forms were employed to create a non-institutional, animated setting. The overall partí was a curious amalgamation of two trends: the industrial aesthetic of high-tech architecture and the anthropomorphism inherent in organic

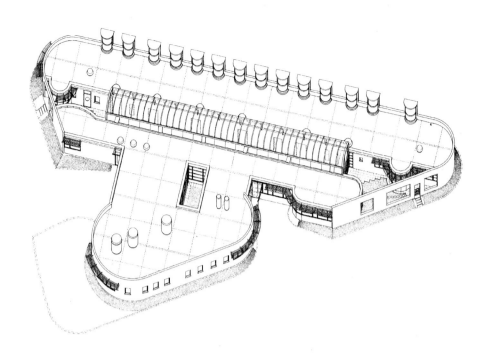

8.52. Health clinic, axonometric view

architecture. Its taut, controlled exterior was softened by curved corners to make it appear more informal (fig. 8.52). The plan was centered on a main entrance from the plaza, leading into an interior pedestrian "street" with a battery of examination rooms along one side and various administrative, community, and support functions at the ends and along the other side of this street (fig. 8.53). The examination rooms all contained skylights, which from the outside could look like the smoke stacks of a factory. On the interior, the light from above made these spaces chapel-like, leading to a sense of seclusion from the main hub of activity, and this impression of isolation was reinforced because the rooms were recessed from the main circulation artery. The main interior street was also skylit from above, and the furnishings were custom-fabricated in wood (fig. 8.54).[68]

Utopianism

In addition to the built work, community-based ambulatory utopian excursions were put forth, some more grandiose than others. Two particular prototypes, developed at precisely the same time, were radically different in intent, scope, and context. The first, the proposal for the Starbright Pavilion (1990) by Kaplan/McLaughlin/Diaz, has evoked debate virtually since its unveiling (fig. 8.55). The Starbright project was initially conceived as an inpatient-outpatient care facility connected to an existing acute-care facility via a bridge; this approach was later rejected because of physicians' fears that the fragile status of the population of pediatric patients with cancer would be disrupted and that problems could rise from the standpoint of infection control. Jain Malkin, an interior designer with considerable experience in health care, wrote of this outpatient superclinic as follows:

> Located in Los Angeles, part of the University of Southern California master plan, the 50,000-square foot Starbright Pavilion is a prototype design for facilities the Starbright Foundation hopes to build around the world. Dedicated to grant-

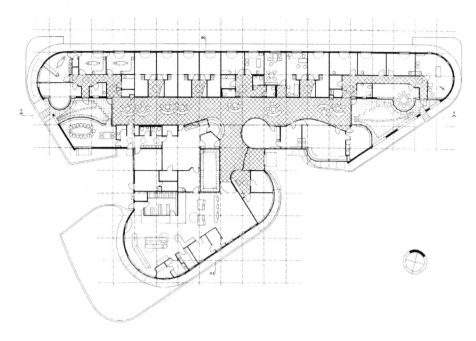

8.53. Health clinic, ground-floor plan

8.54. Health clinic, main circulation artery

8.53. Health clinic, ground-floor plan

8.54. Health clinic, main circulation artery

ing last wishes to children with life-threatening illnesses, the purpose of the building is to integrate some aspects of medical care with entertainment. A communications tower is to broadcast events at the center to locations worldwide via satellite. The imagery of the building was inspired by children's toys and uses bright colors and abstract geometric forms. The pavilion houses a large auditorium with three levels of balconies, child care, indoor and outdoor gardens, an audiovisual library, computer education, dining, case management offices, and therapy spaces for art, music, and play. An unmanned tram rises from the ground level to the third and fourth levels, which have gardens, an outdoor stage, and a petting zoo. This highly imaginative, fantasy environment should delight children and adults.[69]

8.55. Starbright Pavilion (proposal), Los Angeles, 1990

Not all reactions were as supportive, however. One critic, Frances Anderton, described the Starbright proposal as a synthesis of a high-tech entertainment extravaganza and the latest research and treatment procedures in psychoneuroimmunology:

> Planned as a freestanding pavilion in the grounds of an existing hospital, [it] will provide, as a palliative to the traumatic medical treatment received there, only "pleasant, non-painful experiences." . . . Their [the architects'] jolly building, already replete with distractions, will serve as the basis for what might, pending funding and the anticipated involvement of director/producer Steven Spielberg, be an even more excessive environment, and the antithesis of the traditionally tranquil convalescent home.[70]

Anderton continued:

> In accordance with the aim of distracting children totally from hospital experiences, the building is designed to entertain. With the accent on BIG, the sick child is lured by larger-than-life choo-choo trains, doll houses and building-block fountains to a brightly-coloured, sculptural building, ostensibly composed of oversized Meccano and Lego pieces. From the rather abstract exterior to a more theatrical interior, a "magic" key permits entry through a child-size door on to a musical yellow brick road, leading into a four-level atrium which gives on to treatment rooms, playrooms, library, auditorium and more. The Starbright Pavilion boasts not only the natural treats of a flood of light (from the light well and huge skylight above), roof garden, aquarium, aviaries and children's zoo, but also a phantasmagoria of events and visual distractions; climbing trolley, treatment rooms disguised as shopfronts, projected waterfalls, seashores and forests, suspended aircraft, banners and numerous TV screens that constantly beam out—to the 450 Starbright children within and thousands across the world—Disney and (proposed) Starbright channels. (p. 37)

In comparing the Starbright with the socially controlled, completely orchestrated environment of Disney World, Anderton wrote:

> To this end children will evidently never be left to quietly enjoy the many therapeutic and educational facilities—such as art and music, puppet shows and plays [produced by the Los Angeles theatrical community], pets and gardening—but will be constantly wired for sight and sound, chivvied and jollied along by Starbright "mascots" and silly characters . . . surrounded by "child-friendly" gimmicks. . . . This hectic blend of bright building and state-of-the-art communications is an innovative and interesting project, but alarming to those of us who, perhaps fuddy-duddily, thought that edifying surroundings and the company of nice human beings could alone raise the spirits and hence improve health or at least the last days of life. (p. 35)

The Starbright prototype was indeed rather awkwardly composed, with a random-looking assortment of "playful" elements poking and pushing at the

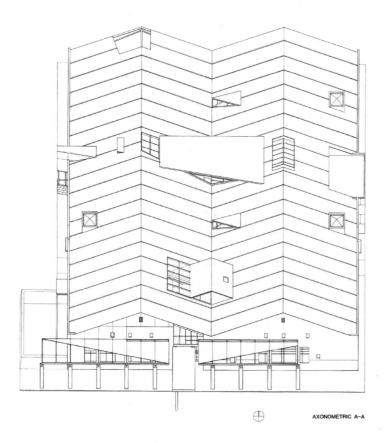

AXONOMETRIC A–A

8.56. St. Tammany Community Health Center (proposal), Slidell, Louisiana, 1991, axonometric view

glass-enclosed atrium like toys strewn across a bedroom floor, all dominated by a tapered, towering telecommunications tower. Most significantly, this design represented the apotheosis of the newfound aesthetic pluralism taken to an extreme: this postmodern machine was the antithesis of the emergent new residentialism.

A radically different, far more contextual, understated approach was taken in the development of the proposed St. Tammany Community Health Center, a prototype community health clinic proposed for a public sector provider in Slidell, Louisiana. The strategy was one of reclamation and recycling of a discarded building type. This unbuilt clinic proposal (1990–91) was developed by R-2ARCH. It consisted of the adaptive use of a former oil field equipment-and-supply warehouse (fig. 8.56). The program called for a community health clinic and offices for an environmental health staff. In response, the warehouse was to be transformed by inserting slotted skylights into the roof, reworking the existing exterior by adding new construction, and incorporating rearrangeable plug-in modules in the interior. The modules could be replaced as needs changed, thus avoiding the need for extensive renovations or relocation. As a result, the interior was to remain an open ground-level "loft space," with demountable modules composing a "kit" of several parts: nursing offices, examination rooms, the laboratory, and modularized clerical and administrative support spaces. The existing concrete-slab floor was to be modified to accommodate plumbing, and all electrical and HVAC systems were to be provided from a support grid attached to an open-grid ceiling above (fig. 8.57).

This prototype, and the larger framework of research on which it was based, was viewed as an appropriate, tempered response to the dilemma of how to reuse the tens of thousands of abandoned buildings that had become the legacy of the Industrial Revolution and, more specifically in the case of the

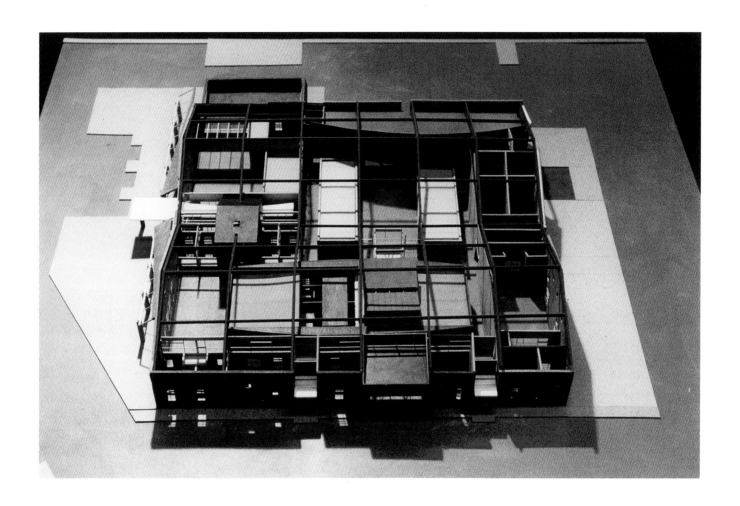

8.57. St. Tammany Community
Health Center, floor plan (model
view)

Gulf South, the many discarded buildings of the "oil patch" economy. The goal was to reclaim a portion of these for such civic buildings as schools, libraries, and health centers.[71] Similarly, the approach of plugging modules into a larger single volume was experimented with at approximately the same time in Japan, in the combination clinic-residence built at Hoya (1991–93) in Tokyo, designed by the Architects' Workshop. There, the clinic examination rooms and support spaces were also designed for disassembly as freestanding, autonomous objects within a larger, minimally differentiated volume.[72]

Convergent or Divergent Ideologies?

Ideological battles waged in the health professions might appear to the casual observer as exclusive of ideological battles waged within the architectural profession. In reality, however, the issues confronting each domain have been intertwined since the beginning of organized medicine. In each realm the debate has typically centered on such bipolarities as ideology versus technique, ephemeralities versus tectonics, or the grand gesture versus austerity. These values, and the inherent tensions they embody, have rendered profound change in both health care and architecture. Since the ancient Greeks, then, developments in architecture and health care have been interdependent. This has been a principal theme throughout this book. The discussion has been centered not on style per se but on those values and attitudes brought to bear on architecture for health. As contemporary health ideology has shifted from sickness to wellness, architecture has mirrored this shift. Similarly, as health ideology has shifted away from technology-for-the-sake-of-technology, so has architecture. As the health economy has shifted from costly inpatient stays to less costly outpatient and community-based care, so has architecture. Accordingly, as ideology in architecture has shifted from modernism to postmodernism and to the current state of pluralism, so have the health professions been engaged in an increasing acceptance of pluralism, gradually embracing not only traditional medicine but also alternative approaches to caring for the sick.

As for the community-based care center as a building type, its continued viability and existence have been questioned: "The health center is an awkward building type: not small enough to be domestic, not big enough to gather much civic presence and, unlike its close relation the primary school, not able to spread itself amid playgrounds and sports fields. Architecturally there might be a case for abolishing the type altogether and letting its various components find separate accommodation in adapted houses or office buildings."[73]

This view, however, discounts the notion of hybridization—the layering of multiple functions within a single entity—and therein lies the ultimate potential of this building type: it is not really a singular type but an amalgamation of "healthcare" and "wellness" purposes, each with a distinct civic mission. By the end of the century, some community-based clinics had achieved the stature of an important civic building, indicative of the dedication of a community or sponsor toward the improvement of the health status of the community-at-large. Unfortunately, relatively few examples among the many thousands of community care clinics constructed worldwide since 1965 would qualify as either true civic landmarks *or* architectural landmarks. Nevertheless, the best and most critically needed of these buildings—particularly in the poorest of communities, where clinics are established out of necessity in makeshift storefronts and abandoned buildings—remain a source of immense pride, determination, and collective achievement, and have much to offer society in the new millennium.

CHAPTER 9

Frontiers of a Transformed Landscape

During the past four decades, healthcare delivery systems have undergone significant transformation on an international scale, and the information revolution is in the process of further altering this landscape. The Virtual Healthscape, the sixth major wave in the history of health care (see Chapter 1), is now emerging. The origins of this sixth wave are based in two main areas of influence: the information revolution and the late-twentieth-century cost-containment movement, specifically the DRGs and the TEFRA mandates of the early 1980s. The widespread impact of these changes on the built environment, however, would not be fully seen until the early 1990s. Around that time, the rise of the Internet and the World Wide Web immediately affected the design and delivery of care. Providers and consumers began to redefine their roles and responsibilities. The increased ability of consumers to monitor their health status from home is just one example of this revolution in the delivery system, signifying a shift from a "single-point" system of care delivery, as typified by the modern medical center, to a "multiple-point," or "multipoint," system of delivery, as typified by a coordinated yet highly differentiated network of care access points. Patients and their families, particularly those in the baby-boom generation, became much more likely than previous generations to question their medical care and to seek alternatives to traditional care.

The multipoint model would consist of at least these five nodes: (1) home, as the focal point of alternatives to the hospital; (2) the workplace, in the form of wellness programs; (3) the community-based healthcare center, with its focus on preventive and primary care; (4) the critical care center (formerly the hospital) for major diagnostic and treatment procedures; and (5) the virtual, that is, the ability for the individual to access health-related information and the provider network from anywhere at any time.[1]

In the United States, the rapid evolution of the for-profit sector in the late 1980s and early 1990s, and its subsequent transfiguration by the close of the century, took many by surprise. The ascent of such corporations as Columbia/HCA during this period was unprecedented. That corporation, however, imploded in 1997 in the face of a Medicare fraud investigation by the U.S. Department of Justice. As a result, Columbia, the largest for-profit healthcare provider in the United States, purposefully downsized and divested itself of many of its facilities and their subsidiaries. Other for-profits, such as National Medical Enterprises (later Tenet) and, in behavioral health, Charter (later Magellan), also reinvented themselves. Other large systems also faced major stress. Kaiser Permanente, for example, had never had a money-losing year (dating from its founding in the 1930s) before 1997, when it lost $270 million. Allegheny Health Services, a massive vertically and horizontally integrated system in Pennsylvania, was declared bankrupt in 1998. Long-standing rivalries transformed into surprising mergers, with the healthcare delivery operations of the University of California (San Francisco) combining with Stanford University's hospitals and clinics. Tulane University, George Washington University, the University of Oklahoma, and other academic institutions sold or leased their healthcare delivery operations to investor-owned chains.

The implications for health architecture of this altered scenario remained unclear at the close of the century. The for-profit providers had sponsored a sizable share of new construction and renovation in the United States while they were developing their networks of facilities. Now, the number of grand-scale capital undertakings would be scrutinized far more carefully than in prior years, both in the nonprofit and the for-profit sectors of the industry.

One way in which providers would combat their fear of overinvestment in updating and new construction would be to work with developers in new types of partnership ventures, whereby, in one scenario among many, the developer would finance and own the facility and lease it back to the provider.

The era of digital health care was in full bloom at the close of the century. Patient records, treatment protocols, medication interactions, surgical procedures, and many other aspects of care were becoming digitally based. Patients, physicians, nurses, and others were thus receiving unprecedented access to information in an interactive fashion in virtually any setting. Communication systems with built-in monitoring functions now enable a greater level of precision than at any time in history. Artificial intelligence promises improved patient outcome across a broad range of clinical interventions. The continuum of care now extends across time—even across one's entire lifespan—allowing for unprecedented information gathering concerning one's health status in times of relative health or in times of illness, thereby giving rise to customized prevention through digitization. On the down side, however, skeptics have warned of the growing influence of an omnipresent Big Brother with the capability of violating individual patient confidentiality.

Virtual healthscape, the term used in this book to describe the current wave in health care, denotes a heretofore unprecedented degree of personal, medical, and technological empowerment, as one can choose the means by which one accesses and receives information and care. The virtual healthscape itself might be conceptualized as six streams, interdependent yet distinct. These extend, amplify, and qualify the five systemic access points listed earlier but are not limited to the usual distinctions by user type, age strata, or building type. The trend since the 1960s to define myriad discrete building types, and for a mini-literature to grow around each type, needs to be supplanted with a literature that intentionally blurs the distinction between building types and stresses commonalities. Thus the following list of six trends within the architecture of the contemporary health landscape avoids such divisions and serves as a set of general conclusions to the arguments made in this book:

1. The reemergence of home-based care and the rise of the "health village," whereby the individual is able to access care in more decentralized settings than in the recent past and whereby community-based care achieves parity with centralized, medical-center-based care.
2. The functional deconstruction and transformation of the acute-care hospital into the critical care center. The reconfigured medical center's primary mission thereby becomes one of providing intensive and semi-intensive care for a somewhat sicker patient population than in the recent past.
3. The dialectical tension between self-determination and provider determination, and the resulting redefinition of access points and service points. The construct of provider empowerment versus recipient empowerment (see Chapter 1) is the hinge upon which the entire system operates, although in the current balance the patient's freedom of choice is, ideally, a more prominent factor than before.
4. Recognition of the necessity of a sustainable landscape based on principles of renewability, flexibility, mobility (where necessary), appropriate construction technologies, and conservation methodologies.
5. Recognition of the necessity of incorporating and sustaining the natural environment as a therapeutic modality in the design, management, and daily experience of health facilities and, beyond, in all buildings and settings for human habitation.
6. The advent of interdisciplinary approaches to address complex health, environmental design, and biotechnical problems at the community, regional, national, and international levels, with particular emphasis on ethics, aesthetic literacy, patient-centered care, and sustainable design concerns.

These six trends will be explored in the following sections.

Home and the Health Village

Until the second half of the twentieth century, the residence was the traditional care setting. The medicine cabinet was analogous to the pharmacy, the bedroom in times of illness was analogous to the patient room, and the kitchen was to the home-based patient what the dietary services department would become to the inpatient care unit in hospitals. The home functioned quite well as a setting for childbirth and minor surgery up to the mid-twentieth century. Yet in the twentieth century, and particularly since 1946, the healthcare industry has done everything in its power to supplant the home as the center of the care universe and to replace it with the hospital or, later, the urban medical center. By the 1980s an entire generation in the United States, England, and other developed nations had become culturally conditioned to turn to the health technocracy first. The near-singular reliance on this system—one becomes sick, one goes to the hospital or medical center, and one is made healthy—proved to be astronomically more costly than a system of preventive home-based care. As the need to contain costs increased, it was logical that renewed emphasis would be placed on less costly, alternative care modalities and treatment settings.

Before the 1980s, hospitals were relatively indifferent to the patient's length of stay from a cost-incurrment or third-party-reimbursement standpoint, but by the mid-1990s the opposite had become true. Financial motivation emerged to keep as many patients out of the acute-care hospital as possible and to provide viable community-based care opportunities. As a result, the home became a center for health education and self-treatment, hence a virtual clinic in and of itself. The useful metaphor of the home-as-clinic is rooted in emerging information technologies and on the interactive capabilities of the home computer, making it possible, for example, for a parent to contact a care provider electronically for advice on the treatment of a child's minor injury. The associated cost savings for providers promise to be significant. As for the home itself, its role as clinic parallels its emerging role as shopping mall for home-based shopping, travel agency for trip planning, or bank for financial transactions vis-à-vis the Internet. The computer space and its multimedia library of reference resources has become an important place within the home and a meaningful part of a family's wellness, adding impetus to the inclusion of interactive libraries—or media rooms—in homes built or renovated in the 1990s. Millions of households use online resources, and this trend will certainly increase exponentially.

Apart from issues of access and use of information technology, the matter of the aging, or graying, of society has given rise to the need to retrofit homes to accommodate universal design principles. Housing is being designed to fit the needs of an increasingly restricted resident; ramps, handrails, adequate lighting, security systems, attention to stair design, technological appliances used to compensate for physical and other disabilities, and adequate door widths have emerged as essential ingredients of a "universal residence." Organizations were formed in the 1990s to respond to this market for professional services, and much research has been conducted on the topic.[2]

Even before the advent of information technologies, the home health movement arose, first in Europe and later in the United States and elsewhere, particularly Japan. The home health industry was a response to the trend away from costly inpatient hospitalization and provided an alternative to frequent outpatient visits. At home, the individual could be in control of events and was near personal possessions, friends, and neighbors. In the area of home health for the elderly, the largest segment of this industry, the market for services grew significantly each year during the 1990s. Elderly persons dependent on some form of home health were projected to reach 14.3 million by 2000.[3] Most important from the perspective of providers, many patients, the elderly in particular, could be cared for in home-based settings at a fraction of the cost of institutionalization.[4]

The home health movement was the second phase in the recentering of the healthcare enterprise away from the hospital, following the success of outpatient care centers during the 1980s. By 1991 there were more than 12,000 home health agencies in the United States, including 1,700 hospice programs.[5] Numerous countries in Europe had operated extensive home health agencies for decades and had found them to provide a necessary support network of services, enabling the aged and others to live independently. Denmark even mandated that disabled persons have a legal right to have their home retrofitted to meet their needs without personal cost, and in England the aged were provided with a multiplicity of home care options.[6] In contrast, the United States recognized the importance of this type of care years after the concept had been used successfully in Europe.

An advantage of virtual, home-based integration of services is that a delivery system can be created without investing huge amounts of capital. Initiatives being explored in the late 1990s centered on new virtual health services that in the past had been provided by home care providers—nutritional education, personal hygiene, wellness care, and so on—thereby extending, ideally, the reach of preventive medicine and primary care.[7] At this time, Community Health Information Networks (CHINs) appeared. The CHIN was a regional, electronic collection of clinical, financial, and insurance data available not only to providers but also to insurers, business coalitions, and other healthcare interests in a given metropolitan area.[8] Electronic health databases such as these have been set up to link the home, the hospital, educational institutions, and the workplace. In addition, thousands of healthcare providers established home pages on the World Wide Web to speed dissemination of their services to the community. The most extensive such network in the United States was established by Columbia/HCA. By mid-1996 Columbia/HCA had established home pages for all 335 of its hospitals and was receiving tens of thousands of inquiries, or "hits," per month. New sites created by providers were turning up at the rate of at least one per day.[9] By the late 1990s, consumer nonprofit coalitions, such as the National Committee for Quality Assurance, had set up Internet-based monitoring programs. Accreditation and quality ratings on the 574 (as of late 1996) HMOs in the United States were now available from one's home-as-clinic. Each provider's Health Plan Data and Information Set (HEDIS) was incorporated as a set of standardized measures, the basis of a health plan's "report card."[10] The architectural and facility-planning implications of making such data available would include the aforementioned information center, which in many homes began to rival the television as the focal point.

The outpatient community clinic had long been poised to take on a more central role in the health landscape but had not come fully into its own until the functional deconstruction of the hospital, near the end of the century. Then such clinics became invaluable as the point of entry, making it possible to provide effective primary and preventive care without involving the costly nearby hospital. But with the rise of the home-as-clinic, the home was on the verge of supplanting the CCC as the principal point of access even though the community-based clinic had been the main testing ground for the new residentialism of the 1980s and 1990s. Ironically, while the clinic emulated the home, the home began to emulate the clinic. In either case, the local community wanted a say in its health care. If community involvement was elicited in the planning and design, a clinic or virtual delivery system stood a much greater chance of community acceptance and use. By contrast, if a clinic or virtual delivery system was planned and designed in isolation from the immediate community, the risk was great that it would fail.

In this spirit, Christopher Alexander, in his seminal 1977 book *A Pattern Language,* advocated a residentialist community clinic at the heart of a small-scale "healthful" village inhabited by persons of all ages: "Gradually develop a network of small health centers, perhaps one per community of 7000, across the city; each equipped to treat everyday disease—both mental and physical, in children and adults—but organized essentially around a functional emphasis on those recreational and educational activities which help keep people in good health. . . . Keep the medical teams small and independent but coordinated with other clinics, such as birth places throughout the town . . . but don't force these facilities to form a continuous 'health park'—knit them together loosely with other parts of the town, such as housing."[11]

In Alexander's cosmology, he placed sickness prevention prominently within a matrix of priorities, as one of many small-scale commercial, recreational, educational, residential, and spiritual amenities that should be within walking distance of most inhabitants of the community. This view would be echoed in 1995 by Victor Papanek, in a call for a community's balanced, centered biotechnology:

> We all sense that something has gone terribly wrong with our communities. Hamlets and cities, slums and suburbs all lack a sense of cohesion. Not only is there no centre there—there is no there. Cities, towns, villages and communities that were designed hundreds of years ago are obviously based upon some basic purpose of living that eludes the designers of our time. Previous ages possessed one great advantage: a precise moral aim that gave meaning and direction to all planning and design. Classical antiquity sought a sense of harmony and balance, the medieval objective was mystic fulfillment, the Renaissance strove for an elegance of proportions and more recent times for enlightened humanism. Builders knew precisely what they wanted. . . . That old towns are charming and new ones are not is due to the fact that city planners of former times . . . did not differ in aims as their age changed, but instinctively always worked toward the one unchanging purpose that has always made people desire to live in urban centres. . . . Aristotle said that men form communities not for justice, peace, defense or traffic, but for the sake of the good life. This good life has always meant the satisfaction of man's basic social desires: conviviality, religion, artistic and intellectual growth [and] politics.[12]

Papanek argued that contemporary culture had lost sight of the need for core communities rich with spatial and functional diversity, and that society had somehow concluded that "every age must have a different purpose." In this view, our age would undoubtedly overemphasize information technology and, by inference, virtual realities, which occur at the expense of real-time and real-space communities—the essence of the culture of daily life.

Apart from the obvious biases of the information age, the call for the renewal of a life-enriching community was in striking opposition to the call for a life-care community. To critics, the life-care community by this time had become unidimensional, lacking in the very richness described by Alexander, Papanek, and others, originating with the great twentieth-century urbanist Lewis Mumford.[13] The life-care movement, personified in the continuing care retirement community, had emerged primarily as a means to segregate the elderly from the rest of society, in what its non-elderly creators assumed would be a "nice place" to live out one's remaining days. According to critics, an entire generation of retired persons in the United States had been misled to fear that no one would take care of them, based on a misdefinition of "community" on the part of care providers, planners, architects, and (by default if not by intent) society at large.

In reality, the life-care movement, until the advent of the new urbanism of the 1980s, was not really about the traditional definition of community but about a near-obsession with the need for the isolated "invalid" to be cared for. Thus, the healthcare industry had triumphed in its struggle to position itself at the heart of contemporary culture. Advocates of the new urbanism and non-age-segregated retirement communities soon began to argue that retirement need not denote isolation. By the late 1990s, efforts were under way to reinforce the traditional fabric of older communities as part of a revitalized urban core, thereby creating neighborhoods where the aged would wish to continue to reside with the presence of sufficient support systems. Care, then, would be but one part of the whole cultural milieu.

Functional Deconstruction and Residentialism

The hospital was thrust into a period of restructuring in the 1980s. Fundamental changes took place in its management, organization, and mix of services. The model of highly specialized services on a single site, with outpatient as well as inpatient services provided at the medical center, had been recast. The breaking apart of the modern hospital into inpatient and outpatient components, and the repositioning of outpatient components to satellite facilities, were well documented. Such buzzwords as "patient-focused care" and "high tech–high touch medicine" signaled the coming paradigmatic shift. But only when hundreds of hospitals faced severe downsizing, closure, and in some cases demolition in the 1990s did the industry fully grasp the gravity of this sea change.

At Francis Scott Key Medical Center in Baltimore, for example, the nursing building was demolished in 1989 (fig. 9.1). In another case, a hospital was completely demolished to make way for a grocery store. The victim was the Lynn Hospital, in Lynn, Massachusetts (the remaining buildings on the site were renamed the AtlantiCare Medical Center), founded in 1892. In 1996 the entire campus was destroyed, including the main administration building, various additions and replacement wings constructed during the postwar period, and the multi-level parking garage across the street. To its out-of-town owner, this institution symbolized fiscal failure and physical obsolescence, largely based on its size and excessive bed capacity. In the eyes of the community and the local historic preservationists, however, its destruction was a significant tear in the historic fabric of the community, once known as a major shoe manufacturing center in the northeastern United States.

The term *functional deconstruction* has been put forth here to describe this process; it is not to be misconstrued as pejorative in any manner, nor is it meant to denote only aesthetic concerns or outward appearance. Further, it is not

9.1. Frances Scott Key Medical Center, Baltimore, implosion, 1989

meant here in the limited sense used by architectural and literary theorists, except to the extent that the hospital was organizationally deconstructed, figuratively and literally, into its constituent parts and reconstituted. Patients could no longer assume that care was always better dispensed from the hospital: bigger was no longer better. Cost containment, market competition, and third-party payer policy dictated that the accepted formula for success was changing. As a result, not only was the premise of the hospital being questioned, its appearance and formal composition were also under scrutiny. By this time, many long-established, highly respected medical centers had disfigured their physical plants through a succession of renovations and expansion projects to the point where the facility's appearance had become chaotic and its scale ungainly. As the demand for bed capacity shrank, and as procedures once performed in the hospital could increasingly be performed on an outpatient basis, functional deconstruction gained momentum. The net effect was a hospital with the responsibility for caring for the sickest of the sick. In other situations, a given hospital would be declared obsolete and then destroyed. Sometimes the decision was made to reinvent on-site: in one case a hospital was actually closed one night and reopened the next day as an outpatient facility.[14] As for the kinds of care provided in the reconstituted hospitals that opted to remain in the enterprise of acute care—the critical care centers—the patient rooms and nursing functions were to be transformational, that is, adaptable to new or modified uses, sometimes in a matter of minutes, as in the case of a postoperative room that could metamorphose into a trauma stabilization station.

The aged also felt the full impact of functional deconstruction and residentialism (see Chapter 7). Although the modern nursing home looked like a typical hospital, it was devoted largely to patient housing and direct-care functions rather than the high-tech surgical, laboratory, and diagnostic functions of the acute-care hospital. Nevertheless, code requirements and, later, accreditation standards of nursing homes were almost identical to those already in place for acute-care hospitals. The medical model of geriatric health care, because of its strong lobbying impact compared to other professionals in the field of long-term care, was the loudest voice in defining the modern nursing home architecturally. To the medical profession it was logical to assume that the nursing home was medically driven and should therefore look like a hospital. The result were skilled-nursing units for twenty-four or more patients, with white walls, ceilings, and floors, and hard surfaces. Lighting was typically fluorescent fixtures overhead, and the furnishings in the bedrooms were nearly identical to those in hospitals. Even the design of the nursing stations was adapted directly from the acute-care medical-surgical unit, and the distance between patient and care provider was minimized wherever possible.

Like the medical profession, the architectural profession as a whole treated the modern nursing home of the 1960s and 1970s with disdain or indifference. Few skilled-nursing facilities for long-term care were published in the professional architectural journals during this period, and the few books that addressed this topic were on the subject of codes and standards, not the subject of design. Moreover, nursing homes were nearly always designed by "hospital architects," meaning architects specializing in acute-care facilities.

Sociologists were the first to sound the alarm regarding the total institutionality that the nursing home had achieved by the mid-1960s. In the United States, Rex Whitaker Allen was one of the first architects to call for a residentially driven alternative to the hospital-driven modern nursing home. His firm, which had also designed innovative hospitals challenging the Hill-Burton standards, led in this search for an alternative approach on the West Coast in the 1960s. These facilities were the forerunners of the high-end, special-care units of the 1980s and 1990s for Alzheimer's patients, and of assisted-living facilities built during the 1990s. While most architects and long-term-care administrators labored over how to best adapt the pavilion model, Allen and others were working to reinvent the nursing home. Their approach included varied ceiling forms, residential roofs, undulating corridors, inviting dayrooms and commons areas, and a more residential scale in keeping with the use of residential materials where possible and allowed by codes.

The mainstream held onto the medically driven, hospital-like nursing home until two countertrends emerged: the CCRC movement and the home healthcare movement. Both had emerged in reaction to the fear that many persons felt when faced with the prospect of placing a loved one in a nursing home. The retirement community boom of the late 1950s and 1960s, with the most famous being Sun City, Arizona, was generally highly regarded in the popular culture. But the nursing home was perceived as the antithesis of independence and choice. The CCRC, by contrast, provided choice and offered the individual a place regardless of health status and abilities, with its pioneering aging-in-place model of care. The home healthcare movement, and the parallel hospice care movement, provided another viable alternative to the nursing home, although both were ostensibly created to provide a maximum level of home-life support. The hospice and its home care counterpart was devoted to palliative care—not cure—in a comfortable setting. The visiting nurse and the social worker, among other professionals and volunteers, were equally vital in the expansion of home-based care for the aged during this period.

Architecturally, neither the hospice nor the CCRC was considered a modern building type; nor were they considered postmodern. In the strictest sense, in fact, few hospices or CCRCs were taken seriously as works of architecture. Their architectural merit stemmed from their rejection of modernist functional planning principles and their conscious incorporation of historicist imagery and forms, such as nineteenth-century British courtyard housing or the country estate manor. Nature also played an important role in these settings, where residents could experience the visual and spatial sensations in moving from building to building, from indoors to outdoors.

Later, the assisted-living movement would flourish as a close-to-home alternative to the nursing home. By the late 1990s the three prevalent types of assisted-living facilities were those on the sites of CCRCs, newly built freestanding facilities, and those adapted from institutional and industrial buildings in urban areas. The popular demand for assisted living resulted in thousands of urban, suburban, exurban, and rural facilities. The assisted-living movement was not the first building type to reject the nursing home; the CCRC, the hospice, and home healthcare programs for the aged had all been based on a residentialist imperative. Yet advocates of freestanding assisted-living facilities argued that they constituted a countermovement to the impracticalities of the CCRC.

A research literature dates from the late 1960s on the topic of environment and aging, at first focusing almost exclusively on the total institutionality of the modern nursing home. In the 1980s the field expanded to include research on congregate care, assisted living, home health care, wayfinding, and other aspects of the long-term-care experience. Since 1965, this residentialist research has had more of an impact on theory and practice than its counterpart research literature in allied domains of the health landscape. Nonetheless, the healthcare administration and medical journals' coverage of architecture, and particularly architecture for the aged, has increased somewhat in recent years, centered on annual design awards programs and annual review volumes published by the American Institute of Architects' Academy on Architecture for Health.

As for research, its application in the fields of healthcare administration, medicine, gerontology, and the design professions has unfortunately been quite uneven and at times paradoxical. For example, a large national chain of assisted-living facilities, perhaps anticipating constructing fifty or more facilities not markedly dissimilar from one another, might not have any interest in incorporating any research, whereas a single-site long-term-care provider might endeavor to take a significant amount of relevant research into account in the planning and design of its sole facility. No external agencies have required that architectural research be a part of the building process for health architecture. Although social scientists were the early leaders in this area of research, they have been unable to communicate meaningfully with designers and facility planners. And designers were often oblivious to the useful information generated by the social scientists. Any real gains made in terms of educating architects and others about the potential merits of incorporating research results into the planning, design, and operation of facilities for the aged were due to two things: first, the particular skills and perseverance of the individual researcher, and second, a newfound awareness on the part of architects, providers, and society of the profound demographic shift taking place in most developed countries.

The new residentialism of the 1980s therefore fueled changes reshaping both the hospital and the nursing home. As the mix of services evolved, the institutionality inherent in modernism was eschewed in favor of an antihospitalist aesthetic. This was not an outright rejection, however. The healthcare establishment tended to be conservative, and architecture, because of its considerable expense, was one of the last areas to be allowed the new freedom already permeating other building types and areas of practice, such as schools. Mainstream health architects were slow to embrace the alternative to modernism, because it posed a new set of questions from the "form follows function" dictum. Postmodern architecture was, in many respects, based on aspects that modernism had rejected fifty years earlier: color, animation, traditional imagery, traditional colors, traditional use of daylighting and incandescent lighting, natural materials, and traditional compositional forms such as barrel-vaulted ceilings—in short, design attributes that would have long been well suited to health architecture, if the will to incorporate them had existed.

By the end of the century, the spread of residentialist health architecture became international in scope. Examples of international residentialism appeared in Africa, Japan, Argentina, Canada, Australia, the Netherlands, and Great Britain, and throughout Europe. Many variants of residentialism became discernible, some based largely on a desire to capture a particular image on the outside of the building, others reflecting a rethinking, from inside out, of the role and meaning of the facility in relation to human health and well-being.

Regardless of whether a building was judged modern or not, the architectural mainstream continued, for the most part, to ignore health architecture. In a major survey of architecture since 1960, published in 1995, only three of seventy-eight projects (3.8 percent) were health facilities. And two of these three projects were designed by architects who had established their international reputations by designing buildings for purposes other than health care.[15] Regardless of the deep-rooted indifference of the architectural mainstream, the hospital by the mid-1990s was being rechristened by leading-edge providers with such new labels as "critical care center" or "diagnostic-treatment center," and even the term *hospital* was on the verge of redefinition, if not extinction. Semantics aside, little doubt remained that a reconstituted building type was needed as successor to the building type traditionally known as the hospital.

Self-Determination versus Provider Determination

In the era of managed care, a decreasing number of providers provided care to ever larger numbers of recipients. The economics of scale had been well documented in the healthcare administration literature. The pooling of staff expertise and resources, larger referral networks, stronger marketing efforts, and the evolution of regional and national markets became the hallmark of the large for-profit chains in the United States. With standardization came questions of quality, although it had been shown to some extent that quality could also be improved when resources were pooled. Critics charged, however, that this standardization brought less choice, less patient self-determination, and a lower quality of care on a per-patient basis.[16] The architectural implications of this trend would soon become apparent: the provider was in a stronger position than ever before to control the architecture at the key access points to their system.

Before the rise of managed care networks in the United States, providers had been somewhat successful in employing architecture as a tool for attracting patients. This had begun in earnest in the mid-1980s, when the appeal of the premodern hospital was reprised in the many impressive atria built at such places as the Brigham and Women's Hospital in Boston, the Tulane University Medical Center in New Orleans, and the Dartmouth-Hitchcock Medical Center in New Hampshire.

The most dramatic architectural effect in the 1990s era of uncertainty and consolidation among providers, particularly the large for-profit chains, was the decrease in building construction budgets, as providers shifted a portion of capital expenditures to more pressing needs such as personnel and equipment. As a result, in order to hold down utilization costs, by the late 1990s the managed care organizations were beginning to control two of the key access points—the community-based clinics and the critical care center—had an increasing degree of control over two of the others—the workplace (in the form of wellness programs) and home—and had achieved even a small level of influence over a fifth realm: *anywhere*, that is, wherever a person could take a laptop computer and access global electronic information networks. A chronic tug of war had evolved between, on the one hand, the consumer seeking a greater voice and degree of self-determination and, on the other hand, the provider seeking to control the flow of health-related information and the flow of care recipients to health facilities. Some indicators even pointed to the emergence of a dialectical or co-empowerment model, where provider and care recipient shared in controlling the flow of goods and services in the health landscape. Relatively few examples of shared control in terms of actual buildings had appeared, however. One innovative program of this type, initiated by the state health agency in Louisiana for less advantaged socioeconomic segments of the state's population, sought to improve the status of its facilities through a statewide architectural planning, design, and post-occupancy assessment protocol involving site selection, assistance in the decision to build a new facility or renovate, and the actual design of community health centers. This protocol proved to be successful, resulting in community care clinics designed based on users' needs and aspirations, both aesthetically and in functional terms.[17]

Meanwhile, "wellness salons," formerly fitness centers, were opening up in fashionable neighborhoods. Such centers as the Definitions Fitness Center II, in New York City, satisfied patrons' health and wellness needs. The design of these centers rivaled that of the trendiest boutiques and restaurants in their upscale neighborhoods, with sophisticated lighting and furnishings and inventive use of materials (figs. 9.2 and 9.3).

For hospitals, the fitness or wellness center emerged as a specialty service to fill the spatial voids created by the process of functional deconstruction. These centers would be to the 1990s what the MRI, VIP patient room, and flexible LDR suites were to the previous decade: "It's been obvious for some time that hospitals in the United States, with an estimated vacancy rate of 40 percent, tend to be overweight and out of shape. Still, it was only recently that the industry began to make the connection that fitness is not only good for people but for hospitals as well. Now wellness and fitness centers are the hot item, and the hospital administrators who have them can't say enough about them. These centers are comparable in every way to other private athletic clubs—the latest in exercise equipment, swimming pools, saunas, personal trainers, health advice, child care. . . . Membership dues compare favorably as well."[18]

Wellness centers were an example of co-empowerment: the medical center was re-empowering itself through renovation and revitalization of its physical plant, and the wellness center was a response to the personal health and fitness movement in the United States. This far-reaching, essentially grassroots phenomenon will likely continue well into the new century.

A Sustainable Health Landscape

The global challenge of creating a sustainable architecture had become a central topic in the environmental design literature by the late 1990s. Efforts to develop biodegradable building products and to use environmentally sensitive building technologies had their contemporary roots in the ecology movement of the late 1960s in the United States and other nations. The development of passive systems, active solar heating systems, and the use of Trombe wall construction were among early steps in this direction. Various passive design strategies were also reappraised, many of which had been rediscovered from vernacular building traditions long associated with folk architecture. Examples included the thickened outer wall of the adobe architecture of the American Southwest as a means to control thermal gains, natural ventilation and lighting systems, and a region's indigenous building materials.

Anti-technologists argued that technology was the reason why the natural resources of the planet had been depleted at such an alarming rate. Without high technology, they argued, the rapid destruction of the rainforests and

9.2. Definitions Fitness Center, New York City, 1995

9.3. Definitions Fitness Center, axonometric view

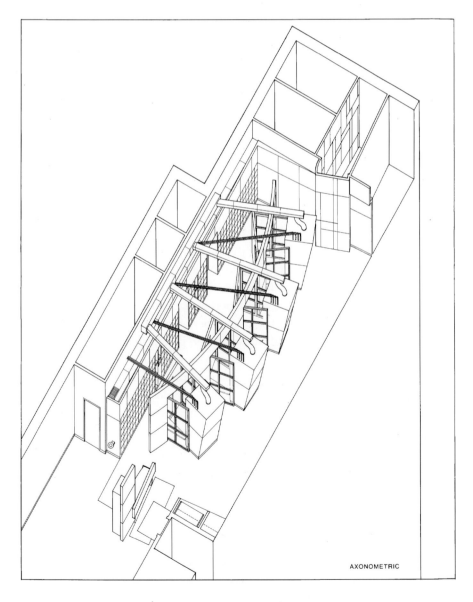

AXONOMETRIC

the paving over of vast areas of farmland for urban development would not have been possible. Advocates of high technology claimed, however, that the problems caused by advanced technology needed to be superseded by even more advanced technologies as a means to eradicate global problems. On the need to move quickly, Victor Papanek stated, "The world we understand goes back only to the Renaissance. The world as we really know it dates back to the Industrial Revolution, and the world we feel comfortable with probably began—depending on our age and feeling for history—sometime between 1945 and 1973. Thus our view of an unlimited future is a chimera. During a lifetime, a decade, a year, or even a day, profound and impersonal dramatic changes take place. . . . We feel that 'normal time' is isolated from such great changes. Yet most of the ecological and possibly irreversible damage has occurred only during the last thirty years. Time is running out."[19]

Architects, though concerned with the coming crisis, were slow to react, mainly because architecture as a field had long been preoccupied with the profundities of various formal theories, its own survival in a competitive professional climate, and growing indifference on the part of the general public. Largely as a result of this inward focus, the sustainability question had received insufficient attention and little serious action. By most accounts, healthcare administrators and the medical establishment were even slower than architects to address the issue of sustainability.[20] The typical administrator was caught up in the daily activities of a rapidly evolving industry, increased cost-containment pressures, and increased competition. The creation of "green" health facilities, for instance, was given little or no priority. Nonetheless, the rush continued to build and renovate, largely based on market-driven concerns; the only relevant architectural input appeared to be that a patient-centered care setting would tend to have a positive impact on a provider's bottom line. In short, providers and architects dealt with their immediate needs and had little time for larger implications. For their part, the public did not seem to care whether their health center or hospital was designed with sustainability in mind. As a result, sustainability obviously could be overlooked in facility planning and design decisions, particularly if it would increase the short-term construction budget. Hospitals were the worst offenders, often with windowless settings where furnishings and fixtures emitted toxins, sometimes causing staff walkouts and protests.[21]

Of the many options available to create a sustainable health architecture, five basic issues dominated the discussion (unfortunately, there was little action) by the late 1990s. First, flexible facilities would be needed, adaptable in ways perhaps unanticipated at the time of initial design and construction. It would not be possible to throw away an obsolete piece of equipment; it would have to be designed from the start to be versatile. In this milieu the concept of planned obsolescence, replacement, and disuse would give way to a climate of adaptation, retrofit, and reuse. Second, "green" building materials and construction assembly processes would be needed to replace those in use in the late twentieth century, particularly those causing indoor air pollution. Third, the use of the natural environment for daylight and ventilation would be reassessed as a means to reduce the building's dependence on costly, artificial environmental control systems. Fourth, it would become an imperative to construct facilities in communities near enough to their constituencies to reduce the dependence on automobiles. At present, the medical center parking garage is the most dominant and often depressing feature of many institutions. It symbolizes an unquestioning acceptance of the role of the automobile in the present and the future. Finally, it would become even more critical for the community to accept the scale, template, and siting of facilities. Location of a new clinic in a wetland area, for example, or on a hilltop site that would destroy a previously undisturbed view, would be unacceptable.

On the need for a new aesthetic in the design of the built environment, Papanek concluded: "Anyone with even a speck of sensitivity will agree that in the 1990s most dwellings, public buildings, means of transport are disturbingly ugly. . . . This dismaying visual pollution signals the imminent emergence of a new aesthetic, and most designers and architects will readily agree that, after Modernism, Memphis, Post-Modernism, Deconstructivism, Neo-Classicism, Object-Semiotics, and Post-Deconstructivism, a new direction—transcending fad, trend, or fashionable styling—is long overdue. New directions in design and architecture don't occur accidentally, but always arise out of real changes in society, cultures and concepts."[22]

In subsequent years, providers, their architects, and others concerned with the planning, design, and construction of health architecture will be challenged to create a sustainable health architecture. In the long run, society deserves no less.

The Natural Environment and Health Architecture

The megahospital was conceived in strict opposition to nature. The interstitialists and others at work building the modern hospital had no interest in the Asclepia as a building type, for its influence had been nearly completely obliterated in hospital form, in favor of a reductivist set of principles. The triumph of minimalism and high technology was everywhere to be found in the modern hospital: the lack of natural ventilation, the shrinkage of the window aperture and a diminution of the total amount of glazed area, adoption of the hermetically sealed building envelope, dependence on artificial lighting over natural daylight, the rise of the block hospital and its rejection of courtyards and other green spaces for use by patients, and a deemphasis on overall patient amenity were but a few technologically driven modern developments. Further, by this time the conquest of religion by high technology was pronounced, with the chapel, once a central feature of the hospital complex, having been reduced to a small room.

The dictates of technology, then, had overwhelmed most remaining traces of the Nightingale movement of the late nineteenth century and the early decades of the twentieth century. Nightingale, whether self-consciously or otherwise, had recaptured many of the basic tenets of classical health facilities, reprising the Greeks' emphasis on the therapeutic powers of nature. Before Nightingale, the emphasis of the Greeks on outdoor therapy, sunlight, water, exercise, and direct contact with nature had been lost for nearly two millennia: hospitals had become places of incarceration, fear, and isolation. To be sick and

9.4. Union Hall Spa-Resort, Saratoga Springs, New York, 1865

9.5. Hospital for Crippled Children, Crippled Children's School, Milwaukee, 1920, sun treatment terrace

frail and in the hospital was to be, in essence, rejected as unworthy of the beauty of nature. Although Nightingale repopularized the amenity of nature in the healing process, the scope of her work was severely limited by nineteenth-century cultural norms.[23]

The nineteenth-century resort spa movement in the United States was the first sustained attempt to recapture nature as a therapeutic modality. During times of epidemics, the wealthy and privileged classes routinely retreated to the refuge of the resort spa. In the North, the area of the Catskills became popular; in the South, there were the antebellum spas in Virginia and the Carolinas, the Ozarks, and later, the California coast. In the 1880s there were more than 850 spas and resorts in the United States.[24] Most of these spas benefited tremendously from the amenity of the natural environment (fig. 9.4). In short, the spa became the premodern equivalent of the Asclepia, minus the spiritual element.

Even the hospital and the tuberculosis sanitarium of the 1920s and 1930s gave way to nature in the form of terraces for "sun therapy," as at the Hospital for Crippled Children in Milwaukee, Wisconsin (fig. 9.5). Such institutions typically had only one level, with a symmetrical floor plan.[25] Terraces were also found in the outdoor solariums at the end of each floor of high-rise hospitals, and as adjuncts to courtyards during the period before World War II. Eventually, the pressures of rising land costs, the urban locations of many institutions, and the accommodation of high technology in the hospital forced out these types of spaces—places where patient, staff, and nature could interact.

As part of the rejection of the modern hospital, a body of research began to appear, indicating the importance of nature for patient and staff well-being in institutional care settings. By the mid-1980s this work would warrant a chapter in a book calling for the reform of hospital architecture through patient-centered planning and design. In this chapter, the research was summarized and a series of design guidelines were presented.[26] Among the most important research in terms of site planning and design were studies on the therapeutic importance of views. Well-being was reported as significantly lower in situations assessed as low in "windowness."[27] Related work examined the relation between contact with the exterior from various points within the circulation network of a hospital, directional signage, and indoor nature, and concluded that a legible hospital configuration with intervals of contact with nature through windows at the end of corridors promoted wayfinding.[28]

Research conducted at about the same time in Sweden found that recovery rates were more accelerated in rooms overlooking nature. Occupants had shorter post-operative stays, took fewer analgesics, and had fewer negative comments in nurses' notes than patients in rooms with views not of nature. More recent research has sought to simulate view representations in laboratory conditions to study this phenomenon further.[29] Research linking dysfunctional physical settings with illness or lessened health status remained scant by the late 1990s. In a thorough review of 38,000 potentially relevant titles from medical databases, researchers Haya Rubin and Amanda Owens identified only 270 articles that appeared to describe investigations into the impact of environmental elements on health outcomes, and only 43 articles or reports were identified as specifically detailing the relation between patient well-being and environmental factors. Many of these 43 documents were concluded to be of limited applicability owing to a host of methodological limitations.[30] Nonetheless, by the 1990s this work had become disseminated among providers and designers, and it was generally accepted that nature content, views, windows, and appropriate colors needed to be a priority in renovation and new construction. Efforts were under way to bring nature indoors in the form of the skylit atrium, fountains, waterfalls, trees, plants, and flowers, and in various representations of nature. Rubin and Owens concluded: "[Investigations] into the effect of environmental manipulations have generally supported the hypothesis that environmental features affect patients' health. . . . Thus, improvements in health outcome are likely to be available through research on this subject, and it is an important topic to pursue."[31]

New facilities in the 1990s routinely incorporated full-spectrum artificial lighting with a mix of incandescent and ambient lighting in patient rooms and other parts of the facility, and surrogate views, which had been called for by researchers, were marketed for use in windowless rooms in both new and older buildings. Such surrogate views included photographic scenes of nature, complete with windowsill panes and blinds. A computer-driven light box replicated the cycle of night and day in the scenic photo transparencies, which were rotatable to reflect the four seasons. Stanford University Hospital was among the first to purchase these windows, to be used in its cardiac transplant ICU, where the real windows had been permanently obliterated by hospital expansion. Patient and staff reaction to the surrogates was positive. The state regulatory agency, which had granted Stanford a provisional waiver to use the artificial windows pending later review based on patient response and outcome, allowed the institution to keep its surrogates.[32]

In the late twentieth century the "wellness retreat," set in nature, became available for those of high social class and position. One facility created for such retreats was the John E. Fetzer Institute Retreat House in Kalamazoo, Michigan (1993–95), designed by Harley Ellington Design. The use of heavy timber construction in the great hall, and the expansive windows, projected occupants into the adjacent woods in an effort to establish a seamless connection between indoors and out (fig. 9.6). Sited near the institute's administration building, which had been constructed in 1988, the new center consisted of a 12,000-square-foot meeting house and four three-level lodging units, each with six single-occupancy apartments. Institute director John Fetzer was deeply interested in the relation between humanity and the earth. Before he died in 1991, he had requested that as little as possible of the forested site be destroyed to accommodate the new building. Accordingly, a forestry consultant was retained, and a 120-foot tower crane with a 246-foot boom was used to "airlift" all the major building materials to the site above the undisturbed forest.[33]

A design for an outpatient counseling and treatment center for mental health and substance abuse, the West St. Tammany Community Health Center by R-2ARCH (1995–96, unbuilt), sought to establish a similarly strong, sustained connection between the interior and the exterior natural environment. The architects provided a number of outdoor and semi-enclosed indoor group spaces with sliding doors for use during mild months of the year, as well as pathways for refuge. A spiral-like structure splayed out from a central arrival point into a two-level volume with group counseling rooms and a balcony overlooking its densely wooded site (figs. 9.7–9.9).[34]

By the mid-1990s, "person-nature transactions" had become a sub-movement within the larger umbrella of the patient-centered-design movement, with research on this topic including reassessment of the therapeutic benefits of gardens in the healthcare experience.[35] Gardens had been used in this way in classical times and in the monastic hospitals of the Middle Ages, and history was slated to repeat itself in the new millennium. By the end of the twentieth century it was argued that not only health architecture but all architecture and design would in the future be concerned with "health,"[36] and person-nature transactions were viewed as a core component in building types not traditionally related to health per se, such as schools, other institutional settings, manufacturing settings, housing, office settings, and so on.[37]

9.6. John E. Fetzer Institute Retreat House, Kalamazoo, Michigan, 1995, main room

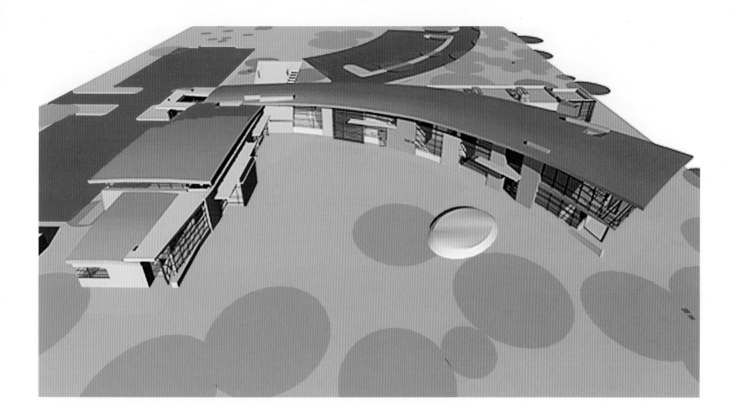

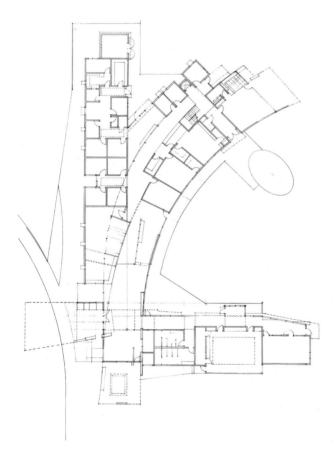

9.7. West St. Tammany
Community Clinic (proposal),
Mandeville, Louisiana, 1996

9.8. West St. Tammany
Community Clinic, first-floor
plan

9.9. West St. Tammany
Community Clinic, interior
perspective

Interdisciplinary Aspects of Health Architecture

In the 1960s the architect, the allied designer, the equipment specialist, the direct-care provider, the administrator, the patient, and the patient's family functioned within separate spheres. Gradually more and more architects and allied designers began to specialize in health architecture. Some architecture schools established areas of emphasis in healthcare design, but these tended to come and go with the shifting interests of their faculty. Similarly, some programs in healthcare administration occasionally offered courses in architecture and in facility planning. Unfortunately, these positive trends were isolated examples. Most professionals trained in health in the waning years of the twentieth century had been instilled with a certain amount of professional egocentrism. The typical curriculum in architecture and in the healthcare fields was highly concentrated, providing specialized training with little time for "enrichment" coursework. In this model of education it was difficult to develop respect and appreciation for the responsibilities and challenges of others being trained for careers in health. The physician was not exposed to architecture at all, and neither were nurses, most administrators, and the myriad technicians and specialists who came to compose the modern hospital staff. As for the architect in training, few schools offered healthcare-specific coursework, and the architect's first commission for a hospital often required learning about the industry on the job. This mutual lack of perspective led to miscommunications between providers and architects, with the worst situations culminating in the firing of the architect.

The situation improved in the 1980s with the creation of new interdisciplinary professional organizations, including the International Facilities Management Association. Other professional bodies, including the American Public Health Association, the Gerontological Society of America, the American Institute of Architects, and the Environmental Design Research Association, began to sponsor sessions at annual conferences on the topic of health architecture. The National Healthcare Design Symposium was the first organization created specifically for this interdisciplinary niche.

This trend was viewed as positive by most observers and critics. Bridges between professions were being built, and more professionals were actively developing an orientation in their teaching and professional work. It was not until the mid-1990s, however, that the mainstream architectural profession acknowledged the contribution of interdisciplinary education in health architecture.[38] In contrast, healthcare accreditation agencies in the United States had been somewhat interdisciplinary from the outset. These bodies, fueled by the growth of the voluntary compliance movement, which formed the framework for establishing minimum performance standards for a provider and its physical facilities, led in 1951 to the creation of the Joint Commission on the Accreditation of Hospitals (in the late 1980s renamed the Joint Commission on the Accreditation of Healthcare Organizations, or JCAHO), by several groups including the American Hospital Association and the American Medical Association. The JCAHO conducted surveys and site visits to applying providers and their institutions. Its standards, along with general suggestions for rendering high-quality patient care, appeared in the JCAHO's Accreditation Manual for Hospitals, issued annually. In developing its inspection criteria, the JCAHO incorporated the standards of such U.S. federal agencies as the Environmental Protection Agency and Occupational Safety and Health Administration.[39]

A second facet of performance assessment was embodied in the postoccupancy evaluation (POE) process. This approach typically consisted of the detailed diagnostic assessment of a building's overall responsiveness to its occupants' needs. Some of the most significant POE investigations in the last third of the century were interdisciplinary, involving the contributions of social scientists, healthcare professionals, administrators, and architects and urban planners. Despite its value as a tool analogous to the case review in law or the autopsy in medicine, by the late 1990s the POE had only marginally found its way into mainstream health architecture. A few firms began to experiment with basing marketing efforts, and even fee remuneration structures, on the assessed performance of the completed building. Typically, an architectural firm conducted an informal POE of a related facility before embarking on the project at hand. Kaplan/McLaughlin/Diaz, for example, conducted a POE of a private psychiatric hospital in Marin County, California, before designing a similar new hospital.[40] This was standard practice for the firm, dating from its origins in the 1960s, although in most firms the custom of conducting POEs in-house remains the exception rather than the rule.

Professional recognition of the value of meeting (and surpassing) minimum accreditation standards, and of the value of the POE, was slow to emerge. Performance assessments are beginning to make professionals more aware of the consequences of their choices, but more such feedback is called for at an earlier stage, during a professional's preparatory training. Education on the value of sustainable and accountable approaches to building and facility operation is urgently needed. The healthcare administrator should have no excuse to remain unfamiliar with the history of health architecture, to remain unaware of the design implications of various care systems, or to be unaware of why some buildings are oppressive and others are not. Neither is there an excuse for the architect to remain ignorant of the provider's organizational culture. Crosstraining should be made available regardless of a student's home field of study. Unfortunately, by the late 1990s only marginal progress had been made in developing truly interdisciplinary educational initiatives, despite the interest of various professional organizations in interdisciplinary "literacy" across the professions affecting the emerging health culture and health architecture.

The Health Culture

Critiques on the current state of health architecture have remained, as stated at the outset of this book, curiously disconnected from a larger context, even though the healthcare system of the 1960s had metamorphosed into the emerging "health culture" of the new millennium, defined as society's unprecedented knowledge of health and health-related information and its bearing on the individual's quality of life. Extended to architecture, the "health culture" denotes a more sophisticated comprehension of the potential of the built environment as a supportive—that is, restorative and palliative—contributor to health and human well-being. With this said, the challenge remains to make the critical connections within the health culture. On the dilemma of formulating valid, reciprocal, well-grounded architectural languages within the broad canvas of a culture-at-large, Charles Jencks stated:

> Architecture expresses passion, religion, and noble thought. Its basic motivations cannot be put any more succinctly. Today the question [is] about what we build—shopping malls rather than agorae, Disneylands rather than cathedrals. Put another way it is a question of style and content—right angles rather than undulating architecture, I-beams rather than organic details, and habitual rather than emergent structures. To ask the embarrassing question, "what style and content shall we build?" implies we have a choice. . . . In times of fast change, such questions are asked, while in peaceful times, people are comfortable with the reigning approach. Curiously, we live today in a conflicted time of both accelerated change and business-as-usual, a time of both transformation and stagnation. . . . Of course it would be silly, after so much twentieth-century evidence to the contrary, to think that architects could change society. They are essentially powerless compared to politicians, developers, journalists, and businessmen. They can only tinker with ecological and population problems set by others. They do, however, have one power that no other profession enjoys: they have some control of the architectural language and the messages sent. A single building can celebrate a better world or signify a change in direction. It has the power to engage the imagination and symbolize the basic truths of the universe.[41]

In the medical sciences, advances in biomedical engineering and genetics have opened up completely new vistas of possibility for humankind, amid growing alarm concerning the possible misapplication of these new technologies. Ethical concerns abound, although they are far from new. Writing in the 1930s, Lewis Mumford had introduced the term *biotechnics* to describe a hopeful trend whereby technology, instead of abstracting and mechanizing human life, would benefit human life by integrating fully with it.[42] But in the 1990s, preoccupation with the reconstructability of genes, organisms, and biochemical pathways had led to the potential to imbalance life itself through preselection, owing to the ability to clone various species, including humans.[43] Yet, at the same time, scientists had made it possible for quadriplegics to be able to write independently, using their eyes with a laser-guided camera, and to activate a control panel enabling them to control the features of the immediate architectural environment as well as key activities of daily living.[44]

The notion of innovation in health architecture and in the administration of health facilities is, however, often somewhat elusive. Most of the examples cited in the previous chapters represented a breaking of new ground, both literally and in symbolic terms, because they involved, or invoked, a certain element of risk-taking. Risk—whether in terms of allowing the architect an unusual degree of freedom to develop a new aesthetic or functional response to a program or a site, or in terms of incorporating new medical technologies—always has its own rewards, but it can also have disastrous consequences if not

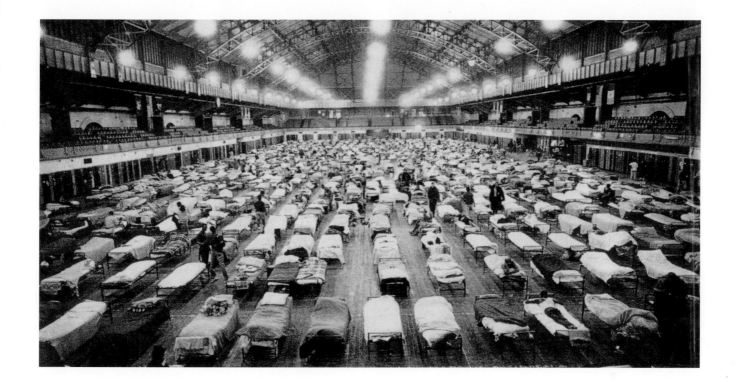

carefully harnessed. Unquestionably, those responsible for innovation in health architecture are to be respected and admired for their willingness to engage in risk-taking even though the easier course of action would have been to continue with the status quo rather than to push the boundaries. This book would not have been possible without those who dared to extend the frontiers of health architecture.

9.10. Seven-hundred-bed makeshift homeless shelter, New York City, 1992

Throughout this period, unfortunately, certain fundamental societal needs remained unmet, as society's aspirations became at times wildly incongruent with those of the health culture. One persistent, troubling case in point was the "network" of vast, warehouse-like homeless shelters created in cities in the United States, such as the immense shelter in New York City (fig. 9.10). Such dysfunctional settings did little besides rekindling public health concerns regarding the reappearance of tuberculosis to an extent not seen in decades. It is this genre of still-unsatisfied obligations of society that the health culture must address in the new millennium.[45]

The health culture will need to aspire to express an encompassing, universal cosmology of its own.[46] Within this cosmology, the patient-provider relationship will be transformed, with the provider rechristened the *carer* and the patient perhaps recast in the role of *carent*. This term should carry with it an entirely new set of connotations—those of empowerment and self-determination, in opposition to the disempowerment and passivity denoted by such words as *invalid* and *patient*. The recent history of the health landscape reveals that, with the emergence of the health culture, the degree of responsibility on the part of both the health provider—the carer—and the carent will be of greater significance than ever before in history, for we all share in the obligation to serve the best interest of our society now and in the future.

Notes

Chapter 1: Introduction

1. Presidential Message, *Congressional Quarterly Almanac* (1965): 1256.

2. Patricia M. Danzon, "Merger Mania: An Analysis," *Health Systems Review* (November–December 1994): 18, 28.

3. Richard L. Miller and Earl S. Swensson, *New Directions in Hospital and Health-care Facility Design* (New York: McGraw-Hill, 1995).

4. A good example of this trend is the large number of technical reference texts concerning the federal civil rights legislation known as the Americans with Disabilities Act of 1990.

5. The technical end of the spectrum is represented in the well-received book by Bettyann Boetticher Raschko, *Housing Interiors for the Disabled and Elderly* (New York: Van Nostrand Reinhold, 1991), and the visual, essentially aesthetic approach to the topic of health architecture is represented in Eleanor Lynn Nesmith, *Health Care Architecture: Designs for the Future* (Rockport, Mass.: Rockport Publishers, 1995). The Center for Health Design, based in Martinez, California, has since 1985 sponsored an annual national symposium on the topic of health facility planning and design. The goal of the organization has been to promote the self-reflective planning and design of patient-centered treatment settings. The symposium proceedings contain essays and case studies from the United States, with some review of international trends and developments. In 1995 a counterpart European organization, ARCHIMED, was created in Paris as a clearinghouse for recent advancements and to focus more singularly on European management and planning issues and their implications for health facilities.

6. John Handley, "Residential Incubator," *Chicago Tribune,* 27 April 1997. In Chicago, the former Francis Xavier Cabrini Hospital, on the Near West Side, an eighty-seven-year-old facility, was transformed into 105 loft apartments, with 28 townhouses built on the site adjacent to the adapted hospital.

7. Since the work in the late 1960s of the Houston firm Caudill, Rowlett, Scott (CRS) and other firms working with similar techniques, the programming phase of a project has been the point at which user input and involvement in the healthcare planning and design process is solicited. And some firms conduct a post-occupancy evaluation to determine how well a project meets the performance criteria identified at the planning process. This process was described in William Pena and Stephen Parshall, *Problem Solving,* 2nd ed. (Washington: AIA Press, 1993). The work of CRS has influenced a generation of architects and facility planners. More recently, research-

based design approaches have been developed as a part of the facility planning and design process; this approach extends the traditional scope of facility programming to include the gathering of information on user needs through survey instruments, extensive interviews, focus groups, and the use of interactive multimedia to document actual settings in use and to elicit user feedback to models and other forms of architectural representation.

8. Abraham H. Maslow, *Toward a Psychology of Being* (Princeton, N.J.: Van Nostrand Reinhold, 1968).

9. J. Howard, "Humanization and Dehumanization of Health Care," in *Humanizing Health Care,* ed. J. Howard and A. Strauss (New York: Wiley, 1975), 57–107.

10. Ibid., 73–84, as cited in Lee H. Bowker, *Humanizing Institutions for the Aged* (Lexington, Mass.: D. C. Heath, 1982), 2–3.

11. The total number of U.S. hospitals has been declining since 1977. Declines were especially rapid in the period from 1985 to 1990, but they have since slowed. Each year reductions in the number of hospitals are offset by new hospital openings and some reopenings.

12. John D. Thompson and Grace Golden, *The Hospital: A Social and Architectural History* (New Haven: Yale University Press, 1975). This book exists only in its first printing. Subsequent discussions of the history of the hospital have been based nearly entirely on the Thompson and Golden book with little new information added; see Leslie McCall Saunders, "Architectural Influences on the History of Health Care Facilities," in *Effective Health Care Facilities Management,* ed. V. James McLarney et al. (Chicago: American Hospital Publishing, 1991), 149–60, and Miller and Swensson, *New Directions,* 19–32.

13. Thompson and Golden, *The Hospital,* xxvii.

14. Ibid., xxviii.

15. Robert Venturi, *Complexity and Contradiction in Architecture* (New York: Museum of Modern Art, 1966).

16. Thompson and Golden, *The Hospital,* 127–39.

17. Florence Nightingale, *Notes on Hospitals* (London: John W. Parker and Son, 1859); and Lucy Seymer, ed., *Selected Writings of Florence Nightingale* (New York: Macmillan, 1954).

18. Alan Katz, "A History of Emergencies," *Tulane Medicine* (Spring 1992): 12–22.

19. James T. Burns, "Corbu's Venetian Contemporary," *P/A Observer* 45 (December 1965): 162–65.

20. Anthony Cox and Philip Groves, *Hospitals and Health Care Facilities: A Design and Development Guide* (London: Butterworth Architecture, 1990).

21. "Introduction to the Virtual Hospital," University of Iowa, 1995, available on the World Wide Web at www.vh.org; also librarian@vh.radiology.uiowa.edu.

Chapter 2: The Hospital as a Machine for Healing

1. Richard A. Miller, "Hospitals: The Race with Change," *Architectural Forum* 120 (April 1964): 82.

2. Herbert Gans, *The Levittowners* (New York: Pantheon, 1967).

3. *Buildings for Best Products,* exh. cat. (New York: Museum of Modern Art, 1979, 22–24). This catalogue also featured an introduction by Philip Johnson, an essay by Arthur Drexler on the work of James Wines and the firm SITE, and the design work of Robert A. M. Stern, Charles Moore, Anthony Lumsden, Allan Greenberg, and Michael Graves.

4. Many histories of the Bauhaus have been written during the past fifty years, most of them sympathetic to its philosophy and teaching objectives. Notable critiques

of the Bauhaus and its indelible legacy include Bruce Allsop, *Towards a Humane Architecture* (London: Frederick Muller, 1974); Peter Blake, *Form Follows Fiasco* (Boston: Atlantic–Little, Brown, 1974); Brent Brolin, *The Failure of Modern Architecture* (New York: Van Nostrand Reinhold, 1976); and Klaus Herdeg, *The Decorated Diagram: Harvard Architecture and the Failure of the Bauhaus Legacy* (Cambridge: MIT Press, 1983).

5. Jon Lang, *Creating Architectural Theory: The Role of the Behavioral Sciences in Environmental Design* (New York: Van Nostrand Reinhold, 1987), 3, 4–7.

6. Ibid., 6–10.

7. Alison Smithson, *Team 10 Primer* (Cambridge: MIT Press, 1968).

8. Jane Jacobs, *The Death and Life of Great American Cities* (New York: Random House, 1961); Herbert J. Gans, *The Urban Villagers* (New York: Free Press, 1962); Martin Pawley, *Architecture versus Housing* (New York: Praeger, 1971); Blake, *Form Follows Fiasco*, 74; Brolin, *Failure of Modern Architecture*, 5–26; see also Lang, *Creating Architectural Theory*, 4–10.

9. James T. Burns, "Corbu's Venetian Contemporary," *P/A Observer* 45 (December 1965): 162–65.

10. Le Corbusier coined the term "modulor man" to describe the relationship of human beings to the principles of architecture he espoused in *Towards a New Architecture*, trans. Frederick Etchells (London, 1927). Le Corbusier's system of proportion, the modulor, consisted of two interpenetrating series of geometrical progressions, the red and the blue, which in a play of geometry and numbers—that is, numbers and their extension in space—form a scale of harmonious measurements of space. In *The Modulor* (1948), Le Corbusier presented his invention to the public. Charles Jencks later discussed the origins of the term and its influence on Le Corbusier's unbuilt hospital proposal for Venice. See Jencks, *Le Corbusier and the Tragic View of Architecture* (Cambridge: Harvard University Press, 1973), 170–72.

11. Burns, "Corbu's Venetian Contemporary," 162.

12. Jencks, *Le Corbusier and the Tragic View,* 171.

13. "A Growing Voluntary Hospital Complex," *Architectural Record* 137 (February 1965): 170–171.

14. "Princess Margaret Hospital, Second Stage," *Architectural Review* 137, no. 820 (June 1965): 426–429.

15. "New Hospital's Expansion Is Suburban Success Story," *Modern Hospital* 105, no. 11 (November 1965): 108–11.

16. This article was part of a special issue of *Architectural Record*, "Medical Facilities: Building Types Study 331," vol. 135 (April 1964): 195–97.

17. Lord Taylor, "The Natural History of Windows: A Cautionary Tale," *British Medical Journal* 7 (March 31, 1979): 870–75.

18. "Finger Plan Hospital Can Grow Up or Out," *Modern Hospital* 104, no. 5 (May 1965): 114–17.

19. "This Small Hospital Even Has an Escalator," *Modern Hospital* 104, no. 2 (February 1965): 105–8.

20. "Eight-Sided Unit Puts Nurse within Six Steps of Patient," *Modern Hospital* 105, no. 10 (October 1965): 118–21. Many of the hospitals featured in *Modern Hospital*'s "Hospital of the Month," besides receiving an award certificate from the magazine's editors, were also evaluated in terms of the performance of the facility. These evaluations were generally informed appraisals conducted by the administrator-in-charge, and as a result might not have always been fully objective. The evaluation appears to have been optional. This practice predated by a number of years the formal "Post-Occupancy Evaluation," or POE, a term first used in the late 1960s to describe a more systematic approach to assessing the performance level of a building-in-use. In her

book *Architectural Programming,* Donna Duerk classifies POES as of three types, or levels of inquiry: (1) indicative, (2) investigative, and (3) diagnostic, with the third type being the most rigorous in the use of scientific data collection and analysis and having the greatest level of depth. Donna P. Duerk, *Architectural Programming: Information Management for Design* (New York: Van Nostrand Reinhold, 1993), 210–15.

21. "Towers Attract the Eye—and Physicians," *Modern Hospital* 105, no. 8 (August 1965): 112–15.

22. "Sawtooth Design Gives Glareproof View," *Modern Hospital* 107, no. 9 (September 1966): 103–6.

23. William B. Foxhall, "Folded Floor Plan with a View for All Patients," in special issue "Building Types Study 356: Hospitals," *Architectural Record* 139 (March 1966): 176–77.

24. "Efficient Nursing Unit in a Triangle," in special issue "Building Types Study 338: Hospitals," *Architectural Record* 136 (October 1964): 190–91.

25. William B. Foxhall, "Adventures in Architectural Services on the Frontiers of Change," *Architectural Record* 147 (March 1970): 107–18.

26. "Innovative Design for a Community Hospital," *Architectural Record* 143 (June 1968): 143–46.

27. "Temple University Health Sciences Center," *Progressive Architecture* 50 (February 1969): 112–17.

28. "Phased Construction Keeps Hospital Revenue Flowing," *Modern Hospital* 112 (April 1969): 88–91.

29. "Hospital Builds in Efficiency with Snowflake Design and Cart System," *Modern Hospital* 112 (July 1969): 78–81.

30. "Centre hospitalier de l'Université 'Libre,'" *Techniques et architecture* 30, no. 2 (March 1969): 71–73. Arthur Q. Davis, as part of the firm Curtis and Davis, would achieve international attention some years later for their design of the state-of-the-art Louisiana Superdome multipurpose sports stadium, which opened in New Orleans in 1975.

31. "Centre hospitalier universitaire, Göttingen," *L'architecture d'aujourd'hui* 150, no. 6 (June 1970): 28–29.

32. "Le nouveau centre hospitalier de Gonesse," *Techniques et architecture* 32, no. 1 (April 1970): 70–72.

33. Patricia Norton, "Hospitals," *Architectural Review* 147 (May 1970): 326–86.

34. Ibid., 334.

35. "General Hospitals," *Architectural Review* 137 (June 1965): 432–433.

36. "Clinique privée, Rome," *L'architecture d'aujourd'hui* 150, no. 6 (June 1970): 94–97.

37. "Complèxe hospitalier et d'enseignement Chandigarh," *L'architecture d'aujourd'hui* 150, no. 6 (June 1970): xlix.

38. "Hospital psychiatrique Tirat Hacarmal, Haifa," *L'architecture d'aujourd'hui* 150, no. 6 (June 1970): xlv–xlvi.

39. "Nouakchott (Mauritania) Hôpital National," *Techniques et architecture* 25, no. 2 (February 1965): 106–7.

40. "Hôpital Marsico Vetere," *L'architecture d'aujourd'hui* 150, no. 6 (June 1970): 74–75.

41. "Women's Hospital, Kuwait," *Architectural Review* 145, no. 866 (April 1969): 293–94.

42. "Bagneux: Clinique chirurgicale," *Techniques et architecture* 25, no. 2 (February 1965): 98–99.

43. "Quibeon Institut de Thalassothérapie," *Techniques et architecture* 25, no. 2

(February 1965): 116–17. The second phase of this facility is described in *Techniques et architecture* 32, no. 1 (April 1970): 79–81.

44. "Slough General Hospital," *Architectural Review* 137, no. 820 (June 1965): 437–38.

45. Patricia Norton, "Hospitals," Special Issue on Manplan 6, *Architectural Review* 147, no. 879 (May 1970): 334–37.

46. "Terraced Hospital under a High-Tiered Roof," *Progressive Architecture* 49 (November 1968): 102–7.

Chapter 3: An Imperfect Machine for an Imperfect System

1. *Architectural Record* 149 (February 1971): 107. Firms remained busy working on healthcare projects, and during this period the firm specializing in health architecture emerged. The trend of some firms to devote the bulk of their energy to healthcare clients dated from the 1920s, but by the mid-1970s firms aggressively began to market themselves in this area, with the rationale that the highly specific, complex requirements of the typical healthcare project were best met by a specialist.

2. *Architectural Record* 151 (June 1972): 117. For more on interstitial space, see Chapter 4.

3. The Co-Struc System, by Herman Miller, was unveiled in *Progressive Architecture* 52 (July 1972): 72.

4. Other firms would soon appear, such as Robert Douglass Associates, based in Houston, and Tribrook Associates, based in Oakbrook, Illinois. H. Robert Douglass, along with James T. Falick of Caudill, Rowlett, Scott (CRS) and later his own firm, the Falick/Klein Partnership in Houston, were frequent contributors to the architectural and healthcare literature during this period.

5. The most notable examples of this approach were such large firms as Perkins and Will, with E. Todd Wheeler, based in Chicago; Kaplan/McLaughlin/Diaz, in San Francisco; Stone, Marracinni, and Patterson, in St. Louis; and Marshall Erdman and Associates, in Madison, Wisconsin. Perhaps the most innovative of this type of firm was CRS, in Houston.

6. "Hôpital Ambroise-Paré à Boulogne," *L'architecture française* 20 (March–April 1971): 79–81.

7. "Le nouvel hôpital de Tarascon-Sur-Rhône," *L'architecture française* 20 (September–October 1971): 73–75.

8. "Centre de readaptation à Vienne-Meilding," *L'architecture française* 22 (November–December 1973): 3–6.

9. This medical center was designed by Roben Matthew, Johnson-Marshall, and Partners, with the consultant team of Llewelyn-Davies, Weeks, and Partners, with John Musgrove as laboratory consultant. The Royal Infirmary and the Western General Hospital formed the nucleus of a comprehensive undergraduate and graduate teaching and research facility and a community hospital. By 1970s, this complex had replaced the entire existing facility, with the exception of the Florence Nightingale Nurses' Home and the Maternity Hospital. The project is reviewed as a work in progress in *Architectural Review* 137 (June 1965): 451–52.

10. "Lakeside Health Centre," *Architectural Review* 152 (August 1972): 73–77.

11. "Clinica Barraquer, Barcelona," *Domus* 593 (April 1971): 16–18.

12. "Medical Centre, Wellingborough, Northants," accompanied by "Critique" by Lance Wright, in *Architectural Review* 155 (December 1974): 382–86.

13. "Natick, Mass.," *Architectural Forum* 135 (June 1971): 43–45.

14. "Hôpital General Docteur Joseph O. Ruddy à Whitby, Ontario," *L'architecture française* 375–376 (November–December 1973): 34–35.

15. "Bertrand Goldberg: Le retour au panoptique," *L'architecture d'aujourd'hui,* nos. 183–85 (January–February 1976): 92–102.

16. Paul-Michel Charoy, "Les malades danse plateau technique," *Techniques et architecture,* nos. 323–327 (April 1979): 42–47.

17. "In Argentina: Tetto d'Ombra Sull 'Ospedale," *Domus* 598 (September 1979): 22–25.

18. Rosemary Stevens, "Pragmatism in the Marketplace: 1965–80," in *In Sickness and in Wealth: American Hospitals in the Twentieth Century* (New York: Basic Books, 1989), 293–94. An excellent review of hospital capital requirements is provided in Uwe Reinhardt and Bradford H. Gray, "Financial Capital and Health Care Growth Trends," in *For-Profit Expertise in Health Care,* ed. Bradford H. Gray (Washington, D.C.: National Academy Press, 1986), 47–73.

19. Henry C. F. Arnold, "The Federal Government and Hospital Construction," *Architectural Record* 158 (September 1975): 63. By the time the program was officially ended, Mississippi, the state with the lowest income per capita, had received the highest allotment of funds per capita over the years. States with high median incomes such as Connecticut, Illinois, New York, California, and New Jersey all received, by comparison, low levels of Hill-Burton funds over the decades.

20. Robert M. Ball, "Problems of Cost—As Experienced in Medicare," in U.S. Department of Health Education and Welfare, *Report of the National Conference on Medical Costs* (Washington, D.C.: Government Printing Office, 1967), 65.

21. "Two California Hospitals by Edward Durell Stone Set a Challenging Pace in Design, and Economics: An Expansion at Monterey; and a New Start at Palm Desert," *Architectural Record* 152 (September 1972): 137–144. The site was donated by the entertainer Bob Hope, and operating expenses have been funded annually to a large extent by the proceeds of the Bob Hope Desert Golf Tournament.

22. See Stevens, "Pragmatism in the Marketplace," 294, and Richard W. Foster, "The Financial Structure of Community Hospitals: Impact of Medicare," in *The Nature of Hospital Costs: Three Studies* (Chicago: Hospital Research and Educational Trust, 1976), 65–68.

23. Stevens, "Pragmatism in the Marketplace," 294.

24. Ibid., 295. Also see "American Hospital Association Surveys of Sources for Funding of Hospital Construction," reported in AHA Hospital Capital Finance, Fourth Quarter 1985, p. 4.

25. The average occupancy rate in U.S. hospitals had increased to more than 75 percent by 1980, and there were two surgical operations for every three admissions. See Stevens, "Pragmatism in the Marketplace," 296–97. Also see "Hospital Statistics," U.S. Department of Commerce, Bureau of the Census, *Statistical Abstract of the United States: 1984* (Washington, D.C.: Government Printing Office, 1983), 115, 117.

26. Stevens, "Pragmatism in the Marketplace," 299.

27. George J. Mann, "Stress Health, Not Hospitals!" *Journal of the American Institute of Architects* 62 (March 1972): 17–22.

28. These data were reported in *U.S. News and World Report,* September 6, 1971. The article also stated that the downturn in use was attributable to the rapidly escalating cost of health care, causing more people not to seek care, more stringent monitoring of Medicare and Medicaid payments to providers, an overabundance of new and pre-existing hospitals for acute and long-term care, and the movement toward outpatient services and away from acute-care facilities. These trends, as well as the start of resource pooling among providers, are cited in H. Robert Douglass, "Health Care: The Fastest Growing Industry," *Progressive Architecture* 53 (July 1972): 53.

29. The call for a system of health care based on time and availability was first

advocated by William O. Anlyan, M.D., vice president for health affairs at Duke University, in an address presented at the annual meeting of the Association of American Medical Colleges in October 1971. Summarizing his model of a patient-focused system, he called for a one-hour maximum time of response to the patient's immediate needs, a two-hour maximum time for an assessment of the patient's secondary specialty care needs, and a five-hour maximum period for the assessment of the patient's tertiary subspecialty care needs. He also called for a self-help and buddy system in junior and senior high schools, where personnel and such instructional aids as videotapes would be available for the teaching of health maintenance and sickness prevention.

30. Mann, "Stress Health, Not Hospitals!" 20. Mann implored architects to carefully assess the fundamental healthcare needs of communities when called upon to consult overseas, and not simply to impose superficial Western solutions or, worse, carbon-copied "templates" that would likely be highly deterministic. He also called for a series of new programs and a research effort within the architectural profession and university departments to address the challenges of creating appropriate health architecture in the 1970s.

31. Bess Balchen, "A New Client: The For-Profit Hospital Corporation," *Journal of the American Institute of Architects* 62 (March 1972): 29–32. The two largest chains at the time were American Medicorp, based in Bala Cynwyd, Pennsylvania, and Hospital Corporation of America, in Nashville (later Columbia/HCA). Combined, they owned more than five thousand beds. Other large for-profits were Beverly Enterprises in California; Hospital Affiliates, also of Nashville; and Extendicare (later Humana), in Louisville.

32. Interview with Thomas F. Batey, director of HCA's Architectural Planning and Construction Division, in Balchen, "A New Client," 30.

33. Interview with architect Jason Frye, in Balchen, "A New Client," 30.

34. The firm of Gresham and Smith handled most of the HCA architectural commissions in the early 1970s. By 1972 the firm had designed seventeen hospitals for HCA, some of them identical. The analysis of need and "role studies" were done by the firm of Hospital Planning Consultants, working with Gresham and Smith's staff. It was no coincidence that HCA was the chief financial interest of Jack C. Massey, the entrepreneur who helped found Kentucky Fried Chicken (now KFC) in the 1960s.

35. Balchen, "A New Client," 31.

36. B. R., "A Healthy Industry," *Interiors* 48 (November 1971): 74–75. The first board of Medicenters of America included Wallace K. Johnson as board chairman and Kemmons Wilson as vice chairman. Both men were top executives of the incredibly successful hotel chain Holiday Inns of America.

37. Stevens discusses the various techniques used by the investor-owned providers to depreciate facilities, finance long-term debt, and restructure debt, and examines the effects of open-market speculation on the relative value of their holdings. "Pragmatism in the Marketplace," 298–309.

38. Elisabeth Kübler-Ross, *On Death and Dying* (New York: Macmillan, 1975). See also H. Feifel, ed., *Death in Contemporary America: New Meanings of Death* (New York: McGraw-Hill, 1977). These seminal works would have a profound impact on contemporary attitudes toward death and dying. Yet it would take nearly two decades for the hospital industry to fully accept the role of hospice care as an adjunctive component to acute care. Meanwhile, the typical acute-care hospital facility made little or no provision for the act of death or for the grieving process.

39. Richard Kolbe, "Inside the English Hospice," *Journal of the American Hospital Association* 51 (July 1, 1977): 65–67.

40. Cicely Saunders, "Hospice Care," *American Journal of Medicine 65*, no. 11 (November 1978): 726–28. Saunders received her nursing training in pain management at St. Luke's Hospital, in the unit for terminal cancer patients. St. Luke's was founded in 1892 as a project of the West London Mission, an arm of the Methodist Church. A detailed account of St. Luke's between the years 1893 and 1921 is provided by Grace Golden in the *Journal of the History of Medicine* (October 1981), 383–415.

41. According to a May 1979 report to the Congress by the U.S. Comptroller General, the contemporary hospice evolved out of the homes for pilgrims owned and operated by religious orders during the Middle Ages in Europe. Institutions of early medicine evolved from these homes and provided care for the sick and dying poor. A group of Catholic widows established a hospice in Lyon, France, in 1842 for poor women with incurable and inoperable cancer. In the mid-nineteenth century a hospice was established in Dublin, and about fifty years later three were founded in London. One of the first of these care centers to reprise those of centuries earlier was called St. Joseph's Hospice; the other two were founded by an Anglican order and a mission of the Methodist Church, respectively. See Comptroller General: Hospice Care—A Growing Concept in the United States, *Report to the Congress of the United States* (Washington, D.C.: General Accounting Office, March 6, 1979).

42. The hospice program generally consists of physician care, nursing care, personal assistance with activities of daily life, medical social work, and companionship and psychological counseling. The team consists of psychiatrists, psychologists, physical therapists, occupational therapists, and legal and financial advisors available to residents and their families. Most hospice patients suffer from either cancer or HIV/AIDS.

43. David H. Smith and Judith A. Granbois, "The American Way of Hospice," *Hastings Center Report* (April 1982), 8–10. Also see H. Peggy Falknor and Deborah Kugler, "JCAH Hospice Project, Interim Report, Phase I, Chicago: Joint Commission on the Accreditation of Hospitals" (July 1981). In 1981, 60 percent of the more than 800 programs reported annual budgets under $75,000; only 10 percent had budgets over $300,000.

44. John L. Ford, "Hospice: A Rediscovered Concept in a Modern Medical World," *Human Ecology Forum* 11, no. 3 (1981): 10–13.

45. Joan Kron, "Designing a Better Place to Die," *New York*, March 1, 1976, 4349. The Connecticut Hospice, the first contemporary hospice in the United States, founded in 1974, operates a statewide home care program and a fifty-two-bed residential facility in New Haven. The hospice maintains a home page on the World Wide Web: http://www.hospice.com.

46. Charles Jencks, *The Language of Post-Modern Architecture* (New York: Rizzoli, 1977).

47. "Martha's Vineyard Hospital," *Architectural Record* 158 (September 1975): 118.

48. "Togane Central Clinic," *Japan Architect* 54 (August 1979): 40–45.

49. Masahiro Ono, "Nakamura Plastic Surgery Hospital," *Japan Architect* 53 (August 1978): 65–69.

50. Martin Filler, "Home away from Home," *Progressive Architecture* 60 (May 1979): 76–83.

51. "Extension pour un hôpital, Baja, California," *L'architecture d'aujourd'hui* (October–November 1977): 29.

52. "Existing Structures Offer Helping Hands to Health Care," *Architectural Record* 161 (November 1978): 121–40. See 122–25 for a description of the project. Also discussed in this article is the "Health Facility Reuse Conference," held in early 1978 at Columbia University. The conference was organized by architect William T. Parker,

the director of Columbia's Health Services Planning and Design Program, and was sponsored by a grant from the National Center for Health Services Research. The conference was divided into six parts: financial feasibility, codes and standards, systems approaches, project implementation, planning strategies, and facility evaluation. A design awards program was linked to the sixth category, with awards given to exemplary examples of buildings adapted to healthcare uses. At about this time the "post-occupancy evaluation" came into the mainstream as a means to assess the performance of a building-in-use. See Herbert McLaughlin, "Post-Occupancy Evaluation of Hospitals: What One Evaluation Produced," *ALA Journal* (January 1975): 30–34.

53. A collection of Ada Louise Huxtable's essays on modern architecture are included in *Have You Kicked a Building Lately?* (New York: Quadrangle/New York Times Book Company, 1976). Huxtable continued this line of inquiry in *Architecture, Anyone?* (New York: Random House, 1986). Norman Mailer and Vincent Scully debated the merits of modernism in the early 1960s. This lively exchange was published in *Architectural Forum* (April 1964): 96–97. The disenchantment with modernism was manifest in protestations against federal urban renewal policies. The irrelevance and superficiality of architectural education were attacked. The general public, never overtly receptive to International Style modernism in the first place, was constantly subjected to watered-down, poorly executed interpretations of the high period of modernism.

54. It is revealing that as of 1978, of the fifty largest hospitals in the United States, only one (Methodist Hospital in Indianapolis) operated a hospice program. This was indicative of the singular disinterest in alternative philosophies of death and dying. The architecture of the high-tech hospital was to symbolize hope and the belief in science; anything other than this attitude was considered virtually subversive. See Donald E. L. Johnson, "Big Hospitals' Expenses Still Soaring," *Modern Healthcare* (May 1978): 34.

55. Jim Murphy, "A Big Toy," *Progressive Architecture* (June 1979): 62–65.

56. Gerald D. Weisman, "Wayfinding in the Built Environment," *Environment and Behavior* 13, no. 2 (March 1981): 189–204.

57. Meyer Spivak, "Sensory Distortions in Tunnels and Corridors," *Hospital and Community Psychiatry* 18, no. 1 (January 1967): 12–18.

58. Frequently, various color stripes would cross over one another, only to be obliterated by a dense congregation of equipment and people at intersections and at vertical circulation points, precisely where users needed the most help. See Janet R. Carpman, Myron A. Grant, and Deborah Simmons, "Wayfinding in the Hospital Environment: The Impact of Various Floor Numbering Alternatives," *Journal of Environmental Systems* 13, no. 4 (May 1984): 353–64. A more detailed discussion of wayfinding is provided in Carpman, Grant, and Simmons, *Design That Cares: Planning Health Facilities for Patients and Visitors*, 2nd ed. (Chicago: American Hospital Publishing, 1993), 65–106. The costs associated with wayfinding have also been analyzed; see K. Christensen, "An Impact Analysis Framework for Calculating the Costs of Staff Disorientation in Hospitals," report, University of California at Los Angeles, n.d. As early as 1971, the "pattern language" developed by Christopher Alexander at Berkeley was applied to making the inpatient setting easier to use by increasing its "legibility." See Argyris Liberakis, "The Human Factor Introduced in Hospital Architecture by the Pattern Language," *Ekistics* 186 (May 1971): 372–75.

59. John Snyder, "Carpeting in the Modern Hospital," *Canadian Hospital* 43, no. 4 (April 1966): 56–68. The cost-efficiency argument was put forth in Pierce, "Carpeting Cuts Maintenance Costs," *Canadian Hospital* 50, no. 4 (April 1973): 55–63.

60. The psychological effects of carpet were studied in F. E. Cheek, R. Maxwell,

and R. Weisman, "Carpeting the Ward: An Exploratory Study in Environmental Psychology," *Mental Hygiene* 55, no. 1 (January 1971): 109–18. Also see A. J. Vestal, "Analysts Discuss Pros and Cons of Carpeting in Hospitals," *Hospital Topics* 50, no. 2 (February 1972): 45–48. Carpet was but one of many points of contention. On other aspects of noise in hospitals, see T. W. Hurst, "Is Noise Important in Hospitals?" *International Journal of Nursing Studies* 3 (1966): 125–35; P. Haslam, "Noise in Hospitals: Its Effect on the Patient," *Nursing Clinics of North America* 5, no. 4, (July–December 1970): 715–24; J. S. Redding, T. S. Hargest, and S. H. Minsky, "How Noisy Is Intensive Care?" *Critical Care Medicine* 5, no. 6 (November–December 1977): 275–76; B. B. Minckley, "A Study of Noise and Its Relationship to Patient Discomfort in the Recovery Room," *Nursing Record Research* 17, no. 3 (May–June 1968): 247–50.

61. "New Hospital Will Offer Private Accommodations in a Semi-Private Room," *Modern Hospital* 117 (October 1971): 84–85.

62. Herbert McLaughlin, "The Monumental Headache: Overtly Monumental and Systematic Hospitals Are Usually Functional Disasters," *Architectural Record* 160, no. 1 (July 1976): 118.

63. Ibid.

64. Ibid.

65. Anon. [Design Lines], "Hospital's Design Enhances Efficiency and Growth, Resembles Region's Historical Architecture," *Hospitals,* March 16, 1979, pp. 38–40. Other hospitals designed by Kaplan/McLaughlin/Diaz during this period were also receiving favorable national and international attention (see "St. Mark's, Salt Lake City: Not a Building but a Village of Medical Services," *Modern Hospital* 122 [March 1974]: 52–58; "Three Hospital Projects by Kaplan/McLaughlin," *Architectural Record* 167 [April 1978]: 101–12). A seminal early article by Jane Jacobs, on the relative merits of the radial nursing unit, cited early research by McLaughlin. This research served as a catalyst for his work in health architecture and provided the foundation for the development of the triangulated nursing unit as a more efficient, flexible outgrowth of the radial nursing unit. See Jane Jacobs, "Hospitals in the Round," *Architectural Forum* 115, no. 1 (July 1961): 98–102.

66. McLaughlin, "Monumental Headache."

Chapter 4: Utopian Excursions

1. Isadore Rosenfield and Zachary Rosenfield, "The Best Answer to Growing Pains Is a Master Plan," *Modern Hospital* 104, no. 3 (March 1965): 112–14. Unless otherwise noted, quotations in the subsequent discussions of Griffin Hospital are from this source.

2. August Hoenack, "Here Are Guidelines for Modernization," *Modern Hospital* 104, no. 3 (March 1965): 91–99.

3. A. C. Parrette, "Modernization Must Face These 'Harsh Facts,'" *Modern Hospital* 104, no. 3 (March 1965): 97. Parrette also noted that a large-scale modernization effort would probably cost more than a replacement hospital, that a long period of disruption would occur during renovation, and that the final product would show traces of its "peculiar manner of growth."

4. Carl A. Erikson, Jr., of Schmidt, Garden, and Erikson, Chicago, writing in a sidebar to Hoenack, "Here Are Guidelines for Modernization," 98.

5. Herman H. Field, "Yesterday's Planning Won't Work in Today's Cities," *Modern Hospital* 108, no. 2 (February 1969): 87–91, 156.

6. Ibid., 89–90.

7. Richard L. Johnson, "Urban Hospitals Face Three Choices: Move, Grow or Change," *Modern Hospital* 106, no. 5 (November 1967): 92–97, 160.

8. Ibid., 93.

9. Ibid., 94.

10. Ibid.

11. Ibid.

12. "Modernization" and "Two Federal Efforts That Help Hospitals," by Harold M. Graning, and "Urban Renewal," by Richard A. Kaiser, in *Modern Hospital* 109, no. 5 (November 1967): 109.

13. Ibid.

14. James C. Downs, Jr., "Society Will Save the Cities, Says Urban Expert, and Hospitals Can Share in the Recovery," *Modern Hospital* 109, no. 5 (November 1967): 98–99.

15. Herbert B. Rubinstein, "Michael Reese Story: The Hospital That Changed Its Community," *Modern Hospital* 109, no. 5 (November 1967): 110–11.

16. "Drive-in Hospital Is Planned for Cologne," *Modern Hospital* 107, no. 6 (December 1966): 68–75.

17. "Independent Outpatient Annex Looks to the Future," *Architectural Record* 49 (March 1966): 172; "Health Center Bridges Hospital and Ghetto," *Modern Hospital* 110, no. 5 (May 1971): 100–101.

18. Herman H. Field in *Modern Hospital* 108, no. 2 (February 1969): 90.

19. The call of researchers for the study of human response to the institutionality of hospitals was articulated in the work of Robert Sommer in *The End of Imprisonment* (New York: Oxford University Press, 1977) and in his book *Tight Spaces* (Englewood Cliffs, N.J.: Prentice-Hall, 1974), in numerous articles appearing in the annual proceedings of the Environmental Design Research Association beginning in 1968, and in the journal *Environment and Behavior,* edited by G. H. Winkel. The work of David and Sandra Canter, in England, focused on psychiatric institutions and patient response to a range of unit configurations. This work is summarized in their book *Designing for Therapeutic Environments: A Review of Research* (Chichester: John Wiley and Sons), 1979.

20. "When Horizontal Movers Come in, Will Hospital Designers Spread Out?" *Modern Hospital* 111, no. 5 (May 1972): 77–84.

21. Robert H. Kennedy, director of the field program of the Committee on Trauma, American College of Surgeons, writing a rebuttal to an article (sidebar) on emergency-room care in *Modern Hospital* 104, no. 2 (February 1965): 41.

22. Charles B. Beal, "Plastic Bubble Isolates Patient Anywhere in Hospital," *Modern Hospital 104*, no. 1 (January 1965): 83–85.

23. Ibid., 85.

24. Maguerite Villecco, "Capsules Replace Hospital Rooms," *Architectural Forum* 41 (May 1970): 54–57.

25. Ibid., 51.

26. E. Todd Wheeler, *Hospital Modernization and Expansion* (New York: McGraw-Hill, 1971), 207.

27. Barbara Koval, "How Technology May Shape Future Hospitals," *Modern Hospital* 109, no. 3 (March 1968).

28. Wheeler, *Hospital Modernization and Expansion*, 209–16.

29. Ibid., 210.

30. Ibid., 212.

31. Ibid., 215.

32. "Now You Can Buy a Packaged Hospital," *Modern Hospital* 105, no. 10 (October 1965): 97–101. At the time of this article the inventor of the system was facing many challenges in marketing his product. He hoped that Atomedic Hospitals would "span the globe and a significant new direction in hospital design and operation would be

taken." But the naysayers had been predicting failure from the start. He had dreamed of full physiological monitoring of the patient, for example, an innovation nonexistent in hospitals at the time. His first prototype was part of a parent hospital (Jackson) recognized as one of the first in the nation to install carpeting in all patient-care areas. One of his main concepts was to have an open central core in response to the needs for multi-task work and the provision of flexible space for treatment and for apparatus to monitor patients' status. In terms of treatment spaces, the surgical area was open, with only a curtain separating it from the laboratory. One day, while giving an informal tour, he was stunned to see that the curtain was being replaced by a six-foot-high fixed metal wall enclosure. This unnerving experience was typical of the many compromises he was forced to make to see his dream hospital become a reality.

33. Robert Kronenburg, *Houses in Motion: The Genesis, History, and Development of the Portable Building* (London: Academy Editions, 1995), 75–76.

34. "Army's Inflatable Hospital Attacked upon Arrival in South Vietnam," *Modern Hospital* 107, no. 6 (December 1966): 148. The U.S. military's interest in portable health facilities would continue to the end of the century. In 1998 the U.S. Army unveiled its high-tech field trauma center, the Airborne Surgical and Trauma Emergency Center, a self-contained modular clinic able to be airlifted into a battle zone and activated for intensive treatment within fifteen minutes of its arrival. Also unveiled was a high-tech, fully automated stretcher, the LIFESTAT. This device contained onboard life-support monitoring capabilities and adaptor plug-in ports to diagnostic and treatment support equipment. CNN Special Report, November 1, 1998.

35. Barbara Koval, "Brazilian Interior Gets a Heath Care Network," *Modern Hospital* 112, no. 5 (May 1971): 104–5.

36. "New Techniques: Real and Unrealized," *Progressive Architecture* 49 (June 1968): 120.

37. "The Healing Machine: Plug-ins and Pre-fabs," *Progressive Architecture* 50, February 1969, 128–29.

38. Ibid., 129.

39. Ibid., 128.

40. J. Peters, "The Healing Machine: The New Hardware," *Progressive Architecture* 50 (February 1969): 118–19. Also discussed are numerous bedside diagnostic and monitoring machines and their automated operating systems.

41. Members of the health facility design team at Caudill, Rowlett, and Scott cowrote the piece "The Healing Machine: Can We Keep Hospitals From Dying?" (*Progressive Architecture* 50 [February 1969]: 122–27) as a vehicle to promote their methods as much as to provide an overview of state-of-the-art thinking on how architects must cope with the rapid trend toward obsolescence among even new hospitals in the 1960s.

42. Ibid., 122. The quotation is from a conversation with hospital consultant Robert Chapman of the firm Chapman and Garber. Unless otherwise noted, all quotations of Zeidler are from the same source.

43. Ibid., 123.

44. Ibid., 126.

45. E. T. Weber, J. Brand, J. B. Balmus, and D. Willinek, "A Prototype Vertical Hospital," *L'architecture d'aujourd'hui* 150, no. 6 (June 1970): 54.

46. John Morris Dixon provided much technical information on this facility in the article "Health Facilities" (*Architectural Forum* 41 [June 1971]: 30–34). For instance, the fifty-five glass-enclosed towers of the hospital were its mechanical shafts, its emergency stairways, and the sole support of its long-span structural system. Steel framing of the towers, covered with cementitious fireproofing, remained visible. The pipes,

ducts, and stairs inside were painted in bright colors coded for each quadrant of building, which was more than six hundred feet long. The structure's four occupied floors, interstitial floors, and tall mechanical penthouses sat on top of a thousand-car parking garage. In the construction of the building, a three-and-a-half-year period of design and a three-and-a-half-year period of construction were telescoped into four years. Construction began in early 1968, and more than 60 percent of the building was completed (in dollar value) before any interior contract work began. This fast-track method allowed for a total of eighteen months of interior design work before any actual interior construction began. The construction cost was $56,918,000, with an additional $10,850,000 for furnishings and equipment; the professional fees totaled $4,800,000.

47. Robert Jensen, "Physician Heal Thyself," *Architectural Forum* 43, June 1973, 30–37.

48. Ibid., 34.

49. E. H. Zeidler and J. F. Mustard, "McMaster: A Rebuttal," *Architectural Forum* 43 (October 1973): 54–57.

50. Kronenburg, *Houses in Motion*, 102–6.

51. Peter Cook, *Archigram* (London: Studio Vista, 1972). An updated, comprehensive review of Archigram in the context of the late twentieth century can be found in *A Guide to Archigram, 1961–1974* (London: Academy Editions).

52. Paul James and Tony Noakes, *Hospital Architecture* (London: Longman, 1994), 30–37. The assumption that it was appropriate to build a facility this large on a single site was questionable from the outset. Its critics in the healthcare community were numerous, even when it was in its early planning stages. In fact, an effort had been made to split the hospital in half, building one half in Houston and the other half in Dallas, which also was in need of an improved facility. By the time it opened, this hospital was nearly twenty years out of step with society and the healthcare industry. Perhaps more than any other building, it represented the last gasp of 1960s utopianism.

53. Lord Taylor, "The Natural History of Windows: A Cautionary Tale," *British Medical Journal* 7 (March 31, 1979): 874–75.

54. Roslyn Lindheim, "How Modern Hospitals Got That Way," *Co-Evolution Quarterly* (Winter 1979–80): 62–73.

55. Jane Jacobs, *The Death and Life of Great American Cities* (New York: Random House, 1961), 63–70.

56. Lindheim, "How Modern Hospitals Got That Way," 71.

57. Ibid., 72.

58. Ibid.

Chapter 5: Reinventing the Hospital

1. "Rather than offering new accounts of the architectural object to replace the one that dominates the disciplines of philosophy and architecture, deconstructive discourse unearths the repressive mechanisms by which other senses are hidden within (rather than behind or underneath) that traditional figure, senses that are already threatening in their very multiplicity. It is the repression of these constitutional enigmas that is the basis of the social contract that organizes the overt discourse about architecture. . . . Inasmuch as deconstructive discourse is the attempt to articulate the unspeakable, but always constitutional, desire of philosophy, it necessarily uncovers a forbidden architecture hidden within traditional discourse. . . . To translate deconstruction in architecture does not simply lead to a formal [physical] reconfiguration of the object or architectural theory. Rather, it calls into question the status of the object

without simply abandoning it." Mark Wigley, *The Architecture of Deconstruction: Derrida's Haunt* (Cambridge: MIT Press, 1993).

2. Leslie McCall Saunders, "Architectural Influence on the History of Health Care Facilities," in *Effective Health Care Facilities Management*, ed. V. James McLarney (Chicago: American Hospital Publishing, 1991), 149–60.

3. Owen B. Hardy and Lawrence P. Lammers, *Hospitals: The Planning and Design Process*, 2nd ed. (Rockville, Md.: Aspen, 1986). Most Hill-Burton funds had dried up by 1968. The Social Security Amendment of 1972 required that providers submit their construction plan to agencies in order to receive Medicare payments. The agency then made a determination of necessity. The Certificate of Need process began as a means to balance the supply of healthcare services with the demand for these services in a given community. The provider submitted an application for a CON permit to a local health systems agency or to the state health planning and development agency.

4. Saunders, "Architectural Influence," 159.

5. Alex Stillano, "Building Type Study 563: Towards a More Humane Healthcare—A Famous Army Institution Builds a Technological Showcase," *Architectural Record* 169 (August 1981): 100–103. As for the Veterans Administration, it would be decentralized in the mid-1990s, long after similar changes had taken place in the private sector. See Jonathan Gardner, "VA Task Force Considers Decentralizing Hospitals," *Modern Healthcare* 24 (November 21, 1994): 42.

6. Marc Emery, "Bronx Developmental Centre," *L'architecture d'aujourd'hui*, nos. 213–15 (February 1981): 23–24.

7. Paul James and Tony Noakes, *Hospital Architecture* (London: Longman, 1994), 30–37.

8. Peter Buchanan, "Alberta Atrium," *Architectural Review* 176 (July 1984): 25–29. Also reviewed in James and Noakes, *Hospital Architecture*, 38–46.

9. Peter Hemingway, "Humanized High Tech—At What Cost?" *Canadian Architect* 29, no. 2 (February 1984): 12–16.

10. Ibid., 12.

11. Eberhard H. Zeidler, "Critic Swims in Confusion," *Canadian Architect* 29, no. 2 (February 1984): 17–18.

12. Richard Rush, "Energy to Recover: Hospital Redesign Strategies," *Progressive Architecture* 64 (February 1983): 136–39.

13. Colin Davies, *High Tech Architecture* (New York: Rizzoli, 1988), 132–39. Similar in scale to the hospital at Aachen was the immense Elias Torres Tur Hospital (1982–87) in Mora de Ebro, a small town sixty-five miles west of Barcelona. Designed by José Antonio Martinez-Lapeña, it was the largest hospital built in Spain in fifty years, and it bore an uncanny resemblance to the Maison Nationale de Charenton in Paris, built a century and a half earlier (1838–45). All three of these hospitals contained symmetrical rows of patient ward blocks set off by central, linear circulation spines. The exterior of the hospital at Mora de Ebro made historicist reference to 1920s International Style modernism, with its formal geometries, flat roofs, stucco exteriors, white exterior, and a large, abstracted clock near the main entrance. See Pierre Mardaga, "Un Ospedale a Morá d'Ebre, di José Antonio Martinez-Lapena e Elias Torres Tur," *Casabella*, nos. 560–63 (September 1989): 24. Also see *Architectural Review* 188 (July 1990): 52–57.

14. Clark W. Bell, "Houston Hospitals on Construction Binge Despite Tough Economy" (editorial), *Modern Healthcare* 17 (July 31, 1987): 2.

15. Cynthia Wallace, "Hospital Can Act as Catalyst to Stem Decay in Neighborhood—Experts," *Modern Healthcare* 15 (July 19, 1985): 46.

16. Elizabeth C. White, "Administrators Shrink Their Hospitals to Withstand

Competitive Pressures," *Modern Healthcare* 15 (November 8, 1985): 66–71. Among the more popular alternative uses of former acute-care inpatient beds were as units for patients with eating disorders (Howard J. Anderson, "Hospitals' Eating Disorders Units Fill Empty Beds with Paying Patients," *Modern Healthcare* 15 [October 25, 1985]: 62–66).

17. David Burda, "Record 81 Hospitals Close," *Modern Healthcare* 19 (January 20, 1989): 2.

18. Lawrence Nield, "Hospitals in the Community," *Architectural Review* 178, no. 1066 (December 1985): 44–45.

19. John Ellis, "West Coast Care," *Architectural Review* 183, no. 1096 (June 1988): 59–65. This hospital was also published in *Architecture + Urbanism* 46 (June 1987): 101.

20. Jean Paul Robert, "Robert Debré Pediatric Hospital, Paris," *L'architecture d'aujourd'hui*, nos. 255–57 (April 1988): 13–19.

21. A second dimension of the port concept was that new specialty units could be plugged in and removed at a later date, if necessary. This anticipation of new technology and the search for a "universal" hospital template was not unlike the quest of the interstitialists for an "infinitely flexible" envelope (see Chapter 4).

22. Peter Blundel, "Cranked Krankenhaus," *Architectural Review*, no. 1184 (October 1995): 74–78.

23. Margaret F. Gaskie, "Acute Care Stacked on Public Uses," *Architectural Record* 187 (June 1990): 94–97.

24. Meisei Publications Editorial Staff, *Medical Facilities* (Tokyo: Nippon Books, 1994), 117–25.

25. Peter Davey, "St. Mary's," *Architectural Review* 187 (February 1991): 24–33. Also see James and Noakes, *Hospital Architecture*, 142–47.

26. Josef Paul Kleihues, "Berlin-Neukolln Hospital Addition," *L'architecture d'aujourd'hui*, nos. 255–57 (April 1988): 27–29.

27. *AIA Health Facilities Review: 1992–93* (Washington, D.C.: American Institute of Architects, 1993), 142–45.

28. Geert Bekaert, "A Provocative Architecture?" *Architectural Record* 175 (July 1987): 128–35.

29. Lynn Nesmith, *Health Care Architecture: Designs for the Future* (Rockport, Mass.: Rockport Publishers, 1995), 80–85.

30. Richard L. Miller and Earl S. Swensson, *New Directions in Hospital and Healthcare Facility Design* (New York: McGraw-Hill, 1995), 10, 151.

31. *Medical Facilities*, 31–38.

32. Andrea Monfried, "Metropolitan Health," *Architecture* 82 (March 1993): 68–72.

33. Margaret Gaskie, "The Picture of Health: Healing Waters," *Architectural Record* 175 (October 1987): 102–7. This was by no means a new idea; one similar setting had appeared in a hotel lobby at the Riverwalk Hilton in San Antonio, Texas.

34. Jain Malkin, *Hospital Interior Architecture* (New York: Van Nostrand Reinhold, 1992), 450–52.

35. Ibid., 192–93.

36. Guido Gigli, "Urology Clinic, Rome University, Guido Gigli," *L'architettura* 40 (October 1994): 680–85.

37. Thomas Fisher, "The Medical Machine—Techniques: Accommodating New Medical Technology," *Progressive Architecture* 64 (October 1983): 108–14. On-site outpatient care centers came to be regarded as saviors of jobs and the prestige of an institution during a period when the hospital would have otherwise suffered as a result of declining bed counts and the rising rate of hospital closures. Fisher addressed the

implications for the architect: "Recent trends mean fewer commissions for new hospitals, but more rehabilitation work to cut hospital costs and a greater emphasis on design to attract more discriminating patients. The future of health care bodes well for architects who can take advantage . . . and we haven't much time to wait, for in the medical profession, with its penchant for change, the future may already be here" (p. 14).

38. "Patients Begin Rehabilitation on Hospital's Easy Street," *Modern Healthcare* 15 (July 5, 1985): 100. By the end of the 1990s dozens of hospitals and outpatient centers in the United States operated variations on the Easy Street model, with many others in the planning stages. However, no empirical data has been presented on a cross-sample, either regionally or nationally, to determine if these treatment settings actually had a positive effect. In the absence of such data, perhaps their most obvious benefit was as a marketing tool to attract patients.

39. Kari E. Super, "Hospitals Build Medical Malls in Hopes 'One-Stop' Concept Will Draw Patients," *Modern Healthcare* 16 (April 25, 1986): 58.

40. Jennifer Fine and Kari E. Super, "Repeal of Some States' CON Laws Spurs Psych Hospital Construction," *Modern Healthcare* 16 (October 10, 1986): 74–76.

41. "CON Elimination Boosts Competition, Capital Costs," *Modern Healthcare* 18 (August 5, 1988).

42. Clark W. Bell, "Free Hospitals from CON Laws" (editorial), *Modern Healthcare* 18 (March 4, 1988): 17.

43. David Burda, "CONspiracies to Crush Competition," *Modern Healthcare* 21 (July 8, 1991): 28–36.

44. *The Number and Cost of Excess Hospital Beds* (Washington, D.C.: American Healthcare Systems Institute and the Center for Finance and Management, Johns Hopkins University, 1990).

45. *Summary of Certificate of Need Laws as of July 1996* (Washington, D.C.: American Hospital Association State Issues Forum, 1996).

46. Charles, Prince of Wales, *A Vision of Britain: A Personal View of Architecture* (London: Doubleday, 1989).

47. James and Noakes, *Hospital Architecture,* 130–35.

48. Ibid., 76–82.

49. Michael Bobrow, "The Arbour Hospital, Jamaica Plain, Massachusetts," *Architectural Record* 171 (June 1983): 94–97.

50. Martin Valins, *Primary Health Care Centres* (London: Butterworth, 1993), 68–74. By this time, *postmodern* was a widely used term, and the Renfrew Center embodied this ideology. Charles Jencks, writing a few years earlier, had stated: "A Post-Modern building is, if a short definition is needed, one which speaks on at least two levels at once: to other architects and a concerned minority who care about specifically architectural meanings, and to the public at large, or the local inhabitants, who care about other issues concerned with comfort, traditional building and a way of life. Thus Post-Modern architecture looks hybrid and, if a visual definition is needed, rather like the front of a classical Greek temple. . . . The architects can read the implicit metaphors and subtle meanings of the column drums, whereas the public can respond to the explicit metaphors. . . . It is this discontinuity in taste cultures which creates both the theoretical base and 'dual coding' of Post-Modernism. . . . [These] buildings show a marked duality [and a] conscious schizophrenia" (Charles Jencks, *The Language of Post-Modern Architecture* [New York: Rizzoli, 1977], 6–7). The Renfrew Center, in true postmodernist fashion, fused the classical pictorial imagery of the English countryside with a contemporary psychiatric institution.

51. Lynn Nesmith, "Homeward Bound," *Architecture* 80 (July 1991): 64–67. This

health facility shared several characteristics with the freestanding hospice facility as a building type: both were avowedly antihospitalist in their appearance and internal organization. For this reason, Shenandoah was a breakthrough in residentialism in the United States: it symbolized a willingness on the part of the provider to break away nearly entirely from modernism and from postmodern classicism, and in turn to embrace architectural influences drawn from the surrounding culture without subverting the role of accepted medical technology.

52. Malkin, *Hospital Interior Architecture*, 307–12.

53. Kenneth Frampton, "Prospects for a Critical Regionalism," *Perspecta: The Yale Architectural Journal* 20 (1983): 147–62. Frampton, the most vocal advocate of critical regionalism, had stated some years earlier: "The fundamental strategy . . . is to mediate the impact of universal civilization with elements derived indirectly from the peculiarities of a particular place. It is clear from the above that Critical Regionalism depends upon maintaining a high level of critical self-consciousness. It may find its governing inspiration in such things as the range and quality of the local light, or in a tectonic derived from a peculiar structural mode, or in the topography of a given site." Kenneth Frampton, "Towards a Critical Regionalism: Six Points for an Architecture of Resistance," in *The Anti-Aesthetic: Essays on Postmodern Culture,* ed. Hal Foster (Port Townsend, Calif.: Bay Press, 1983), 21. The term *critical regionalism* was coined by architect Alexander Tzonis and historian Liane Lefaivre in the essay "Why Critical Regionalism Today?" (*Architecture and Urbanism*, no. 236 [May 1990]: 22–33). They provided an overview of regionalism in the twentieth century and defended its existence, defining it as present when a building is "self-reflective, self-referential, when it contains, in addition to explicit statements, implicit metastatements." The authors acknowledged a debt to Lewis Mumford, the internationally known architectural and urban historian. In Mumford's writings of the 1940s, he was similarly concerned about the crass domination of mass technology and automation, the rapid loss of sense of place in community after community, and the inherent limitations of the International Style. Also see Kate Nesbitt, ed., *Theorizing a New Agenda for Architecture: An Anthology of Architectural Theory, 1965–1995* (New York: Princeton Architectural Press, 1996), chap. 11, 468–92.

54. Lynn Nesmith, *Health Care Architecture*, 124–27.

55. Judith Sheine, "Oasis of Healing," *Architecture* 80 (July 1991): 47–49.

56. Brad Collins and Juliette Robbins, *Antoine Predock, Architect* (New York: Rizzoli, 1994). Also see Brad Collins and Elizabeth Zimmermann, *Architectural Journeys: Antoine Predock* (New York: Rizzoli, 1995).

57. Karin Tetlow, "Dream into Reality: NBBJ Creates a Unique Hospital Especially for Children," *Interiors* 152, no. 12 (1993): 70–75. This hospital has been criticized for its cartoonish expropriation of local vernacular traditions and construction techniques, particularly in relation to Frampton's definition of critical regionalism. Also reviewed in Nesmith, *Health Care Architecture*, 138–43.

58. Nesmith, *Health Care Architecture*, 76–79.

59. Malkin, *Hospital Interior Architecture*, 105–6.

60. *Medical Facilities*, 136–43.

61. Ibid., 61–67.

62. Nesmith, *Health Care Architecture*, 128–33.

63. Mitchel Green, "How the American Hospital Changes its Image," *Architecture + Urbanism*, no. 201 (June 1987): 101–26.

64. "Architecture for Psychiatric Treatment," *Progressive Architecture* 73 (January 1992): 94–95.

65. Margaret F. Gaskie, "Building a Caring Community," *Architectural Record* 178

(June 1990): 91–93. Also see Martin Fiset, "Freeport Hospital Health Care Village," *Canadian Architect* (March 1990): 28–32.

66. Nesmith, *Health Care Architecture,* 64–67.

67. Sandy Lutz, "Epic to Renovate Shuttered AIDS Hospital," *Modern Healthcare* 19 (April 7, 1989): 5; and Steve Taravella, "Innovative Nursing Facility Scheduled to Open in Seattle," *Modern Healthcare* 22 (June 22, 1992): 42.

68. "The Aga Khan Awards for Architecture," *Inland Architect* 39, no. 5 (November–December 1995): 16.

69. Lester B. Knight, "Housing the Sick," *Chicago Tribune,* March 3, 1996.

70. Sandy Lutz, "Columbia Will Roll On, Leaving Turmoil in Wake," *Modern Healthcare* 26 (January 1, 1996): 40.

71. Miller and Swensson, *New Directions in Hospital and Healthcare Facility Design,* 190–92.

72. Stephen Verderber, transcript of interview with Elbert Garner, vice president of Design Development and Equipment Planning, Columbia/HCA Healthcare Corporation, Nashville, March 1, 1996, pp. 15–16.

73. Michael J. Crosbie, "Village, Not: The Unfulfilled Promise of Yale's Psychiatric Institute," *Progressive Architecture* 74 (June 1993): 101–6. The problems requiring retrofitting were: the windows from counseling rooms overlooking the adjacent sidewalk compromised patient privacy, security measures were ineffective because access to the site was difficult to control, and certain program requirements had changed since the project's inception.

74. Marie Christine Loriers, "Centre d'long séjour de l'Hôpital Charles Foix," *Techniques et architecture,* nos. 391–93 (March 1991): 57–58.

75. Heidi Landecker, "Local Colors," *Architecture* 81 (December 1992): 46–53.

76. Janet R. Carpman and Myron Grant, *Design That Cares: Planning Health Facilities for Patients and Visitors,* 2nd ed. (Chicago: American Hospital Publishing, 1993). This book consists of a series of vignette research studies carried out throughout an existing university-based medical center in Ann Arbor, conducted parallel to the facility programming and schematic design phases for a replacement hospital. The chapters addressed exterior and interior wayfinding, waiting and reception areas, diagnostic and treatment areas, inpatient rooms and baths, the therapeutic functions of access to nature and elements of the natural landscape within the facility, and the needs of such specialized user constituencies as the physically challenged, the aged, and children. In the foreword to the second edition (1993), Margaret Gaskie, former senior editor of *Architectural Record,* stated, "First, the book [the first edition, which appeared in 1986] made accessible an unprecedented wealth of reliable information. . . . [Health architecture] is a field where objective documentation is sparse and planners too often rely on intuition, anecdotal evidence, or the unexamined 'rules' of conventional practice" (p. ix).

77. Most mainstream health architects were quick to point out the failings of the modern hospital but were at a loss to provide genuine leadership in the new era of health architecture. Their meandering yet vitriolic critiques centered on scale, image, flexibility, and internal issues at the expense of the larger picture. These critiques lacked sophistication with respect to architectural theory, eschewing informed references to postmodernism in particular. See Jerry Breakstone, "History Offers Architectural Guidance to Hospitals," *Modern Healthcare* 17 (October 23, 1987): 60. Breakstone at the time was vice president and principal in charge of design for the firm Stone, Marraccini, and Patterson, St. Louis. His firm was responsible for some of the largest, most complex megahospitals ever built in the United States, and it was ironic that these stalwart modernists suddenly started calling for a renewed appreciation of history. These statements appeared superficial and not grounded in any substantive theoreti-

cal position. A commentary similar in tone is Shannon P. Kennedy, "As Care Delivery Evolves, Facility Design Must Change," *Modern Healthcare* 24 (March 21, 1994): 38.

78. Robert Gutman, *Architectural Practice: A Critical View* (New York: Princeton Architectural Press, 1988), 39–42. Gutman provides a detailed discussion of three major types of architectural firms: strong idea firms, strong service firms, and strong delivery firms. Into this typology he inserts the client (in this case, the healthcare provider) as antagonist, the key decision maker with increasingly sophisticated wants. One problem with this approach, in his view, has been that the client has come to "instrumentalize" the facility—to commodify it as if it were identical to almost any other item bought and sold in the course of conducting a healthcare business.

79. Clifford Pearson, "Healthcare Facilities: Whither the Hospital?" *Architectural Record,* Building Type Study 749 (May 1997): 165–67.

80. Wanda J. Jones, "Hospitals of the Future," *Architecture* 82 (March 1993): 39.

Chapter 6: Reinventing the Patient Room

1. John D. Thompson and Grace Golden, *The Hospital: A Social and Architectural History* (New Haven: Yale University Press, 1975), 207. Thompson had long favored small wards for from four to six patients. See John D. Thompson, "Patients Like These Four Bed Wards," *Modern Hospital* 85 (December 1955): 84–86.

2. Lucy Seymer, ed., *Selected Writings of Florence Nightingale* (New York: Macmillan, 1954), 166.

3. Thompson and Golden, *The Hospital,* 208.

4. S. S. Goldwater, *On Hospitals* (New York: Macmillan, 1949). Goldwater had for many years been the administrator of Mount Sinai Hospital in New York City and had cultivated a deep interest in hospital-planning issues. See S. S. Goldwater, "A Plan for the Construction of Ward Buildings in Crowded Cities," *Transactions of the American Hospital Association* 12 (1911): 178–85. He wrote and spoke extensively on issues of hospital planning and had a strong influence on the post–World War II generation of hospital planners and architects.

5. "Paris: Porte de Choissy Centre Medico-Chirurgical de la FNMFAE," *Techniques et architecture* 25 (February 1964): 136–39.

6. "Four American Hospitals," *Architectural Review* 137, no. 820 (June 1965): 464–65. In a commentary on this hospital, the editors noted that the exterior sawtooth pattern was rather banal, and that the effort of the architects to develop a unique solution to issues of bed-window adjacency was not based on any evidence that maximizing the window-bed ratio was of any benefit to the patient.

7. "Efficient Hospitals: Success of Private Room Plan at Temple, Texas," *Journal of the American Medical Association* 74, no. 7 (February 14, 1920): 479. The seventy-five-bed King's Daughters Hospital (1908) provided private rooms for the poor and wealthy alike. But hospitals eventually could not cope with the increased operational costs of private rooms. Only the larger urban institutions of the early twentieth century were able to afford them, and then only as part of a mixture of private and semi-private accommodations.

8. Ted Isaacman, "The Patient Arena: A Ward by Any Other Name," *Modern Healthcare* 5 (March 1976): 29–32.

9. "Universitatsspital Zurich, Augenklinik und ORL-Klinik, Case Study," *Werk, Bauen & Wohnen* 226 (September 1994): 1–6.

10. "Metropolitan Health, Guggenheim Pavilion," *Architecture* 46 (March 1993): 60–73.

11. Christian Dupavillon, "Maison de Cure Sainte-Perrine," *L'architecture d'aujourd'hui,* no. 214 (April 1981): 72–73.

12. "Reassessing Goals: H. Lee Moffitt Cancer Center and Research Institute," *Progressive Architecture* 67 (August 1986): 81–85. This hospital received a citation in the 1983 *Progressive Architecture* Awards Program 64 (January 1983): 107–9.

13. Normand E. Girard, "Room Clusters Facilitate Nursing Care," *Modern Healthcare* 8 (June 1978): 46–47.

14. Ibid. Also, letter from Zachary Rosenfield to S. Verderber, dated November 22, 1996, where additional details of the genesis of the cluster concept were outlined.

15. Girard, "Room Clusters Facilitate Nursing Care."

16. "'Cluster' Design Gives Staff Ready Access to Patients," *Hospitals* 57 (December 16, 1983): 16–18.

17. Ernst Hubeli, "Das andere Krankenzimmer: Bezirksspital," *Werk, Bauen & Wohnen,* no. 4 (April 1989): 4–8. One of the earliest U.S. nursing units to include corridor-to-room windows was at the Mercy Medical Center in St. Joseph, Michigan (1987). It is highly probable that a number of U.S. hospitals built in the mid- to late 1980s used a version of this idea.

18. *AIA Health Facilities Review, 1992–93* (Washington, D.C.: American Institute of Architects, 1993), 82–83.

19. D. Kirk Hamilton, ed., *Unit 2000: Patient Beds for the Future* (Houston: Watkins, Carter, Hamilton, 1993).

20. Ibid., 253–63.

21. In the period from 1933 to 1965, Hill-Rom introduced the following products: the first bedside patient-room lamp (1936), the first crank single-pedestal overbed table (1940), the first swinging-arm bedside table (1945), a fracture bed (1946), the first low-back chair with adjustable back height (1947), the first Hi-Lo bed (1948), the Trendelenburg Spring and the first bed with partial siderails (1949), the first combination wood-and-metal patient-room furnishings (1950), the first bed rated by Underwriter's Laboratory and the Electric Hi-Lo bed (1952), the first mattress guard and the recovery bed (1955), the first all-electric Hi-Lo bed (1956), the first labor bed (1957), the first permanent flameproof cubicle curtains, the first bedside cabinet lamp, and a radio-isotope bed (1958), a bed with full controls on both sides (1960), the first intensive-care bed (1961), the "walkaway chair" and the first pediatric intensive-care bed (1962), the first fully retractable bed (1964), and a "patient-centered" bedside cabinet (1965).

22. In the period from 1966 to 1996, Hill-Rom introduced the following products: the first vacuum-controlled bed (1968), the first prefabricated wall unit approved by the Underwriters Laboratory (1970), a double insulated bed (1971), tuck-away siderails, first siderail controls, and the first central brake and steering system (1974), the first freestanding integrated wall-unit power column (1977), the first patient telephone integrated with the bed (1982), the high-tech Centra Bed (1984), a second-generation high-tech bed known as Century and the Horizon integrated headwall system (1986), the first freestanding wall system for the neonatal intensive care unit (1987), a modular wall unit with hidden controls and functions (1988), a birthing bed with siderail controls and a siderail communication panel (1989), the Advance 2000 bed with adjustable comfort and pressure controls (1990), the Advance 1000 upgradable bed to eliminate bed obsolescence (1991), the Affinity birthing bed and the Enhancemate bed-integrated system enabling the patient to control the bed and the room through voice-activated commands (1992), a pivoting power column with movable monitor arms and gas rails (1993), a pneumatic air surface with heel-pressure relief for patients at risk or requiring treatment for pressure ulcerations, and the Composer digital nurse-patient communication system with automated, hands-free visual and audio communications (1994), and a pneumatic bed that provided continuous lateral rotation therapy for the at-risk patient, a "bariatric" patient-care system ergonomi-

cally designed for the obese patient, and a second-generation (replacement) pneumatic mattress (1996).

23. Nora Richter Greer, "Redesigning Health Care," *Architecture* 75 (April 1986): 68–70. An insightful narrative of the origins and growth of Planetree was presented by Robin Orr, former vice president and national director of hospital projects for Planetree, in a talk given at the Fourth National Symposium on Healthcare Design, Boston, Mass., 1991, and reprinted as "The Planetree Philosophy," in *Innovations in Healthcare Design,* ed. Sara O. Marberry (New York: Van Nostrand Reinhold, 1995), 77–86. In an article appearing a few months earlier (Cynthia Wallace, "Hospital's 'Personalized' Care Unit May Boost Share, Patient Satisfaction," *Modern Healthcare* 15 [January 3, 1986]: 36–38), the industry was first alerted to the potential profits for providers using the Planetree concept. The article ended with a cautionary note to providers: the objective of the hospital of the future would be to keep people out of the hospital.

24. Roslyn Lindheim, "How Modern Hospitals Got That Way," *Co-Evolution Quarterly* (Winter 1979–80).

25. Michael Wagner, "90s Alert: Healing Revolution," *Interiors,* no. 150 (December 1990): 96–97.

26. Greer, "Redesigning Health Care," 68.

27. Margaret F. Gaskie, "Joint Assets: Mercy Memorial Medical Center Addition, St. Joseph, Michigan," *Architectural Record* 174 (June 1986): 126–27; Andrea O. Dean, "Children's Ward Made into a Friendly 'Village,'" *Architecture* 76 (January 1987): 40–41.

28. Jill Cohen and Marti Dorsey, "Midwifery Today: Online Birthing Center," www.efn.org/djz/birth/MT/MTindex.html.#top. Also see Richard W. Wertz and Dorothy C. Wertz, *Lying In: A History of Childbirth in America* (New York: Schocken, 1977), 80–84, 154–67. In the early decades of the twentieth century, the infant death rate due to medical complications rose in the United States. Not surprisingly, hospital births cost a lot more than home births, and few health plans covered maternity care. By the 1930s, the number of hospitals had dramatically increased, and 60–75 percent of births in the United States took place in hospitals. After 1945, practically all births occurred in hospitals.

29. Wertz and Wertz, *Lying In,* 159–67.

30. Leslie Kanes Weisman, *Discrimination by Design: A Feminist Critique of the Man-Made Environment* (Chicago: University of Illinois Press, 1992), 52.

31. Wertz and Wertz, *Lying In,* 171.

32. Susan Doubilet, "The Fittest Survive," *Progressive Architecture* 68 (May 1987): 98–103. The healthcare administration field was introduced to the Cottonwood birthing unit and other "early" patient-focused care initiatives in hospitals at about the same time as the architectural journals began to provide coverage of this new wave. See Cynthia Wallace, "Hospitals Should Tailor Services to Meet Local Needs—Experts," *Modern Healthcare* 32 (July 5, 1985): 160–64.

33. Margaret Gaskie, "Patients First," *Architecture* 82 (March 1993): 99–105.

34. Hill-Rom "Genesis Bed" and "First Impression Series" maternity headwall sales brochures, 1989.

35. Stephen Verderber, interview with Elbert Garner, March 1, 1996.

36. Stephen Verderber, "Dimensions of Person-Window Transactions in the Hospital Environment," *Environment and Behavior* 18, no. 4 (July 1986): 450–66.

37. Stephen Verderber, *Windowness and Human Behavior in the Hospital Rehabilitation Environment* (Ann Arbor: University Microfilms International, 1983); Stephen Verderber and David Reuman, "Windows, Views, and Health Status in Hospital Therapeutic Environments," *Journal of Architectural and Planning Research* 4, no. 1 (1987):

121–33, and "Editor's Errata," *Journal of Architectural and Planning Research* 5, no. 1 (1988): 89–90.

38. Roger Ulrich, "View Through a Window May Influence Recovery from Surgery," *Science* 224, 420–21.

39. Beatrice Loyer, "Aménagements hôpitaliers," *Techniques et architecture* 420 (June–July 1995): 108–9.

40. Ibid., 110.

41. Atelier 5 (Red), "Sichtbar Konstruiert: Krankenheim Bern-Wittigkofen," *Werk, Bauen & Wohnen*, no. 11 (November 1990): 36–41.

42. Karin Tetlow, "Dream into Reality," *Interiors* 152, no. 12 (December 1993): 70–75.

43. Jain Malkin, *Hospital Interior Architecture* (New York: Van Nostrand Reinhold, 1992), 83.

44. Ibid., 89.

45. Kim Carter, "Computerized Bedside Terminals Will Be in Use Soon at N.J. Hospital," *Modern Healthcare* 16 (March 28, 1986): 102.

46. Kim Carter, "Point of Care Approach Applied to Bedside Computing System," *Modern Healthcare* 16 (September 26, 1986): 72–73. Also K. Carter, "Bedside Patient Care System Gains Support Among Nation's Hospitals," *Modern Healthcare* 17 (January 30, 1987): 38.

47. Elizabeth Gardner, "IBM Introduces Bedside Workstation," *Modern Healthcare* 19 (March 12, 1990): 49.

Chapter 7: Architectural Environments for the Aged

1. Mary A. Mendelson, *Tender Loving Greed* (New York: Random House, 1974).

2. Peter H. Millard, "Long Term Care in Europe: A Review," in *Care of the Long-Stay Elderly Patient*, ed. M. J. Denham (London: Croom Helm, 1983), 206.

3. Robert B. Kebric, "Aging in Pliny's Letters: A View from the Second Century A.D.," *Gerontologist* 23, no. 5 (1983): 538–45.

4. Pliny, *The Letters of Pliny the Younger*, trans. B. Radice (1963; reprint, New York: Penguin, 1978), 139.

5. D. H. Fischer, *Growing Old in America*, rev. ed. (New York: Oxford University Press, 1978). Greco-Roman society generally defined old age as life after sixty. A. M. Sherwin-White, in *The Letters of Pliny* (Oxford: Oxford University Press, 1966) notes that many of the nine emperors who ruled during Pliny's lifetime lived into "old" age: Galba (A.D. 69) was assassinated at the age of seventy-three, Vespasian (A.D. 69–79) died of fever at sixty-nine, Nerva (A.D. 96–98) was about sixty-eight when he died, and Trajan (A.D. 98–117) died of a stroke at sixty-four. None of these men came from a royal background, and therefore they did not lead particularly privileged lives. Long lifespans are also indicated by a general census taken during the reign of Vespasian, in which eighty-five males gave their ages as one hundred or older. Pliny himself died in his early fifties.

6. Martin Valins, *Housing for Elderly People: A Guide for Architects and Clients* (London: Architectural Press, 1988).

7. In England during the Reformation the convents and monasteries were closed or destroyed, leading to the secularization of care. The creation of the Poor Laws led to the establishment of public agencies in each community charged with providing care for the aged and infirm. Gradually, small communities joined together and large institutions called workhouses were built to care for indigent orphans, the sick, and the old. In the early decades medical care per se was not provided in these institutions. The pattern was to provide dormitory bedrooms and segregation of the sexes. Even-

tually, infirmary wards for the aged who were chronically sick or infirm had to be established. The poorest were assigned to large overcrowded wards. Millard writes: "Concern over conditions in the workhouses led, at the end of the nineteenth century, to laws being passed to give every resident the right to keep some personal possessions in a locker and for husbands and wives not to be separated even if one was infirm" ("Long-Term Care in Europe," 207).

8. Ibid., 209.

9. David J. Hoglund, *Housing for the Elderly: Privacy and Independence in Environments for the Aging* (New York: Van Nostrand Reinhold, 1985).

10. Joseph A. Koncelik, *Designing the Open Nursing Home* (Stroudsburg, Penn.: Dowden, Hutchinson and Ross, 1976). For further background information, see Thomas L. Coffman's excellent review of twenty years of forced relocation of the aged, "Relocation and Survival of Institutionalized Aged: A Re-Examination of the Evidence," *Gerontologist* 21, no. 5 (1981): 483–99. The architectural environment of the nursing home is cited as having a potential adverse impact on well-being in instances where the setting is deemed too harsh, or "disintegrative," in addition to the direct effect of relocation per se.

11. Millard, "Long-Term Care in Europe," 211.

12. "Residence d'anciens les Floralies: Et Centre International de Gerontologie a Bagnolet," *L'architecture française* 21 (January–February 1972): 61–65.

13. "Foyer de personnes agées à Waiblingen," *L'architecture française*, nos. 365–66 (November 1973): 60–62.

14. Leon Goldberger, *Housing for the Elderly: New Trends in Europe* (New York: Garland, 1981). In this book Goldberger reviewed recent projects from Austria, Belgium, Denmark, Eastern Europe, West Germany, France, England, the Netherlands, Norway, Sweden, and Switzerland and discussed policy, planning, and design guidelines.

15. "Forbes Pavilion Nursing Home Is in and of the City," *Architectural Record* 141 (October 1967): 176.

16. "Geriatric Building for a Mental Hospital, in Building Types Study 331: Medical Facilities," *Architectural Record* 135 (April 1964): 192–93.

17. "Maison de Retraite à Spiez-Faulensee," *L'architecture française*, nos. 365–66 (November–December 1973): 41–43.

18. "Foyer pour personnes agées à Wangen," *L' architecture française*, nos. 365–66 (November–December. 1973): 45. It is noteworthy that this project received only one page in a special issue devoted to the state of the art in health architecture. By contrast, more orthodox modernist projects, particularly those most strongly influenced by Le Corbusier, received much more coverage in the issue.

19. "Building Types Study 331: Medical Facilities: Nursing Home Criteria Based on Patients' Needs," *Architectural Record* (April 1964): 188.

20. Noverre Musson and Helen Heusinkveld, *Buildings for the Elderly* (New York: Reinhold, 1963). This book focused on what had been built and what was in construction at the time of its publication. Given that limitation, it appears that scant attention was devoted by architects toward visionary schemes for nursing homes during the early 1960s. William N. Breger was an exception to this pattern. In addition to his proposal for Warsaw, Indiana, he also developed a radial prototype for a ninety-bed nursing home for the Rockland Nursing Home and Cottages, in a rural community near New York (*Architectural Record* 135 [April 1964]: 187–88). This project was never built. Architects apparently were not intrigued by the prospect of creating visionary proposals for nursing homes. Their attention was drawn toward hospitals, perhaps because the hospital was a much more direct expression of high technology than the

nursing home. Other possible explanations for architects' inattention include a lack of client funding for research, or a disinterest on the part of architects in marketing their services in this specialized area of practice.

21. Rex Whitaker Allen, "New Concepts in Nursing Homes: The 'Custodial Facility' Gives Way to Design for Active Extended Care," *Architectural Record* 142 (October 1967): 175.

22. Ibid., 170.

23. "Otterbein Lets Patients Live the Way They Can," *Modern Healthcare* 1–2 (May 1974): 58–62.

24. "A New Concept in Housing and Nursing Spaces," *Architectural Record* 135 (April 1964): 189–91. This facility was the first U.S. limited for-profit facility for the elderly to combine residential living with medical care on the same site. The financial and administrative aspects of this nursing home were also reported as innovative in the healthcare administration literature ("Isabella: Three Levels of Care, Two Buildings, One Administration," *Modern Healthcare* 1–2 [June 1974]: 54–55).

25. U.S. Congress, Senate Subcommittee on Long Term Care, *Nursing Home Care in the US: Failure in Public Policy,* Supporting Paper no. 1 (Washington, D.C.: GPO, 1974). It was reported that despite the large infusion of federal dollars, one-half of all nursing homes offered a substandard level of care, untrained staffs, inadequate provision of health care, unsanitary conditions, poor food, unenforced safety regulations, and excessive profiteering. This was set against the statistic that although only 5 percent of the population aged sixty-five or older would be in a nursing home at any one time, almost one-quarter of the aged would reside there at some point before death. After years of lobbying on the part of advocacy groups, in 1965 Congress passed the basic legislation that created the Medicaid and Medicare programs. Medicaid was to provide a safety net for those who did not have the resources to pay for their care, and Medicare was established to support the needs of the population over age sixty-five. These federal entitlement programs fueled a major expansion of the long-term-care industry. By 1980 there were nearly 18,000 nursing homes, housing 1.4 million persons. A significant share of these were found to provide a substandard level of care.

26. Colleen L. Johnson and Leslie A. Grant, *The Nursing Home in American Society* (Baltimore: Johns Hopkins University Press, 1985), 3. By 1985, nearly 1.4 million persons resided in nursing homes. The number of nursing-home beds doubled between 1963 and 1973. By 1985 there were nearly three times more nursing homes than general hospitals, and consequently nursing homes contained more patient beds and patient-stay days than hospitals.

27. Martin Gornick, "Ten Years of Medicare: Impact on the Covered Population," *Social Security Bulletin* 39, no. 7: 3–21. Four reasons for the dramatic increase in healthcare expenditures for the aged were cited by the early 1980s. First, biomedical advancements enabled people to live longer than in the past. Second, because of the absence or shortage of an intermediate level of care in the community, many families were forced to turn to nursing homes at the point when care could no longer be provided by the family at home, or when an elderly relative could not live independently. Third, changes in the family structure occurred, including the rise of two-career families, the rise in the divorce rate, and increased mobility of offspring. Fourth, public resistance to the nursing home lessened, so more families opted for this type of care. For a more detailed discussion, see B. D. Dunlop, "Need for and Utilization of Long-Term Care among Elderly Americans," *Journal of Chronic Diseases* 29 (1976): 75–87; and B. D. Dunlop, *The Growth of Nursing Home Care* (Lexington, Mass.: Lexington Books, 1979). Between 1966 and 1975 nursing home expenditures rose 500 percent. In 1977 the combined public and private expenditures were $12.6 billion, ten times the level in

1965. Over this period the percentage of healthcare dollars for the elderly in nursing homes rose nearly 23 percent. The cost of these federal entitlement programs would continue to increase exponentially through the end of the century.

28. B. C. Vladeck, *Unloving Care: The Nursing Home Tragedy* (New York: Basic Books, 1980).

29. Dunlop, in *The Growth of Nursing Home Care,* noted that the U.S. government, from 1935 on, prohibited the use of federal funds to cover care in old people's homes, and only when custodial care was needed were the elderly covered for care in the forerunners of the contemporary private nursing home. The Social Security Act of 1935 was designed to empower the aged to pay for their own care. Reimbursement for institutional care fueled the transformation of boarding homes and homes for the aged into nursing homes because more people than ever before wanted to live independently until they needed nursing care, and no viable living options provided a level of care between those of the home and the institution.

30. Johnson and Grant, *The Nursing Home in American Society,* 6–8.

31. Ibid, 9.

32. Erving Goffman, *Asylums* (Garden City, N.Y.: Doubleday, 1961).

33. Jules Henry, *Culture Against Man* (New York: Random House, 1963).

34. Lee H. Bowker, *Humanizing Institutions for the Aged* (Lexington, Mass.: D. C. Heath, 1982), 3. Although Goffman viewed all these institutions for the aged in extremely negative terms, he cited three "dimensions" crucial for the degree of totality of institutional life: the extent of role differentiation, the resident's mode of recruitment, and the institution's permeability. In Bowker's words, "Role differentiation refers to division of the residents into differing but interlocking social roles. Mode of recruitment varied among residents, some of whom freely entered homes for the aged, while others [were] forced by social, economic, and medical circumstances into entering these institutions. Permeability refers to the degree of contact between the institutionalized aged and members of the larger community. . . . The general implication of his work is that many [of these] negative effects are due to structural properties that are common to all institutions rather than to actions of individual administrators" (4).

35. Henry, *Culture Against Man,* 474.

36. Ibid., 405.

37. Jaber F. Gubrium, *Living and Dying at Murray Manor* (New York: St. Martin's, 1975). Gubrium's case study stands as one of the major efforts to describe the daily life of a nursing home, including its physical environment. In Bowker's excellent review of the literature on the 1960s-70s debate on the effects of institutionalization of the aged (Bowker, *Humanizing Institutions for the Aged*), he cites two schools of thought during this period. On the one hand were the studies that tended to classify all nursing homes as total institutions. These include William Alders, "The Idea of a Home for the Aged: A Re-Appraisal," *Journal of the American Geriatrics Society* 9 (1961): 943–46; David J. Vail, *Dehumanization and the Institutional Career* (Springfield, Ill.: Charles C. Thomas, 1966); Richard M. Garvin and Robert E. Burgar, *Where They Go to Die: The Tragedy of America's Aged* (New York: Delacorte, 1968); and Andrea Fontana, "Ripping Off the Elderly: Inside the Nursing Home," in *Crime at the Top: Deviance in Business and the Professions,* ed. John Johnson and Jack Douglas (New York: Praeger, 1978), 125–32. On the other hand was literature that tended to differentiate among different types of nursing homes and their varying levels of institutionality. Examples of this type include Peter Townsend, *The Last Refuge: A Survey of Residential Institutions and Homes for the Aged in England and Wales* (London: Routledge and Kegan Paul, 1962); Morton A. Lieberman and Martin Lakin, "On Becoming an Institutionalized Aged Person," in *Processes of Aging: Social and Psychological Perspectives* 1, ed. Richard

H. Williams, C. Tibbets, and W. Donahue, (New York: Atherton, 1963); and Morton A. Lieberman, "Institutionalization of the Aging: Effects on Behavior," *Journal of Gerontology* 24 (1969): 330–40.

38. Rex Whitaker Allen, "California Retreats," *Architectural Record* 142 (October 1967): 170.

39. "Nursing Home in Zurich," *Architecture + Urbanism* 169, no. 10 (October 1984): 27–36. A common practice was to construct mid-rise nursing homes in order to preserve as much open space as possible on the site. As a result, many facilities were much taller than neighboring buildings, thereby setting the nursing home awkwardly apart from its community context. This pattern was apparent in the nursing home built in Spreitenbach, Switzerland (1978–80), designed by Urs Burkhard with Adrian Meyer and Max Steiger. The six-level building towered over the small bungalows in the neighborhood ("Home for the Aged in Spreitenbach," *Architecture + Urbanism* 168, no. 10 [October 1983]: 101–3). This disjunction between the resident in the nursing home and his or her former neighbors could be unsettling. This site-planning strategy, however, was little different than that used in hospital site planning and design during these years.

40. "Sichtbar Konstruiert," *Werk, Bauen & Wohnen* 23, no. 11 (November 1990): 36–41.

41. "Residenza per anziani a Campdevanol, Girona," *Domus* 56, no. 776 (November 1995): 18–25.

42. Herman Hertzberger, "Residenza per anziania, Almere-Haven," *Casabella,* no. 508 (December 1984): 52–63.

43. Peter Buchanan, "Old People's Home, Almere, Netherlands," *Architectural Review* 177, no. 1058 (April 1985): 27–35.

44. Yuzuru Tominaga, "Kofuen: Nursing Home and Day Service Center," *Japan Architect* 63 (May 1988): 59–63.

45. Paul James and Tony Noakes, *Hospital Architecture* (London: Longman, 1994), 155–59.

46. P. Buchanan, "Lambeth Community Care Hospital," *Architects' Journal,* Special Issue 182 (October 1985): 23–32.

47. Stanley Mathews, "Quality Care," *Inland Architect* 37, no. 7 (January–February, 1993): 46–47. In addition, Jain Malkin highlighted the Dolan Center in the chapter on long-term care in her book *Hospital Interior Architecture* (New York: Van Nostrand Reinhold, 1992), 400–403. Malkin discussed the innovative dining area, the ongoing research program, the contributions of Margaret Calkins as an on-staff architect and environment and aging specialist, the use of natural materials and wood in particular to delineate areas, and the residential ambiance created in the bedrooms. Also, various works of tactile interactive art were cited by Malkin as able to be manipulated by the residents. For example, one painting featured a tennis shoe that could be tied or untied by the viewer. Innovative designs for wandering paths, acoustical control, color schemes, and furnishings were cited.

48. Mathews, "Quality Care," 47. Frank Lloyd Wright founded two schools, Taliesin East, in Spring Green, Wisconsin, and Taliesin West, in Scottsdale, Arizona.

49. American Association of Homes for the Aging and Ernst and Young, *Continuing Care Retirement Communities: An Industry in Action: Analysis and Developing Trends, 1989* (Washington, D.C.: American Association of Homes for the Aging, 1989). Also see American Association of Homes for the Aging, *National Continuing Care Data Base Update, 2: May 1990* (Fairfax, Va., 1990). Experts on the CCRC movement generally agreed by the 1990s that the boundaries of a CCRC were rapidly changing, and that a need existed for a clear definition. Anne R. Somers and Nancy L. Spears, in *The Con-*

tinuing Care Retirement Community (New York: Springer, 1992), defined three essential components of a CCRC: (1) some form of congregate housing; (2) some communal social supports and activities in the absence of one's family; and (3) assured long-term-care services to help supplement the gap left by Medicare and other U.S. health insurance, which had been generally restricted to reimbursement for acute care (p. 11).

50. American Association of Homes for the Aging, *National Continuing Care Data Base Update.*

51. J. Wiener, "Which Way for Long Term Care Financing?" *Generations* 14, no. 2 (1990): 5–9. By 1990 a total of nearly 225,000 residents lived in CCRCs in the United States, with the largest concentration of CCRCs in three states: Pennsylvania, California, and Florida.

52. Valins, *Housing for Elderly People,* 44–47.

53. Daralice D. Boles, "P/A Inquiry: Aging in Place in the 1990s," *Progressive Architecture* 59, no. 11 (November 1989): 84–91.

54. Albert Bush-Brown and Dianne Davis, *Hospitable Design for Healthcare and Senior Communities* (New York: Van Nostrand Reinhold, 1992), 112.

55. Boles, "P/A Inquiry," 88.

56. Ibid., 91.

57. Ibid., 86.

58. The U.S. Census Bureau in 1989 reported that by the year 2030 the 65-plus population in the United States will have more than doubled, from 31 million to 65 million. These estimates were later revised upward, and by 1996 the Census Bureau reported that the 85-plus age group represented the fastest-growing segment of the population, with their ranks expected to increase from 3.3 million in 1990 to 5.7 million by 2010 and 15 million by 2050.

59. Boles, "P/A Inquiry," 88.

60. The net effect for users of this increased competitiveness was that the elderly and their families had an increasing responsibility to assess the strengths and weaknesses of the various alternatives, and especially to compare for-profit and not-for-profit providers. For the architect and planner the increasing number of alternatives was a sign that design and construction budgets would become tighter and more restrictive, thus making it more of a challenge to build high-quality facilities.

61. Victor Regnier, *Assisted Living Housing for the Elderly: Design Innovations from the United States and Europe* (New York: Van Nostrand Reinhold, 1994). The term *assisted* denoted a higher level of independence than the term *personal care.* Personal-care facilities had their origins in the nursing-home industry. Regnier cited other influential quasi-residential settings, including sheltered housing, residential care, assisted care, catered living, service flats, adult-care homes, homes for the aged, and rest homes. He further distinguished between a medical model of care and a residential model of care. The medical model, according to Regnier, dominates nursing homes and tends to foster the dependency of the patient, whereas residential models of assisted-living care tend to foster the independence of the resident. Daralice D. Boles wrote: "[As] an outgrowth of the notion of personal or in-home care the assisted living unit bridges the gap between independent living and skilled nursing, serving those who are somewhat frail and may need assistance in dressing, eating, bathing, and other daily functions" ("P/A Inquiry," 86).

62. Elder-Homestead received much attention for its contextual scale, although the grouping of units in pairs with recessed alcoves overlooking a central atrium was not particularly successful.

63. Daralice D. Boles, "Congregate Manor," *Progressive Architecture* 55, no. 8 (August 1985): 99–103.

64. Regnier, *Assisted Living Housing for the Elderly,* 10.

65. *Design for Aging: 1992 Review* (Washington, D.C.: American Institute of Architects, 1992). The results of the post-occupancy evaluation were presented as part of the "Assisted Living" workshop held at the Annual Meeting of the Environmental Design Research Association, Salt Lake City, June 1996.

66. Daralice D. Boles, "P/A Inquiry," 89.

67. Bush-Brown and Davis, *Hospitable Design,* 147.

68. Such states as Oregon, Massachusetts, and Illinois experienced an explosion in small one-off assisted-living facilities. In the case of Oregon, the state decided to grant operating licenses to independent for-profit providers seeking to open assisted-living residences of only six to eight beds each. These facilities were typically bare-bones operations, with minimal amenities in terms of personal care and recreational activities. Critics labeled these as nothing more than scams—a new version of the old board and care facilities of the 1940s and 1950s.

69. Such adaptability entailed equipping the units with appliances, accessibility standards, furnishings, fixtures, electronic devices, and security systems in anticipation of the later stages of residency, without rendering an overtly institutional image.

70. Jon Nordheimer, "Elderly Get a Needed Assist with Hybrid Housing," *Chicago Tribune,* May 19, 1996. Meanwhile, the growth in the ccrc and assisted-living movements continues. Upscale providers, such as the U.S. national hotel chains, have aimed for the most affluent segments of the market. Marriott's Brighton Gardens chain alone is expected to have more than two hundred assisted-living and ccrc facilities by 2000. Most are predicted in the northeast United States, where demand will be greatest. By 2000 it is estimated that there will be nearly 75,000 assisted-living facilities and board and care residences in the United States, a combination of new construction, adaptive use of such former institutions as schools, adapted industrial and commercial buildings including motels, and adapted private residences. In 1996 several companies that had recently gone public were frantically expanding: Assisted Living Concepts of Portland, Oregon, which in 1996 operated 25 facilities, added 55 more in 1996 alone and intends to have 160 more by 2000; Sterling House Corporation of Wichita, Kansas, with 52 facilities as of 1996, added 55 in 1997; arv Assisted Living of Costa Mesa, California, had 37 facilities in six states as of 1996 and will expand, through acquisition and construction, to 132 by 2000. Amid all the optimism, however, critics warned that stiff opposition from the powerful nursing-home industry, overbuilding by inexperienced operators, and hundreds of poorly built facilities could result by 2000. As of 1997 state and federal regulation was minimal, owing to the lack of widespread public outcry, and most assisted living was privately financed, with little or no Medicaid or Medicare money defraying the costs. Therefore, the main concern of providers was meeting state and local fire codes. On the other end of the sociodemographic continuum, the nonprofits, such as the Daughters of Charity, based in St. Louis, opted to compensate for larger trends, addressing the needs of the poor, the lower-middle-class, and the middle-class aged populations. Many states were expected to allow such nonprofit providers to use Medicaid to subsidize assisted-living care. If this occurs, industry accreditation, regulation, and staff-training standardization would result, and costs would likely escalate. These events would symbolize the end of the first era of the assisted-living movement in the United States. What most experts in the field agreed on as the new century approached was the continued demand for expansion of this type of health facility as a cost-effective, appealing alternative to the institutionality of the nursing home.

71. T. L. Coffman, "Relocation and Survival of the Institutionalized Aged: A Re-Examination of the Evidence," *Gerontologist* 21, no. 5 (1981): 483–500.

72. M. Powell Lawton, *Environment and Aging* (Monterey, Calif.: Brooks/Cole, 1980). Lawton and his colleagues developed the theory of environment press-competency, which postulated that the level of press inherent in the built setting is a function of the individual's physical competency level and level of personal choice and autonomy. An overly pressing setting is one within which it is too difficult to function. A widely published chart illustrated the optimal balance between press and personal competency: individuals function successfully when they are able to engage in daily activities of living that are neither too overpressing nor underpressing. Useful examples of this theory in practice were provided in a 1985 article by Lawton ("The Elderly in Context: Perspectives from Environmental Psychology and Gerontology," *Environment and Behavior* 17, no. 4 [1985]: 501–19). At the "Assisted Living" workshop at the Annual Meeting of the Environmental Design Research Association in Salt Lake City in June 1996, Lawton predicted that specific design standard regulations for assisted living would be established nationally by the turn of the century.

73. Leon A. Pastalan, "The Empathic Model: A Methodological Bridge between Research and Design," *Journal of Architectural Education* 30, no. 2 (1977). Before this work, Pastalan, with Daniel H. Carson, co-edited the groundbreaking book *Spatial Behavior of Older People* (Ann Arbor, Mich.: University of Michigan and Wayne State University, Institute of Gerontology, 1970), a collection of essays in the emerging field of environment and aging that amounted to an attack on the total institutionality of the modern nursing home. Topics included personal space needs, human territoriality, the design of spatially stimulating long-term-care settings, and the importance of patients' exposure to nature in long-term-care settings. Later, after founding the National Center on Housing and Living Arrangements for Older Americans at the University of Michigan, he continued to argue for the deinstitutionalization of the nursing home ("Six Principles for a Caring Environment," *Provider* 12, no. 4 [April 1986]: 4–5). The empathic model has also been used in the teaching of nurses (Andrew H. Malcolm, "Nurses Get a Taste of an Elderly Patient's Life, *New York Times*, October 24, 1992).

74. Gerald D. Weisman, "Wayfinding in the Built Environment," *Environment and Behavior* 13, no. 2 (March 1981): 189–204. This work would lead Weisman into the area of health architecture. Lorraine Hiatt extended this argument in a chapter entitled "The Resource of Environmental Design" in a book primarily written for providers (Anne C. Kalicki, ed., *Confronting Alzheimer's Disease* [Owings Mill, Md., and Washington, D.C.: Rynd Communications with the American Association of Homes for the Aging, 1987], 133–64). This was soon followed by the first book intended for designers on the topic of special-care units for Alzheimer's patients (Margaret P. Calkins, *Design for Dementia: Planning Environments for the Elderly and the Confused* [Owings Mill, Md.: National Health Publishing, 1988]).

75. Thomas O. Byerts and Paul S. Taylor, eds., "Curriculum Development in Environment and Aging," entire special issue of *Journal of Architectural Education* 31, no. 1 (1977); Thomas O. Byerts, Sandra Howell, and Leon C. Pastalon, eds., *Environmental Context of Aging: Life Styles, Environmental Quality, and Living Arrangements* (New York: Garland STPM Press, 1979); Sandra Howell, *Designing for Aging: Patterns of Use* (Cambridge: MIT Press, 1980); John Zeisel, Gale Epp, and S. Demos, *Low Rise Housing for Older People: Behavioral Criteria for Design*, HUD Publication no. 483 (Washington, D.C.: GPO, 1977); Victor Regnier and Jon Pynoos, eds., *Housing the Aged: Design Directives and Policy Considerations* (New York: Elsevier, 1987); Uriel Cohen and Gerald Weisman, *Holding on to Home: Designing Environments for People with Dementia* (Baltimore: Johns Hopkins University Press, 1991). Numerous other books and articles have been published on this subject. The bibliographic sections of the aforementioned texts provide a wealth of additional references.

76. Rudolf H. Moos and Sonne Lemke, *Group Residences for Older Adults* (New York: Oxford University Press, 1994). This book summarized years of work on assessing the quality of life in more than three hundred long-term-care settings for the aged. The first step involved the testing of measures for articulating key attributes of these care settings. This phase resulted in the Multiphasic Environmental Assessment Procedure.Descriptive data on the physical resources, policies and services, and social climate of facilities were used to determine the extent to which various aspects of the physical setting were interrelated, and how these care settings might be improved through changes in management and design.

77. Victor Regnier, *Assisted Living Housing for the Elderly.* Based on the findings of research conducted on assisted-living facilities, Regnier presented twelve summary environment-behavior principles: privacy, social interaction, control/choice/autonomy, orientation/wayfinding, safety/security, accessibility and functioning, stimulation/challenge, sensory aspects, familiarity, aesthetics/appearance, personalization, and adaptability. This research received recognition in the Thirty-first Annual *Progressive Architecture* Research Awards Program, 1994.

78. Malkin, *Hospital Interior Architecture.* Malkin stated that among the plethora of writing and research on this topic, at least twelve useful books for designers and healthcare providers had been published by 1992.

79. *Design for Aging: 1992 Review,* 88–89.

80. Bush-Brown and Davis, *Hospitable Design,* 135–36.

81. "Mountain Trace Nursing Center: Quality Care in a Lush Garden Setting," *Provider* 20, no. 9 (September 1994): 34.

82. Claire Cooper Marcus and Marni Barnes, *Gardens in Healthcare Facilities: User, Therapeutic Benefits, and Design Recommendations* (Martinez, Calif.: Center for Health Design, 1995).

83. Bush-Brown and Davis, *Hospitable Design,* 230–32.

84. Ibid., 234–39. This community is also presented in the final chapter of Richard L. Miller and Earl S. Swensson, *New Directions in Hospital and Healthcare Facility Design* (New York: McGraw-Hill, 1995).

85. Stephen B. Meyers, "Pittsburgh Convents Take on New Meaning," *Provider* 12, no. 4 (April 1986): 22–24.

86. Martha Levisman, "Casa di accoglienza per anziani a Montecchio (Terni)," *Domus* 39, no. 699 (November 1988): 14–15.

87. Valins, *Housing for Elderly People,* 21.

88. Beatrice Houzelle, "La vie protégée: Residence pour personnes agées: Kiuruvesi, Finland," *Techniques et architecture,* no. 424 (February–March 1996): 42–45. The precedent established by Aalto at Paimio was included in an excellent retrospective of his work: see Richard Weston, *Alvar Aalto* (London: Phaidon Press, 1995), 50–51.

89. "Colton Palms Apartments," *Architecture + Urbanism,* nos. 265–67 (November 1992): 44–49.

90. Joseph Koncelik, *Designing the Open Nursing Home,* 6–7.

91. Roslyn Lindheim, "Environments for the Elderly," *Ekistics,* no. 240 (November 1975): 356–59. This article was excerpted from R. Lindheim, "Environments for the Elderly: Future-Oriented Design for Living?" *Journal of Architectural Education* 27, nos. 2–3 (June 1974): 14–23.

Chapter 8: The Community Care Clinic

1. Nancy B. Solomon, "Advice from Healthcare Experts," *Architecture* 81 (July 1991): 75–81.

2. Jeff Goldsmith, "A Radical Prescription for Hospitals," *Harvard Business Review* (May–June 1989) 104–9.

3. Ibid, 109.

4. Sara O. Marberry, "How Reform Is Shaping Up," *Architectural Record* 182 (May 1994): 98–99.

5. John Allen, "Finsbury at 50: Caring and Causality," *Architectural Review* 183, no. 1096 (June 1988): 47–50.

6. Allen, "Finsbury at 50," 47.

7. Ibid., 50.

8. Ibid. The account of the planning and design process was the subject of an article published upon the building's completion. See "Finsbury Makes a Programme," *Architectural Review* 46 (January 1939): 23–38.

9. Ibid., 51.

10. Peter Coe, *Lubetkin and Tecton: Architecture and Social Commitment: A Critical Study* (London and Bristol: Arts Council of Great Britain and University of Bristol, 1981).

11. Ibid., 37–38.

12. "Capsule Clinic," *Architectural Review* 169, no. 1010 (April 1981): 206–10.

13. Peter Buchanan, "Middle East Modules," *Architectural Review* 169, no. 1010 (April 1981): 211–13.

14. "From Middle East to East End," *Architectural Review* 169, no. 1010 (April 1981): 214–16.

15. "Space Age Clinic Boosts HMO's Walk-in Enrollment," *Modern Healthcare* 14 (December 1984): 76.

16. James S. Russell, "Not Just for Warehouses Anymore," *Architectural Record* 177 (September 1989): 110–11. Tilt-up casting is similar to precasting concrete, but the crucial difference is that the panels are cast on site, then tilted up and hoisted into place using a crane. This becomes a cost-effective technique when the building slab itself becomes the mold face, saving the costs and limitations of mold fabrication, factory production schedules, and shipment to the site. However, finish and color options are far more limited than with other techniques, and complex shapes are difficult to cast on site.

17. "Mobile Scanners Ready," *Modern Healthcare* 7 (January 1977): 20.

18. Mary Wagner, "Mobile Mammography Tries to Enhance Its Image and Revenue through Strategic Ties," *Modern Healthcare* 19 (January 8, 1990): 78.

19. "Peace Dividend," *Modern Healthcare* 24 (January 2, 1995): 56.

20. Robert Kronenburg, *Houses in Motion: The Genesis, History, and Development of the Portable Building* (London: Academy Editions, 1995), 73–80.

21. Stephen Verderber, interview with Robert Seeber of Perspective Enterprises, March 11, 1996. These units, which were generally much cheaper than a conventional, permanent-site building, were becoming a popular alternative for cash-strapped providers in both the public and the private sectors. Mobile vans were used for such operations as blood donor programs, kidney dialysis clinics, immunization clinics, and women's health clinics, and as ancillary semi-detached appendages on the sites of medical centers, particularly for use as temporary facilities during periods of expansion and renovation of permanent quarters.

22. Francesco Moschini, "Distaccarsi dar Padre," *Domus*, nos. 660–62 (May 1985): 12–15 (project synopsis in English).

23. Martin Filler, "The Recent Work of Arata Isozaki: Part II," *Architectural Record* 172 (May 1984): 170–83.

24. Anthony Vidler, "Wiel Arets Centro Medico e Casa d'Abitazione, Hapert/Olanda," *Domus*, no. 715 (April 1990): 38–45.

25. Jo Coenen, "S. G. E. Health Center in Eindhoven," trans. Ady Steketee, *Architecture + Urbanism,* nos. 214–15 (September 1988): 103–8.

26. Martin S. Valins, *Primary Health Care Centres* (Essex: Longman Group and John Wiley and Sons, 1993), 120–28.

27. Shin Takamatsu, "Clinique Nishina," *L'architecture d'aujourd'hui,* no. 231 (February 1984): 86–89.

28. "Pharaoh," *Japan Architect* 59 (October 1984): 13–18.

29. Sally Woodbridge, "P/A Portfolio: New Japanese Design," *Progressive Architecture* 68 (October 1987): 94–95.

30. Ibid., 95.

31. Chris Fawcett, "Beware of Architecture," *Japan Architect* 59 (October 1984): 19. The term *unfocused-focused* denotes a building of constituent parts drawn from multiple building types, both past and present. The term *ultimate* in this context is part tongue-in-cheek, as if to say, "This architect's vision is so daring that anything is possible." The same goes for the phrase *New Order,* referring to a new aesthetic language for a future architectural order.

32. "Clinique Kazura, Chiba, Japan," *L'architecture d'aujourd'hui,* no. 224 (December 1982): 22–23. In an accompanying article, "Atelier Mobile Team Zoo," the firm was described as antihierarchical, informal, and a framework where the "disposition" of each team member determined the composition of each project team. This was a participatory process, where the individuals collaborated closely within these working teams. Their ideology was antiformalist and inclusive, that is, open to alternative yet refined modes of production and design.

33. *Medical Facilities* (1994): 170–75.

34. Many of Kurokawa's projects have been widely published, including his Helix City Plan for Tokyo (1961), the Nakagin Capsule Tower (1972), his Floating City proposal for Kasumigaura (1969), the Sony Tower (1976), and Capsule House K (1973). He wrote *Metabolism in Architecture* (London: Studio Vista, 1977) and *The Philosophy of Symbiosis* (London: Academy Editions, 1994), among other works.

35. "Himeji City Health and Welfare Center," *Japan Architect* 70 (Summer 1995, part 2): 90–95.

36. Yasumitsu Matsunaga, "H Clinic," *Japan Architect* 63 (January 1988): 48–51. The Hirayama Clinic was reviewed to a greater extent in Valins, *Primary Health Care Centres,* 77–82.

37. *Medical Facilities* (1994): 189–94.

38. Itsuko Hasegawa, "Sugai Clinic," *Japan Architect* 62, no. 360 (April 1987): 24–29.

39. *Medical Facilities* (1994): 200–209. A large number of provocative clinics were built in Japan during the 1980s and 1990s. They might be classified as falling into three types: (1) residentialist, such as the wood-sided quasi-American vernacular of the Sumiyoshi clinic-residence (1981–83), by Yuzuru Tominage and FORM SYSTEM Institute (*Japan Architect* 58, no. 10 [October 1983]: 63–68); (2) restrained late modernist, such as the all-concrete, austere clinic-residence in Osaka (1979–81) by Yasuyuki Takaguchi and Atelier Zoka (*Japan Architect* 57, no. 304 [August 1982: 47–51]; Arata Isozaki's Etoh Clinic; the concrete capsule-shaped Jin'nai Clinic (1979–81), by Tetsuro Kurokawa and Design League (*Japan Architect* 58 [August 1983]: 52–57); and the Matsushita Pediatric Clinic; and (3) postmodernist in one of two veins, either the flamboyant expressionist iconoclasm of the Ark and Pharaoh clinics or the colorful "decorated box," as in the Sugai Clinic.

40. Arthur Wortman, "An Orthodontist Practice," *Architecture + Urbanism,* no. 287 (August 1994): 56–65.

41. John D. Thompson and Grace Golden, *The Hospital: A Social and Architectural History* (New Haven: Yale University Press, 1975), 80.

42. Valins, *Primary Health Care Centres*, 46–54.

43. Pierre-Alain Croset, "D. A. Studio: Three Projects in Czechoslovakia," *Casabella*, no. 548 (July–August 1988): 4–15.

44. Valins, *Primary Health Care Centres*, 149–54.

45. Rory Spence, "Health Centre, Kensington, Melbourne," *Architectural Review* 178, no. 1066 (December 1985): 88–89.

46. Valins, *Primary Health Care Centres*, 107–12.

47. Colin Davies, "East End Avanti," *Architectural Review* 183, no. 1096 (June 1988): 18–24; and the architect's account published in the same issue, p. 25.

48. Justin de Syllas et al., "Surgery Creates a Local Landmark," *Architects' Journal* 200 (July 13, 1994): 39–44. Peter Scher's account of the Church End Medical Centre appears in this article.

49. *Medical Facilities* (1994), 164–69.

50. Stephen Verderber and Ben J. Refuerzo, "On the Construction of Research-Based Design: A Community Health Clinic," *Journal of Architectural and Planning Research* 19 (Winter, 1999). This case study consisted of a thorough programming phase followed by design guidelines that became the basis for the design.

51. Stephen Verderber and Ben J. Refuerzo, "Empowerment on Main Street: Implementing Research-Based Design," in *Power by Design,* proceedings of EDRA 24, ed. R. M. Feldman, Graham Hardie, and David Saile (Washington, D.C.: Environmental Design Research Association, 1993).

52. Margaret Gaskie, "Care for a Caring Community," *Architectural Record* 74 (June 1986): 130–31.

53. Marina Waissman, "Miguel Angel Roca, Argentine Architect," *Architecture + Urbanism* 275, no. 8 (August 1993): 73–92. See also Annie Zimmermann, "Ponctuation urbaine: Equipments de quartier à La Paz, Bolivie," *Techniques et architecture,* nos. 400–402 (February–March 1992): 100–104; and Dorothy Roworth, "Bolivian Beacons," *Architectural Review* 191 (October 1992): 36–42.

54. Elizabeth Kendall Thompson, "Buildings for a Broad Spectrum of Health Care," *Architectural Record* 149 (March 1971): 135–47.

55. Julian Wolpert, Michael Dear, and Randi Crawford, "Satellite Mental Health Facilities," *Ekistics* 240 (November 1975): 342–47.

56. *Community and Migrant Health Centers: Critical Components of Health Reform* (Washington, D.C.: National Association of Community Health Centers, 1992).

57. Leslie Kanes Weisman, *Discrimination by Design: A Feminist Critique of the Man-Made Environment* (Chicago: University of Illinois Press, 1992), 56–60.

58. Ibid., 59. In the United States in 1989, the average cost of comprehensive maternity care offered by birthing centers was $2,111, compared with $3,960 for a private physician and a two-day hospital stay. Because Medicaid did not typically reimburse birthing centers, however, low-income women could not afford this less expensive alternative. But because the cost savings were often in excess of 50 percent, by the mid-1990s most private insurers, such as Blue Cross and Blue Shield, supported birthing centers. The situation had become virtually the opposite of the case in Japan, where such centers are encouraged and adequately funded, as the U.S. medical profession lobbied against birthing centers and advocated the return of birthing to the hospital setting. This trend was furthered by the economic hardships faced by rural U.S. hospitals, many of which were forced to close their maternity units. Further, by the mid-1990s most states had not established code and licensing requirements for this new building type. It fell between the cracks of institutional occupancy codes, with

their strict requirements for an overnight stay, and business occupancy codes, which lacked such requirements. Therefore birthing centers cost much less to build and operate than most other kinds of medical outpatient facilities.

59. Elisabeth M. Meyer, "Plan More Hospital Outpatient Units," *Modern Healthcare* 7 (March 1977): 50–51.

60. Sandy Lutz, "Ambulatory-Care Centers Grow by 18.2 Percent," *Modern Healthcare* 19 (June 2, 1989): 68–80.

61. John Burns, "Outpatient Care Growing Both in Numbers, Scope," *Modern Healthcare* 24 (May 23, 1994): 81–84.

62. Julie Franz, "Mall Motif Turns Office Building/Clinic into Medical Arts Shopping Center," *Modern Healthcare* 13 (May 1983): 76–77.

63. Peter Meijer, "Mall Medicine," *Inland Architect* 37 (January–February, 1993): 44–45; Sandy Lutz, "Ambulatory Care of the 1990s Stretches the Imagination," *Modern Healthcare* 20 (December 10, 1990): 24–34.

64. John Burns, "Move to Outpatient Settings May Boost Medical Hotels," *Modern Healthcare* 22 (June 8, 1992): 57–58.

65. "American Hospital Supply Forms New Company to Build Modular E.C.F.s," *Modern Healthcare* 113 (November 1969): 24–25. The argument for a facility type that would be a cost-effective, less technologically driven alternative to the costly acute-care hospital had been sounded in some quarters as early as the mid-1960s. Soon, proposals emerged for step-down facilities for persons in need of a less care-intensive level of hospitalization. One effort in particular was noteworthy not only for the unique nature of this new type of building, but also for its architects. In 1969, Harry K. DeWitt, the president of American Hospital Supply Corporation, commissioned the Office of Mies van der Rohe in Chicago to develop a prototype Extended Care Facility for construction on the grounds of existing medical centers and in certain satellite locations. A new subsidiary, American Health Facilities, was to oversee this effort. The resultant design (unbuilt) was characteristic of Mies's oeuvre—basically a glass-and-steel box, with brick end walls. The building was to be two levels in height, with dimensions of 226 by 77 feet.

66. "Centro sanitario holistico," *L'architectura* 40, no. 459 (January 1994): 32–34.

67. Frances Anderton, "Northcote Community," *Architectural Review* 189, no. 1128 (February 1991): 38–39.

68. Raymund Ryan, "Dutch Diagnosis," *Architectural Review* 196, no. 1172, (October 1994): 62–67.

69. Jain Malkin, *Hospital Interior Architecture* (New York: Van Nostrand Reinhold, 1992), 171–72.

70. Frances Anderton, "L. A. Care," *Architectural Review* 89, no. 1128 (February 1991): 34. The next two quotations are also from this source.

71. "Community Public Healthcare," *Progressive Architecture* 73 (January 1992): 94–95.

72. *Medical Facilities* (1994): 176–83.

73. Colin Davies, "East End Avanti," 20.

Chapter 9: Frontiers of a Transformed Landscape

1. Nicholas Negroponte, *Being Digital* (New York: Knopf, 1995). The term *virtual reality* initially was meant to describe the simulation of a "real-time" experience in nonreal terms via information technology. Whereas the filmmaking industry had developed advanced methods of representing reality vis-à-vis the abstracted medium of film, the personal computer has been associated with the cybernetics of virtual reality in terms of software and hardware development. Although the term was much misused by the mid-1990s in the popular press, in architecture its earliest usage denoted the wearing of a headset to capture the sense of a "walk-through" of a proposed building or sequence of spaces. Interior

and exterior simulated building representations became possible. With this tool, healthcare planners and architects could, for the first time, convey their proposed "reality" to the client, staff, patients, and others. The term *virtual* calls for definition as it is used in the context of health architecture. Architects and designers, always fascinated with simulation and the process of representing future "reality" to clients of yet-to-be-built projects, made some progress by the 1990s in terms of meaningful applications of virtual reality in the field of health architecture, but the widespread dissemination of this technology has been limited by its high cost. The largest health architectural firms, such as Perkins and Will/Nix-Mann Partnership, and Kaplan/McLaughlin/Diaz, are in the late 1990s beginning to experiment with virtual walk-throughs using computer-aided design programs.

2. Such clearinghouses as the Center for Adaptive Environments, at the University of North Carolina at Chapel Hill, conducted research and disseminated information on universal design to the general public.

3. J. M. Keenan and K. W. Hepburn, "Home Care Needs Physician Leadership," *Group Practice Journal* (March–April 1991): 14–23.

4. Cynthia A. Leibrock, "Residential Design: The New Frontier in Healthcare Design," *Journal of Healthcare Design* 4 (1992): 207–10. The National Association of State Units on Aging reported that by 1991 20 to 40 percent of the elderly population in nursing homes or long-term-care facilities could be cared for in less intensive settings, including the home. And nearly 90 percent of elderly persons living in the community-at-large received some form of assistance with activities of daily living.

5. Charles Honaker, "Home Healthcare Renaissance," *Group Practice Journal* (March–April 1991): 8–12.

6. Leibrock, "Residential Design," 209. In Denmark, kitchens have been the most frequently retrofitted space, followed by bathrooms. Doors and hallways are often widened, and ground-floor units are made barrier free. Elevators are installed when necessary. Demonstration centers in most districts display various design and project equipment options. In England, individuals pay rent for their sheltered housing, and care is provided in three categories: minimum services, in which care is provided by neighbors; institution-sponsored services, including one meal per day in one's home; and partial nursing-home care. Most elderly people with dementia are cared for at home with home-agency assistance.

7. "Virtual Healthcare: Linking Firms to Form All-Star Teams," *Modern Healthcare* 26 (March 18, 1996): 42–47.

8. John Morrissey, "The Future Starts Now for Regional Data Link-Ups," *Modern Healthcare* 24 (May 9, 1994): 52–60. In the United States, the Chicago area established a CHIN among the ninety-three-member Metropolitan Chicago Healthcare Council. Among the chief concerns in the early phase of this collaborative effort to share data and expertise were issues surrounding patient confidentiality.

9. Mary Chris Jaklevic, "Columbia Is Biggest on the Web, Too," *Modern Healthcare* 26 (January 1, 1996): 51. This article highlighted the importance of Web sites as marketing tools and touted the success of Columbia/HCA's effort. By mid-1996 Columbia was attracting 100,000 visitors per month to its corporate home page, which provided disease-specific information, physician-to-physician information, bulletin boards, and other changeable content.

10. Stuart Auerbach, "Sign On for Health Care Data," *Times-Picayune* (New Orleans), December 28, 1995.

11. Christopher Alexander et al., *A Pattern Language: Towns, Buildings, Construction* (New York: Oxford University Press, 1977), 252–55.

12. Victor Papanek, *The Green Imperative: Natural Design for the Real World* (London: Thames and Hudson, 1995), 105.

13. Lewis Mumford, *The City in History: Its Origins, Its Transformations, and Its Prospects* (London: Harcourt, Brace and World, 1961).

14. John Morrissey, "Hospital Becomes Ambulatory Facility," *Modern Healthcare* 24 (June 20, 1994): 20.

15. Alexander Tzonis, Liane Lefaivre, and Richard Diamond, *Architecture in North America since 1960* (Boston: Little Brown, 1995). This assessment of architecture was primarily a coffee-table treatment, but its slighting of health architecture was typical of the mainstream architectural profession, which had long ago written off health architecture as an area of aesthetic innovation, particularly in the United States as opposed to England, Japan, France, and Scandinavia. The three projects cited in this book were the McMaster University Health Sciences Center (1967–72), by the Zeidler Roberts Partnership; the Bronx Developmental Center (1970–76), by Richard Meier; and the Cedars-Sinai Comprehensive Cancer Center (1990–91), by Morphosis.

16. Editorial, "In Search of the Quality HMO," *Chicago Tribune*, April 21, 1996. The effort of the NCQA was praised for its rigor: as of 1996, only one out of every three HMOs had been granted full accreditation by this industry watchdog group.

17. Stephen Verderber and Ben Refuerzo, "Empowerment on Main Street: Implementing Research-Based Design," in *Power by Design*, proceedings of EDRA 24, ed. R. Feldman, G. Hardie, and D. Saile (Washington, D.C.: Environmental Design Research Association, 1993), 281–83.

18. Chuck Hutchcraft, "Hospitals Muscle In on Fitness Craze," *Chicago Tribune*, February 9, 1997. As of the end of 1996 there were 343 hospital-based fitness centers in the United States.

19. Victor Papanek, *The Green Imperative*, 28.

20. Richard Ingersoll, "The Ecology Question," *Journal of Architectural Education* 45, no. 2 (February 1992): 125–27.

21. In *American Journal of Nursing* 94 (October 1994): 83–98, it was reported that a group of nurses left their jobs at Brigham and Women's Hospital in Boston over an apparent epidemic of asthma, bronchitis, sinusitis, rashes, chest pain, nausea, headaches, and other symptoms associated with poor indoor air quality. In *Asclepius* 4, no. 1 (Winter 1995), it was reported that hospital administrators responded by thoroughly cleaning the affected spaces and reducing the use of many chemicals.

22. Victor Papanek, *The Green Imperative*, 236.

23. Florence Nightingale, *Notes on Nursing: What It Is, and What It Is Not* (Boston: W. Carter, 1860), and *Notes on Hospitals* (London: Keegan Paul, 1858). Also see Florence Nightingale, *Florence Nightingale at Harley Street: Her Reports to the Governors of Her Nursing Home, 1853–54*, intro. Sir Harry Verney (London: Dent, 1970).

24. H. W. Lawrence, "Southern Spas: Source of the American Resort Tradition," *Landscape* 27, no. 2 (1983): 10–12.

25. W. E. Campbell, "Work of the Crippled Children's Hospital," *Modern Hospital* 15, no. 5 (November 1920): 424–25.

26. Janet R. Carpman and Myron A. Grant, *Design That Cares: Planning Health Facilities for Patients and Visitors* (Chicago: American Hospital Publishing, 1986).

27. Stephen Verderber, "Designing for the Therapeutic Functions of Windows in the Hospital Rehabilitation Environment," in *Knowledge for Design*, proceedings of EDRA 13, ed. Polly Bart, Alexander Chen, and Guido Francescato (Washington, D.C.: Environmental Design Research Association, 1982); S. Verderber, *Windowness and Human Behavior in the Hospital Rehabilitation Environment* (Ann Arbor: University Microfilms International, 1983). This work was reported in a series of journal articles, including S. Verderber, "Dimensions of Person-Window Transactions in the Hospital Environment," *Environment and Behavior* 18, no. 4 (July 1986): 450–66; S. Verderber and David Reuman,

"Windows, Views, and Health Status in Hospital Therapeutic Environments," *Journal of Architectural and Planning Research* 4, no. 1 (1987): 121–33; and "Editor's Errata," *Journal of Architectural and Planning Research* 5, no. 1 (1988): 89–90. It was found that insufficiently informative views, and those lacking in nature content, were least preferred by patient and staff respondents in six Chicago-area hospitals. The resulting design recommendations emphasized the importance of hospital form that maximizes the relation of the patient to windows, views, and the natural environment, incorporates surrogate views and windows that include nature scenes, and includes plants, flowers, water, and other nature content in the patient's room and throughout the facility.

28. Carpman and Grant, *Design That Cares*.

29. Roger S. Ulrich, "Visual Landscapes and Psychological Well-Being," *Landscape Research* 4, no. 1 (Spring 1979): 17–23; "View through a Window May Influence Recovery from Surgery," *Science* 224, no. 4647 (April 1984): 420–21.

30. David O. Weber, "Life-Enhancing Design," *Healthcare Forum Journal* (March–April 1996): 3–11. The survey of research literature was conducted by Maya Rubin and Amanda Owens of the Johns Hopkins University Program for Medical Technology and Practice Assessment, and was commissioned by the Center for Health Design. In addition to their less-than-favorable review of the research literature, this compendium of information focused on a limited review of the work of a handful of sponsoring health architectural firms toward the advancement of patient-focused-care philosophies and design approaches. The philosophy and work of Wayne Ruga's Center for Health Design was the heart of the article. See Haya R. Rubin and Amanda J. Owens, *Progress Report: An Investigation to Determine Whether the Built Environment Affects Patient's Medical Outcomes* (Martinez, Calif.: Center for Health Design, 1996).

31. Rubin and Owens, *Progress Report*.

32. John Morrissey, "Room with a View," *Modern Healthcare* 20 (April 9, 1990): 60. Each window surrogate cost twenty thousand dollars, and the state regulatory agency was the California Office of Statewide Health Planning and Development.

33. Kristen Richards, "Retreat House," *Interiors* 49 (October 1995): 54–59.

34. *AIA Health Facilities Research Review* (Washington, D.C.: American Institute of Architects, 1997): 15–20.

35. Clare Cooper Marcus and Marni Barnes, *Gardens in Healthcare Facilities: Uses, Therapeutic Benefits, and Design Recommendations* (Martinez, Calif.: Center for Health Design, 1996). This movement dates from the 1960s ecology movement and was carried forward in the mid-1990s in the efforts of various environmental conservation groups, such as those listed in *Earth, Healing the Mind* (San Francisco: Sierra Club, 1995). In a call for a new symbiosis in person-nature transactions, it advocated a view of the natural world not as removed or apart from humans but as existing within the human spirit and mind. A disturbed "outer world" of nature, it was reasoned, if allowed to continue to be viewed as existing apart from humans, would lead to a disturbed inner world of the human.

36. Wayne Ruga, president of the National Symposium on Healthcare Design and CEO of the Center for Health Design, founded in 1991, was a leading advocate of patient-centered design, including person-nature transactions. The organization's national symposia, held annually; its quarterly newsletter, *Asclepius*; and its annual *Journal of Healthcare Design*, based on the annual meeting, focused attention on the value of humanistic, anti-institutional design in the healthcare experience—that is, the shift in values expressed in the new residentialism.

37. Stephen Verderber, Stan Grice, and Patrice Gutentag, "Wellness Health Care and the Architectural Environment," *Journal of Community Health* 12, nos. 2–3 (1987): 163–75.

38. A sequence of courses taught to students in the School of Public Health and Tropical Medicine and the School of Architecture at Tulane University was honored in the 1995 AIA Education Honors award program. These courses were summarized in "Architecture, Health, and Society: A Framework for Interdisciplinary Seminar Education," in *On Honoring Teaching Excellence* (Washington, D.C.: American Institute of Architects, 1996). Stephen Verderber was the recipient of this award. Also see the October 1996 issue of *Metropolis* magazine, devoted to the topic of well-being, and a review of university curricula on the subject of health architecture (Barbara Lamprecht, "The Gap between Design and Healing," *Metropolis* 77 [October 1996], 123–30).

39. Douglas S. Erickson, "Codes, Standards, and Regulation Compliance," in *Effective Health Care Facilities Management*, ed. V. James McLarney (Chicago: American Hospital Publishing, 1991).

40. Craig Zimring and Polly Welch, "POE: Building on 20/20 Hindsight," *Progressive Architecture* 69 (July 1988): 55–56, 58–60.

41. Charles Jencks, *The Architecture of the Jumping Universe* (London: Academy Editions, 1995), 21.

42. Lewis Mumford, *Technics and Civilization* (New York: Harcourt, Brace and Company, 1934), 353.

43. Edward Yoxen, *The Gene Business* (New York: Harper and Row, 1984), 4. The field of genetic engineering is thoroughly reviewed by Sheldon Krimsky in *Biotechnics and Society: The Rise of Industrial Genetics* (New York: Praeger, 1991) and in a series of essays edited by Anthony Dyson and John Harris, *Ethics and Biotechnology* (London: Routledge, 1994). A review of recent genetic research in the transformation of animal species was provided by Michael W. Fox in *Superpigs and Wondercorn: The Brave New World of Biotechnology and Where It All May Lead* (New York: Lyons and Burford, 1992). The ethical implications of the field were further examined in a series of essays edited by Frederick B. Rudolph and Larry V. McIntire, *Biotechnology: Science, Engineering, and Ethical Challenges for the Twenty-first Century* (Washington, D.C.: Joseph Henry Press, 1996). In 1997 the first successful cloning of a sheep was announced in the scientific literature, and this development opened the door for the cloning of other mammal species, including humans.

44. "Paralyzed Can Write with Their Eyes," *Chicago Tribune*, February 25, 1996.

45. Geoffrey Cowley, Elizabeth A. Leonard, and Mary Hager, "Tuberculosis: A Deadly Return," *Newsweek*, March 16, 1992: 53–57.

46. Jencks, *The Architecture of the Jumping Universe*, 167. Jencks posits eight directions for the function of architecture within a mode of practitioner-based reflective action: (1) building close to nature and natural languages; (2) representation of the basic "cosmogenic truth" of self-organization, emergence, and jumps to a greater or lesser degree of complexity, based on architecture's ability to express both harmony and disharmony; (3) attainment of a higher aesthetic and functional order that at once is orderly and chaotic—that is, a higher order achieved out of order *and* chaos; (4) the celebration of diversity, variety, and bottom-up participatory alliances; (5) the injection of collage, superimposition, and eclecticism in unexpected ways in the design of buildings; (6) an acknowledgment that architecture must establish a compelling agenda that includes ecological sustainability in a culturally and politically pluralistic context; (7) the incorporation of an aesthetic language that laypersons can relate to and that also expresses the larger scientific realm of complexity theory and chaos theory; and (8) an awareness of the transcendent laws of science in order for architecture to remain unencumbered by fashion and the pressures of thoughtless, unreflective actions.

Index

Musson, Noverre, 231, 375n.20
Mustard, J. F., 124

Nakamura Plastic Surgery Hospital, 87
Narcus, Claire Cooper, 268
National Association of Assisted Living, 265
National Association of Childbearing Centers, 316
National Committee for Quality Assurance, 333
National Gallery of Art, 200
National Healthcare Design Symposium, 348
National Health Service. *See* British National Health Service
National Medical Enterprises, 330
nature. *See* environment
NBBJ Architects, 177, 188, 218
Nebraska Methodist Hospital, *22*
needs assessment in health care, 6
Nemtin, Steve, 251
neoclassicism, 11
Nesmith, Lynn, 169
Netherlands: assisted-living facility in, 240–45; community health centers in, 291, 321–22; orthodontist clinic in, 301–2
Neumatic Portable Satellite Unit (NPSU), 104, *104*
New Age health movement, 318–20
New Age Hospice, 85
new residentialism, 134, 167–75, 184, 338–39; in assisted-living facilities, 263, 264; in community health clinics, 306–12; in nursing homes, 228, 239–53
Nield, Lawrence, 143
Nightingale, Florence, 11–13, 343
noise levels, 90–91
nomadic clinics, 289–90, 383n.21
NORR Partnership, 182, 183
Northcote Community Health Centre, 320
Northwest Community Hospital Wellness Center, 320
Northwestern University Medical Center, 70, 72
Norwick Park District General Hospital, 50, *52*, 58, 60
Notes on Hospitals (Nightingale), 11
Notes on Nursing (Nightingale), 11
Nouakchott National Hospital, 55
Nuclear Magnetic Resonance (NMR). *See* Magnetic Resonance Imaging

nursing homes, 6; architecture of, 336–38; and assisted-living movement, 258–67; and continuing care retirement community movement, 253–58; dehumanizing aspects of, 237–38; and environment, 267–69; evolution of, 235–36; international residentialism in, 269–77; modernist aesthetic applied to, 238–39; new residentialism in, 231–32, 239–53; precursors of, 223–31; social critique of, 235–38; utopian visions for, 231–35
nursing units: clustered, 44, 201–8, 220; plan typologies, *75, 76*; postmodern, 209–14
NVO, 271
Nycum Architects, Ltd., 268

Odell Associates, 156
O'Donnell Wicklund Pigozzi and Peterson, 143, 264–65, 320
On Death and Dying (Kübler-Ross), 84
Ono and Associates, 87
Operation MUST (Medical Unit, Self-contained, Transportable), 112
organic hospital, 106–7
Otterbein Home, 234–35, 251
Oud, J. P. P., 56
outpatient facilities, 81, 135, 333, 367–68n.37. *See also* community health clinics
Overturf, Harrison, 232
Owens, Amanda, 344–45, 389n.30
Oxford Architects, 112

Pacific Presbyterian Medical Center, 211–13, *212*
Paimio Sanatorium, 271
Palle Svensons Tegnestue A/S, 228
panopticon, 73
Papanek, Victor, 334, 342, 343
Parette, A. C., 97, 362n.3
Parker, William T., 360–61n.52
Parker Architects, 312
parking, 97
Pastalan, Leon, 267
patient beds, 208
patient-care unit: plan typologies, *75, 76*
patient empowerment paradigm, 5–6, 7, 351
patient rooms, 10; clustering of, 44, 201–8; design trends, 74, 195–96; furnishings of, 208–9; horizontal designs, 201; pri-

vate, 196–200; semi-private, 196–97; standardization of, 91; transformational, 214–17; windows for, 217–19
Pattern Language, A (Alexander), 334
Pawley, Martin, 21
Payette Associates, 86
Pearce Corporation, 264
Pei, Cobb, Freed, and Partners, 160
Pei, I. M., 160, 199–20
Peichl, Gustav, 66
Pelli, Cesar, 50
Percy Thomas Partnership, 167
Perkins, Dwight, 250
Perkins, Geddis, and Eastman Architects, 263, 268
Perkins and Will Partnership, 44, 102, 109
Perry, Dean, Stahl, and Rogers, 87
Perspective Enterprises, 290
Pharaoh, 292–96, *294, 295*
Philadelphia Geriatric Center, 235, 267
Philips Electrical Corporation, 291
Phoenix Memorial Hospital, 165
Pickworth, Herbert, 184
Pine Lake Medical Center, 187
Planetree concept, 211–14, 221
Planetree Health Resource Center, 211–12
platform hospital, 48–56
Pliny the Younger, 224
Plug-In City, 125, *125*
Pomerance and Breines, 31
Pomperaug Woods, *254, 255*
Pope Pius XI Clinic, 53, *54*
Porte de Choissy Medical and Surgical Center, 197, *197*
Portman, John, 158
postmodernism: in community health clinics, 302–6; defined, 368n.50; in health architecture, 7, 9, 14–15, 86–88, 90, 133–35, 338. *See also* functional deconstruction
post-occupancy evaluations (POES), 203, 349, 353n.7, 355–56n.20
Powell and Moya, 27, 58, 60
Powers, Gordon, 41
Poyet, 11
Prague, Czech Republic, children's clinic in, 305–6, *306, 307*
Prairie School, 177, 250, 265
prefabricated medical units, 112–15, *112, 113, 114*, 364n.34; in community health clinics, 287–89; used in the Middle East, 286–87, *288*
preferred provider organizations (PPOS), 136

Illustration Credits

Leader: Prof. Robert Wischer; Hospital Consultant: Gordon A. Friesen International, Inc.

Fig. 4.7: Henri Colcob, G. Philippe Architects

Figs. 4.8–4.9: Empyrean Diagnostics

Figs. 4.10–4.11: Breger Terjesen Architects

Figs. 4.12–4.16: By E. Todd Wheeler with permission of Perkins & Will

Figs. 4.17–4.20: Dr. Hugh Maguire, Atomedic Hospitals, Inc.

Fig. 4.21: Garrett Corporation, American Hospital Supply, Douglass Aircraft

Fig. 4.22: Cashion Horie Architects, Pomona, Calif.

Fig. 4.23: Theodore F. Mariani FAIA

Figs. 4.24–4.25: Photo by Eugene Dwiggins

Fig. 4.26: Gordon A. Friesen International, Inc.

Fig. 4.28: Courtesy of Zeidler Roberts Partnership

Fig. 4.30: H. Stubbins & R. Allen

Fig. 4.31: Courtesy of Zeidler Roberts Partnership

Figs. 4.32–4.34: Photo by Panda/Croydon Associates; courtesy of Zeidler Roberts Partnership

Figs. 4.35–4.36: Courtesy of Zeidler Roberts Partnership

Fig. 4.37: Kallman McKinnell & Wood

Figs. 4.41–4.42: Courtesy of Stone Marraccini Patterson Architects

Fig. 4.43: Photo by Aker Photography; courtesy of Stone Marraccini Patterson Architects

Page 132: Photo by David Richmond

Figs. 5.1–5.2: Courtesy of Stone Marraccini Patterson Architects

Figs. 5.3–5.4: Photo: © Ezra Stoller/Esto; Architect: Richard Meier Architects

Figs. 5.5–5.6: Photo by Balthazar Korab; courtesy of Zeidler Roberts Partnership

Figs. 5.7–5.8: Weber Brand & Partner

Fig. 5.8: Weber Brand & Partner

Fig. 5.9: Photo: Max Dupain; Architect: Lawrence Nield & Partners

Fig. 5.10: Lawrence Nield & Partners

Fig. 5.11: Kaplan/McLaughlin/Diaz

Fig. 5.12: Photo: Sophie Ristelheuber; Architect: Pierre Riboulet

Fig. 5.13: Pierre Riboulet, Architect

Fig. 5.14: Courtesy of OWP&P Architects, Inc.

Fig. 5.15: Photo by Howard N. Kaplan, © 1996 HNK Architectural Photography, Inc.; courtesy of OWP&P Architects, Inc.

Fig. 5.16: Domenig, Eisenkock & Egger Architects

Fig. 5.17: Photo: © Donna Kempner; Architect: Kaplan/McLaughlin/Diaz

Figs. 5.18–5.19: Atelier Kan '90

Fig. 5.20: Photo: Yoshiaki Miyoshi '90; Architect: Atelier Kan '90

Fig. 5.21: Photo: Terence Charles Grimwood; Architect: Ahrends, Burton, Koralek

Figs. 5.22–5.23: Ahrends, Burton, Koralek, Architects

Fig. 5.24: Photo: Martin Charles; Architect: Ahrends, Burton, Koralek

Fig. 5.25: Ahrends, Burton, Koralek, Architects

Figs. 5.26–5.29: Architect: Joseph Paul Kleihues, Kleihues & Kleihues

Fig. 5.30: Photo: David Ramsey; Architecture/Engineering: Odell Associates Inc.

Fig. 5.31: Photo: C. Bastin and J. Evrard; Architect: Charles Vandenhove

Fig. 5.32: Photo: Jean M. Smith; Architect: Shepley Bulfinch Richardson and Abbot Inc.

Fig. 5.33: Photo: © 1993 Gary Knight: Gary Knight & Associates, Inc.; Architect: Earl Swensson Associates, Inc.

Fig. 5.34: Photo by Tohru Waki; Architect: Tohru Funakoshi and ARCOM R&D Architects

Figs. 5.35–5.36: Photo by Shin Koyama; Architect: Ellerbe Associates, Inc. (later Ellerbe Becket Architects)

Fig. 5.37: Courtesy of Ellerbe Becket

Fig. 5.38: Photo: © Steve Rosenthal; Associated Architects: Tsoi Kobus & Associates and Kaplan/McLaughlin/Diaz

Fig. 5.39: Photo: Stephen F. Verderber; Associated Architects: Tsoi Kobus & Associates and Kaplan/McLaughlin/Diaz

Fig. 5.40: Photo: © Grant Mudford; Architect: Morphosis

Fig. 5.41: Morphosis

Fig. 5.42: Photo: © Grant Mudford; Architect: Morphosis

Fig. 5.43: Photo: Trepal Photography, Inc.; Architect: Dalton, Dalton, Newport

Fig. 5.44: Photo: Lars Hallén, Design Press; Architect: Bo Castenfors, Arkitektkontor AB

Fig. 5.45: Photo: Paul Ferrino; Architect: Graham/Meus Inc.

Fig. 5.46: Photo: © Tom Bernard; Architect: Atkin, Olshin, Lawson-Bell and Associates

Fig. 5.47: Atkin, Olshin, Lawson-Bell and Associates

Fig. 5.48: Photo: © Tom Bernard; Architect: Atkin, Olshin, Lawson-Bell and Associates

Figs. 5.49–5.50: Photo: © Peter Mauss/Esto; Architect: Richard Rauh & Associates

Figs. 5.51–5.53: Richard Rauh & Associates

Fig. 5.54: Photo: Stephen F. Verderber; Architect: Kaplan/McLaughlin/Diaz

Figs. 5.55–5.56: Photo: Brian Vanden Brink © 1997; Architects: Cannon Architects

Fig. 5.56: Photo: Brian Vanden Brink © 1997; Architects: Cannon Architects

Fig. 5.57: Photo: © Allan Weintraub; Architect: Kaplan/McLaughlin/Diaz

Fig. 5.58: Kaplan/McLaughlin/Diaz

Fig. 5.59: Robert A. M. Stern, Architect

Fig. 5.60: Photo: Akira Nakamura; Architect: Ars Design Associates

Fig. 5.61: Photo: Greg Hursley; Architect: HKS Inc.

Fig. 5.62: HKS Inc., Architect

Fig. 5.63: Photo by Greg Hursley; Architect: HKS Inc.

Fig. 5.64: Photo: Ben J. Refuerzo; Architects: R-2 ARCH (Research to Architecture), Los Angeles/New Orleans

Fig. 5.65: Photo: William Santillo; Architect: NORR Partnership

Fig. 5.66: NORR Partnership

Fig. 5.67: Photo: Kamran Adle; Architect: Fabrizio Carola; ADAUA (Association pour le développement et architecture d'une urbanisme africaine)

Figs. 5.68–5.69: Fabrizio Carola; ADAUA (Association pour le développement et architecture d'une urbanisme africaine)

Fig. 5.70: Photo: © Jeff Goldberg/Esto; Architect: Frank O. Gehry & Associates

Fig. 5.71: André Bruyère, Architect

Fig. 5.72: Photo: Paul Warchol; Architect: NBBJ Architecture Design Planning, continuing from the Rosenfield Partnership

Figs. 8.14–8.15: Shinkenchiku-sha

Fig. 8.16: Kazura Clinic, Team Zoo

Fig. 8.17: Shinkenchiku-sha

Fig. 8.18: Photo: Tomio Ohashi; Architect: Kisho Kurokawa Architect & Associates

Fig. 8.19: Kisho Kurokawa Architect & Associates

Figs. 8.20–8.23: Shinkenchiku-sha

Fig. 8.24: Photo: Jan Derwig; Meyer en Van Schooten Architecten BNA

Fig. 8.25: Meyer en Van Schooten Architecten BNA

Fig. 8.26: Photo: Ed Hershberger; Architect: Broome Oringdulph O'Toole Rudolph Boles & Associates PC (BOOR/A)

Fig. 8.28: Broome Oringdulph O'Toole Rudolph Boles & Associates PC (BOOR/A)

Fig. 8.29: Photo: Ed Hershberger; Architect: Broome Oringdulph O'Toole Rudolph Boles & Associates PC (BOOR/A)

Fig. 8.30: Photo reproduced by permission of Pavel techa; D.A. studio s.r.o.

Figs. 8.31–8.32: D.A. studio s.r.o.

Figs. 8.33–8.35: Photo: Reerso/Karsten Vibild; Architect: Karsten Vibild M.A.A./P.A.R.

Fig. 8.36: Photo: Leanne Temme; Architect: Ashton, Ragatt, Dougall Pty. Ltd.

Fig. 8.37: Photo by Martin Charles; Avanti Architects Ltd.

Figs. 8.38–8.39: Avanti Architects Ltd.

Fig. 8.40: Photo by Keith Parry; Avanti Architects Ltd.

Figs. 8.41–8.42: Avanti Architects Ltd.

Fig. 8.43: Photo by Atelier Kidera; ALSED (Architectural Laboratory for Systems Environment Development)

Fig. 8.44: ALSED (Architectural Laboratory for Systems Environment Development)

Fig. 8.45: Photo: Stephen F. Verderber; Architects: R-2 ARCH, Los Angeles/New Orleans

Figs. 8.46–8.47: Photo: Stephen F. Verderber; Architect: Coffee, Crier and Schenck

Figs. 8.48–8.49: Architect: Donald Hoppen

Fig. 8.50: Photo: Dennis Gilbert; Architect: Julian Wickham, A and H van Eyck & Partners

Figs. 8.51–8.53: Julian Wickham, A+H van Eyck & Partners

Fig. 8.54: Photo: Dennis Gilbert; Architect: Julian Wickham, A+H van Eyck & Partners

Fig. 8.55: Kaplan/McLaughlin/Diaz

Figs. 8.56–8.57: Photos: Ben J. Refuerzo; Architects: R-2 ARCH, Los Angeles/New Orleans

Fig. 9.1: Implosion performed by Controlled Demolition Incorporated, Phoenix, Maryland.

Fig. 9.2: Photo by Brian Ross; Thanhauser & Esterson Architects

Fig. 9.3: Thanhauser & Esterson Architects

Fig. 9.6: Photo by Gary Quesada, © Korab Hedrich Blessing; courtesy of Harley Ellington Design

Figs. 9.7–9.9: Photos: Ben J. Refuerzo; Architects: R-2 ARCH, Los Angeles/New Orleans

Fig. 9.10: Photo by Melchior Di Giacomo

The authors have made a sincere attempt to identify the source of each illustration included in this book. In a few cases, however, we have been unable to locate an illustration's source. We therefore wish to apologize if we have inadvertently failed to credit any person or organization.